PRAISE FOR

THe v sociETy

The True Story of Rebel Vigin~Girls

"I loved it! . . . it will inspire anyone who reads it, most importantly, college-aged girls who need to hear something other than the voice of the hook-up culture."

— Megan Palos
Student & Vice President of True Love Revolution Club at Harvard College

"I really liked the rawness of the book and the fact that it covered topics that are normally avoided in Christian groups and settings. It brings up topics that may be difficult for girls to bring up on their own for fear of being embarrassed or judged. I liked that it took a very real look at what college life is like for an 18-22 year old girl, and addresses very real circumstances."

— Laura Wong
Student & Former President of Alpha Delta Chi Sorority at University of California, Berkeley

"I really connected with this book . . . it's challenging to try to remain on the path of our sexuality that God wants us to be on! I think a lot of girls could really relate to this book and feel so good about what they are reading! . . . I don't know how many times I laughed out loud! . . . It made me feel like I was reading my best friend's diary or something!"

— Jessica A. Jenkins
Student

ORDER COPIES TODAY!
TELL US WHAT YOU THINK ABOUT THE V SOCIETY.

VSOCIETYBOOK.COM FACEBOOK.COM/VSOCIETYBOOK

AUTHOR'S NOTE

MEMORY IS A FUNNY THING.

I can barely remember what I did yesterday. I got up and hustled my daughter, who moves in slow motion, into the car with a giant chocolate-chip pancake and a car cup full of juice. The winter sky hovered, luminous and white, as I began my twenty-minute drive to her school. En route, the freeway jammed with more traffic than I expected, and I realized that Christmas would arrive in three weeks. I hadn't yet bought a single gift. I returned home and busied myself doing something. What exactly? I don't recall; the entire day is a blur.

But *some* things and some people you remember forever. You carry them with you wherever you travel, and just the thought of them— while you sit in your car waiting for the light to flash green—makes you smile. For no reason at all, you're suddenly staring through your windshield, cheesing, with a big stupid-happy grin.

The thought of college and the wildly original people I met there makes me smile as I sit impatiently behind the steering wheel. Sometimes I think of them and the things we did, and I laugh loudly to myself—like a crazy person.

One day, because I had nothing better to do—the economy languished and I hadn't worked full time in over a year—I started to write.

I started writing about the outrageous bunch of school friends that kept me up until three in the morning. I remember our conversations, my feelings, and their faces more clearly than I remember yesterday.

With the passage of time, some details about college have grown foggy; I don't always remember the exact day of the week that a rowdy escapade transpired. In my recollection, Tuesdays sometimes get confused with Wednesdays. And an entire week can seem to have passed in a single day.

But as I typed, the details of those adventurous days and late nights, tumbled forth rapidly. Once I began recording my memories, I simply couldn't stop.

Some underemployed people become addicted to television, job search websites, or sleep. I fell in love with my computer keyboard. It helped me produce this unbelievable record of a time I remember fondly. I wrote everything down in the same imperfect manner in which the memories dwell in my mind—condensed, soaring, and epic.

The affair with my keyboard ended one year after it began. My hard drive boasted the rough draft of *The V Society: The True Story of Rebel Virgin-Girls.*

This is my story—and the story of the peculiar companions who accompanied me on a journey of self-discovery, faith, and love. They helped me formulate and solidify the ideas and principles that I hold today; in many ways, they were my teachers. This memoir is a tribute to them and the gift of their friendship.

I hope you will enjoy our story.

THE

Society

THE TRUE STORY of
REBEL VIRGIN~GIRLS

A MEMOIR

Adele Berry

30·AD
MEDIA

edgy, modern, relevant media for the spiritually-hungry

The V Society: The True Story of Rebel Virgin-Girls

Copyright © 2011 by Adele Berry

Cover Design: Deb Harrison, PogostickStudio.com

Author Photo: Jeffrey Fiterman

Published in Castro Valley, California, by 30AD Media Inc.

1 2 3 4 5 6 7 8 9

ISBN 13: 978-0-9834816-0-7 (pbk.)

ISBN 10: 0-98348-160-1 (pbk.)

Printed in the United States of America

FOR MY DAUGHTER S.B.

V Society Rebel Yell: "Rebel from the ways of this world, and be transformed by the renewing of your mind. Then you will be able to test and approve what God's will is—his good, pleasing and perfect will!"

— ADAPTED FROM ROMANS 12:2

CONTENTS

THE cast

{Supporting Cast}

Mandy Johnson

Red-haired, laid-back dorm resident advisor from the Midwest. Pre-med major. V Society member.

Nick Wilson

Adele's friend from high school. Big flirt, cross-country runner, and zealous liberal at the University of California, Berkeley. Political science major.

Justin Greco

Übersmart, Wall Street–bound, cute Bible study leader from New Jersey. Adele's big brother in the coed honor fraternity. Business and communications major.

Noel Jean-Baptiste

Prank phone caller and originator of the term "nuns from hell." Globe-trotting sorority girl from Haiti. Senior-year roommate of V Society girls.

Ryan McAlba

Good-natured, fun-loving, strapping surfer from Northern California. Torn between a post-college career as a professional comedian and joining the marines. Sociology major. Honorary V Society member.

Prelude to Act Three

senior year

Chapter One

THE APARTMENT

{August, First Semester of Senior Year}

KISS HIM? OR TIE HIM UP ON THE TRAIN TRACKS?
Extreme? Maybe.

I asked myself questions like that all the time without thinking them the least bit odd. I was twenty years old and starting the wild adventure of my last year of college. We students lived and breathed to write our own recipes for extreme. From late evening to early morning, we reveled with friends and laughed until our sides burst, trading myths and revelations about boys and men. If I managed to sleep sometime in between, that was extremely good. If not . . . Oh, well. I'd just be extremely tired and hope none of my professors would catch me dozing off in the middle of a lecture.

Looking back, nearly seventeen years later, I realize that every experience at the University of Pennsylvania that year burst forth like a robust new anthem. Every day broke sparkling and pure, untainted by history and regrettable memories. Each moment rang wondrously different from the last, offering us a blank canvas to paint new melodies and tap esoteric, never-before-heard rhythms.

My dorm apartment on the twenty-first floor of High Rise South seemed the most captivating place on earth. Most everything that went on there was extremely something—outlandish, exhilarating, inventive.

Seldom were things serious. But on rare occasions, they were. Sometimes I had extreme choices to make.

Room 2110 of High Rise South was the social hub and command center for my eccentric bunch of friends. This was where the V Society was birthed—a secret women-only society. The most interesting people I'd ever met congregated here on a regular basis: Keri and Michelle, my roommates and best friends; and Milan, the wily, perplexing, foreign-born boy-man who sparked our curiosity and conversation.

Here, with votes amongst V Society members, we determined the most intriguing people on campus, the coolest places to see and be seen, and the year's best TV shows. The previous year's V Society notes were all intact, stored in a photo album with corresponding pictures and hidden away in my closet.

V Society Best of the Best List
Junior Year

Note: Brackets { } indicate special nominations by individual V Society members.

MOST INTRIGUING PEOPLE
Milan
Noah (aka Boy-Girl)
Ken (aka Greasy II) {Stephanie}
Alan (filmmaker guy)
Sexy (aka Greasy I) {Adele}
Doug {Michelle}

BEST HANGOUTS
Milan's Room
College Green

2110 High Rise South
Beanie's Coffee House

BEST TV SHOWS
Beverly Hills 90210
Life Goes On
In Living Color
Saturday Night Live {Stephanie}

As on most early evenings, after we'd finished our afternoon classes, Keri, Michelle, and I lounged in the living room of our apartment, with our usual guest Milan, spinning our creative wheels.

"So, I just saw this article about the artist Christo," Milan relayed with enthusiasm. "Have you heard of Christo?"

Milan sat in our red canvas Ikea chair, in front of the large bank of windows that ran across the back of our white-walled apartment. Each word he spoke with his appealing Serbian accent had an engaging resonance.

"Who?" Keri asked, as she turned from gathering cooking ingredients on the narrow kitchen countertop. Our kitchen and living room were joined in one large studio-style living space.

"No. Never heard of him," Michelle added.

Michelle sat cross-legged on the sofa in her signature, three-sizes-too-big jeans. She wore a thick brown leather belt that insured that her jeans didn't accidentally slide off her slender figure. Even in her giant jeans, surrounded by stacks of lecture notes and books, you couldn't overlook Michelle's near-perfect features. She stood several inches taller than me, with long, wavy light-brown hair and a beautiful oval-shaped face. When she spoke, her pouting, pink cherub lips barely moved. She had a tiny beauty mark just below her mouth.

"Umm, I think I've heard of him. Doesn't he wrap up stuff in large public places?" I asked.

I sat on the sofa, next to Michelle, with my own lecture notes sprawled nearby.

"Yes. Exactly!" Milan exclaimed. "I was just looking at these pictures of some of his work. He wrapped a medieval tower in Italy—an entire building—in plastic and ropes. He wrapped over a mile of coastline in Australia with plastic."

"No way!" Keri shot back. "You're lying." Her hazel eyes flashed with interest, and her curly dark brown hair swung with the quick turn of her head.

"No, I'm totally serious," Milan declared.

"You're not making that up?" Michelle asked in disbelief.

The image of large objects wrapped in polyethylene jogged a memory from an art history book I'd seen some time ago.

"Right—I remember. He wrapped up a bunch of islands with pink plastic," I recalled. "It was super cool—"

"Exactly," Milan interjected, happy to be vindicated.

"*We* should wrap something up and call it great art," I declared.

"Great idea. I love it! What should we wrap?" Keri asked looking at me and then at Milan. We were the most likely culprits to come up with the most bizarre—and thus the most ideal—suggestion.

"Let's wrap up Milan!" I exclaimed.

The thought of Milan wrapped up and immobile thrilled me. I suspected that it would be equally satisfying to the other two women in the room.

"Let's use Saran wrap," Keri suggested.

"Perfect!"

I ran down the short hall to get my camera out of my bedroom.

"Here, Mich," I said, when I returned, giving Michelle my camera. "Will you take pictures while Keri and I wrap up Milan?"

"Of course," she laughed.

Milan stood in the middle of the living room in his khaki slacks and dark-blue polo shirt. A grin spread across his handsome, clean-shaven

face. He put his arms straight down at his sides, so Keri and I could
begin wrapping.

Keri and I armed ourselves with separate rolls of kitchen plastic wrap.
I started from Milan's shoulders and wrapped down, while Keri began
from his feet, wrapping upward. We met triumphantly in the middle,
tore off the last strips of plastic wrap from the roll and then stood back
to admire our "great art."

The image of Milan unable to move—and unable to disappear in and
out of our apartment at will as he usually did—was altogether cathartic
for Keri, Michelle, and me. For the next minute, as he stood bound, he
couldn't exasperate us. For the first time since we had met him junior
year, our roles had reversed. He was our captive, and we were no longer his.

As I stepped back to observe our artwork, I couldn't help wishing
I could keep Milan contained like that for the rest of the school year.
He was beautiful, almost male-model pretty—a pleasure to behold. His
dark Serbian features, a harmonious blend of Slavic and Mediterranean
characteristics, came together in a divinely sculpted masterpiece—al-
most-black eyes, shapely lips, olive skin, and wavy black hair. Wrapped
up, he became relatively harmless. Saran wrap was like magic. All his
sultry charm seemed safely encapsulated in a plastic cocoon. He became
temporarily incapable of spinning the web that drew fellow students to
him like flies. I savored our creation for an entire two minutes before
Michelle warned us of the health risks of our little art endeavor.

"It's dangerous for his skin to stay covered up like that for too long.
His body can't take in oxygen through his skin pores, so he could suffocate eventually," Michelle stated flatly.

"Okay, you got a picture, right?" I asked her. "Oh—one more.
Get Keri and me standing next to him," I requested.

Snap. The heavy click of my camera shutter resounded. "Yep, got it,"
Michelle answered.

"Okay," Milan smiled. "I'm coming out."

He began to shred the plastic, and soon wriggled free. My moment
of containment ecstasy ended.

"Whew, that was *good*," Milan sighed, handing Keri and I wads of balled up plastic wrap.

"That *was* good," Keri smiled.

Her broad grin filled up half her face. Her almond-shaped eyes lit up her always-radiant features. She reminded me of an ancient portrait, like the ones of content women pictured at the Turkish bath—full bodied, all curves and no corners, with nice proportions, and a lovely, cheerful face.

While Michelle went back to reviewing her study notes, Keri made her way into the kitchen and began chopping up vegetables for our favorite sweet-and-sour chicken. With a handful of fresh vegetables, some diced chicken, a jar of grape jelly, and a jar of chili sauce, Keri could make enough sweet-and-sour chicken for a week of meals. All she had to do after that was cook fresh rice in her rice cooker each day.

Just then Stephanie, our fellow V Society member, came flying through the door—her round face exuberant and her mane of sandy-brown hair trailing behind her like an untamed shadow. Stephanie was our honorary roommate. I didn't actually know for sure where her dorm room was. If I needed to find her, I usually never had to look much farther than my living room.

"Mike Myers is on *Saturday Night Live* tonight!" she gushed.

"Hi, Stephanie!" we all called out, with the exception of Milan, who purposely ignored her. The previous semester, Stephanie, possessed by a vampire-like urge, had bitten Milan while he slept in his dorm room. Now her presence—or rather, that of her teeth—agitated him, evoking the memory of awakening suddenly from sound rest to incisors planted in his flesh at three o'clock in the morning.

"I can't wait to see him!" she exclaimed. "Oy vey, I'm feeling verklempt!"

None of us cared one bit about Mike Myers. But we knew he was Stephanie's true love, in close running with Elvis and Kurt Cobain, the lead singer of Nirvana. Only her two other great loves, the outlaw Jesse James, and all things country western trumped them. Stephanie's fascination with Kurt Cobain and Mike Myers, like most of the V Society members' favorite things, was documented in the official notes from the previous semester.

V SOCIETY, MARCH 14
Junior Year

RUMORS OF THE DAY

Stephanie married Kurt Cobain and now wears trashy babydoll (kinderwhore) dresses.

SCIENTIFIC EQUATION OF THE DAY

$$\text{Number of Times Stephanie Mentions Mike Myer's Name per Day?} = \lim_{x \to \infty} \frac{X^{10} X^8 X^2}{2}$$

Stephanie peeked at the concoction Keri swirled in a big pot on the stove and then seated herself on the floor.

"Mike Myers," Stephanie repeated dreamily as though saying his name might cause him to materialize right in the middle of our dorm room.

Milan rose from his seat and scooped his black backpack up from the floor. His face had melted from cheery to cold and disinterested.

"I don't have time to talk crap," he stated evenly as he headed toward the door.

"You are so moody," Stephanie mumbled under her breath.

"What?" Milan asked, showing vague interest in Stephanie's hushed complaint.

"She said, 'You're moody,'" I repeated. "Worse than all four of us *combined* in the throes of our most psycho PMS mood swings."

Keri, Stephanie, and Michelle snickered, trying to stifle bursts of laughter. Milan was outnumbered and guilty as charged. He could only scowl gingerly at his persecutors before admitting defeat and smiling at the friendly accusation.

"So what time does the party start tomorrow?" he asked, changing the subject.

"Seven sharp," Keri replied.

With that, Milan disappeared down our long dorm hall and out into the night.

Act One

JUNior year

{Six Months Earlier}

Chapter Two

THE V SOCIETY

{March, Second Semester of Junior Year}

No one remembers the details of the colorful, rollicking conversation or the unruly, electric spark that inspired our secret society. Often it proved difficult to pinpoint the origins of our inventions—each spewed forth without warning, the unexpected by-product of a conversational tornado. Our roommate conversations romped and spun wildly, touching down and then sucking in and synthesizing all sorts of unrelated ideas. Keri, Michelle, and I probably dreamed it up one typical weekday in a spirited banter that began on one side of the world and ended on a distant planet.

KERI: What's that playing on the stereo?

ME: I don't know. It's the school radio station. The DJ just put it on.

MICHELLE: Where's Tajikistan?

KERI: What? This song is called, 'Where's Tajikistan'?

MICHELLE: No, where's Tajikistan on the map, butthead?

KERI: I really like this song.

ME: It's cool, huh?

KERI: Totally cool.

ME: What are you reading?

KERI: *Women in the Bible.*

MICHELLE: Hey, where's my little green Tupperware container?

ME: I don't know. Maybe in the fridge somewhere.

KERI: Oh, oh… oh, disgusting… Can you close that refrigerator door? It smells like something died in there!

ME: Oh my gosh, that smells worse than Mich's feet.

KERI: No, that smells ten times worse!

MICHELLE: What's this song called?

ME: Who knows? It's on the radio.

KERI: What radio station?

MICHELLE: Eww—who put the rotten pasta in the fridge? It's totally green and moldy.

ME: Oops… sorry. I was wondering who ate my pasta. Yeah, I cooked that last semester… then I couldn't find it.

KERI: Hey, I think what's-his-name is kind of cute.

ME: Who?

KERI: That singer from the Underground Café.

MICHELLE: Do my feet really smell?

KERI: Of course, *everyone's* feet smell. But the rest of you smells okay, so don't worry about it.

MICHELLE: You mean that folk-singer guy?

ME: This is a good make-out song.

MICHELLE: Maybe you should ask out what's-his-face from the Underground.

KERI: Very funny.

ME: You'd probably make his day.

KERI: Have you ever been in love?

ME: No. Have you?

MICHELLE: Well, yeah, I guess so.

ME: I haven't been in love, but I've had a zillion crushes.

KERI: So… have you ever done it?

MICHELLE: Done what?

KERI: *It.*

ME: No. Have you?

MICHELLE: You're a virgin? No way? Me too!

KERI: Me three!

ME: Cool.

MICHELLE: We're all virgins?!

KERI: We should form our own sorority or something.

MICHELLE: Not a sorority… maybe a club?

KERI: What kind of club?

ME: One with good snacks.

KERI: Yeah, snacks from Tajikistan.

ME: Where *is* Tajikistan?

KERI: It should be a funky club.

ME: Like a secret society.

MICHELLE: The Virgin Society?

KERI: How about the V Society?

ME: Oh yeah, that's perfect!

I can't say for sure, but the V Society probably came kicking and screaming into the world like that. Keri, Michelle, and I conjured up our little club during the spring of our junior year. That year began my most memorable time in college. I'd found my place—making films and pursuing photography; and I'd found my people—Keri and Michelle. For the first time, I began to think of my dorm room as home, rather than a randomly assigned, rented room that I tolerated until I could return to my parents' house in California—my real home.

The society had five official members. In addition to my roommates, our friends Mandy and Stephanie completed the society's roster. The society had strict membership requirements. You had to be female, and you had to fit our definition of cool and funky. Most important, you had to be a virgin—and committed to abstinence.

Collectively, the five of us encompassed a vast range of experiences in our darting and dancing encounters with the opposite sex. Our game plays had spanned from "never up to bat" to "almost stole home." But, without saying it, we understood—in the tacit way that only close friends understand each other—that past encounters, even the ones lingering around second and third base, were forgiven. The V Society symbolized commitment to a reborn chastity, and the expectation—at least in my mind—to hover somewhere between "never up to bat" and "first base."

All spring the society operated covertly, remaining a guarded secret from everyone. Everyone except Milan.

"I want to join the V Society," he complained.

"*You?* That's funny. You are *definitely* not a virgin," Keri replied.

"You can lose your virginity more than once," he shot back.

"More than once? Clever, aren't you?" I said.

"It doesn't matter, anyway," Michelle interjected. "You have to be a woman to join the V Society."

Later we came up with a plan that would embrace Milan as part of our ragtag bunch.

"You can't be in the V Society, but you can join the Elevator Society," Keri announced.

"The Elevator Society is the new parent club of the V Society," I explained.

"How do I join?" he asked.

"You have to ride in the elevator from our floor—the twenty-first floor—to the lobby and do the Elevator Dance," Michelle explained.

The Elevator Dance was an unrehearsed, seizure-like dance performed entirely behind closed elevator doors. You had to make the dance as wild and uncontrollable as possible but appear completely still and calm when the doors opened. Your dance was nullified if anyone caught a glimpse of you mid-seizure when the elevator doors opened. Milan was game for that.

The V Society had bylaws, a motto, and meeting notes that our secretary, "the Secret-Keri" typed.

V SOCIETY {THE UNTOUCHABLES}
Junior Year, Spring
The Virgin Society is a female bonding subgroup of the Elevator Society
founded at the University of Pennsylvania
Motto: Chaste No Haste!

V SOCIETY ALTERNATIVE TITLES
No Entry Zone
Chastity Belt Girls/Women
Penisn't
VIP (Virgins in Practice)
Legs Crossed Nothing Lost
The Impermeables
Trust Not Lust
Virginity is for Lovers
P . . . Not

PREREQUISITES FOR MEMBERSHIP
1) Must be a woman
2) Must be a virgin
3) Must be funky (eccentric-funky, not smelly-funky)
4) Must be invited to join and unanimously accepted by members

INITIATION
An initiate is simultaneously initiated into the parent group, the Eleva-
tor Society. The initiation requires the presence of the majority of the

present members. The initiate joins members in the execution of the Elevator Dance. She must find her own expression within the dance, but all members and initiates end the dance with the customary crossed legs and crossed arms making the "V" sign with one's first two fingers on both hands. At this point the initiate becomes a member (a ride in the elevator following the initiation is optional).

CHANGES IN MEMBERSHIP STATUS

Any member who violates any single or combination of the first three prerequisites before marriage is automatically disqualified as a member. Any member who marries automatically receives alumna status.

CURRENT MEMBERS OF THE VIRGIN SOCIETY

Michelle Schroeder
Stephanie Schwartzbaum
Adele Moore
Keri Zelman
Amanda Johnson

CURRENT MEMBERS OF THE ELEVATOR SOCIETY

Michelle Schroeder
Stephanie Schwartzbaum
Adele Moore
Keri Zelman
Amanda Johnson
Milan Zorić

Chapter Three

---- ❧ ----

PARTY of FIVE

{Autumn, First Semester of Junior Year}

JUNIOR YEAR HAD BEGUN THAT AUTUMN, WITH ME, MICHELLE, Keri, and Allison Lee moving into High Rise South together. High Rise South, along with High Rise North and High Rise East, anchored the west end of campus, known as Superblock. Superblock also consisted of clusters of varied low-rise dorms with different themes. Modern Language House housed students who wanted to speak foreign languages regularly in their residence. Many black students resided in W. E. B. Du Bois House. And there were the high-rise dorms, right smack in the middle, three towering, twenty-four-story, giant concrete monoliths that resembled housing projects.

Aside from the gloomy gray architecture of the high-rise buildings, Superblock itself was lovely. The dorms perched in the midst of vast, green, well-kept, park-like lawns. Graceful, tall, flowering trees and shade trees, peppered the greens and arched over benches along the edge of the lawns, where students often sat and read.

As the name indicates, Superblock was huge. It took up an entire city block. A modern, three-story-tall, welded-steel sculpture painted scarlet red loomed in the middle of the block. The sculpture, officially named *Covenant*, resembled oversized pieces of falling, fighting, and overlapping cylindrical metal rods. It towered above the park, a monstrous display of abstract art gone berserk. We all called it *The Dueling Tampons*.

Locust Walk ran east to west through the middle of the university, and cut right through Superblock, connecting it to the rest of campus via a broad pedestrian bridge over busy Thirty-Eighth Street. Penn was its own world: pristine, picturesque, awe-inspiring, and insular. People often praised it as one of the most beautiful urban campuses in the Northeast. The school consumed limitless acres of property in every direction. Freshman year, I left campus only a few times to go downtown. A self-contained city, the university had everything you needed: innumerable dining options and nonstop entertainment—athletic fields, a swimming pool, an ice skating rink, free film showings, and more than twenty thousand students.

A distinct, almost tangible division ran between the university and the urban community of West Philadelphia that surrounded it. Once you crossed Fortieth Street and left Superblock, you left behind the spotless lawns for the lively, cluttered, colorful, churning inner city. I had never lived in an urban environment before, and I relished the West Philadelphia grit that tempered the spotless, modern classrooms and intermingled with the 150-year-old historic buildings at the center of campus.

Houston Hall, the student center, perfectly blended inner-city Philadelphia with the heart of university life. The cashiers in the student store where I bought my dad a "My daughter and all my money go to the University of Pennsylvania" T-shirt, wore three-inch, gold-colored hoop earrings with their initials hanging in the middle of each loop. Many of the West Philadelphians who worked in Houston Hall were bold, confident black women who greeted the wide-eyed students with disinterested gazes.

West Philadelphia embodied a peculiar mix of inner-city hardiness, sprinkled with inconsequential restaurants, bars, and an Urban Outfitters, where students regularly congregated. Just past Fortieth Street, where West Campus poured into West Philadelphia, students frequently rented clusters of brownstones interspersed with almost-identical row-houses that West Philadelphia natives had inhabited for generations.

At the grocery store nearest to my dorm, on Forty-Second Street, thick, six-foot-high bars surrounded the perimeter of the supermarket entrance. For the life of me, I never understood why the grocery store didn't allow customers to push their carts into the parking lot. The bars disabled me from pushing my groceries to the corner of Forty-Second Street before abandoning my cart at the edge of the lot to carry my over-stuffed grocery bags back to campus.

That fall, our fourth roommate, Allison, rarely hung out at home. As a nursing student, she probably studied even more than Michelle—an amazing feat. No one seemed to give nursing students credit, but they worked as hard as, if not harder than, the business school undergraduates did. While we liberal arts majors had time to relax in cafés, conduct impromptu dorm-room photo sessions, discuss the campus's most intriguing people, and write songs, Allison knocked herself out in study groups.

"You guys always have all the fun when I'm not here," Allison said in her sweet voice. Most everything she said came out kind and sincere. Even when she rightly accused us, it didn't sound like a complaint. I looked at her cute, round face and felt badly. Keri, Michelle, and I loved Allison. She was short, with thin-rimmed little glasses and medium-length black hair. She and Michelle kept our apartment mascot, Bud the tadpole, in their room.

"Allison, we never leave you out on purpose," Michelle said, wrapping her long arms around Allison's small frame in a big hug.

"Definitely not," Keri stated.

"You're just never here," I submitted.

"I know," she said, "but I showed some people the pictures you guys took in Adele's last photo session, and everyone wanted to know why I wasn't in any of the pictures."

When Allison left, Keri, Michelle, and I worked out a resolution to the situation.

"Okay, let's plan the next photo session," Keri suggested. "We'll plan it when Allison is here. We'll have a complete roommate photo session with all four of us."

Planning was a new element in our V Society activities. Generally, we rarely planned anything that we did, except dinner parties and social soirees. All of our activities burst forth spontaneously as we gathered in the apartment and imagined new endeavors for ourselves.

"Good idea," agreed Michelle.

"Okay, I'll find out when is a good time for Allison," I volunteered.

"That's good," Keri added.

"Allison is right. We don't have any pictures with her," said Michelle.

It was true. Whenever I needed models to try out a new lighting technique or new backgrounds, I always counted on Keri and Michelle to model for me. They often hung out in the apartment when I was home, and they made good photo subjects. Several days later, our roommate photo session came to life. I had purchased an extra-long shutter release cable so I could put my camera on a tripod and snap a picture of all four of us, with me in the frame. In the living room I set up my black backdrop—a big black sheet taped and tacked to the wall—and my studio lights. The four of us dressed in a coordinated array of jeans and similar-colored tops. We blasted U2's latest album on the stereo and laughed our heads off as Michelle tried in vain to look vampy.

"Come on," I coaxed. "Look like you're Kate Moss and you're super *hot*."

Michelle looked uncomfortable trying to imitate a supermodel and couldn't stop cracking up. I had better luck getting her to look morose.

"Okay, look depressed then," I told her. All fashion models looked depressed.

I took pictures of each of my roommates alone. Then I photographed all three of them together—looking melancholy, looking cheerful, and looking plain goofy. Michelle had perfected goofy. She liked to contort her face in weird expressions. We laughed all the harder watching her face transform into various ridiculous rubber-like faces. Finally, I took pictures of all four of us, with me inserted in front, close to the shutter release cable, which lay hidden under my backdrop.

When I'd finished the third roll of black-and-white film, I called it quits.

"Okay, that's a wrap," I called out.

U2's "Mysterious Ways" boomed out of the stereo speakers. Keri, Michelle, and I began singing at the top of our lungs and dancing wildly. Allison looked on with amusement.

When we got to my favorite verse, I jumped on the sofa and held up the wooden spoon I had swiped from the kitchen countertop like a microphone. I jumped back down to continue performing my mad, whirling boogie with Keri and Michelle. We danced, exhilarated, swept upward in the inebriating fever of youth, while Allison looked on. The song ended, and so did our war dance. Another successful photo session came to a close.

Michelle and I had met freshman year at a nondenominational Christian retreat.

"Hi!" I said to the most interesting-looking girl in the room.

"Hi," she replied dryly.

I couldn't tell: Was she shy? Or was she completely disinterested in the conversation I had started? I didn't care. I had a goal in mind, and her lack of enthusiasm didn't put me off.

"I like your T-shirt," I continued.

"Thanks."

"I love the Cure! So, you're a Cure fan?"

"Yes."

She certainly wasn't the talkative sort, but anyone who would wear a Cure concert T-shirt at a Christian retreat had to be interesting. Even without the Cure T-shirt, she stood out. She was five feet ten and the best-looking student in the entire recreation room of sixty students.

The Cure ranked as one of my absolute favorite New Wave bands. The lead singer, Robert Smith, used whole cans of hair spray and mousse to stand his tangled black hair on end. It stood straight up—a six-inch immovable sculpture. It looked like a bird's nest on crack. The Cure was revolutionary in New Wave circles. In the music video for "Close to Me," Robert Smith violated all social norms and wore smudged red lipstick and gray eye shadow. I loved it! Their pop-band-royalty status made it perfectly acceptable for normal guys to wear eyeliner. Guys in makeup were never as cool as at a Cure concert. Elated to find another Cure fan at a Christian retreat and bolstered by our mutual affection for Robert Smith, I pressed on, determined to force a pleasant conversation with this tall, pale, quiet girl.

"I went to their concert last year!" I exclaimed. "We had really bad seats. We were way up in the nosebleed section for the first half, but at intermission we moved up to seats on the floor. I went with my friend Sebastian. It was so funny, all those guys with Robert Smith hair! You know Robert Smith said his concerts trip him out because the people at his concert look more like him than he looks like himself."

I waited for her to laugh. She didn't.

Undeterred, I kept on. "Yeah, I love *Disintegration*," I continued, referring to the Cure album I'd just bought. "Do you like that one?"

"Yes." She smiled. I was making progress.

"Oh, I'm Adele, by the way."

"I'm Michelle," she replied as another small smile flitted across her lips and then faded almost as quickly as it appeared.

"Nice to meet you, Michelle." I smiled and stuck out my hand.

She shook it awkwardly, as I continued. "Yeah, I just heard this rare Cure B-side a couple months ago. Have you heard 'Breathe'? It's amazing!"

"No."

"Really, you should hear it. It's so good!"

I started to repeat myself and thought I'd better quit while I was ahead. I didn't want to appear too eager. I had successfully established common ground. Despite her monosyllabic answers, I was sure we'd eventually become friends. I didn't detect a hint of coldness or pretension in her demeanor. She actually seemed quite nice—just at a loss for what to say next.

We were both fans of the same alternative British pop band, and we were both freshman who had checked "yes" on a little form outside the dining hall that asked, "Are you interested in a Bible study?" That's how most freshmen ended up here, at the fall retreat on the nippy, clean white beach of the New Jersey shore.

For the rest of the weekend retreat I flowed in and out of conversations with other freshman. I chatted with friendly upperclassmen and quickly identified the only two other students from California. Most everyone else seemed to be from the Northeast.

"I'm excited to experience real seasons," I told Kristin, a freshman from Massachusetts. "We have year-round temperatures of seventy degrees," I joked. "And our leaves don't change colors in the fall—unless you count green to brown. In California we miss that colorful transformation to autumn entirely."

I ate with different people at each meal and made the rounds, chatting a little with everyone. By the end of the weekend, I'd met everyone and made a thorough assessment. The students were all friendly enough, but I'd decided no one was quite as interesting as my fellow Cure fan. The only cute guy on the entire retreat was already engaged to a mousy-looking senior, and he didn't even go to our school. His girlfriend had invited him.

I observed Michelle as our paths crossed in small groups and at meals. I noticed she rarely initiated conversation with anyone, though she never spoke unpleasantly. I hardly even saw her talk to Jim, a tall, lanky, pointy-faced guy. "That's her boyfriend," someone told me. While I jumped at the opportunity to share my opinion in small groups, Michelle said very little all weekend. Unlike me, she didn't see the weekend as an opportunity to expand her social circle as widely as possible and meet cute guys.

I met Keri at an on-campus Christian social gathering later in the year. She was the first Messianic Jew I had ever met. Like me, Messianic Jews believed in Jesus as the Jewish Messiah—the Son of God; however, she didn't go to church as Christians did. She went to a Messianic synagogue. By junior year, I had gone to services with her enough times that I could recite the beginning of the traditional Jewish prayers, "Baruch atah Adonai Eloheinu Melech ha-olam." Translation: "Blessed are you, O God, our Lord, King of the Universe."

As the only twelfth-grade student at her synagogue's tiny Messianic school, Keri supplemented her high school coursework at a local Christian school. We affectionately called her Book Woman. Oblivious to the latest fashion trends and pop culture icons that influenced the culture of most American high schools, Keri displayed her own unique sense of style. Her wardrobe fused a dizzying kaleidoscope of neo-hippie style with indigenous people's craftiness. When she went to class, Keri carried a bright, multicolor Guatemalan textile backpack. You could see it from far off, with its thick, interwoven red, purple, yellow, orange, and green thread. To finish off every outfit, she often wore short, sagging, tasseled black suede booties. I don't know where she found those shoes.

Keri loved books and surrounded herself with feminist reading. She often lost me in deep conversations espousing the virtues of feminism. I didn't feel oppressed, and I didn't see the relevance of feminism in my everyday life.

I knew Keri and I would be good friends when we rode together on a spring break missionary trip to Daytona Beach, Florida, from Philadelphia. We laughed almost the entire time on the fifteen-hour bus ride.

Three hours into our nonstop dialogue, Keri began relaying the details of an anthropology ethnography she'd read.

"Did you know there's a tribe in Papua New Guinea where the men wear penis gourds? That's it—that's all the clothing they wear," Keri declared.

"What? Really?"

"Yes, the men in the tribe have dressed that way for generations. That's been their traditional tribal clothing for, like, forever."

"Isn't that uncomfortable?"

"Maybe at first."

"I guess you just get used to it."

"But how does it stay on?"

"I think there's a string or something across the back that keeps it strapped on."

"Yeah, but what if the string gets caught on a tree or something? That has to hurt."

We looked at each other—and then busted up in whopping howls.

"I bet the gourd is itchy."

"No kidding, and you can't even scratch, 'cause the gourd is covering everything up."

We were beside ourselves with uncontrollable laughter and nearly fell out of our seats as we imagined itchy, uncomfortable tribesmen. My merriment filled me like a warm, incandescent glow. It emanated from the depths of my abdomen and rippled out to the tips of my fingers. I was oblivious to the upperclassmen I otherwise might have tried to impress with a feigned show of maturity and sophistication.

"Can you imagine if all the guys at school dressed like that?"

"Ewwwwwww!" we squealed loudly in unison.

We paused long enough to catch our breath and attempt to lower our voices as an upperclassman in the seat across from us shot us a "Quiet down, you crazy, giggling freshman" look.

"You know what else I read?" Keri tried hard to whisper and muffle a hoot. "Did you know urine is a great antiseptic?"

"No way!"

"Really, it's documented."

"But pee is full of germs. How can it be an antiseptic?"

"Indigenous people in several remote regions of the world use it as an antiseptic."

"And it works?"

"Sure does."

"Do you know how much money we could make if we could market that idea? It could be the first all-natural antiseptic." I couldn't contain myself. Chortles and snorts caught in my throat. Soon they escaped without my permission. "We could start off small—you know, a little family business at first!" I cried.

"We'd just sell our own pee to start," Keri giggled.

"Just think about it. Our company would explode overnight. There's an unlimited supply of urine in the world."

"We'd have almost no overhead costs for production."

Urine was never so worthy of discussion as in conversation with Keri. Everything she said seemed hilarious. We fed off each other, finding each idea more hysterical than the last. Our exchange seemed to float us both on a natural high, void of all sensibility and restraint.

"We just need to come up with really cool packaging to sell the idea," I suggested.

"Like a little pee-perfume spray bottle."

I choked through my cackling. I wanted to double over, my sides hurt so badly. "And a good slogan like, 'Spray pee every day—keep the germs away!'"

Finally, our sleepy bus, full of road-weary college students and two tireless, chattering freshmen, stopped at a nondescript chain restaurant for breakfast.

We finished eating, and the server began clearing the table. As he reached for the butter dish, Keri exclaimed, "Wait!" She reached out and, with a single swoop of her hand, scooped up a pat of partially melted butter. All eight of us around the table looked at Keri, startled.

"Butter is a great moisturizer," she offered as an explanation.

Then she rubbed the butter into her elbows and her arm. This girl definitely marched to the irregular rhythm of some funky folklore drummer. Our friendship was sealed from then on.

I met Stephanie, the V Society's primary lyricist, at a Penn Film and Video Club meeting junior year. Initially, Stephanie had worked my last patient nerve. She talked incessantly about things I cared nothing about. In every other sentence she mentioned musicians I disliked, such as Johnny Cash and Willie Nelson. She went on and on endlessly about Elvis, Kurt Cobain, and Jesse James. She always talked about Mike Myers's film *Wayne's World*. I couldn't stand that movie. It was so goofy; I couldn't understand how she could sit through the whole thing.

Stephanie and I had introduced ourselves when the Film Club members broke out into small groups to collaborate on a new project. For some reason that completely escapes me, I agreed to work on a small film with her. One day, after an exasperating but brief meeting with cheerful, yakking Stephanie, she came with me back to my apartment. Stephanie met Keri and Michelle and lingered at our place for a little over two hours—two very *long* hours. For some reason, Keri and Michelle liked her. In fact, Keri found her delightful.

I came home several days later and found Stephanie comfortably situated in my living room, deep in conversation with Keri.

"Really, you're a Zionist?" she asked Keri. "Wow—I don't think I could live in Israel. I mean not for years and years and years! Won't you miss it here?"

At twenty-two, Stephanie was two years older than the rest of us. Although good-natured, her dopey jokes and giggly-little-kid laugh affected me like fingernails scratching a chalkboard. Over the next few weeks, she attached herself like a permanent fixture in our place. She'd found a home. I could do nothing about it. She wasn't going away. I had to get used to her if I wanted to keep my address at 2110 High Rise South.

But the more I got to know her, the more I began to like her. She possessed a mischievous wit and wrote hilarious daily commentary about our V Society adventures on the large dry erase board that hung in our living room by the phone. We used the dry erase board to take phone messages, but Stephanie used it to draw telling caricatures of each of us. Single-handedly she invented the Rumors of the Day and the infamous Scientific Equation of the Day. We welcomed her into our little gang.

V SOCIETY, MARCH 14
Junior Year

SCIENTIFIC EQUATION OF THE DAY

$$\text{Adele's Estimate of the Number of Milan's Lovers} = \frac{\text{Actual Number of Milan's Lovers}}{10}$$

{Note: This is an approximation +/– 20.}

RUMORS OF THE DAY

1. *Allison never wakes up when we're too loud.*
2. *The essence of Milan should never be contacted between 11:00 p.m. and 6:00 a.m. (It's a male cycling thang. 4:00 a.m. testosterone is highest. 8:00 p.m. testosterone is lowest.)*
3. *Stephanie converted to the Temple of B'nai Milan.*
4. *Adele got a three-record deal with MCA records.*
5. *Michelle froze into an abstract sculpture, Aerobic Woman.*
6. *Keri cracked corn, and I don't care—Yeeeeehah (Triscuits, tuna casserole, and Velveeta recipes)!*

The fifth and final V Society member, redheaded, easygoing Mandy Johnson, worked as an RA (resident advisor) in High Rise East. RAs received free room and board for serving as community social organizers and peacemakers on their dorm floors. It was a good deal for Mandy; it saved her thousands of dollars in exorbitant school fees. Though High Rise East was physically within close proximity to High Rise South, it was a world apart. I never went to High Rise East, and I rarely saw Mandy. She was usually preoccupied planning floor events—pizza parties, study groups, and the like—for the students on her floor. Mandy had been Michelle's roommate sophomore year, and was more Michelle and Keri's friend than mine.

Mandy didn't enthusiastically participate in our livelier V Society activities. She was earnest and kind, but I felt compelled to behave myself in her presence. I had a much harder time inciting Keri and Michelle to rambunctious behavior whenever Mandy came around. She was the most straightlaced of the five society members and not very tolerant of the passive-aggressive protests I launched when I didn't get my way in determining our V Society social calendar. Michelle and Keri generally overlooked my obvious faults.

Keri, Michelle, Mandy, and I had all chosen liberal arts majors in the College of Arts and Sciences; Stephanie was the only Wharton student among us. The four of us, all but Stephanie, aligned ourselves under the same Judeo-Christian spiritual beliefs and pursuits.

In college, students established societies and clubs for all sorts of reasons—political, moral, religious, and social. Sometimes they emerged out of a desire to foster dialogue or promote a way of thinking through the formation of a vocal, visible club. They had banners and matching T-shirts and registered with the university. We didn't do any of that. The V Society arose without a public agenda. We weren't trying to change anyone's mind or make a statement. Our goal was apolitical. We were all aware of the double standard that encouraged our male peers to recklessly pursue every carnal urge imaginable but demeaned women for behaving in the same manner. But our abstinence wasn't a protest of this hypocrisy either. We simply made the right choice for us. We rarely discussed our sexuality or our choice outside the V Society. For us abstinence was a very private matter.

But if you asked any one of us why—"Why wait?"—you'd receive a fiery earful. Keri would gladly and passionately deliver her personal manifesto: "I take literally the commandments to have sex only within the boundaries which God defined for it—the marital relationship. That means no sex as an unmarried person and no sex with a partner other than your spouse. I believe this is the best way for one's soul to remain pure and focused on what is good and right and to prepare for a healthy, happy, lifelong marriage, if that is part of God's plan, or for a healthy, happy life of celibacy if necessary. I oppose the rampant idea that you have to try on men like you try on a bathing suit before investing in it, as though, somehow, you would know by sleeping with an uncommitted boyfriend, or stranger, that this man—that you might love—wouldn't be able to develop with you into a good lover. And if not, couldn't you stand by him through therapy or whatever?"

Keri viewed our virginity the way most people perceived celebrity status—as something enviable, almost divine. "We stand out among our peers who are screwing each other endlessly—and rather indiscriminately—despite the fear of STDs and all the other unpleasant consequences," she declared.

Keri believed the five of us had artistic leanings and open-minded attitudes, which generally aligned with wilder, freer sexual mores. Yet we rebelled against free-for-all sex as well as all uptight, repressed views. "We don't fit into either image. And we don't accept either image," she stated. "We're unique individuals, interested in aesthetics—film and art of every form, as well as languages, cultures, and food. We appreciate people other than ourselves without judging or alienating them."

And so Keri embarked on a personal mission: "I want to redefine the image of the virgin, not as prudish and naïve, but as super sophisticated, tuned in, consciously choosing the best and actually demonstrating self-control. Imagine that! I kind of think of it as a kid in a candy store just shoving everything in sight in her mouth versus a mature young woman discriminately choosing one piece of 60 percent cocoa content Belgian chocolate."

Michelle, Mandy, and I felt similarly. We also thought of sex as something wonderful and sacred—not something you dished out freely with casual abandon. You had one chance to give away the treasure of your virginity. After that, you could never get it back. We believed that one time should be chosen carefully. No woman should throw away a treasure on some guy that didn't deserve it and wouldn't appreciate the gift he'd been given.

I don't think faith or any spiritual reason compelled Stephanie to maintain her V status. I believe she was in search of true love—the Right One. She refused to give it up to some random guy she barely liked for some casual, meaningless hook-up. She held the simple belief that sharing yourself intimately with someone ought to mean something. It should be an experience shared with someone important—someone you loved.

Mandy, Michelle, Keri, and I abided by an unwritten but understood code in which we refused to date guys who were not fully committed to their own personal relationships with God and thus our like-minded spiritual equals. Too much heartache ensued by getting involved with someone who didn't share our core values. For starters, we were steadfast on staying abstinent. That eliminated most of the university's male population as potential boyfriends. We only knew a few men also committed to abstinence. They were friends of ours from various Christian student groups on campus. But none of those men seemed to fully embrace our zany capers. I suspected we were a little too nonconformist and peculiarly opinionated for them. On top of that, we were a package deal of sorts. Keri, Michelle, and I were fairly inseparable, so if you dated one of us, you'd better like the other two of us, because we'd certainly be around.

All of us were on the lookout for our ideal embodiment of Mr. Right. Maybe he sat several rows behind us in the lecture hall or rode the same packed elevator in our dorm. Maybe he'd just zipped past us on the wide steps of Van Pelt Library. Who knew? Like explorers on an epic voyage, each of us aimed to seek and find him—wherever he might be. And I wasn't just looking for a boyfriend who would share my spiritual beliefs; I also wanted someone to be my creative collaborator. My ideal man was a brilliant, slightly insane artist who would challenge me creatively. I wanted someone who could work side by side with me to imagine brave new art.

V SOCIETY, SPRING
Junior Year

F-A-T C-O-W-S RENDITION
BY MANDY JOHNSON & KERI ZELMAN

Faithful

Available

Teachable

Christian

Outgoing, Osculating, Outré, Orgasmic, Overqualified, Off-Beat, Omnivorous, Oviferous, Outta hand, Outta sight

WomenS

Chapter Four

MILAN

{March, Second Semester of Junior Year}

PENN FILM AND VIDEO CLUB FIRST CAME ROARING INTO MY life when I spotted a meeting announcement in the student paper. I opened the *Daily Pennsylvanian*, and saw the invitation: "Come to the first meeting of the new Penn Film and Video Club." It seemed the perfect place to explore my interest in filmmaking. I wasn't sure if I wanted to be a photographer or a film director or both.

I spotted Milan almost as soon as I walked in the door. He stood against the wall of the lofty, wood-paneled room in Houston Hall. An artsy-looking girl with short reddish-brunette hair stood next to him. He wore a dark long-sleeve T-shirt, a black beret, and the latest style of worn faded jeans. I took one look at him and thought, *I'm going to like Penn Film and Video.*

Milan caught my eye again at the second Penn Film and Video meeting. This time we struck up a conversation.

"This club seems pretty cool," he said.

"Definitely. I've been wanting to make films for a while."

"Do you have some ideas for a film?"

"Not really—I mean, not yet, anyway. How about you?"

"I have a few ideas."

We paused our conversation to listen to a brief presentation by the student officers of the Film Club. A curly-haired guy with sharp features and big, brown, cascading locks delivered the introduction.

"The club owns a video camera and several Super 8 cameras that you guys can check out. We have a number of film projects going on, and we're looking for help; so be sure to sign up on the sheet in the back. Let us know what you're interested in. If you want to help out on a film project, write that next to your name and phone number. Also make a note of your film experience, if you want."

Milan and I introduced ourselves to another student sitting close by and started tossing around concepts for a short film. As the meeting ended, Milan suggested, "Let's get something to eat, and talk about more ideas."

"Yeah, I'm starving," I agreed.

"Me too," the other student said.

The three of us headed to lunch together in the Hall of Flags, which filled the entire back side of Houston Hall. It housed the immense two-story dining area at the heart of the student center. Downstairs, around the perimeter of the hall, resided a small food court with different varieties of fast food—pizza, sandwiches, and the like. The second story of the hall formed an open three-sided balcony. You could sit at tables on the quiet second floor and look down onto the rows of tables populating the noisy food court below. Enormous flags hung along the edges of the balcony representing Penn and its seven Ivy League sisters: Harvard, Yale, Princeton, Dartmouth, Cornell, Brown, and Columbia.

I placed my order at the bagel sandwich shop and pulled up a chair at a big round table with Milan and the girl from the Film Club meeting. I recognized her from one of my communications classes, and thought her name was Wendy—but I wasn't positive. She wasn't the red-haired girl that had been with Milan at the first meeting. She was brunette and plump and not nearly as animated as Milan and me. She ate her lunch quickly and left, leaving me sitting alone with Milan.

We continued to toss around haphazard film ideas. I'd ordered a tuna melt on a raisin bagel—not the best choice. I was glad Milan had sat across from me at the wide table. He wasn't close enough to smell my tuna breath. I liked looking at his pleasing face, with its strong, dark features. He spoke elaborately in an unrehearsed manner about absurd films he intended to make. His ideas grew more fantastic with each film he described, as if he were testing himself to see just how bizarre an idea he could concoct. Completely engrossed, he described the elements of a film that would make him the number one offender on some animal rights activist's hit list.

"Let's take a chicken and throw it from the top of my dorm in the winter. We'll film it as its blood splatters in the snow," he said excitedly but as though he didn't believe a single word he said. He stopped for a moment and looked at me expectantly, waiting for a reaction. Would I be disgusted, or would I reply enthusiastically as though I took him seriously?

"That's very interesting," I replied flatly. "But where are we going to get a chicken in the middle of the winter in Philadelphia?"

Although unrealistic and extravagant if he really intended to make movies, he certainly wasn't dull. If I listened to only half of what he said, he even seemed sane. Perhaps the sum of his seemingly contradictory characteristics made him so engaging. He seemed worldly and street-wise, but at the same time, fresh and candid. He exhibited an unspoiled boyishness in the way he spoke so freely and expressed his thoughts in such an undisciplined fashion.

"The summer before I came here, I lived in England. I showed up with one suitcase and a couple hundred British pounds. I sold fake art— well, replicas—in London," he explained. "I had to do something until I figured out a way to pay to come here."

"You were there just to work for the summer?"

"No, taking some classes in a summer program. But I had to work so I could get by."

After lunch, we headed outside. I hesitated, temporarily blinded by the flood of sunlight washing over us. My eyes quickly adjusted from Houston Hall's dark corridor to the brilliance of the courtyard outside. Ornate, black metal café tables, occupied by sprinklings of unhurried students, dotted the walkway's mammoth gray stone slabs. The distinct, lavish glow of spring encapsulated all of campus like a radiant, effervescent umbrella. The very atmosphere felt new, cleansed of mire and the sediment of winter. Everything icy and lethargic had vanished into a vacuum—the occasion emerged anew.

"Where are you headed?" Milan asked.

"High Rise South."

"Are there computers there? I need to type a paper."

"Yeah, there's a computer lab on the first floor."

"Cool, can you show me where it is?"

"Of course."

We headed down Locust Walk, toward West Campus. Our gaits kept pace in leisurely, matching strides. As Milan walked next to me and continued to relay ridiculous movie plots, I felt a budding sense of admiration. He was undoubtedly more compelling than the other guys I knew.

"So, do you know anyone in the Film Club?" I asked.

"No. Do you?"

"No, this is only my second meeting."

"Right, I think I saw you at the first meeting."

"Yeah, I think I remember seeing you there. Weren't you with someone?" I asked, feigning only a mild interest in his answer.

"No, I don't think so."

"Oh, I figured you knew some people in the club. You were standing next to a girl at the meeting."

"Really, what did she look like?"

"I don't know . . . She looked pretty cool. Kinda reddish hair."

"Hmm," he paused, appearing to wrack his brain. "I don't know. She was with me?"

"Oh, I don't know," I replied dismissing my initial inquiry.

"I have no idea," he shrugged. "I don't remember coming to the meeting with anyone."

I was pretty sure I had seen him standing side by side with the red-headed girl. It was the kind of proximity that indicated familiarity. You wouldn't just walk up to a stranger and stand that close. But I could be wrong. Who knew? I didn't have any reason to doubt him. Maybe he was just being friendly to some random student who was also into film-making.

I loved walking down Locust Walk in the springtime—one of my favorite times of the year. I never fell out of love with the month of March as long as I lived in the Northeast. Throughout all the semesters I lived in Philadelphia, March signified a substantive change, unlike in Northern California where I hardly noticed the climate's five-degree transition out of winter into the new season. Here Spring became a recognizable persona, a character that transformed the entire university into a grand canvas of sheer beauty. The lawns perked up and showed off their decorative clusters of bright, budding flowers and little shrubs. The forms of bare, fruitless ginkgo trees arched over the wide, weathered brick walkway at the heart of campus. In the spring, the ginkgo biloba fruit didn't drop and stink as onslaughts of students heading to class crushed them into mush underfoot. The campus pulsed with renewed vitality. The paralyzing, freeze-this-California-girl-to-death winter chill had broken. I still had my lined leather gloves stuffed in the pocket of my coat, but I didn't need to wear them.

"Here it is," I said as I pointed toward the entrance of the computer lab inside my building.

"Great, thanks."

"Yeah, we should stay in touch—you know, to work on a film project," I remarked.

"For sure. Here, give me your number," Milan requested. He wrote my phone number on a page of notebook paper.

"Cool. What's yours?" I asked. I scribbled his number on the back of my Penn Film and Video flyer. "All right, see you around."

"Yep, I'll talk to you later." He smiled.

A couple of days later, Milan returned to my dorm to visit. I introduced him to Keri and Michelle. I think they found him just as fascinating as I did.

"Where do you live?" I asked him. I expected him to say off campus. Living off campus represented certain independence; it subtly implied that you were above safe, university-governed, housing department–controlled dorm living.

"The dorm across from the food court," Milan replied.

His dorm, nicknamed the Hole, was the farthest east, at the opposite end of campus from Superblock. It wasn't exactly a cool place to live. Mostly freshman and some sophomores lived there. Even though it was located close to the heart of campus, it stood the lone dorm on that block. It sat adjacent to a huge, open, half-acre-sized lawn area where outdoor rock concerts materialized during Spring Fling. If you weren't going to the dining hall there or didn't know someone who lived there, you pretty much forgot that it existed. It wasn't like Superblock, packed with thousands of students and simmering with activity.

The high-rise complexes were self-contained social spheres. High Rise South housed a student commissary in the basement, where I occasionally bought a late-night pint of chocolate fudge brownie ice cream and ate half the carton during a V Society study session. High Rise North accommodated the low-lit, espresso-slinging Underground Café. All the high-rise buildings contained multiroom apartments, most with four student occupants. Milan's dorm didn't have a café, a commissary, or apartments, only two stories of single and double studio rooms and its own dining hall.

Milan and I began hanging out pretty regularly; he was interesting to talk to, and I enjoyed his twisted sense of humor.

"So, I found a place where we can get live chickens to star in our film," he said seriously one day.

"You're kidding, right? Where are you going to keep a stupid chicken? In your room? You can't keep a live, squawking bird in your dorm room. Your RA will kill you!"

Milan broke into a huge smile. "Kay eye dee ding," he said.

"What?"

"K-I-D-ding—*kidding*."

"Oh, right," I replied, returning the smile.

A few days later, I stopped by Milan's room for a short midday visit.

"Hey, let me show you something," he said. "You can get into my room without a key."

The tall, narrow window at the end of Milan's room faced an un-adorned outdoor rooftop enclosed by walls and windows of identical dorm rooms forming a grey industrial courtyard. In the hallway, around the corner from Milan's room, stood three tall, narrow windows that opened and swung outward toward the enclosed roof area. The windows measured about a foot and a half wide and five feet tall.

Milan took me to the window in the hallway and pushed it open. Then he ducked and stepped through it onto the safely enclosed roof-top. He walked diagonally across the corner of the rooftop, less than twenty feet, to the first window on the left. He gently pushed it open and stepped through it into his room.

"I never lock it," he said. "You can get in this way whenever you want."

All university students had access to all the dorms on campus. At any time, I could simply slide my student ID card and get into Milan's dorm. Once inside, I simply had to walk to the hallway Milan had showed me, and I could visit him unannounced whenever I liked. Soon me and my two cohorts, Keri and Michelle, were descending uninvited upon Milan's poorly lit, untidy dorm room. The three of us sprawled across his small twin bed, leaving him to sit in the only chair in the room. A sheet of paper hanging on the wall with chewed-up, stuck-on green gum amassed in a dripping linear pattern simultaneously appalled and fascinated us.

"What is that?" Keri asked, pointing at the chewing gum assemblage.

"Consider it a work of art," Milan replied.

"And that? What's that?" Michelle pointed at the black–and–white collage of stark, abstract curves hanging next to the gum paper.

"Oh, that's called *Bipolar Connection* . . . or *Oral Sex* collage, if you please," Milan stated matter-of-factly.

An unannounced visit to Milan's room always elicited endless post-visit discussions. One night, Keri, Stephanie, and I prattled on for twenty minutes, about the pretty, slightly intoxicated African American student who had knocked on Milan's door at eleven o'clock as we left his room. Stephanie checked in on sleeping Milan at ten o'clock the next morning and reported to us that the evidence of his not-so-discreet tryst had been laid to rest in his dorm room garbage can.

"Can you believe the breakfast burritos in Milan's trash can this morning?" she exclaimed, referring to the two used condoms that she had seen lying on top of the trash in Milan's garbage can when she stopped by. "It was the girl that came by last night," she guessed.

"So I asked Milan if he slept with her," Stephanie went on.

"*No, you didn't!*" said Keri, surprised by Stephanie's audacity.

"Yes, I did—and guess what he said . . ." Stephanie's face turned pink and shining beneath her unruly hair. Her mouth and nose quivered as she tried to hold back her laugh and then exploded. She could hardly finish her sentence, she laughed so hard.

"He said—*no!*" Stephanie cried, in near hysterics. "Did her, bagged her, had her, got some!" Stephanie cried, mocking Milan's fib.

"Don Juan Milan," Michelle stated dryly.

All four of us shrieked with uncontrollable ear-splitting peals of laughter.

On my way to the library the next afternoon, I took a detour and dropped in on Milan.

"Hey, what's up?" he greeted me cordially as he opened the door.

"What's going on?" I said casually, trying to mask my newly acquired knowledge of his escapades. I sat down in his desk chair and dropped my book bag on the floor. I wondered what he'd say if I teased him, "Late night Tuesday? How was your little slumber party?" Would he turn red with embarrassment, or would he deny it with a straight face, as he'd done with Stephanie?

"Just heading to a study session in a few minutes," he replied. "Oh, Jenn thought you were cool."

"Who?" I asked.

"Jenn. You know, the girl that stopped by the other night when you were visiting."

"Oh, I didn't remember her name. Yeah, she seemed nice."

Milan laughed. "Yeah, she was like, 'Why don't you date her? She seems really cool.'"

He waited for a reaction. I didn't know what to say. What *could* I say? He was sleeping with her, right? And she had asked why he didn't date *me*—in fact, she had suggested it. Tongue-tied, I did what I always did when a guy said something that left me speechless: I pretended not to hear him and changed the subject.

"What study session are you going to?" I asked.

"Econ."

"Cool. Well, I'll catch you later."

"Yep, okay later," he said.

I headed out and crossed the street, back on course to Van Pelt Library at the center of campus.

Several days later, Michelle, Keri, and I sat in our living room listening to one of our favorite CDs and talking about our favorite subject: Milan.

Keri: "He's so funny. Why do you think he showers twice a day?"

Michelle: "I don't know. He's just *different*."

Me: "Stephanie likes to sniff him."

Michelle: "No kidding?"

Me: "Does he smell good?"

Keri: "I don't know."

Me: "Maybe I'll try to smell him next time I see him."

Michelle: "I've never heard of a guy shaving his armpits either."

Keri: "I know. What's up with that?"

Michelle: "Who knows?"

"I luhv Lah-teeno, blahk, and Per-shun woh-mahn," Keri said with a Serbian accent, mimicking the declaration Milan had made earlier that week. Somewhere in the midst of one of our wild, rambling conversations, he'd let that slip.

Noh, I luhv ahl bee-u-tee-fuhl woh-mahn," I said, completing the rest of his statement with my best Serbian accent.

That evening, we couldn't decide what to do with ourselves for the night. Often we went to the Underground Café in the basement of High Rise North and listened to emerging student musicians rock the microphone. We'd gone there several times to drink lattes and listen to Marc Zola, a folksy guitarist and singer that Keri loved. We also liked to frequent Beanie's, a new café just off campus, not far from Milan's dorm. Our favorite other pastimes were praying and reading the Bible. And, of course, aside from that, we often amused ourselves by telling jokes that were funny only to V Society members.

Stephanie liked to dabble at the guitar and write songs. She often performed impromptu guitar concerts for us. When she wasn't singing, she authored things like the Alliterated Allegations of the Day. She didn't come over that night though. We were on our own to amuse ourselves.

V Society, Spring
Junior Year

ALLITERATED ALLEGATIONS OF THE DAY

1. *Michelle matriculates into a myriad of majors metamorphosizing into a mega-metalhead musically mastering the meringue to Metallica.*
2. *Keri kraps korn in a kaka-kolored kar with Karen from Konstantinople.*
3. *Adele and Allison anticipate action from an amorous art aficionado with an accentuated appendage.*
4. *Milan's many moods make marvelous mountains of magnificent madness.*

Keri, Michelle, and I deliberated for a few more minutes and then decided to make the trek to Beanie's, on the opposite side of campus. It took ten minutes to walk there. We arrived and ordered hot drinks. We sat down at one of the round tables, and I quickly surveyed the room for signs of any of our top ten most intriguing campus men. No one interesting lingered in Beanie's that night. After about thirty minutes of chatting, we grew bored of the lackluster café scene.

Recently, Milan's room had risen to the top of the V Society's Favorite Hangouts list. His place drew us in like an addictive compulsion. In the daytime, it looked like nothing more than a tiny, poorly lit studio—slightly disheveled and ordinary. We didn't know that after sunset, Milan had the power to will his room into wielding beguiling, magical powers.

"Let's go visit Milan," Keri suggested.

"Great idea," Michelle and I chimed in.

Milan's dorm stood only a half block away and across the street. We slid our student identification cards into the card readers at the entrance and pushed through the waist-level turnstile that enabled entry into the dorm. We charged upstairs and into the hallway near Milan's room. I considered the three of us crawling through his window and then thought better of it. It was nine thirty at night and not such a good idea to be crawling through his window. He might have company already. From the hallway, his window looked dark. He probably wasn't home.

Michelle knocked on his front door, and we waited. Nothing. I knocked again louder, and soon Milan opened the door. His lights were off, his hair tousled. He stood fully clothed with his shoes on. He let us into the room without much of a greeting and flicked on a small desk light.

"I was sleeping," he grumbled, clearly in one of his PMS moods. "Where are my cigarettes?" he mumbled to himself as he picked through odd items littering his desk.

His grumpiness didn't discourage us. I sat down on top of the tangled mess of sheets strewn across his bed. Michelle and Keri sat down next to me. Milan sat across from us, slouched in the desk chair and said nothing. He just sat there and looked at us. I started talking about our less-than-exciting night out. Soon he seemed to warm to our intrusion. He smiled a little as I talked, but mostly he just sat there in the dim room—quiet—carefully studying the three of us. He didn't say a word, but his wheels were clearly turning. He was thinking *something*.

The longer we stayed in the room, the more I became aware of an undeniable, visceral feeling, like an electric undercurrent. The room had a clear and present vibe, as noticeable as an aroma in the air. It enveloped me stealthily, like invisible steam. I entered a Bermuda Triangle. A strange supernatural force pulled at the depths of me like a tractor beam sucking me into another dimension. Silent, uncommunicative Milan continued to sit, his dark eyes locked on us. We stayed in the room another twenty minutes before we grew tired of his unresponsiveness and left.

The next day, I sat at my desk reading my new favorite book of the moment, *The Confessions of Saint Augustine*. Saint Augustine wrote deeply—and candidly. I liked this guy. I had only started the book and had never finished reading it. But *Cliffs Notes* broke it all down. St. Augustine was honest. Abstinence wasn't easy or fun. It went against the very wiring programmed inside my DNA. I didn't stay abstinent because it came easily—it didn't. I stayed abstinent because it was the right thing to do. God commanded it, so I obeyed it.

I knew from reading the Bible that bad stuff went down when people ignored God's commandments. Entire nations disappeared off the face of the earth when they disobeyed God's instruction manual. Some of the Old Testament rules in God's playbook were pretty straightforward, like wash your hands before you eat. Duh. The Middle Ages' bubonic plague might not have wiped out one third of Europe if people had paid attention to that one. The Jewish people stayed in bondage to heathen nations and in slavery for decades because they thought they had a better way to do things than God did. Then of course, there were the dead firstborn and the plagues of locusts and the blood-colored water—all completely unnecessary when a "Yes, God, we'll do it your way" would have sufficed. In the long run, things worked out better when you did it God's way and generally with a lot less unnecessary drama.

I didn't want to be one of those foolish people that found myself in some harrowingly unpleasant predicament because I had given God the middle finger and decided to do it my way. God tried to help us out, "Hey, Earthlings, here are some rules to make life a little easier." He created Ten Commandments, not Ten Suggestions. God invented sex, so He probably had a better idea of what I was supposed to do with that gift than I did.

Besides everyone had the same old arguments against abstinence: "It's unrealistic," "If it feels good, do it," "It's not for modern people," "It's unnatural *not to* . . ." Blah, blah, blah. Abstinence *was* unnatural.

Just like eating tofu or riding an airplane—both completely *un*natural—but modern people did both all the time. People made decisions to do *unnatural* things every day. Abstinence was a decision of choice—a mind-over-matter commitment to exercise self-control *despite* natural, God-given human impulses.

It all boiled down to one simple question: "Is truth absolute, or is truth relative?" Many people say that truth is relative: you have your truth, and I have mine. The problem with relative truth is that it's based on convenience. Modern people love convenience; we prefer to invent morality based on what suits our desires. Yet, when someone wrongs us, we'll protest that truth is absolute: "You stole my wallet—that's wrong!" We'd dismiss the thief as a lunatic if he replied, "I can take anything I want. It's my right." Many of the same people who declare truth is relative would argue that it's *absolutely* wrong to steal someone's wallet.

But I believe that Truth is *always* absolute—even when it's inconvenient. I believe that Truth is defined by a single, almighty, all-powerful God. In His Truth there is Light. In that Light, there is Life. When we make the decision to follow that Light, we become light—shining brightly in a fatally flawed world. Though we live within the dominant culture of relativity, we live transformed—at odds with the world. I believe Jesus was the greatest nonconformist to walk the face of this earth. He lived at odds with all of mainstream culture. I believe He is the Light. He illuminates the way to live *in* this world—but in nonconformity to its values.

One of my roommates had just come in from class. I could hear her making lunch in the kitchen. I walked out of my bedroom and down the short, dark hallway. During fall semester, Keri and I had shared the large double bedroom at the end of the hall. Allison and Michelle shared it now. According to customary dorm etiquette, the four of us had switched rooms at the beginning of spring semester. That way each roommate would have one semester in her own room and one semester sharing the double bedroom. My room had a brown faux-wood desk, accompanied by two rows of mounted wall shelves, a desk chair, and an extra long twin bed. My old double room had two desks and a metal-frame bunk bed.

"Hey, Mom," I greeted Keri cheerily. Lately, we'd begun calling each other Mom. My mother called weekly, and Michelle always summoned me to the phone by saying, "It's your mom." For some reason, she began using that line for every caller—Milan, Stephanie, Mandy; regardless of who called, Michelle said, "It's your mom." Naturally, Keri and I found that amusing. From then on all three of us assumed the nickname. I plopped down on the sofa, ready to talk her ear off about Saint Augustine.

"Hey," she replied. She stopped making lunch and came to sit down next to me on the sofa. She looked me directly in the eyes, her gaze steady and her demeanor serious. At the same time, she looked at me lovingly, almost maternally.

"I want you to promise me something," she said.

"Ummm . . . yeah?"

"Promise me you won't go to Milan's room alone at night," she said.

"Umm . . . yep, okay," I promised.

Then she got up and went back to making lunch.

Keri was truly my dearest, closest friend and a wise woman. She knew me, in some ways better than I knew myself. She had been there the previous night. She had felt the peculiar and powerful undercurrent, as had Michelle. She knew that I had felt it as well and suspected that its draw resonated the strongest in the depths of me. We never discussed it again. She said the one thing that needed to be said, and I heeded her gentle reproof. Thank God I had this V Society sisterhood. Thank God, Keri perceived my greatest weakness, long before I admitted it to myself.

V SOCIETY, APRIL
Junior Year

SCIENTIFIC EQUATION OF THE DAY

$$\text{Range of Hours Milan Should be Avoided} = \frac{\lim AM}{x \to 6} \quad \frac{\lim PM}{x \to 11}$$

{Note: Extreme caution must be used in contact during these times. We warned you!}

MILAN'S FOUR COMMANDMENTS

1. *Sex is bad.*
2. *It is the moon.*
3. *It is a pencil sketch.*
4. *Jupiter is a god.*

A FILM ABOUT MILAN

WORKING TITLES
Milan and the V Society or The Elevator Society

FAVORITE MILAN QUOTES
"I don't have time to talk crap."
"I'm kidding—K-I-D-ding."

NOTES ON MILAN

- *Always making business plans*
- *Spends too much money*
- *Elevator Dance*
- *Chicken off the roof*
- *Wears black beret*
- *Doesn't wear underwear sometimes*
- *Showers all the time*
- *Chewing gum art*
- *"Behind Black Eyes" (sung by the V Society chorus)*
- *Cigarettes (before hello)*
- *Sex and breakfast burritos*
- *Bipolar Connection collage (aka Oral Sex collage)*
- *Latino, black, Persian—and all beautiful women*
- *Naps fully clothed with shoes on*
- *Dated two British women at once, in the same dorm, without either knowing*
- *Boat to travel around the world unbound by any country's laws and borders*
- *People always bring him things (fresh squeezed OJ, spring water, vitamins)*
- *Rakija (Balkan moonshine) and friends*
- *If sad or injured, he cares*
- *Moody. What is PMS?*

Chapter Five

~❦~

EYE CANDY

{March, Second Semester of Junior Year}

THE CROWD ROARED. ONLOOKERS CLAPPED. CONTESTANT NUMBER *One stood on the stage—waiting patiently for the judge's decision. "What is the final score?" the announcer's voice boomed loudly, reverberant and clear over the loudspeaker. "Contestant Number One earned a perfect ten!" I proclaimed. The crowd exploded. Deafening cheers and applause filled the air. Another male supermodel was born.*

That scene played in my head.

Obviously, something was the matter with me. I was sick and wrong. I should appreciate a man for his character. But strolling down Locust Walk in between classes, with a constant flux of contestants passing me in droves, I couldn't assess character—only exterior. I could only answer one question: "Good model or bad model?" In the onslaught of possibilities, the split-second decision reigned supreme.

At that very moment, as he whizzed past me, I decided whether a guy qualified as model beautiful or not. It was terrible—I knew that. But I deflected any criticism with the justification that men had judged women that way since the beginning of time. I excused my affection for physical beauty by claiming a photographer's exemption. As New York and Europe's next great fashion photographer, I had committed myself to the artistic pursuit of worthy photography subjects.

It didn't take me long to figure out that fashion photography enabled me to come into direct contact with the most beautiful men on campus. I wasn't bold enough to walk up to a good-looking guy and ask him to model for me. I didn't seek out rejection. However, I did have enough sense to spot a great potential model and then ask around until I found someone that knew him. Then I would have that person ask him to model. If Potential Model Guy seemed interested, my contact would introduce us. If Potential Model Guy was not interested in modeling, my contact would report back to me, and I'd remain anonymous. Potential Model Guy would never know that I was the photographer seeking to immortalize his physical attributes on film.

I couldn't help myself. I enjoyed looking at beautiful men. I told myself it was no different than the way I cherished spending an afternoon in an art gallery, gazing at a splendid painting or an arresting sculpture. I appreciated the way magnificently designed features and complementary proportions culminated in a masterpiece. I liked eye candy. I just wanted to look—not touch. I probably would have wet my pants if one of those drop-dead beautiful guys had actually made a move on me. I was pretty good at subtly signaling that an advance would be quickly rebuffed. I was always cordial toward my newfound models, but also very professional—never flirtatious. Photo shoots were all business. Most models could tell that my interest lay in getting the perfect shot—not a date.

I looked forward to every new photo shoot with excited anticipation, dying to stand behind my camera and give direction to my latest supermodel.

"Turn left and lower your chin a little. Lean back on the motorcycle and look aloof. Good. That's it."

Snap. My camera shutter fired.

"Don't show so many teeth when you smile. No, that's not quite it. Okay, imagine you're on the cover of *GQ* magazine. I need *sophistication*. Don't look like you're the friendly neighborhood paperboy. Good!"

Snap. Snap. Snap.

But after every shoot, I always sighed with anxious relief when Model Guy and I went our separate ways. Extremely beautiful men made me nervous.

Once, I arranged a photo shoot with the second-hottest guy on campus—OJ, a gorgeous black student and a Castle brother. He had the same light-brown skin tone as me, with tightly curled black hair. He had the ideal model build—about six feet tall and physically perfect—with the exception of his skinny pencil legs.

OJ's fraternity, known as the Castle, had prime real estate in the middle of campus. The building, true to its name, resembled a Gothic castle. The entrance of the Castle sat right at the edge of College Green, forming the perimeter of a picturesque circle of great Gothic-style buildings.

College Green anchored the main artery of the university. I had come here as a fresh-faced first-year student to feel the pulse of two hundred and fifty years of tradition. College Green intimately connected me to my romantic notions of great thinkers and storied alumni who had walked the grounds generations before me. Its open acreage, manicured lawns, and giant, arching trees formed a picture-perfect vision of East Coast college life. Students lounged on the grass in the fall and spring; and teaching assistants conducted small class seminars on the greens.

The office of the university president in College Hall inhabited the quad to the right of the Castle, across the rolling emerald turf. College Hall perched, stately and monumental, looking quintessentially collegiate. Massive stone steps and a colossal statue of Penn's founding father, Ben Franklin, marked its entrance. Tall, arched windows, decorated with ornate cinquefoils, adorned the four stories of College Hall's gray-green facade. The iconic Furness Building rose up at the far end of College Green, directly opposite the Castle. Furness soared above the green, as impressive as College Hall, but characterized by dark orange-red stone. Tom Hanks had filmed a portion of his Academy Award–winning performance in *Philadelphia* inside the Furness library. Directly across from the office of the university president, north of the Castle, sprawled the main university library. There Keri, Michelle, and I sometimes attempted to study together, unsuccessfully, before abandoning our course packets and lecture notes for nonacademic social studies.

The Castle's enviable geographic location alluded to its inhabitants' many other notable characteristics. From what I observed, Castle brothers hailed from the top American and international prep schools. They ranked well above average in physical attributes and descended from some of the wealthiest families in the world. They differed from their rival fraternity Saint A's in their racial diversity. Saint A's mirrored Abercrombie: homogenous, all-American, and very white. The Castle reflected a United Nations: multiethnic, multicultural, and richly poetic in its various shades. Castle brothers always loitered on the front steps of their house. Their presence reminded every passerby of their princely status.

"The Castle has the best parties," Stephanie proclaimed.

She voted theirs best party in our V Society poll. I regarded the Castle with a sort of love-hate disdain. The Castle housed many Eurotrash students. Euro boys secretly enamored me. If a good-looking guy had a charming foreign accent, wore neat sideburns, smelled of the intoxicating elixir of cigarette smoke and expensive cologne, and dressed like he had just arrived from Fashion Week in Europe, he rated as 100 percent Eurotrash. My roommates and I affectionately referred to all cool-looking, fashionable male students as *Euro*. The term *Euro* wasn't an accurate description, since the majority of the guys we called *Euro* weren't European. We used *Euro* loosely to include handsome, stylish black American guys and a handful of striking Pakistani students. The term also applied to some alluring Israeli students and a small bunch of South Americans. We only knew one guy—a cute British student infatuated with Michelle—who *actually* qualified geographically as a Euro boy. All the other requirements were optional. The term had everything to do with international fashion and street savvy—and nothing to do with European origins. *Eurotrash* isn't exactly the politically correct term; that would be *male fashionista*.

In theory, I liked the Castle; it brimmed with worthy photo subjects. But in reality, it reminded me of the rarely mentioned but widely understood social hierarchy at school. The Castle made me uncomfortable. In the V Society world, my friends and I were the cleverest girls we knew. In our world, we were attractive and incredibly interesting. In the Castle world, we didn't exist.

I went to a Castle party one night with Stephanie and stayed for all of about five minutes. I probably wouldn't have been admitted except that Stephanie knew someone at the door. I recognized one of the girls at the door; she had been in the same dorm as me freshman year. I'm not sure she remembered me; I remembered her because she was one of the most stunning black students in the freshman class.

Once inside, Stephanie and I made our way into a spacious and dark room with high ceilings. Well-dressed, attractive students stood around, mingling and drinking. The room smelled strongly of beer, and music blared from hidden speakers. As soon as we entered the room, a short Pakistani fashionista-guy made eye contact with Stephanie. He seemed to know her; she walked over to him, leaving me standing alone.

Up until the time I entered the Castle party, I had felt pretty cute. I wore my urban hipster, nod-to-grunge clothes (the Seattle rock band Pearl Jam's grunge style permeated American fashion)—secondhand, worn, dark dyed jeans from Urban Outfitters, and a Gap shirt. But suddenly, I felt oppressively inadequate. No one here looked like they shopped at Gap. No one wore twenty-three-dollar, secondhand jeans from Urban Outfitters. I had never heard of the luxury brands from the high-end boutiques where these students probably shopped. I didn't know the names of the cocktails they drank. I'd been to St. Croix and St. Thomas but had no idea where St. Barts was—or wherever these kids vacationed.

Everyone at the party looked like they had just rolled out of their parents' overstuffed wallets. Their clothes fit better than mine did; my jeans were baggy, held up by an inexpensive leather belt. Up until that very second, I had thought baggy jeans were in style. All the girls there looked casual—but *perfect*—with a studied, styled sort of ease. None of the women appeared to be wearing makeup, except some eyeliner and light lipstick. They didn't need to wear makeup; their faces seemed naturally flawless, as if none of them had ever had a pimple in their entire lives. I had little makeup on too, but I had an aggressive Retin-A, acne-fighting regimen that kept my skin blemish free.

I looked for Stephanie—to rescue me. She stood talking to the fashionista-guy. He seemed to be looking over her shoulder, at me, with a disdainful curiosity. Man, I was getting paranoid—he couldn't *possibly* be looking at me. I couldn't wait to get out of there. Finally, after what seemed like a year, Stephanie came back over.

"Can we get out of here?" I asked, almost pleading.

"Already?"

"Yes!" I yelled, making sure she could hear me over the screaming music.

We left the Castle party, and I breathed in deeply, as we headed through campus back to my dorm. We'd returned to my world. I began to feel cute again.

"Who was that?" I asked Stephanie.

"Oh, that's just Abbas. I hadn't seen him in a while." Then she went off on a tangent: "Abbas asked about my friend Claudia. I told Abbas that she played soccer on the team. He said, 'Girls don't play soccer.' So stupid!"

"Is that all he said?" I asked, trying to bring her back to the issue at hand.

"Oh, he was just wondering why I haven't been around." Apparently, Stephanie had hung out with Abbas and his friends the previous semester, before she joined up with the V Society in the spring. No wonder she was on a first-name basis with the whole clan of well-off Pakistani fashionista-guys.

"I told him I had new friends," she said, referring to me and the rest of the V Society. "Then he asked where I was getting my *new* friends from."

Stephanie didn't mean the comment as an insult to me. She just relayed the message honestly, without filtering. I knew what the comment meant. Abbas, like me, knew that I had no business at a Castle party.

But, unaware of my hostile sentiments toward his fraternity, OJ, the Castle brother, stopped by my dorm room a couple weeks after my photo shoot with him to pick up copies of his pictures. He sat in my apartment and chatted for twenty minutes. It thrilled me to be sitting in the same room as him and talking as if he were a regular guy, not the second-most beautiful man on campus. Sophomore year, we'd enrolled in the same Spanish language seminar, only a dozen students, and he hadn't noticed me sitting behind him the entire semester.

"So, how did you become interested in photography?" he asked.

"I took a class when I was ten. It was fun. It was a college-for-kids program at this junior college, back home. But then, the class ended, and I went to the darkroom a couple times, but kinda lost interest. Then last year—do you remember that photo exhibit that came to campus? It featured celebrity portraits by big-name advertising photographers. It amazed me. That got me interested in photography again."

"I think I must have missed the exhibit. Was it here long?"

"No, only a few days. It traveled to colleges all over the country," I replied.

"So, you want to be a professional photographer?"

"I'm not sure. Maybe. I can't decide if I want to be a film director or a photographer. How about you? What do you want to do?"

"I think I want to be a teacher. I'd really enjoy something like that."

OJ's fellow Castle brother, Kamau, was in my opinion the hottest man in the entire school and the most beautiful black man I'd ever seen. He was two shades darker than me, with perfect, chiseled features— definitely cover-of-*GQ* worthy. Kamau made every celebrity, every teen idol, and every rock star look like day-old bread. Once, as I stood in the food court just off campus, someone came up behind me and covered my eyes with both hands. I turned around and saw OJ, accompanied by Kamau. I nearly died.

I felt honored that OJ hadn't just picked up his pictures and left. But at the same time I kept thinking, *Why is he staying so* long? *Why is he here in my room talking to me? I wish he would hurry up and leave!* I felt out of my league. I figured the less time he talked to me, the less obvious it would be that I didn't have anything clever or flirtatious to say to him. I had only flirted once before—with a German exchange student, in high school. I was such a flirting novice, that I was probably the *only* person who would have even recognized that I was flirting. But I figured most women probably did flirt with OJ—who wouldn't?—except me.

He was extremely pleasant to talk to, but I sighed with relief when he finally left. He'd been sitting in my bedroom. When he first came into the apartment, I went to my room to retrieve his photos, and he had followed me. I had thought he'd take the pictures and be out the front door before I could say "Bye." I hadn't known he'd grab a seat and visit. After he left, I needed a moment alone to process the amicable visit from gorgeous Model Guy. The next semester, OJ studied abroad in Spain and immediately landed professional modeling gigs.

A couple weeks later, my friend Helena, who lived in the dorm room next to OJ's room (he didn't live in the Castle house), revealed that he had commented, "Adele is the kind of girl I'd marry. But I'd never date someone like her now because I wouldn't treat her right." The comment shocked me. Had it not come from Helena—a completely trustworthy source—I wouldn't have believed that OJ said any such thing. I never thought of myself as on the radar of guys like OJ. I wasn't on his radar *really*, but I felt reassured that he had stayed and talked to me those twenty minutes because he had actually enjoyed our brief, nonflirtatious conversation.

V SOCIETY, BEST OF THE BEST LIST
Junior Year

BEST PARTIES
The Castle {Stephanie}
Pi Lam {Adele}

WORST PARTIES
The Castle {Adele}

That spring, my roommates and I plunged into all sorts of adventures, zipping around Philadelphia in Stephanie's silver Audi. Few undergraduates kept cars on campus. It was too much hassle to find parking; and common sense dictated that you wouldn't park a nice car on the crime-prone streets of West Philadelphia. Stephanie had made an arrangement with one of the on-campus fraternities to park her car in their tiny lot. She paid them a monthly sum to guarantee secure campus parking, close to her dorm.

On one particular night in March, Keri, Michelle, and I waited patiently inside Stephanie's car, while she ran inside the Wawa corner market. In a few minutes, Stephanie returned to the car carrying a carton of eggs. Keri, Michelle, and I had initially agreed to accompany her on this excursion to egg the Tabard house, but as we pulled out of the lot, I couldn't think of a single reason to visit misfortune on a Tabard member. First of all, I had never been to the Tabard house and didn't even know the names on the Tabard Society roster. Second, the one girl that I thought might be in Tabard, who had lived in the same dorm as me freshman year, was quite nice—friendly and unassuming.

"I can't stand Tabard," Stephanie griped. "They're a bunch of elitist moneybags." Our car pulled up to the ordinary-looking Tabard Society house, and Stephanie exited with the carton of eggs.

So why was I sitting in Stephanie's car about to be an accomplice to undeserved meanness? For Pete's sake, Stephanie could have been the president of Tabard. I remember the first time she drove me out to her parents' house on Long Island to film some footage for the short film we were making. I had only visited a few such homes in my life. We pulled off a main street in a residential neighborhood and drove up a long—very long—gravel driveway. As we drove past enormous maple trees, an expansive, palatial dwelling came into view. Stephanie parked the car at the top of the driveway, next to a door on the side of the house.

"This is your place?" I asked, trying to sound nonchalant.

"Uh-huh," she replied, preoccupied, as she dug in her trunk to pull out a video camera.

For whatever reason, Stephanie had awoken to her social cause that school year. She had temporarily turned her back on friendships formed on the bond of like tax brackets and excessively expensive New York private school educations. Michelle, Keri, and I had become her new running buddies, middle-class girls from middle-class suburbs, with white-collar parents, but without sports cars or near-limitless lines of credit.

Why did Stephanie have such disdain for Tabard? I don't think Tabard girls had ever done anything to her directly or indirectly. They hadn't blacklisted her during rush, as they had one of my freshman-year acquaintances. As far as I knew, no one in Tabard had ever barred Stephanie from attending their parties, or had done anything malicious to her. Maybe the sheer fact that her new friends, middle-class girls like Michelle, Keri, and I, wouldn't be accepted into the ranks of Tabard Society riled her up. And so Stephanie mounted her political protest to right the wrongs of monetary elitism.

In any case, Keri, Michelle, and I stayed seated in the car while Stephanie got out and cracked eggs all along the sills of the three windows closest to the street. In a few minutes, she jumped back into the driver's seat of her car, and we rapidly left Tabard behind.

"That will show them," Stephanie laughed.

Show them what?, I thought.

Chapter Six

roots

{The Childhood Years}

So, what crazy catalyst spawned my commitment to abstinence? Why would any normal, red-blooded girl choose to forgo sensual pleasure—especially when it's served on a silver platter and beautifully packaged in the form of deliciously good-looking Ivy League boys? Well, we have to go back—way back to well before college—to answer that question.

Growing up, I wasn't exactly normal. I approached life differently than the other kids—*much* differently.

"Boy? You're not a boy. Why does your T-shirt say 'boy'?"

In high school, strangers asked those kinds of bewildered inquiries about my clothing. I didn't dress like the other kids.

"Boy" stood for Boy London, an alternative, punk-inspired clothing company. In my mind, wearing normal clothes showed a lack of creativity. Showing up at school in trendy department-store clothing indicated that you probably felt afraid to express yourself—or worse, you had nothing interesting to say. My clothes and hair signified my *art*; they broadcast to the world in a shrill, screaming chorus that I did *not* want to fit in.

Once, while shopping in downtown San Francisco with my mother and brother, someone stopped me.

"Are you someone famous?" the friendly thirtysomething woman asked me. My jacket had caught her eye. You either had to be a celebrity or orbiting your own special planet to wear a coat that drew attention to itself like a third eyeball.

My absolute favorite jacket in the world had become an extension of me—the unbridled, tangible essence of me at sixteen. Even teachers who never taught me, and students who didn't have classes with me, knew me by my cropped black military coat with its large silver buttons and impossible-to-ignore external leopard-pattern shoulder pads, edged with three-inch, dangling, sparkling silver tassels. My Spanish teacher Mr. King fondly named it the "Sergeant Pepper's jacket." I was a generation too young to know that he referred to the Beatles album, the cover of which featured the famous pop band wearing similarly-styled, absurd-looking military jackets. That jacket, decorated with my old ice-skating medals and military bars from a thrift store, was my pride and joy.

If my clothes didn't cause people to do a double take, my hair usually did the job as my greatest asset in expressing my nonconformist attitude. My parents wouldn't let me shave the sides of my head—one of their few creative restrictions—so I had a classmate braid the sides of my hair in cornrows that lay flat against the sides of my skull, and then connected them in a single, short, flat braid down the back of my head. The sides of my hairstyle resembled parallel rows of shaved black hair. I straightened the hair on the crown of my head so it stood erect. It looked like a fusion between Grace Jones's 1980s flattop and the tangled bird's nest the lead singer of the Cure wore.

All through high school, I remained head over heels in love with anti-establishment counterculture—the clothes, the music, the films. *Mainstream* rung like a dirty word in my vocabulary. I divided my world into two groups: "cool and interesting people" versus "not-so-cool, not-so-interesting people." Cool and interesting people were blatant nonconformists. They each possessed a vivid and uniquely ingenious fashion sense. They marched to their own drummers and dreamed up wildly original personal manifestos.

My friends and I shopped for funky attire in vintage clothing stores and sought out even funkier music—soundtracks for our
suburban revolt. We loved buying esoteric music imports and rare B-sides
on Telegraph Avenue in Berkeley. We scoured Haight-Ashbury in San
Francisco, the famed former hippie headquarters of Janis Joplin and
other sixties legends, for peculiar shoes, spiked bracelets, and inspiration
from New Wave, punk, and ska music.

We unearthed beloved, colorful plotlines and eccentric characters
in independent films, foreign movies, and art flicks. I joined my high
school's film club where the futuristic, hypersurreal film *Brazil* dazzled
me. Set in a not-too-distant, Big Brother-esque future society, *Brazil*
embodied all the fantastic, bizarre, artistic anarchy that aroused every
creative bone in my body.

My friends and I consumed whimsical esoteric films, visionary
surrealist movies, and dark, twisted films.

"*Clockwork Orange* is one of my favorite movies," my friend Sebastian
told me. He owned more B-sides and imports than any other sixteen-
year old I knew. We'd been friends since seventh grade. He had wonderful parents who got along well with my parents. He was kind and well
mannered—just the kind of agreeable boy everybody's parents loved.
At his recommendation, I watched *A Clockwork Orange* and nearly
lost my lunch. It portrayed glorified ultraviolence—rape and random,
brutal beatings—as the favorite pastimes of the film's young male stars.
In the end, the film's star submits to treatment for his violent behavior;
but, from my fifteen-year-old point of view, the journey on his way to
rehabilitation was harrowing and disturbing.

Once my parents almost caught me and a group of friends watching
a sordid, semipornographic movie.

"Hey, this is supposed to be a great film," my classmate Eric said as
he and several of our school friends squeezed together on a sofa at my
house. Eric popped in the R-rated movie, and for the next hour, the
group of us sat, glassy-eyed and mesmerized, as we watched the twisted
New York tale of a female art gallery assistant and a wealthy business-

man embarking on an impersonal, highly sensual relationship based on sexual obsession and manipulation.

"Oh, no!" one of my friends gasped suddenly. "Where's the remote control? Adele, I think your parents are home!"

Someone launched for the remote and switched to a TV sitcom—just before my parents could walk through the door and ask, "What on earth are you watching?" When they retreated upstairs, we all sighed with relief and watched the film's conclusion.

The funny thing is that my parents rarely told me *not* to do anything as a teenager. I knew I had no business watching that movie—my conscience, not my parents, told me that. In fact, I don't ever remember my parents saying things like, "Don't drink. Don't smoke. Don't have sex. Don't watch raunchy movies." They did say, "We won't always be around. *You* have to be responsible for *yourself*." That worked for me.

If my parents said be home by 9:00 pm, I came home by 8:45. When they said, "Do your best," I worked to bring home good report cards. They gave me a tremendous amount of freedom as long as I remained trustworthy. They passed me the baton of sacred trust, and with it, personal responsibility. I couldn't lie to them—I'd feel like I had violated their trust. A friend of mine told her parents she would spend the night at a girlfriend's house and then spent the night at a boy's house. Another friend of mine hid a boy under her bed most of the night, until he could sneak past her sleeping parents in the wee hours of the morning. I couldn't do something like that with a clear conscience.

In our household, I had so many incentives for respecting my parents' wishes that it didn't make sense *not* to listen to them. As long as I complied with their few requests, I could pretty much do whatever I wanted and hang out with whatever friends I chose. It was win-win. Besides, I liked my parents; they were pretty cool as far as grown-ups went. A lot of kids griped about their parents, but I honestly couldn't think of anything to complain about. They never protested or seemed to mind when I left the house every day dressed like a New Wave circus freak.

Once, during my junior year of high school, my parents let me sleep over at my best friend's house. He was a boy. It just so happened that he was gay, but my parents didn't know that. They let one of my junior prom dates and another guy friend of mine, stay over at our house on prom night too. Both slept in my brother's room. My parents didn't freak out about things like that, the way other kids' parents did. They used excellent reverse psychology. With all that freedom, I felt compelled to behave responsibly.

Sophomore year of high school, my parents allowed me to go to a keg party, and I was disappointed to find it populated by mainstream kids— no cool and interesting kids in sight. Not a single one of my fellow crazy-dressing, alternative-music-listening friends stopped by for even a moment. It also helped that by the time I was fifteen, I already knew two kids in Alcoholics Anonymous, though I never saw either one touch a drink. Some of my friends dabbled in drinking and drugs, but they didn't engage around me. They knew it wasn't my cup of tea. I had way too much fun without that stuff, assembling my alarming wardrobe.

Don't get me wrong, though. My parents weren't pushovers who let my brother and me run wild. My mom was just about the sweetest woman you'd ever meet. She never raised her voice or threatened, and she never cursed. Trim and energetic, she always kept a step ahead of my busybody brother and me. But, beneath Mom's reassuring warmth and kindness, lived an old-school black mother from the South. Mom didn't play. Unless I went stark raving mad, I wouldn't dream of talking back to my mother, or rolling my eyes at her, without simultaneously imagining my eulogy: "Adele was a nice girl. She had a bright future. Too bad she lost her mind and rolled her eyes at her mother . . . Foolish child, may she rest in peace."

Mom was the primary disciplinarian in our house. But Dad was always home and always present. Throughout my childhood, my father often hung out upstairs at his desk, quietly working away at something on paper or on his computer. He always made himself available to help with homework and helped reinforce the few rules Mom laid down.

Every Sunday, our family attended church. We went to The Church by the Side of the Road—a nondenominational Christian, traditional African American church in Berkeley. The congregation at The Church by the Side of the Road was my extended family. They loved me, and I loved them. I don't know where the name of the church came from. I never thought much about it until I mentioned the name to a friend in high school and he laughed his socks off. "What kind of name is that?" he asked. I think the name was meant to be inviting—a sort of open invitation to anyone passing by: *Come on in. Join us. We're just a friendly little neighborhood church on the side of the road.*

Shortly after I turned eight years old, my television set changed my life. I watched the movie *Jesus of Nazareth*. Everything I had learned in Sunday school up to that point suddenly crystallized. The supernatural made sense—that God would send someone, Jesus, to guide us on our spiritual journey through life. Right there in front of my big, brown TV set, with two big antennas sticking up, I acknowledged and accepted Jesus as my Lord and Savior. I wanted a personal relationship with God.

Suddenly the Bible became interesting. It no longer seemed a sleepy old book, with nice stories about things that had nothing to do with everyday life. I began to read it, looking for *something* to satisfy my newly blossomed curiosity about God. Dad had given me a little white Bible with my name embossed in silver. For years, it collected dust on my shelf. But now I couldn't read enough of it. It was a King James Version with lots of *thees, thous,* and *begats.* I started at the beginning, Genesis, and read through the first several books before I discovered some really good stuff further back in the books of the New Testament.

In Mark 7:21 I came across the word *fornication.* What on earth was that? Thank goodness we had dictionaries all over the house. Fornication meant sex outside of marriage. No problem. I got it. Sex was designed for marriage. I accepted it as a good rule to live by. Much later in life, I heard a wise pastor break it down this way: "Sex is the *benefits package* for the *job* of marriage. You wouldn't go to a job interview and expect the benefits package—medical insurance, paid vacation, and all the other perks—without ever committing to the job."

I'm not actually sure who first told me about the birds and the bees. In grade school, I discovered reproduction in the encyclopedia. It contained a full explanation of all the crucial details and colored illustrations as a bonus. Several times, I snuck out the R volume of the encyclopedia whenever I wanted some provocative reading.

When I turned twelve, Mom gave me the birth-control talk. "We're not raising any more children in this house," she stated firmly. As a high school teacher, she foresaw the bundle of raging hormones bound to overtake me. That one brief talk was the only time I remember either of my parents ever mentioning sex. But Mom didn't know I had already worked it out. I had fully committed to abstinence until marriage; that was 100 percent effective, foolproof birth control.

In junior high and high school, when it came to sex, I had no worries. I embraced abstinence as another opportunity to rebel against mainstream culture. It wasn't that I wasn't interested in sex—I had been curious ever since I became tall enough to reach the *Playgirl* magazines on the top shelf at the bookstore in the mall where I took ice skating lessons. I'd also done my fair share of playing doctor and you-show-me-yours-and-I'll show-you-mine in kindergarten and elementary school. I started to like boys in the fourth grade. That's when I started to outgrow my tomboy tendencies and realized that I might like to kiss a boy instead of beating him up.

My best girlfriend in junior high had an adventurous spirit and sometimes embroiled me in her escapades. We attended a Depeche Mode concert when she was thirteen; I had just turned fourteen a couple months earlier. Our parents allowed us to go to the concert, unsupervised, at the large outdoor Greek Theatre at the University of California, Berkeley, otherwise known as Cal.

"He's cute," my friend said, checking out the guy sitting in front of us. The guy was more than cute; he was model beautiful.

"He sure is," I agreed.

"How old are you?" my friend asked him after the concert.

"Nineteen," he replied. "How old are you?"

"I just graduated," she replied, implying she'd just graduated from high school, not eighth grade. Soon after, Cute Depeche Mode Guy, his friend, my best girlfriend, and I stood inside an empty recreation hall on Cal's campus.

"I'll be right back," my friend said before disappearing into a dark room with Cute Depeche Mode Guy. I lingered in the hallway, trying to ignore his friend. She emerged five minutes later.

"I got a little freaked out when he unzipped his pants. I told him I just graduated from eighth grade," she whispered. By sophomore year of high school, her fear disappeared. She had enough sex for both of us. While I steered clear of make-out sessions and hookups with guys, she changed out her boyfriends and flings on a regular rotation. It always made for amusing outings together—me trying to keep it platonic with guys, while she stoked the flames of romance at every opportunity.

Many years after high school, my best friend from junior high made a startling comment: "I wish I'd had a V Society," she remarked.

"Really? Why?" I asked, surprised. When we were teenagers, she had rarely seemed unhappy with her decisions about guys.

"I never told you this. I haven't told many people really . . . ," she began. "Sex was always my realm; I knew what I was doing. I always used protection. It was no big deal. But when I was twenty, I slept with this guy, and the condom broke. Fine. I made an appointment with the doctor. They gave me the morning-after pill. Problem solved—I thought. The morning-after pill was supposed to eliminate any possibility of pregnancy. They told me I had to come back in six weeks to make sure the pill had worked. I didn't even see the point of going back, but I made the appointment anyway. So, six weeks later I went back. They told me that the pill hadn't worked. If I continued with the pregnancy my baby would be severely deformed. There would be part of a child growing inside of me—not a whole, complete, healthy child—but a *partial* child. There's a small percentage of cases where the morning-after pill isn't 100 percent effective. I fell into that small percentage."

The doctors had surgically removed the deformed fetus.

"I'd killed my baby. I felt so guilty. It was absolutely awful. And the guy that got me pregnant—he hadn't even stuck around. It was devastating. I was so depressed." She paused.

"That's what no one tells you," she continued. I never thought that could happen to me. I was always careful."

I listened quietly—speechless. I had always assumed she had no regrets. I had no idea. It was hard to envision her being depressed about anything. All through junior high and high school she'd been my most upbeat friend—always fun and cheerful—Little Miss Positive. I couldn't imagine how utterly excruciating the horrible ordeal had been for her. To make things worse, she'd probably had to behave cheerfully the entire time so no one would know the predicament she was in. Meanwhile, her heart and conscience secretly crushed into millions of tiny, brittle shards, like a windshield in a head-on collision.

My friend from junior high is married now. She and her husband have two great children.

"But when I look at my kids, even all these years later, I still feel guilty sometimes. Because there are two of them, and I remember my third one, their brother or sister, who isn't here anymore—gone. I had to use fertility drugs to get pregnant with the two I have now." The abortion had messed up her reproductive system, so she couldn't get pregnant naturally. All those years, I'd never known. She'd guarded this secret for almost two decades.

When the two of us were in high school, all my romantic interests fell into one of two categories: major crushes—that applied to any guy that I liked for longer than two months—and minor crushes, which the hands of a watch could measure. Through most of high school, I rounded out major crushes with simultaneous minor crushes. I couldn't focus my affections on any single guy for a long period of time when the sea overflowed with so many fish. But the simple fact that most of my major crushes were out of reach aided my chastity. Freshman year, I became enamored with a six-foot-tall, strapping senior on the varsity football team who already had a girlfriend. Sophomore year, five minor crushes (a record for one school year) and one major crush bowled me over. My big heartthrob, an artsy, talented creative type, came out of the closet later that year. Senior year, a Turkish exchange student visiting from Germany captivated me. He was 100 percent male-fashionista and the lead singer of a German New Wave band. His plane touched down in the States and then took off again before I could make a move; we were never alone since his host student, my friend Eric, always stayed nearby.

"I just need twenty minutes alone with him," I told Eric, while he, the German student, and our friend Shawna kicked it at my house. The four of us had been consuming some obscure independent film.

"Okay," Eric agreed with a knowing chuckle. "I'll be back in twenty minutes." Eric and Shawna disappeared in Eric's convertible beetle and returned in forty-five minutes. I hadn't budged; the wacky art film filling the television screen completely engrossed the German student and I. I was so into the movie, I'd completely abandoned my ploy to instigate a make-out session.

Chapter Seven

———— ✦ ————

SPRING FEVER

{March, Second Semester of Junior Year}

SPRING FEVER DETONATED RANDOM ACTS OF AFFECTION AND dissension, like a string of igniting firecrackers.

"That's it," Keri declared. "I'm through. I am not doing it! It's misguided and misogynistic, and I refuse to participate in these oppressive rules imposed on women!"

"What's oppressive?" I asked. "What are you talking about?"

"Shaving!" Keri declared. "Shaving is oppressive to women. It's a misogynistic society that forces women to shave. God gave women hair. So why should I shave my natural God-given hair?"

"Nobody is forcing you to shave," I remarked.

"That's my point. I'm taking a stand. I'm not shaving anymore," she declared. "I'm *not* shaving my legs, and I'm *not* shaving under my arms."

"Fine with me," I shrugged. Personally, I liked my razor; we had a good relationship. Keri could *not* shave all she wanted. I planned to shave.

That same week, Michelle joined Keri in the civil uprising against unnecessary hair removal.

"I'm not shaving either," Michelle announced. She deprived her legs of a razor for three whole weeks before she gave in. "I was just getting... well, too hairy," she explained.

Keri's no-shaving act of civil disobedience lasted a bit longer.

"I think I'm going to start shaving again," she announced after a very long, hairy stint. She'd already resumed shaving under her arms sometime earlier. "I was just getting too hot and uncomfortable not shaving my armpits," she admitted.

The edge of winter still pinched the warming days of spring. In our uniform of sweaters and jeans or skirts with tights, Keri and Michelle's antishaving protest remained hidden under a layer of clothing. I was glad about that and especially pleased that it wasn't summer. As much as I loved Keri and Michelle, I wasn't sure I wanted to be subjected to bearded legs and underarms peeking out from cut-off jean shorts and frilly tank tops.

Then again, Michelle might have stopped her most persistent suitor dead in his tracks had she flashed her bewhiskered legs at him. One night that spring, Mich and I accompanied Stephanie to a house party several blocks from our dorm. Though my roommates and I didn't drink beer—the main pastime at most parties—we loved to socialize. We were always up for a friendly party. No sooner had we entered the front door then we spotted him: Slimy Alex! Michelle's most ardent admirer stood chatting on the other side of the room. But just as we spotted him, Michelle tripped his radar, and it was too late to duck into the crowd— he'd seen her. Stephanie, Mich, and I tried to sequester ourselves among a few familiar faces on our side of the room. We succeeded for about fifteen minutes before Alex made his move.

"Ugh, he's so slimy," Michelle complained.

"Slimy? How is he slimy? He's totally cute," I argued.

"Yuck. He is *not* cute."

"He has great style."

"Whatever," she sighed.

"Well, how about that cute British accent?" I reminded her.

No go. Michelle wasn't having it. I didn't know why she wouldn't at least have coffee with the guy. He seemed perfectly fine to me. I'd go out with him once—just once so I could look into that adorable face. I'd want to know for sure that he was certifiably slimy before I wrote him off. I would meet him at one of the cafés just off campus to enjoy some lively conversation, have some laughs, and ask subtle questions to unearth the truth. If it turned out he just wanted to get some action, then right after I finished my drink and downed a dessert, I'd start my speech.

"Alex, I just don't think this is going to work out. We're coming from very different places, with very different expectations . . ." I'd let him down nice and easy. And if he didn't take the bait, then I'd pull out my secret weapon: "I really think we should just be friends. I'm not planning to have sex until I get married." I only had to tell a guy that once, years later. It worked extremely effectively. As much as he liked me, we both agreed he'd be miserable in a relationship with me. There was nothing like telling a guy that he could *never* have sex with you to stop him dead in his tracks. This easily jettisoned even the most sincere but incompatible suitors. A guy that stuck around after that disclosure usually made an interesting friend. And if I were Michelle, I'd genuinely want to be friends with Alex. He could come over and sit in my living room anytime. I'd love to come home and find him parked on the sofa. But Michelle wasn't hearing it. None of it.

Within moments, Alex crossed the crowded room full of mirthful, partying students, and soon stood face to face with Michelle. He ignored me and began talking to her as if they were the only two people in the room. I stepped aside and joined a small group of students I knew toward the back of the room. From where I stood, I had a clear view of Alex and Michelle. I could call the shots like the last round of a knockout boxing match.

Poor guy. He'd been talking to Michelle less than five minutes, and he didn't know he'd just received a quick series of jabs from a lightweight champion. He was barking up the wrong tree. He wouldn't even get her phone number. He'd tried at least three times to get Michelle to go out with him. She'd barely talk to him, much less go with him *anywhere*. The conversation was completely one-sided. His mouth kept moving; hers stayed clamped shut.

It was coming—the knockout blow. Poor, poor Alex. He kept talking. He couldn't see it. Michelle was extremely subtle. He missed all the signs screaming, "Bail! Duck and cover! You're about to be TKO'd!" As Alex leaned in, trying to capture her full attention, Michelle leaned away from him and took a small step backward. She looked for a polite way to exit the conversation and flee. Alex wasn't making it easy. His jaw kept flapping. The more he talked, the more irritated Michelle became. Then, there it was. Finally. She delivered the knockout blow. She crossed her arms, and her naturally pouty lips turned into a tiny, barely distinguishable pout. That was it. Alex was down for the count. Two seconds later, she pivoted abruptly away from him and headed toward me at the back of the wide room.

Then Alex did the unthinkable. The defeated, bloody, pulpy former contender rose from a heap on the floor and followed her across the room. As Michelle crossed the room and arrived in front of me, I leaned in quickly and whispered a warning, "Here he comes."

"*What?*" She whirled around as he closed in on her. "I'm going to the bathroom," she huffed.

Just as he was about to pick up where he had left off, she made a getaway into a nearby bathroom and locked the door behind her. Even persistent Alex couldn't follow her in there. She was too kind to tell him outright to take a hike. Why couldn't he take a hint? Unbelievable. He loitered around near the bathroom door, pretending to talk to some students nearby, waiting. Finally, Michelle emerged, and we made a run for it. Michelle, Stephanie, and I jetted like rockets out of the party and emptied ourselves into the alley outside.

"That was too much," I laughed.

Michelle didn't look amused. She said nothing the first few minutes of the walk home. I couldn't figure out her type. She never specified exactly what kind of guy she liked. Keri and I had a list. We could deliver a full rundown on our ideal guy—everything from his height to his hair color to his preferred hobbies and interests.

Keri listed very particular requirements. There could only be one or two men in the world who met her checklist and shared her unique worldview. Keri had given me her rundown several months before: "My husband has to be Jewish and Messianic. He has to be a Zionist and committed to living in Israel. And of course he should be fluent in Hebrew, because we have to speak the language if we're going to live in Israel," she explained. Keri was nearly fluent in Hebrew already. Years earlier, Keri's Hebrew teacher had introduced her to a pen pal named Erez, a slightly older American Messianic Jewish guy already living in Israel. They wrote to each other so Keri could practice her Hebrew.

"And don't forget he has to be a feminist," I'd added.

"That would be a plus," Keri laughed.

"Oh, and I love hairy men," Keri confessed. "So my husband has to be hairy."

"Really? You don't mean those guys with the hairy backs do you?" I asked, picturing some modern incarnation of Sasquatch.

"Not a hairy back, but I love hairy chests," she replied.

Well, at least I knew I'd never have to worry about us both liking the same guy. I did not intend to become Mrs. Sasquatch.

But walking down Locust Walk the next day after the party, I did consider for a split second the possibility of becoming Mrs. Sexy. Walking toward me was a guy I'd never seen before—*Mr. Sexy*—ambling down Locust Walk. I liked the peculiar cadence of his stride—uneven, confident, and original. He embodied the quintessential male fashionista—smartly dressed, perfectly accessorized, and sloppily groomed. He stood out easily amidst the preppy, J. Crew–clad student body.

"I saw the most a-maaaaa-zinnnng guy today. Seriously, you should have seen him!" I exclaimed to Michelle and Keri as I burst through our front door. I plopped down in one of the wooden chairs around the square table in our living room.

"Who?" Mich asked eagerly.

"Yeah, who is he?" Keri pressed as she leapt into the chair directly across from me. She and Michelle were all ears, anxiously waiting for me to spill the details.

"I don't know his name. He was just so, so . . ." My voice trailed off in search of just the right word. "Sexy. He was sooooo sexy."

"Sexy?" Michelle echoed. "Did you talk to him?"

"Are you kidding?" I squealed. "No way! Of course, I didn't *talk* to him. I just saw him walking down Locust Walk."

"Well, what's his name?" Keri asked. "Do we know him?"

"I have no idea what his name is. No—I don't know him. Maybe *you* guys know him?"

"Well, what does he look like?" Michelle asked excitedly.

"Sexy. Super duper sexyyyyyyyyyy!" I cried, almost jumping out of my seat.

The three of us accelerated into a fever pitch of animated conversation, sounding like someone had pressed the fast-forward button on an old cassette player.

"He wore black motorcycle boots," I began, my voice shrill with delight.

"Yeah?" Michelle and Keri replied in unison, leaning in close so as not to miss a single word. Michelle jumped into the third chair, taking a front-row seat in the ensuing hyper triangle of cross talk.

"What else?" Keri inquired enthusiastically.

"Guys look so good in motorcycle boots," I rambled. "He has longish, almost black hair and sideburns. Big sideburns, but not like the crazy, Elvis lamb-chop ones. Know what I mean?"

"Yeah, yeah!" Keri cried.

"Um, he's a decent height, probably six feet or close to that. He wore a suede jacket—brown—a brown suede jacket, nice sunglasses, black jeans. And he carried a European-style leather school bag; you know, kind of a cross between a messenger bag and an attaché case. Have you seen him?" I begged with a pleased shriek. I was unable to contain my excitement as my roommates egged me on with their shared enthusiasm.

"I don't think so. He doesn't sound familiar," Keri replied.

"No," Michelle agreed, still smiling.

"Do you think he's a believer?" Keri asked excitedly, referring to the fact that none of the three of us would date a guy that wasn't as serious about his personal relationship with God as we were.

"I don't know," I replied thoughtfully. "How cool would that be!" I cheered. "I just want to have coffee with him. Then I could find out."

"Yeah," Keri smiled broadly.

"You'll have to show us Sexy the next time you see him," Michelle encouraged.

"Oh, definitely," I cried. "You'll know it's him by the big 'HOT' sign on his forehead." Our laughter consumed us as we looked at one another and each imagined our version of Motorcycle Boot Guy with a glowing neon sign plastered across the front of his face.

As our conversation died down, Keri and Michelle disappeared into their rooms. I began foraging in the fridge for something to eat. I compiled random items for a snack and sat down to munch, extremely pleased with my day so far.

"What is *that*?" Michelle asked suspiciously, as she reappeared in the room and looked at me devouring my snack.

"Uh . . . it's cheese and crackers," I replied. I couldn't figure out why she looked so alarmed.

"I can see the cheese and crackers," she replied. "But what's *that* in between the cheese and crackers?"

"Mayonnaise," I replied, still not sure where she was going with all the questions.

"Ewwww!" Michelle said, wrinkling up her nose in disgust.

Almost on cue, Keri emerged from her room to join in the snack discussion.

"Adele's eating processed American cheese on saltine crackers with mayonnaise," Michelle declared.

"No way," Keri said, moving in to inspect my plate of cheese slices folded into quarters to fit the square crackers. "Delie, that is so gross!" she exclaimed.

"What's the matter with mayonnaise?" I asked, baffled.

"Nothing's the matter with *mayonnaise*. It's the combination of crackers, cheese—*processed cheese*—and mayonnaise that's the problem. That's totally disgusting!" Michelle laughed.

"Where did you come up with that combination?" Keri teased.

"Oh, whatever," I replied as I lifted another cheese-and-cracker sandwich from my plate. They were right. It wasn't the most palatable combination. But who cared? It was quick and cheap and not *completely* unhealthy. As long as they didn't tell my mom what I ate, I'd be fine. It had taken me two years to convince my mom to take me off the school meal plan. I didn't like making the inconvenient trek to the dining hall for every meal, and after freshman year most of my friends had dropped their meal plans. I definitely didn't want to be one of the lone juniors eating in the dining hall, solo amidst a sea of freshman.

"You're going to eat balanced meals?" my mom pressed before she would agree to cancel my meal plan.

"Yes, Mom," I agreed. Cheese, crackers, and mayo were *almost* balanced. This combination covered two food groups—the bread group and dairy. That wasn't bad. It wasn't like I was having a candy bar for lunch.

A rapping knock on the door interrupted us. Michelle opened it. Milan.

"Hey, what's up?" he greeted her.

"Nothing much," she replied and let him in. "What are you up to?"

"Nothing. I was just on this side of campus, so I thought I'd stop by," he said as he stepped into the living room and greeted me and Keri. "Hey, what's going on?"

"Nada," Keri answered.

"Nothing," I replied.

Milan fell back onto the sofa and dropped his backpack on the floor nearby. He studied each of us momentarily before a sly smile played on his lips. "You girls look awfully pleased with yourselves," he stated curiously.

"Adele's just having a good day," Michelle replied sweetly. Her reply aptly distracted from the elation I'm sure I failed to hide on my face.

"Yep, just having a good day," I chirped, trying to look unflustered and collected.

"Hmm . . . ," he said as he leaned into the padded sofa back. He continued looking at us with interest, his gaze roaming from me to Mich to Keri and then back again. He expected to hear the details of my good day. *Yeah, right*, I thought. *Like I'm going to tell you about Sexy. Please.*

"So, hey, didn't you want to start filming this week?" I asked, deliberately redirecting the conversation.

"Oh, yeah. We said this weekend, right?" Milan said.

"Yeah, Saturday afternoon is fine with me," I replied.

"What are you filming?" Keri asked.

"Just some random scenes," Milan answered. "A kind of surrealist film with cool imagery."

"And a funky soundtrack," I continued. "If we like what we film, we'll use it in the promotional short we're making for the Film Club." This time around Stephanie would be joining us as well. I turned to address Milan. "I have the video camera. I checked it out yesterday. It has some sweet special-effects features. I haven't really played around with it much, though."

"You filmed us yesterday," Michelle corrected.

"Yeah, but that doesn't count. We were just fooling around. I can't use that in the promo. You two"—I nodded toward Michelle and Keri—"making weird faces and dancing around the apartment with moisturizer caked on your faces . . . that's hardly fitting for the promo," I scoffed.

"The slow-motion feature is really nice," I informed Milan. "I'll show you on Saturday."

We agreed to scope out downtown so we could get some cool urban footage of cars in motion, people, different cityscapes, and then Milan reminded me that he wanted to film in the cemetery too.

"I like the cemetery idea," I agreed. "I did a photo shoot this past summer at a cemetery back home. We rode around on my friend's motorcycle and got great shots. Those old mausoleums always have such great architecture."

"Let's shoot at the cemetery next week," Milan suggested.

"Works for me," I replied before turning to Michelle and Keri and asking, "Hey, can one of you model for us in the cemetery?" The graves alone would be drab. It would be much better if there were a muse—an undead hovering above the corpses six feet under.

"You can be an apparition haunting the graves," Milan stated coolly. I could see his creative wheels starting to spin rapidly. I loved the synergy of our spontaneous brainstorms as we carelessly piled abstractions on top of each other; our ideas usually synched well together.

"You can dance around in a flowing white gown like a beautiful ghost," I added.

"Mich would be a great ghost," Keri agreed.

"That's true. You could do a little dance around the tombstones," I declared.

"Dancing around tombstones? What kind of dance?" Michelle shot back.

"Break dancing of course," I replied with a straight face. "You could do a head spin on top of the mausoleum, then moonwalk over several graves."

Milan, Keri, and Michelle started cracking up.

"You break dance?" Milan asked Michelle.

"Are you kidding? She was the break-dancing star of her junior high!" I teased. "She won the national flare competition."

"Shut up," Mich snarled with an expression as fierce as a puppy. She rose and grabbed me in a big hug from the side, squeezing me tightly. "You little turd."

"You big turd," I retorted, laughing.

Keri, Michelle, and I rarely said "I love you" outright to each other. It was way too mushy. We preferred to call each other "turd" and "butt-head" and then hug a lot. I was much more comfortable with that than with any sort of heartfelt outpourings—girly, emotional stuff made me uneasy. Keri and Mich were the only two people in the world that I'd let call me those names and get away with it. In return, they were the only two people for whom I held those names aside to express affection.

"What's a flare?" Milan interrupted.

"Mich's best break dancing move," I joked. "No, but seriously," I continued, turning around toward Michelle, "will you be in our cemetery film?"

"Of course I'll be in it," Mich replied. "But I'm *not* break dancing."

"That's fine," Milan assured her.

Mich turned and headed out of the living room, disappearing down the hall.

"Hey, where are you going?" Keri called after her.

"I have a study group in an hour," Mich called back, her voice muffled by the thin walls of her room.

"What's the rush?" I yelled around the corner. "You have a whole hour. Stay awhile."

Mich's head popped out of her room's doorway. She looked at me and then emerged again and reseated herself in the canvas chair. I grabbed a cup of water from the kitchen and sat back down on the sofa, next to Milan.

"What's the study group for?" Milan asked.

"I have an organic chem exam tomorrow," she replied.

"Whew, science is not my thing," I stated. "Seriously, I think my parents' science genes completely skipped me. They're both scientists, but I barely made it through physics in high school."

"I thought your mom was a math teacher?" Michelle asked.

"She is now. But before that she was a chemist," I replied.

"Really? I didn't know that," Michelle answered. "Did she do research?"

"I think so. She worked in a lab at a university. Before I was born, though, so I'm not too sure."

"Yeah, I'm definitely more of a right-brain person than a left-brain, science-math person," Keri commented.

"Yeah, I'm all right brain, no left brain—at all," I agreed.

Milan leaned toward me on the sofa. "You have the best forehead," he stated and cupped his warm palm around my forehead.

"Uh . . . thanks?" I replied.

"No, really," Milan restated, his hand still resting on my forehead, "I like your forehead." What should I say to *that*? It was such an odd compliment, observation, or whatever it was. It was endearing, I guessed . . . Right? Who knew? It was one of the many peculiar affinities that blossomed in the Elevator Society that spring. From that day on, Milan gave himself permission to occasionally reach over and rest his hand gently on my forehead whenever the urge arose. I didn't mind.

The four of us sat around shooting the breeze for a while longer before Milan bid us good-bye and took off. As the door closed behind him, Michelle looked at me and laughed. "I love your forehead," she teased.

"I know! What was *that* all about?" Keri joked.

"How should I know? Guys are so weird," I mumbled.

V Society, Best of the Best List
Junior Year

FAVORITE OBJECTS
Adele's forehead
Breakfast burritos
Keri's books
Stephanie's guitar

The following day I trekked over to the Furness Building, home of the magnificently picturesque Fine Arts Library. I needed to use their flat-art copy station to copy my new photography installation onto slides. The flat-art copy station was a simple lighting setup with a camera mount. It allowed you to place artwork face up on the table, light it evenly, and then snap photographs of the artwork. I wanted all my photographs in slide format so I could project them onto a large movie screen in a dark room.

Several weeks before, I'd begun an avant-garde black-and-white photography series that posed the question, "If death is inevitable . . . why do you live?" I'd named it *La Question d' L'Artiste,* "the question of the artist" in French. My friend Patrick had just returned from his fall semester in France, and we both agreed that regardless of how ridiculous a work of art might be, it always sounded serious and esoteric when you gave it an arbitrary French title. I set the photography series to the Yaz song "In My Room," an entrancing New Wave ballad with the Lord's Prayer recited in the background.

The completed slide show, set to the music, simulated a music video, with black and white images flashing by rapidly. In one image, I sat in my room with a documentary photograph I'd taken of a New York phone booth behind me. Someone had pasted a "Believe in Jesus" sign over the Camel cigarette ad on the side of the phone booth. My death occurred in the next few slides, followed by the recurring question flashing boldly in white, handwritten letters against a sea of black: "Y," "Do U," "Live," "?".

La Question d' L'Artiste opened with a festive private screening among my roommates and some friends in my apartment, and then traveled on to public screenings on campus and finally to the Black Filmmakers Hall of Fame screening in Oakland, California. *La Question d' L'Artiste* represented my first little breakthrough in the photography world. Its success was one of the highlights of that spring.

After I finished copying all my photographs, I packed up my things and strolled home from the Furness Library.

The following evening was Saturday night. The Christian student fellowship that Michelle and I attended regularly had received an invitation to a dance from a fellowship at Drexel University, a small school that abutted the northeastern corner of Penn's campus.

"So, do you think we'll meet anyone at the dance?" Keri asked.

"I hope so," I grinned.

"I know . . . It would be nice to meet a really cool guy," Michelle mused.

"No kidding," I agreed.

The three of us and Mandy, our usually absent V Society member, set off on the twenty-minute walk from Superblock. We made our way to Drexel and found the dance location, guided by a Xeroxed campus map that had accompanied the invitation.

"I am so ready to dance," I said, smiling as we heard muffled music thumping behind closed doors. Mandy swung the door open, and I expected to see a dimly lit dance floor packed with students getting down to some good beats. No such luck. The four of us stood looking into a practically empty room, with all the lights turned on and some jacked-up music with no discernible drumbeat sadly streaming over an antiquated speaker system.

"What on earth are we listening to?" I whispered. I hoped someone would suggest that we turn and run. Less than twenty students dotted the large room. In one of the upper quadrants of the room, four students who clearly heard a rhythm indiscernible to everyone else shook in some strange fashion that simulated dancing. The tallest of the four, a gawky, slender guy, swung his arms and legs in a wild free-for-all. I had to give him credit for his obvious self-confidence. Most people with those dancing skills would have been afraid to show themselves in public.

I didn't mind that only four people populated the dance floor. If the music had been good, I would have been perfectly content to dance the night away with Keri, Michelle, and Mandy. I loved to dance. But the tunes pumping out over the loudspeaker were sickeningly disheartening. I couldn't even identify the music genre; it was some kind of tame, sappy, melody-free, beatless rock song.

"Well, are you coming?" Mandy asked, looking at the three of us. She had already stepped through the door. It was too late to bolt straight back to Penn's campus and leave Drexel, the cheerless mishap of a night gone wrong.

"Yep, we're coming," Michelle said as she followed behind Mandy. Keri lingered, but just for a moment. I couldn't see her face, only the back of her head, and I wondered if she was also reviewing a quick list of possible exit strategies. Unwillingly, I followed Mandy, Michelle, and

Keri into the room. We made our way to the front. I forced a smile at some of the wallflowers standing around in clusters. Soon we caught the attention of the tall, skinny guy on the dance floor. He came over and greeted us.

"Hi, I'm Mike," he said with a warm smile.

"Hi," we each responded, one after the other, offering our names as we shook Mike's hand.

"Are you from Penn?" he asked.

"Yes," Keri replied.

"I'm so glad you could come," he replied. "When we invited your student group, we weren't sure anyone would actually show up. I'm one of the organizers of this dance." He was so welcoming and earnest that I knew we were trapped. We'd have to stay and pretend to have a good time. It was the least we could do to repay his gratitude.

"Well, come join us on the dance floor," he beckoned as he moved back toward the tiny group bobbing and swerving around out of step with the music.

"Okay," Michelle agreed.

The four of us followed him over to the group. He introduced us and then we joined them in attempted dance. After five minutes, I gave up. I tried not to look at the four students moving to the absent rhythm, each one bouncing and veering like a rubber band shooting in twenty different directions. It was disconcerting. I was not accustomed to no-beat, no-rhythm dancing. It offended all my memories of the Saturdays I had spent watching *Soul Train*, the popular R & B dance show, as a kid. *Soul Train* taught me to flow fluidly to a pounding bass. I tried to focus on Michelle, who had a decent sense of rhythm, so I wouldn't be distracted by the seemingly disjoined arms and legs lurching around me. It was no use.

"I'm going to rest," I said and retreated to a chair against the wall. A moment later Keri joined me.

"I'm ready to go," she confessed.

"Me too," I agreed heartily.

"How long do you think Mandy and Michelle are planning to stay?" she asked.

"I don't know. I'd feel kind of bad if we left right now, though," I replied.

"I know. Me too. That guy—what's his name . . .?" Keri began.

"Mike," I answered.

"Yeah, Mike seems really glad we're here," she continued.

"I know," I sighed.

"So, I guess we're stuck," she stated, flatly resigning herself to our fate.

Eventually, a couple of the students dancing with Mike came off the floor, and we stood around chatting politely with them. Finally, Mike, the other Drexel student, Michelle and Mandy, joined us. Some of the other bystanders had already begun to clear out. The whole thing seemed to be winding down early. I sighed in relief.

"Hey, why don't you come back with us to the dorm to hang out?" Mike suggested.

"Okay," Mandy replied, eliminating the possibility of a polite, immediate getaway. We followed Mike and his friends back to a small studio dorm room. There we grabbed seats wherever we could find them, on the floor or leaning against a desk. I plopped down next to Keri, comforted that I was not alone in my sentiments.

Mike had clearly taken an interest in Michelle and was chatting her ear off about alternative rock bands. Always the cordial guest, Michelle nodded and looked interested. Finally, I heard the words I'd been waiting for ever since we arrived.

"Well, I think we should be getting home," Michelle announced. We were free at last. Thank God Almighty! Keri and I rose quickly, ready to say our friendly good-byes and be on our way before someone began a new conversation.

"Oh, of course . . . ," Mike replied. Obviously, he wanted to continue his conversation with Michelle, but our rising cued him of our determined departure. Realizing that Michelle was about to disappear with us from Drexel forever, Mike did what any smart guy would do.

"Let me give you my number," he told Michelle.

"Okay," she replied. He scribbled it down and handed it to her, setting the stage for his next request.

"And let me have yours?" he asked, handing her a blank scrap of paper and a pen. She wrote her number down and gave the paper to him.

"Okay, nice meeting you," Keri said as she smiled at Mike and his friend. The rest of us followed with our quick good-byes and left. Within five minutes, we were back on the familiar outskirts of Penn's campus.

"So, are you interested in Mike?" Keri asked Michelle.

"Just as a friend," Michelle replied, confirming what Keri and I already suspected.

"Ugh, another horrid Christian dance!" Keri declared.

It was true. Every school year we ended up at some dance sponsored by a Christian student fellowship. We always went to those things hoping we'd meet someone who might spark our interest. It never happened. Without fail, the music stunk. Usually the same guys we already knew stood around, most completely disinterested in dancing.

A vicious cycle kept repeating. Every school year we went to the same retreats, the same fellowship meetings, and the same giant northeastern spring collegiate conference, all sponsored by Christian student groups. The objective wasn't to find boyfriends, but it certainly would have been a nice fringe benefit. But even at the annual spring conference, where a couple hundred students from Penn, our seven sister schools, and several other Northeastern colleges congregated for an extended weekend of teaching, reflection, and worship, nothing ever blossomed. The spring conference always seemed the perfect place to meet guys and exchange phone numbers. Each year, after the first evening, I'd already surveyed all the conference attendees and decided whom I'd most like to have ask me for my phone number. But guys from other schools rarely uttered a word to any of us, much less asked to stay in touch. The Drexel dance didn't surprise us. Similar scenarios had played out many times before. The four of us meandered slowly home.

Still early for a Saturday, my watch barely showed ten thirty. We dropped Mandy off outside High Rise East. Then Michelle, Keri, and I climbed into the High Rise South elevator and let ourselves into the apartment. Michelle threw a CD on the stereo—decent music at last—and we settled down with some edible allies. With a half-pint of Ben and Jerry's chocolate fudge brownie in hand, I became a happy camper once again. Immediately, we turned to one of our favorite topics—men.

"What's the most serious relationship you've ever had?" Keri asked.

"Well, it wasn't all that serious, but when I was fourteen, I dated a nineteen-year-old. My parents didn't even freak out. They let me go out with him," I replied.

"No way! Your parents let you date a nineteen-year-old?" Keri interrupted dubiously.

"I know . . . Pretty wild, huh?"

"Where did you meet him?" Michelle asked.

"Riding the bus," I answered sheepishly. I knew I'd be heckled.

"On the bus? The city bus?" Mich laughed. "You never told us you used to pick up guys on the city bus."

"Let the record show that I did *not* pick him up," I declared, imitating a superior court judge. "He started talking to *me* first and asked for *my* phone number," I continued jovially. "He was on the bus with his younger brother. I don't know. He seemed—well, looked nice. So, we talked on the phone a couple times, and then he came by my house to visit. My mom said, 'You can go out with him, but I don't want you having sex. I'll tell him myself the next time he comes over.' Can you believe that? I thought she was kidding."

I paused for effect. Keri and Michelle listened, wide eyed.

"So, the next time he came over, my mom says 'Zac, you can see Adele, but I don't want her to be sexually active with you.' . . . Seriously, she said that right to his face—I just about died."

Keri and Michelle looked at me in disbelief.

"Yeah, I would have died too if my mom said that to my boyfriend," Michelle agreed.

"I was so embarrassed; I left the room and went into the kitchen while my mother finished talking to Zac. When I finally got the nerve to go back a few minutes later, my mom was saying, 'Are we clear?' to Zac, and he was nodding. 'Yes, Mrs. Moore.' My mom was so calm and cool. I died. So after my mom left, Zac said, 'Why did you leave the room?' Duh. I was fourteen—and totally embarrassed. My mom just had a sex talk with my boyfriend. How weird was that?"

"How long did you date him?" Keri pressed.

"Like two minutes," I replied.

"Seriously?" she laughed.

"I'm serious. I dated him for about four or five weeks before I broke up with him," I explained. "He was super flaky. I couldn't deal with that. He called me up once and said he was coming over to take me out. That was around four o'clock in the afternoon. So, I got dressed up and sat around the living room—waiting. Fifteen minutes passed, then a half hour. Five o'clock came, went, and still no Zac. Another half hour passed—and not even a phone call. That was it, I was through."

"Well, did he have a good reason? Was he in an accident or something?" Michelle asked.

"Well, he did have a motorcycle accident while we were dating, but that was earlier. That wasn't why he was late."

"So, why was he late?" Michelle asked.

"He gave some lame reason, but who cares? I wasn't sitting around waiting for some guy who couldn't keep his word. Besides, that was just the straw that broke the camel's back. It wasn't just that he was flaky. There were other issues."

"Like what?" Keri asked.

"Well, half the time we were dating I was on vacation with my parents because it was summer, so we agreed to write each other. I wrote him three times, and he wrote me once. His letter had bad grammar and spelling mistakes."

Keri and Michelle snickered.

"You're too much Adele," Keri laughed.

"Well, he'd already graduated from high school, and I was only a sophomore in high school. He ought to have had a better command of the English language than I did—right? I mean, seriously, English was his first language. He wasn't an exchange student or something."

Keri and Michelle cracked up.

"On top of that, he liked watching football. I can't stand watching sports. I don't mind playing football. Powder-puff football—sign me up. But *watching* sports—forget it. I only went to one football game in high school—because of him. So, you know—flaky, bad grammar, *and* football. Three strikes. He was out," I declared.

The truth of the matter was that I had broken up with Zac when his ex-girlfriend, the mother of his child, called me. Keri, Michelle, and me had no secrets—but I couldn't share that detail. The two of them were still trying to wrap their minds around the fact that I had dated an adult when I was a minor. This additional bit of information was best left a state secret. I had never even told my parents about Zac's child. My dad might have shot him the next time he showed up at our front door.

Zac never tried to hide the fact that he was a father. After the no-show date, he eventually called later in the evening to chat and apologize. Somewhere in the conversation he said, "Something came up with my son's mother." I was sure I hadn't heard him correctly, and I dismissed the words. Something was the matter with my phone receiver.

But, a day or two later, the phone rang at my parents' house.

"Hello," I spoke into the receiver.

"Hi," a woman's voice replied. "Adele?"

"Yes," I replied. "Who am I speaking to?"

"Uh, this is Rhonda. You don't know me. But I'm the mother of Zac's child," the voice said.

I sat frozen and silent.

"Are you still there?" the voice continued calmly.

"Yes," I replied.

"Well, Zac has been talking about you a lot. And I just wanted to warn you—be very careful. He's not all he pretends to be."

I remained quiet.

"Are you still there?" the voice asked again politely.

"Yes," I returned.

"I just wanted you to know. That's all," she finished.

"Uh, thank you," I replied and hung up the phone.

The phone call, the baby, his ex, and *football*—it was too much. The next time he called, I told him it was over.

"So, you weren't in love with him?" Keri asked.

"Heck no. How could I be in love with someone who likes to watch football?" I sassed.

"You're so bad," Michelle smiled and shook her head.

"Give me a break. I was fourteen," I shrugged.

"So, did you kiss him?" Keri asked.

"Sort of," I replied.

"Sort of? You can't sort of kiss someone," Michelle balked.

"Well, I did—*sort of*," I returned. "You know someone should have warned me about the whole tongue thing," I interjected.

"What?" Keri asked looking perplexed.

"Well, we're sitting in my parents' family room, with all the lights turned on full blast, no music playing or anything. It was absolutely the most *un*-romantic moment of my entire life, and then he says, 'Can I kiss you?' And I said, 'Sure.' No big deal, right? I'd seen it on TV a zillion times. So he leaned forward, I leaned forward . . . and—*whack!*—my nose totally smacked his. Hard. So now all I can think is, 'Watch out for the nose, watch out for the nose!' So, take two. I'm thinking, *Isn't he supposed to tilt his head or something?* And then I forgot to close my eyes because I was looking for his nose. It was so awkward; my lips couldn't hit the target. I'm thinking *Close your eyes! No, navigate the nose!* And then . . . all of a sudden out of the blue, he licked the inside of my head!"

"What?" Keri shrieked.

"Huh?" Michelle exclaimed.

"This giant tongue tried to slurp up my entire head. He totally grossed me out!"

Keri and Michelle almost fell off their seats, dying with laughter.

"It was *not* funny. He should have warned me that was coming," I replied seriously.

"So, you didn't really kiss him?" Keri clarified.

"I said *sort of.* I wasn't really into him—I only said yes because I was curious. Then he does the freaky tongue thing, and I *knew* I wasn't really into him. It wasn't a French kiss; it was more like a French vacuum."

Keri and Michelle howled.

"So why did you go out with him if you weren't really into him?" Michelle asked once she recovered from laughing.

"He was totally hot," I replied.

"Yeah, well, that's what you get for picking up totally *hot* guys on the bus," Michelle exclaimed as she nearly fell over with laughter.

We continued talking and divulging all our past crimes and misdemeanors of passion. We drew out the evening with colorful recountings of darting and dancing encounters with the opposite sex.

Guys, kissing, sex—Keri, Mich, and I were open books to one another on all things related to men. In retrospect, I realize that our conversations were far more than stimulating late-night conversation. Our rambling, uninhibited discussions functioned like a machete in a dense rainforest, helping us to slice through the entangled vines of the campus's constantly beckoning sensual world and set a clear path to our collective destination. We relied on each other to unravel the unknown and clarify the murky. Anything that came to mind was fair game to question, contemplate, and discuss. (Is it normal for women to get to know themselves, or is that just a guy thing? Is it moral? How often do couples have sex?) We discussed every topic of the day relentlessly, with the same uncensored, free-flowing flood of opinions as we discussed our favorite classes. Every far-fetched inquiry and bizarre observation was fair fodder for serious examination as well as irreverent ridicule. Taboo simply didn't exist. We held nothing sacred except God Himself—and, of course, the hope of V Society alumnae status.

"Hey, Allison," Keri said to our roommate in a very serious tone as we milled about in the living room. "I have a lot of hairs on my breast, and I'm concerned that maybe one day my children will refuse to nurse or something. Do you have any professional literature on the subject?"

Allison, the nursing student, replied sincerely, "I don't know, but I'll look up some information on that for you."

Keri was joking of course, but Allison took her seriously. We often joked about random stuff like that.

When Keri eventually headed back to her room, I followed her and lingered for a while in her doorway.

"Do you ever wonder when you'll meet your husband?" I asked.

"Of course. All the time," she replied.

"I wonder what he's doing right now—right at this exact moment," I reflected.

"I know. Isn't that a weird thought? Somewhere, he's out there, wandering around doing his thing," she relayed quietly.

"Then, just think, one day out of the blue your paths will cross in some divine, serendipitous encounter. Like at a grocery store or something."

"I don't think I'll meet him at a grocery store," Keri countered.

"Okay, fine. So you're sitting in synagogue, and all of a sudden you turn to look over your shoulder, and there's some tall, dark, and beautiful Israeli guy checking you out from the pew two rows back."

Keri smiled. "That would be nice," she replied. She paused as though turning the thought over repeatedly in her mind. "Do you believe in love at first sight?" she asked.

"No, I don't think so. I mean, just because he *looks* good doesn't mean he *is* good. I've heard some serial killers are very charming and handsome."

Keri laughed.

"I do believe in *like* at first sight, though," I clarified.

We chuckled.

"Good night." I smiled and turned to head to my room.

"Good night," she replied.

In all of my far-flung conversations with Keri and Michelle, it was strange that I talked to my roommates about abstinence, but never chastity. *Chastity* was a foreign word to me. In fact I'd only heard it used once or twice in my entire life. I don't remember the first time I heard the word used—maybe in church—but I couldn't be sure.

The second time someone mentioned the word *chastity* occurred during high school. For several weeks during my freshman year, two Mormon missionaries stopped by my parents' house once a week to talk to us about their faith and the Church of Jesus Christ of Latter-Day Saints (the Mormons). My parents had no intention of converting to Mormonism, but we were curious about what they believed. We'd heard all kinds of rumors and wanted to get our facts straight.

So one day, the two Mormon missionaries, both guys in their early twenties, stopped by our house for their regular weekly visit. Usually, my mom let them in, but on that particular day she was out. So I mimicked what I'd seen her do; I let them in, told them to sit in the living room, and offered them glasses of water. They sat patiently waiting for Mom to arrive. After a half hour she still hadn't come home, so the missionaries began their weekly lesson without her.

"Do you know what chastity is?" the first missionary asked. I flushed with embarrassment. I should have known what it meant, but I couldn't muster up a working definition to save my life. To my horror, the missionary proceeded to *explain* chastity to me. I felt awkward and kept wishing Mom would appear. Suddenly, it seemed rather *un*-chaste to be sitting in the living room, alone with two guys that I hardly knew, while my parents were out. After that, I blocked out chastity. I associated it with an uncomfortable, one-sided conversation that I had with two older guys when I was thirteen. Besides, it seemed like an ancient concept; no one even used that word on regular basis.

In my mind, abstinence equaled chastity. I didn't realize that chastity ran deeper than avoiding hookups. Our actions resulted from our thinking. True chastity sought purity of mind, which, if practiced, resulted in purity of thought *and* purity of action. Jesus said that if you were angry with someone—angry enough to kill him, it was the same as committing murder. Entertaining murderous intentions equaled murderous action. According to that teaching, if I lusted after a guy—actually imagined hooking up with him—it was the same as committing adultery. Entertaining lustful thoughts equaled committing lustful action—even if it was only in my head.

But I hadn't wanted to sleep with my ex-boyfriend Zac. I had just wanted to make out with him to satisfy my curiosity. I thought—wrongly—that that was okay. I failed to realize that my motivation lacked purity. My thought process didn't differ from the one I suspected many guys had when they justified sleeping with a girl—out of curiosity. He'd ask himself, "Would she be fun to hook up with?" I'd asked myself. "Would Zac be fun to make out with?" In retrospect, I could see that I had used him—and then made fun of him to my roommates. The fact that he was older than me didn't automatically make him the villain and me the innocent. I didn't mean to use guys, but sometimes I did—unconsciously. I didn't truly grasp purity *of mind* at all.

Stephanie stopped by the next day. It was early Sunday afternoon. Finally the temperature outside had warmed enough to slide open a window. A faint breeze wafted into the living room, reminding us that soon we could store our sweaters away as spring tiptoed into summer.

"You know Penn-Film-and-Video Josh?" Stephanie asked as she sat on the floor with her guitar resting on her knee.

I lay at an angle on the sofa, my feet kicked out over the edge and my head resting against Keri's arm as she dozed in and out of a light sleep. Keri, Michelle, and I had stayed up late again the previous night. The lack of sleep was finally getting the best of Keri. Exhausted, she tried to stay engaged in the conversation, but her eyelids fought against her.

"Yeah, I know who he is," I replied.

"Is he cute?" she asked with a little giggle. "I can't decide. I keep look-ing at him, and sometimes I think, 'He's cute.' Then I look at him again, and I think, 'He reminds me of a Tootsie Roll,'" she declared.

"*A Tootsie Roll?*" I exclaimed. I assumed the Tootsie Roll reference had something to do with Josh's compact build. He was vertically challenged. But Stephanie wasn't very tall either; she was the shortest of all of us. Josh was a couple inches taller than she, but still a bit shorter than the average guy.

"I can see how someone would think he's cute," I assured her. Penn-Film-and-Video Josh was 100 percent clean-cut, J. Crew–wearing, East Coast college guy. I could easily see how someone (other than me) would find him attractive. He had short, dark hair and a roundish but distinct face with nice features. He helped organize the Film Club, maybe a club officer—I wasn't sure.

"Yeah, I don't know," she mused. "Tootsie-Roll Josh," she murmured in a distracted manner, as her thoughts turned inward and her eyes focused somewhere on a distant plane beginning and ending outside the bounds of the room. She still seemed to be deliberating whether he resembled the chewy, cylindrical candy.

"I can't decide if he's nice, though," she added turning her focus back to me again. I couldn't find any truthful, reassuring words to encourage her. I'd only spoken to Josh a few times, and he seemed okay, not par-ticularly nice, but not entirely unpleasant.

For the rest of spring, Stephanie waxed and waned in her preoccupa-tion with Penn-Film and-Video Josh, but I couldn't tell if she harbored a secret affection for him or if she disliked him. She mentioned him only slightly less than Mike Myers from *Saturday Night Live*. In the forth-coming weeks, he seemed to evolve into the subject of disdain. Finally, she wrote him into the Rumors of the Day. I assumed she'd made her final decision about him.

V Society, March 16
Junior Year

RUMORS OF THE DAY

1. *Stephanie bought all the Tootsie Rolls in West Philly and burned them in protest of Mr. Josh Penn-Film-and-Video.*
2. *Michelle went on a date with Slimy Alex.*
3. *Allison is doing a paper on Keri's breast hair. (Keri told her that she had veritable forests growing on her breasts especially since she let her underarm hair grow, and what did she think as a nurse—would it affect her children negatively to drink hairy milk? Allison was sufficiently grossed out.)*

The next day, Keri and I sat in Milan's room talking to him about nothing in particular, indulgently wasting away a fine afternoon, as we often did when our study load became light.

"Man, I need to do my laundry," Milan grimaced. His mind had jumped from the subject at hand to the chores he'd sorely neglected. "All my underwear is dirty—I haven't worn any for a couple days."

Keri and I couldn't help but laugh. The laundry room ranked as one of my least favorite places in the dorm. It was a necessity, but I tried to spend as little time there as possible. Everyone did.

"That has to be uncomfortable," Keri said, turning her head toward me and away from Milan with a funny expression that read, *What's the matter with that boy?*

"Seriously, you need to do your laundry," I advised.

"I know this guy that just turns his underwear inside out and wears it again when all his laundry is dirty," Milan replied matter-of-factly.

"That is so gross," I returned. "No woman would ever do that!"

"Yeah, definitely a guy thing," Keri agreed, hardly masking a look of repulsion.

I amused myself by thumbing through Milan's music collection. He didn't have many CDs, but the ones he had were all interesting— an eclectic mix of varied artists and different genres from around the world.

"Hey, can I borrow this one?" I asked, holding up a compilation.

"Sure," he replied without even looking to see which CD I held up. It was one of those perfect, peaceful, temperate afternoons when our idle thoughts roamed to and fro. If any one idea in particular held our attention for more than a split second, we uttered it aloud, seeking collaboration. At times like these, Milan's armor of moody detachment cracked and he absentmindedly divulged information about himself.

"Did I ever tell you that I used to wear really wild clothes when I lived in Belgrade?" he asked as he sat slightly reclined on one side of his bed, propped up on an elbow. Keri sat relaxed at the other end of his bed, her back and head leaning against the wall.

"No," I replied as I finished rummaging through his music collection and seated myself in his desk chair. I wondered if his wardrobe looked as ridiculous as my New Wave punk–inspired, circus-freak high school get-up.

"Yeah, I used to wear these hippie-style clothes, and my father always tried to get me to quit dressing like that. So one day he put my clothes on and wore them around," he continued.

"What did you do?" Keri asked.

"I quit dressing like that. He made his point," Milan finished.

"That's funny," I said. "Yeah, that would freak me out too if my parents wore my clothes from high school."

"Do you think the dorms here are better or worse than other schools?" Keri asked as our stream of consciousness conversation continued trickling forth.

"I don't know. The only other dorms I've stayed in were in LA and Massachusetts. They were okay, not much different than these. In high school, I stayed in a dorm in England on this school trip we had. They weren't bad," I volunteered. "We had some good times when we were in this one dorm," I said with a laugh.

"Do tell," Milan returned.

"We tied sheets together and climbed out of the second-story window after curfew," I admitted.

"How about you?" I asked Milan. "What's the craziest thing you did in your dorm?"

"Uh . . ." He hesitated. "When I was in England, I dated two girls in the same dorm."

"Did they know about each other?" Keri asked.

"No," Milan replied.

It was an elite British school; I couldn't believe he'd pulled that off easily with smart women. "Weren't they suspicious?" I probed.

"Hey, which CD did you want to borrow?" Milan asked, just then seeming to register my previous question.

"The compilation with the Psychedelic Furs on it," I replied.

"Yeah, no problem. Of course you can borrow it," he returned. We forgot our questions about the double girlfriends in the shifting sea of thoughts spilling out and washing ashore.

"I've got to get something to eat," I said.

"Me too," Keri replied. "I haven't eaten lunch yet."

"Do you have anything to eat in here?" I asked.

"Yeah, a few things. Orange juice and vitamins, you know—different stuff," he replied lazily.

"That's not lunch. Let's go to the Middle Eastern food truck," Keri said, looking at me. Just past our dorm on Fortieth Street, a row of mobile food trucks served up everything from falafel to Chinese food for next to nothing.

Keri and I rose to our feet and scooped our backpacks up and on. We headed out the door.

"We'll catch you later," I called to Milan.

"Bye," he replied, his face suddenly more serious and grave. Instantaneously his armor seemed to reappear, walling him behind his impenetrable fortress.

"Bye," Keri echoed.

The next day I swung by Gap and bought a two-pack of men's boxers. I let myself into Milan's empty room through the window and dropped the GAP stamped gift box on his bed with a signed note, ". . . until you do your laundry."

V SOCIETY, MARCH 16
Junior Year

RUMORS OF THE DAY

1. *Said Milan, "Did her, had her, bagged her, double timed her, got some..." as he happily sat upon his red bowl pee pot.*
2. *Adele got falafel on the Walk, and they laughed at her because she wasn't Jewish. She told them she was an Ethiopian Jew.*
3. *Keri cooked chicken and rice for the Serbian boys choir.*

Hours later, long after our falafel binge, I sat alone in my room, studying. Kate Bush's ethereal voice cooed at low volume from my stereo speakers. I dug her album, *The Sensual World*, but I always had to pass up the title song with its stirring, seductive lyrics. That song got my mind spinning in the wrong direction. Instead I always skipped straight to track two, "Love and Anger." That I could deal with.

Keri walked in just as I finished packing up my study notes and tidying up my desk.

"Hey, as long as we've been roommates, I've never seen you change your sheets," she stated plainly.

"Uhhh . . . ," I started, wracking my brain for the last time I'd washed my linens. "It's not like they're really dirty," I offered.

Keri looked at me skeptically.

"I mean, no one *else* is sleeping on them except me, and I take a shower every night before I go to bed," I said, attempting to defend my laundry-deprived bedding. "It's not like anything is going on to make them dirty . . . exactly."

Keri just looked at me. I felt like a child whose parents had discovered that she only brushed her teeth once a week. I honestly couldn't remember the last time I'd washed my sheets. I couldn't believe she actually noticed how often I washed—rather, *didn't wash*—my sheets. Great, just what I needed—more laundry to do.

V Society, March 17
Junior Year

RUMORS OF THE DAY

Adele received a $2,000 scholarship award from the
Clean Sheets Council.

Two days later, after Keri had left for the morning, I stripped my bed hastily and stuffed the sheets and pillowcase into a laundry bag. I didn't want her to think she had anything to do with the unexpected trip my sheets took to the washing machine. I headed down the hall with my dirty clothing and bedding and filled up three washing machines with my things. I sniffed my sheets before tossing them in the washer. They smelled fine—what was the big deal? Anyway, Keri was right. It was probably a good idea to wash my sheets more than once a semester. Besides, I definitely wanted to avoid any future discussions about my not-so-fresh linens. After that, I stripped my bed regularly and hauled my sheets to the laundry room with my usual wash runs.

Just before spring break, Keri developed a painful cyst on her back-side. She couldn't sit normally or rest her weight evenly on both sides of her bottom. Instead, she had to sit leaning on one hip and then alternate and lean on the other. That inspired Keri's most famous lullaby.

V SOCIETY, MARCH
Junior Year

SPRING BREAK DITTY BY KERI ZELMAN
"PAIN" TO THE TUNE OF YAZ'S "WINTER KILLS"

Pain in my butt

Feels so cruel

And very spiteful

Sobs n' sighs flow delightful

Come dreary nightfall

Now that Keri's cyst had become a regular topic of our roommate discussions, related butt topics inspired our daily dialogue.

"What are you having for dinner?" Keri asked Michelle.

"Poop-on-a-stick," Mich replied without cracking a smile. Of course, that sent Keri and me into whooping laughter. Clearly, we were all sick and wrong. But from then on buttlore flourished, and we documented it systematically in our V Society notes.

V Society, March 14
Junior Year

RUMORS OF THE DAY

Michelle made a one billion dollar deal with McDonalds
to market her patented "Poop-on-a-Stick."

Amidst laundry woes and butt aches, Michelle regularly fielded calls from Drexel Mike who couldn't seem to understand that she just wanted to be friends.

I met up diligently with Milan and Stephanie to shoot footage for our budding avant-garde film. Some days Milan and I filmed on our own. Other times Stephanie and I set out to capture footage together. Stephanie and I usually shot scenery that involved her car. We liked road trips. Occasionally, Milan joined us, and all three of us hopped in Stephanie's car and filmed together using a couple different cameras.

"I'm going to visit my cousin Sandra at Dartmouth over spring break," Stephanie informed Keri and me one evening. "I think I'll do some filming up there. Do you want to come?"

"I'd love to!" Keri exclaimed before Stephanie could finish the sentence.

"How about you?" Stephanie asked me.

"Thanks, but I signed up to build houses with Habitat for Humanity over break."

"Really? Who's going with you?" Keri asked.

"I have no idea. Some other Penn students, I guess. There was an announcement posted that students could help build homes for families in North Philadelphia."

"So, you don't know anyone else that's going?" Stephanie inquired.

"No. It should be fun, though. Besides, it's only a week," I replied.

"Are you going to go back and forth from campus every day?" Keri asked.

"No, we're all staying out there, at a rectory a few blocks from the building site," I answered.

"Can I take the video camera with me to Dartmouth?' Stephanie asked.

"Of course," I replied. "What are you planning to film there?"

"I don't know. Once I get up there, I'll just film whatever looks interesting," she replied.

"You can take the camera with you after this weekend," I told her. "I won't need it again till after break."

Stephanie left late that evening, leaving Keri, Michelle, and me sprawled out in our living room. For some reason, the three of us waxed more philosophical and pensive than usual. Perhaps we'd exhausted our daily quota of jokes and jests.

"You know," Michelle said thoughtfully, "I think pride is the root of all sin. Think about it. What sin isn't the result of pride?"

"What made you think of that?" Keri asked.

"Nothing in particular. I was just thinking about it," Mich replied.

"Hmm," I deliberated aloud, "that's an interesting point, Mich." I had never thought of sin that way before.

"Name a sin," Michelle requested.

"Greed and lust," Keri replied.

"Isn't pride at the root of greed and lust?" Michelle suggested. "Both are based on the belief that you deserve to possess something you don't have."

"Anger. Malice," I posed.

"Anger—you believe you've been denied something you're owed, and so you lash out. Or you believe someone has wronged you, who does not have the right to wrong you. Again, pride is the culprit," Michelle surmised.

"And malice," Keri began. "To be malicious you have to believe that the other person is not worthy of better treatment. That requires that you consider yourself better than that person."

We continued down a list of sins: lying, fits of rage, stealing . . . It was true. At the root of each of those lay pride, a belief in one's own entitlement.

"You are so right, Mich," Keri agreed.

"That's deep," I concurred as we sat quietly reflecting.

Spring break came upon us before we knew it. Stephanie and Keri took off in Stephanie's car, headed up to Dartmouth. Michelle and Mandy secured short-term jobs at the Philadelphia Flower Show and commuted there from school every day. I packed a bag of my oldest, grubbiest clothes to wear for my short-term construction gig in North Philadelphia.

In total, about nine of us from Penn choose to spend spring break pounding nails and wielding power drills. I made two new friends: Rob, an easygoing frat brother in a fraternity I'd never heard of, and Amy, an upbeat English major. This was my first visit deep into the heart of North Philadelphia. In many ways, it resembled a war zone. On our short walk from the rectory to the building site, we passed several row homes completely gutted and ravaged, each caving in on itself as though a bomb had been dropped through the ceiling. In the attached row house next door to the home we worked on, a family went about its daily business, paying no attention to their neighbors' obliterated residence and the overflowing refuse that exploded out of the blown-out door and windows.

I took some beautiful photographs there. On my way back to the rectory from work one day, I snapped a brightly painted red-brick home with green trim. It stood cheerful and erect, in bold contrast to the paint-chipped, dilapidated house next door. A tiny child peeked out of the second-story window and gazed down at the sidewalk below.

"Hey, lady!" a gregarious little boy about six years old called out to me on the street. "Take my picture!" He was too cute to resist as he assembled his playmates for a group picture of five lively, larger-than-life kids flashing radiant Hollywood smiles.

My week in North Philadelphia ended as quickly as it had begun. We'd help jump-start three new homes toward completion. On the last day, we packed our few belongings up and jumped in cars shuttling us back to West Philadelphia.

Chapter Eight

COMING UNDONE

{April, Second Semester of Junior Year}

"Owww! What the hell? Ugh—MAN!" Milan exclaimed, frustrated and baffled. He sat up with a disgusted "Ughh!" and slid off the bed in the dark room.

"What?" I said, roused from my dozing. "What happened?"

"Stephanie bit me!" he retorted, clearly vexed.

"What? Stephanie bit you?" I asked.

"Sorry," Stephanie said, trying to stifle a giggle. "I couldn't help it."

"She bit me on the shoulder!" Milan barked. His voice simmered with agitation.

I tried not to laugh as I imagined Stephanie's face pressed against the back of Milan's thin T-shirt: Her nose, brushed by the hair on the back of his head, peeked just above the back of his shoulder. Her lips aligned with the back side of his shoulder blade. Unexpectedly, a primordial urge overcame her. She was filled with an otherworldly, mischievous desire to sample Milan like a piece of watermelon.

Tired and inconvenienced, Milan was not enthusiastic about our spontaneous slumber party. Stephanie, Keri, and I had popped in on Milan for one of our unannounced late night visits. Keri had left after an hour since she had to wake up early for an exam. Stephanie and I stayed. We entertained ourselves by playing Milan's CDs on his stereo.

We twirled each other around in waltzes and busted our best dance moves in the small floor space. Stephanie lip-synched, and Milan and I egged her on with cheers and clapping. Milan served as resident DJ and recommended different CDs we might find intriguing.

Milan had inserted an obscure-sounding title into the stereo, and the room filled with heavy percussion and the distinct pinging sound of a Balkan stringed instrument. A strong dance beat soared, and an unidentifiable foreign language emerged from the background. Then another set of harmonizing vocals in a foreign language overlaid the earlier sound.

"This is great! What is this?" I asked Milan.

"Goran Bregović—he's a Serbian musician. He's a bit of an avant-garde, folk, independent-type composer. Sounds like a soundtrack, right?"

"It does. Where's the CD?" I asked, as Milan took his turn on our makeshift dance floor.

"Over there," he replied, pointing to the shelf where the stereo sat.

I immersed myself in examining the Goran Bregović CD cover.

I paused to look up at Milan who was flowing in an inebriating and soulful melodic rhythm. He moved with ease, boldly yet gracefully to the pounding base. Every hip-swaying step synchronized with a subtle but decisive arm motion in a harmonized, effortless slow jam. His dancing mesmerized me—not because I'd never seen anyone dance like that before—but because I'd never seen a *white* boy dance like that. How could a distant foreign land imploding in violent ethnic tensions between Serbs and Croats produce such an embodiment of black urban swagger? With each movement, he hit every beat. His face exuded measured self-assurance as he exercised exacting control over every body muscle, as though to contain the simmering fire that boiled fiercely beneath the surface. He was an incredible dancer.

"No way!" I exclaimed in sheer delight. "You did *not* pick that up in Belgrade!"

A huge grin broke out across Milan's face. "I hung out with the *brothas* when I was in England," he replied smugly.

Clearly, he'd been hanging with the brothas well before London. It had taken me years, studying the *Soul Train* dancers and dancing in front of a mirror, to learn to move like that. Milan danced as if he had been fed on a strict diet of Motown and hip-hop—not British New Wave music like me.

By three in the morning, Milan looked spent.

"Hey, I'm beat," he mumbled.

Fully dressed, in jeans and a T-shirt with his socks and shoes still on, Milan stretched across his bed. He turned toward the wall, away from the room lights and us.

Stephanie turned to me. "Well, it's too late for us to walk home."

She was right. Milan's room was on the far east side of campus. We lived in the dorms farthest west, on the opposite end of campus. The university police and Penn Safety provided a campus safety escort service for free until two in the morning. When you called the campus safety line, male student volunteers of football-player proportions met you at the place you requested and walked you safely to your destination. Or you could ride the Penn Shuttle, a free van that safely taxied students to and from distant areas of campus and the surrounding West Philadelphia community. With a recent mugging and an assault just off campus, students knew to be cautious. The university police warned of the lurking danger for unaccompanied female students who walked through campus late at night or early in the morning.

"We'll just stay here," Stephanie resolved. "Okay?" she asked Milan.

"Yeah, fine," he replied, half asleep.

Stephanie took her shoes off and lay next to Milan on his twin bed. I removed my shoes and squished onto the few inches on the edge of the bed next to Stephanie.

"Turn the lights out," Milan grumbled.

Stephanie sat up and flicked off the desk lamp at the foot of the bed. I got up and walked over to the switch by the door to turn off the main room light. Then I resettled myself in the sardine sleeping arrangement.

I couldn't relax on my three inches of mattress and despite the thrill of Milan being asleep just one person away from me, I couldn't help wondering when he had last washed his sheets. Thankfully I was sleeping on top of the sheets with a layer of clothing between the bedding and me.

I reached across Stephanie and put my hand on Milan's forehead.

"Whose hand is that?" he barked.

"Mine," I replied.

"Oh, okay," he returned, his voice instantly mellowed and agreeable.

I dozed off, thinking about my tidy dorm room, with freshly washed sheets on the bed, and the clean ivory pillows I'd brought from my parents' house in California. I must have been out for fifteen minutes before Milan's howl startled me awake. The bite had roused sleep-deprived Milan into full-scale-curmudgeon Milan.

"I can't sleep like this," he growled and snapped on the desk lamp. His face twisted in a dark frown, his rage palpable.

He expelled us.

The two of us half jogged, half speed-walked down the well-lit but abandoned Locust Walk, which ran east to west through the center of campus. We were giddy with the image of a shocked and bitten Milan replaying in our heads. We laughed with nervous energy and looked over our shoulders for muggers as we sped home.

"Stahfahnee beet me!" I exclaimed in my best Serbian accent, mocking Milan.

"I can't believe we're doing the walk of shame from Milan's dorm— it's not even a cool dorm," Stephanie joked. The infamous "walk of shame" occurred in the early hours of the morning as college women trudged back to their dorms and respective homes from frat houses and other boys' dwellings.

Stephanie and I couldn't wait to relay the biting incident to Keri and Michelle when we were all back together again the following afternoon. They nearly fell off their chairs, letting out irrepressible howls of laughter. The previous night was so vivid and thrilling in its peculiar events and explosive outcome—yet so bizarre that it seemed unreal.

"He was so mad!" I proclaimed.

"I've never seen him that angry before," Stephanie added gleefully.

Maybe it was Milan's unbridled show of emotion that made the night so unforgettable. He was always so guarded—so seemingly emotionless—yet so full of energetic fervor that it was obvious his emotions ran deep, regardless of how well he hid them. Even a show of anger indicated his capability to express some sort of raw, heartfelt outpouring.

V Society, Best of the Best List
Junior Year

FUNNIEST MOMENT
Stephanie Biting Milan {Adele}

I saw Milan a couple days later as I hurried past Van Pelt Library, returning from a lecture.

"Hey!" he called out.

"Hey, what's up?" I returned. His face looked somber and reserved, though a quick smile revealed he wasn't unhappy to see me.

"Where are you headed?" he asked.

"I'm headed to Le Bus to read," I replied. Le Bus was a casual café-style restaurant just off campus—a popular eatery for students.

"I'll join you," he said.

We ambled past the giant, ivory broken-button sculpture in front of the library. College Green buzzed with students headed in fifty different directions, trickling out from the library, lounging on the lawn, and spilling out from the vast doorways of innumerable buildings dotting the perimeter. We found a small table in a quiet corner at Le Bus. I put my hot tea down on the table and slung my backpack over the back of the chair. He plopped his drink in front of him. We sat down.

I hadn't seen Milan since Stephanie had chomped his shoulder. Not anxious to bring up that night's misadventure, I was glad he didn't mention it. We chatted briefly about our current load of assigned reading and papers, upcoming exams, and our progress on the film short. Then he paused shortly to take a drink, before looking back at me again. His face appeared serious, but his voice was gentle.

"Hanging out with you, Michelle, and Keri all at once is too much," he told me in an exhausted tone. "It's like feeding one speaker through three amps."

He was getting at something, but I wasn't sure exactly what. I only half listened to him. What would my roommates and I do on a random Tuesday night if we couldn't all drop in on Milan for an impromptu visit? What was he talking about? I couldn't—*we* couldn't—erase him, his room, and our visits from our roaming. It would be like taking the fizz out of soda. Junior year would be flat. But maybe that wasn't what he meant. I couldn't be sure. Maybe he meant that I could drop by but I should quit bringing my cohorts with me. Was he asking me to help him shed the very friends that were inseparable from me? Impossible. I liked Keri and Michelle with me all the time. Besides, he didn't know it, but I'd promised Keri I wouldn't hang out in his room alone at night. I had safety in numbers.

My expression gave him the impression I was listening, but everything he said went in one ear and out the other. He didn't make sense. If our collective presence taxed him so much, why did he come by our room to visit all the time? He seemed to be saying that the three of us, all the time, all at once, overloaded his senses. Then add Stephanie to the mix, with her prattling and quirky sense of humor, and it made him crazy. But what could I do about that? As he continued trying to make his point, I ignored him.

Milan grew surlier as the school year lumbered toward the end of the semester. But he still couldn't stay away. We continued to see each other several times a week. He still dropped by the apartment, though less frequently.

Eventually, his gripe unveiled itself. Milan forced the space he needed from the V Society by systematically carving it out. Stephanie became the first casualty. He openly turned a cold shoulder toward her. Before the biting incident, he would listen to her with interest; now he showed none. When she knocked on his door, he discouraged her visits with an incredulous expression and a stern nongreeting. The message was clear. He didn't want to be her friend—at least not right now.

But Stephanie doted on Milan. So did Mich and I. As much as he bewildered and frustrated us, we could not imagine a single week passing without him. Milan's purposeful indifference cut Stephanie to the heart. She openly mourned the loss of him in song and tears.

V Society, Spring
Junior Year

RUMORS OF THE DAY

1. *Milan is smiling and feeling good! His favorite song is "Don't Worry, Be Happy!"*
2. *Stephanie chipped her incisor tooth on Milan's left clavicle.*

RUMOR OF THE YEAR

*Milan thinks Stephanie is the greatest person and would
take his own life if he couldn't see her twice a day.*

SCIENTIFIC EQUATION OF THE DAY

$$\frac{\text{Number of Tears Stephanie Shed Over Milan}}{} = \frac{\lim\limits_{x \to \infty}}{} \frac{x^{2000}}{1}$$

The balance had changed; the Elevator Society no longer remained a happy, dysfunctional family, accepting each other's peculiar idiosyncrasies. We were coming undone and realigning under new allegiances.

Milan captivated all of us—except Keri—like no other. Keri thought him too random and abstract for her taste. But he was a riddle I couldn't unravel. I tried to make sense of him. We all tried to figure him out. It was like fitting together the fragmented pieces of a complex, moving puzzle. He sat in the apartment regularly, talking and telling us political jokes about disintegrating Yugoslavia. Yet much of him remained buried beneath a shiny, impenetrable veneer, as though what lay beneath the surface was so fragile it might crumble if exposed. Occasionally I saw an indication that behind the grouchy boy there might be a deep, warm man. But, like a tortoise after popping its tender head out for a quick peek, Milan always retreated into his hard shell.

We discussed him tirelessly and often recorded our observations about him in a concerted effort to piece him together. It was like therapy—a healing exercise to prevent him from making us mad as hatters. Of all the guys we knew on campus, only he commanded that kind of hold on us. Michelle, Keri, Stephanie, and I had other male friends. Different guys often stopped by the apartment to visit and hang out. And, of course, I still recruited male models regularly. But the other guys in our lives seemed far easier to read—even the most complex, intelligent, and introspective of them failed to confound us, so we rarely discussed them and seldom wrote them into our V Society notes.

V Society, April 18
Junior Year

QUOTE OF THE DAY
Michelle: "It's Milan. When are you ever sure?"

This element of intrigue propelled me involuntarily toward Milan. In every encounter with him, a tacit risk that I wouldn't admit to myself or to anyone—thrilled and electrified me. He wasn't safe. One foolish move on my part would send my tumbling over the precipice at light speed.

The next week the phone rang. Keri answered. It was Milan. She remained quiet; he talked to her at length—a rarity for Milan. As he spoke, Keri's face grew cloudy in a concerned frown. Curious, I lingered close by, hoping to get a hint of the conversation in her response. But Milan did most of the talking. Keri remained silent except for an occasional "uh-huh" followed by another frown. I tried to wait around for some indicator of what he'd been saying but after more than a few minutes of loitering, I retreated to my room to finish the project I'd started. Finally, Keri hung up. I went to see what the matter was.

"What's going on?" I asked nonchalantly.

"Milan converted to some religion where he wears a turban," she said.

"A turban?" My immediate thought was that his rolling waves of dark hair were so nice, why would he cover them with a turban?

"You're joking." I smiled at Keri.

"No, I'm serious," she replied, looking genuinely concerned.

"He's lying," I assured her. "He's not interested in faith of any kind. Trust me."

"No, he's very serious," she countered. "He said he met this guy that revealed all these amazing things to him and now he's joined this religion."

"What?" I replied, dumbfounded. Milan was not easily persuaded of anything. He had to be pulling Keri's leg. "He's not lying?" I insisted.

"No, he just spent the last twenty minutes explaining his conversion to me. He's very serious," Keri restated firmly.

I still couldn't believe it, though Keri's expression began to convince me. I'd spoken to Milan about my faith before, and it had elicited absolutely no response. None. He seemed impervious to absorption of anything in the spiritual realm. The guy who had converted him must have been one gifted salesman.

"So, what did he say exactly?" I pressed.

"He wants to meet us in a little while at Beanie's to tell us about his new religion," she explained.

"That's it? He must have said more than that," I insisted.

"Well, he asked if I still wanted to be friends or something like that."

"What? I don't get it?" I balked.

"He asked if I still wanted to be friends," she repeated.

"And what did you say?" I asked, distracted by the questionable chain of events.

"Well, I was going to say yes, but then he started talking about something else before I could really answer," she replied.

It didn't matter to me what religion he followed either. Without a personal relationship with God through the risen Savior, the outcome was the same; he remained eternally separated from fellowship with God.

"When are we supposed to meet him?" I asked.

"In about an hour," she replied.

"Okay," I agreed. Something wasn't right. The whole thing seemed implausible. I believed Keri, but I couldn't believe Milan's story. It didn't add up. He wasn't someone who would wake up one day and join some religious group because someone told him a good tale—especially some guy he just met. Who was this guy anyway? He never mentioned any turban-wearing friends to me. I anxiously waited to hear his side of the story at Beanie's.

Michelle's key turned in the door. She swung it open and entered the room.

"Hi," she said and sank into the closest wooden chair as she allowed her backpack to slip off her arm into a sagging heap on the floor. She looked beat.

"Hi," I replied. "What's up?"

"Nothing," she said. "I just finished a lab." Suddenly, she noticed the look on Keri's face. "What's the matter?" she asked Keri. She sat straight up. All signs of fatigue vanished as her attention refocused entirely on Keri.

"Milan just called. He joined some religious group and is wearing a turban." Keri repeated the abbreviated story to Michelle. "So, be ready to go with us in about ten minutes to meet him," Keri added.

Keri, Mich, and I arrived at Beanie's. No one in a turban was present. We ordered drinks and sat down. My curiosity burst out of control. (What had convinced him? Would he really wear a turban every day? What faiths required followers to wear turbans? Sikhism? Could you become a Sikh overnight? I didn't think so. Every faith that I knew of with the exception of following Jesus required that you *do* something to become a follower. You had to go through a ceremony, memorize doctrine, or take classes—*something*.)

Only in the pursuit of Christ, could you make a confession of faith and be a full-fledged child of God. He couldn't have secretly studied to join this faith—whatever it was. He would have told me, wouldn't he? I could only think of one person I'd seen on campus wearing a turban. That took me back to my initial question: Where did he *meet* this guy? My inquiring mind ran amok. Caught up in my thoughts, I scarcely said a word to Keri or Michelle. Finally, Keri and Michelle looked toward the door. I followed their gazes—Milan. His silhouette filled the front door. He wore a big, dark turban wrapped around his head.

I studied his face quickly for cues, still suspecting a joke. But Keri appeared absolutely correct. All the telltale signs—an impish grin, the far-reaching possibility that he'd be wearing a "Belated April Fools'" T-shirt instead of a turban—were absent. He joined us, his face solemn and his demeanor noticeably subdued. He looked odd, yet the same. I couldn't decipher the expression he wore. His face gave no hint of his thoughts. This was a big deal. How could he look so passive and unanimated?

"Hi," he said and sat in the empty chair at our table.

"Hey," we each replied.

I tried to act as though everything were normal. I remained quiet as I waited to hear from Milan.

"So, you converted to this new religion?" Keri asked.

"Yes," he replied. He looked at Keri, then me, then Mich.

I tried to keep my face expressionless. I'm not sure I succeeded. To my relief, Milan gave no indication that my face revealed utter shock.

"Actually, I didn't tell you the entire story," Milan began. "What did Keri tell you?" he asked us.

"Just that you met some guy and that he told you something. Now you've joined this religion," Michelle recounted.

"And what do you think about that?" he asked.

"Nothing," I replied.

"Nothing?" He looked perplexed.

"I don't think anything about it," I repeated. "You're free to believe whatever you want." Why was he wasting time asking me questions? I came to hear from him, not give an opinion.

Michelle shrugged in agreement with me.

"Like I said, I didn't tell you the whole story," Milan started.

"I just wanted to see if you were really my friends," he said quietly. Then he took the turban off.

"What?" Michelle asked. She spoke for the whole bewildered group of us.

"You didn't join some religious group?" Keri asked. Her eyes flashed, her face ablaze with heated disbelief.

Milan turned to meet Keri's incredulous glare with an equally confrontational scowl. "I thought you said you didn't want to be friends," he stated in an icy, low voice.

"I never said that," Keri replied.

But Milan didn't seem to hear. Keri remained quiet. I could tell she was evaluating the most judicious response. It wouldn't be effective to call Milan on his tremendous lie. In his worldview, lying was not a sin.

Likewise, she couldn't address the fact that he'd manipulated us. He saw it as an ends to a mean—a necessary tool to assess loyalty. It was a trap designed to serve his purpose. He needed distance. Now he had it. First from Stephanie. Now from Keri. She'd failed his Turban Friend Test. A tiny wedge now existed between them.

I wondered if Milan weren't also using his little charade to test the depth of our character and the substance of our faith. Were our beliefs based on rigid religious doctrine and self-righteous rules of exclusion that would cause us to spurn a friend if his beliefs conflicted with ours? Would we cast him out if he worshipped a god other than ours? Or would we embrace him with the same warmth we always had, regardless of what he believed? Ultimately, would we extend to him the same grace our God extended to us?

The next evening, Stephanie sat in our living room with her guitar. Keri retold the events of the afternoon before. What could we do about Milan? Finally, Michelle summed it up best.

V Society, April 18

Junior Year

QUOTE OF THE DAY

Michelle: "Milan—can't live with him, can't shoot him."

In the end, we decided to forgive him and let the matter go. What else could we do—besides write a song? Penning lyrics was always cathartic. It made us laugh our heads off, and that always made me feel better.

V SOCIETY, APRIL 21
Junior Year

"WE STILL LOVE HIM" TO THE TUNE OF "I USED TO LOVE HER" BY GUNS N' ROSES

Chorus

We used to love him
But we want to kill him.
We still love him
But we want to kill him.

Verse 1: Michelle

We gave so much
He won't be touched
He won't let us know his pain.

Verse 2: Stephanie

He's so moody
Want to kick him in the booty
But I guess he's okay anyway

Verse 3: Keri

Young women beware
Of his love lair
The Trojan horse is at the gate.

Verse 4: Stephanie

Will he care
If I'm shaped like a pear?
I hope I don't gain that much
weight.

Verse 5: Adele

You're far from home
But you're not alone
Even though you may feel that way.

Verse 6: All

We're disenchanted
'Cause he took us for granted
He should show us how much
he cares.

Optional Verse 7: All

Think he uses Nair
That old Serbian bear
Body hair is personal anyway.

Optional Verse 8: All
He doesn't like hugs
And he does lots of drugs
Losing love and brain cells are
his way.

Optional Verse 9: All
What's in the closet over there?
Don't you wash your underwear?
You can't join the panty parade!

During the third week of April, Spring Fling arrived—a university-sponsored outdoor funfest ripe with entertainment and food. Many black students preferred to skip Spring Fling, in favor of the Penn Relays, a huge track and field event; but I could think of nothing worse than spending an afternoon at a sporting event. I liked Spring Fling—simply another excuse to procrastinate from studying in exchange for a couple lazy days goofing off with my friends. When it rolled around, the entire V Society assembled together to eat at the outdoor stands and leisurely enjoy whatever free entertainment Penn placed at our disposal.

Soon after Spring Fling ended, Hey Day breezed in. My twentieth birthday arrived on Hey Day, the school-wide celebration where juniors officially became seniors. On the last day of classes, in a long-standing Penn tradition, the entire junior class—nearly two thousand of us, donned scarlet-red, university-issued class T-shirts, bamboo canes, and fake straw hats made of Styrofoam. Keri, Mandy, Allison, and I—all of us except Michelle and Stephanie—dutifully put on our matching T-shirts and hats and carried our canes to the meeting place. Michelle and Stephanie, the little rebels, joined us but insisted on wearing their own clothes. The six of us congregated in the lower courtyard of the Quad, a tremendous, venerable brick dormitory spanning the length of an entire block. It ranked as the most popular dorm for freshman. The Quad appeared to be one sprawling, majestic building with several internal grassy courtyards. But it actually encompassed thirty-eight interlocking houses, the first of which had been built in the 1890s.

The six of us, along with the most raucous assemblage of our class that I could remember, swarmed inside the far-reaching courtyard of the Quad's walled perimeter. Our classmates gathered on the lower quad, the connecting steps, and the broad Junior Balcony above. I saw hall mates from freshman year that I hadn't seen since we had all lived in the Quad as first-year students. One of my freshman-year pals, who could barely stand up on her own, accosted me. Apparently, the campus-wide binge drinking that usually began in the evenings started early on Hey Day.

"Hey, how are you?" I grinned as we embraced. I hesitated to let go of her arm, afraid she'd fall flat on her face. She steadied herself. Her eyes rolled around, unable to focus on me.

"Haw-rrrr-ya-ahdel?" she slurred in a friendly greeting. Thankfully, another friend came alongside her and acted as a temporary support.

A bacchanalian spirit encompassed the whole celebratory affair. I considered it a blessing that no one puked on my shoes before the class march began. At the designated time, our entire class marched, waddled, or staggered from the Quad, down Locust Walk to College Hall at the center of campus. There we jubilantly obeyed the tradition and raised our canes high above our heads, noisily tapping them against one another in a boisterous cacophony. Then as the tradition decreed, we grabbed each other's hats and took large bites out of them. You hadn't fully celebrated Hey Day until your Styrofoam hat resembled Swiss cheese, full of irregular, gaping holes. Hey Day escalated to its peak when the university president emerged from the front door of College Hall, where his office resided. He welcomed the incoming senior class with a short speech. We greeted him like a band of hooligans with whooping hoots, whistles, and howls. As the rambunctious crowd of newly minted seniors dissipated, the group of us migrated back to Superblock. I felt lighthearted and expectant—senior year lay just a couple months away. I couldn't believe I only had one year left.

Since it was my birthday, Hey Day marked the beginning rather than the end of our celebration. My mother had mailed me a small, dense chocolate cake that waited to be devoured back at the apartment. Unknown to me, Michelle and Keri had prepared their own birthday surprise. I'd made the mistake of telling them about a birthday tradition my friends and I had kept in high school. On our friends' birthdays, our high school gang showed up at the birthday person's house in the wee hours of the morning and kidnapped her. We dressed the birthday person in ridiculous clothes and then ferried her off, blindfolded, for display in public places. Of course, we planned and executed all this in collusion with the birthday person's parents. Our friend's parents let us in the house, allowed us to sneak into her room, and force our victim into absurd attire. We high school kidnappers outfitted ourselves as make-believe suburban mobsters, wearing black-and-white clothing and funny nametags labeled with "Biff" and other aliases.

The Saturday morning before my sixteenth birthday, five of my high school friends rushed into my room and ordered me to wear a ludicrous concoction reflecting the fashion sense of a pattern-blind bag lady— a floral, pink, ruffled kitchen apron; black spandex workout pants; giant brown bear-claw slippers; a large red king's crown; a sweatshirt; assorted mismatched striped and polka-dot scarves; and a rainbow umbrella they instructed me to carry everywhere. Then they blindfolded me and drove me to a huge mall in a nearby town where my crush of the moment worked after school and on weekends. He was one of our classmates, and perhaps in collaboration with the kidnappers—I can't be sure. They led me blindfolded across smooth floors through some unidentifiable location. When they finally removed the blindfold , there *he* (my crush) stood behind the counter of a mall store, smiling. The kidnapping excursion always ended with breakfast at IHOP or some other local breakfast spot.

Keri and Michelle seem to have remembered only the dress-me-up-and-humiliate-me part of the story. They forgot to arrange a meeting with my crush of the moment and treat me to breakfast. After the morning's Hey Day festivities died down, we arrived at the apartment, and they commanded me to dress in a heinous mismatched outfit—a red and black ski mask; turquoise and black polka-dot leggings on top of swirly-patterned blue leggings; saggy, mismatched ski socks; dorky white athletic sneakers; cut-off, pink, checkered pajama pants; a bright-orange bowling shirt; Mardi Gras beads; and a green army jacket, all topped off with a giant straw sombrero. Then they forced me into the elevator and onto Superblock for pictures with my fellow society members. Thank goodness I had that ski mask on—no one could identify me.

"Come on, let's go walk around," Keri urged.

"Are you kidding? I'm not going anywhere dressed like this! What if someone recognizes me?" I moaned.

"You look so cute. Who cares if anyone recognizes you," Michelle goaded.

"I look like a bank robber that ran away from the circus. Can I go back inside now . . . please?" I begged.

"Oh, come on," Mandy piped in. "You look great."

"The sombrero and ski mask are a nice combo. Those colors are really working for you," Stephanie joked.

"My favorite is those sexy shoes," Michelle continued.

"You guys are so mean," I groaned.

"Let me get more pictures of you, Delie," Keri chuckled.

They outnumbered me. I stood obediently for more pictures while students passing by stared, amused at the nutcase in the middle of Superblock.

"Now, can I go back and change?" I pleaded.

"Yes, cutie," Keri agreed.

Finally, they released me. I changed back into normal clothes and borrowed a cute jacket from Stephanie. I snatched up my camera and Mich, Keri, Stephanie, and I hit the town, roaming West Philly for food and mischievous photo ops for ourselves. We took pictures of each other posed in alleys and doorways contorted into abstract sculptures.

We stayed up late celebrating the arrival of my twentieth year. My head didn't hit the pillow until early the next morning.

Throughout all of April, I saw Sexy more frequently. Finally, he appeared while Michelle and I sat on College Green, catching a bit of sun and soaking in warmth, for the first time in months. He walked past us among the throngs of students filing down the Walk through the center of campus.

"There he is!" I exclaimed in a loud whisper to Michelle.

"Who?"

"Sexy!"

"Where?"

"Right there . . . with the dark sideburns and the newsboy cap."

"Oh, I see him," she answered evenly. Michelle was never much for words, so I didn't press her with more exclamations. (*Isn't he fascinating? Don't you love the way he walks?*)

Twenty minutes later, Keri and Stephanie joined us on College Green.

"You just missed Sexy," I informed them.

"Really?" Keri replied, looking genuinely disappointed.

"More like Greasy," Michelle replied in that endearing fashion of hers that made even criticisms sound nonjudgmental.

"Greasy?" I asked.

"I don't think he washes his hair every day," she observed. She was probably right. The Seattle rock band Pearl Jam had catapulted its signature grunge style into American youth culture. At the time, style dictated that fashion-conscious men cut back on daily hair washings as part of the grunge-inspired runway look. They aimed to look stylishly disheveled and androgynous.

"Stephanie has a Greasy too," Keri chimed in.

"I rode in the elevator with him yesterday," Stephanie declared excitedly.

"Who is he?" I asked.

"I don't know," she replied. "But I think his name is Ken."

"Nice. Now we've got Greasy I—Adele's greasy, and Greasy II—Stephanie's greasy," Michelle announced.

"I just want to have coffee with my Greasy," I sighed.

V Society, Spring
Junior Year

RUMORS OF THE DAY

Adele got a new prescription for her glasses and now knows that Sexy (a.k.a. Greasy) is ugly.

Chapter Nine

WORLDLY EDUCATION

{December, Winter of Junior Year}

ALL THE EXCITEMENT OF JUNIOR YEAR CULMINATED IN THE spring, but that winter, before the fun of second semester's warmer days, I reflected on the past several months, recalling a number of memorable events that had occurred earlier in the year. Over winter break, after we finished the fall semester, Keri came to visit me in California, her first visit to my house in the San Francisco Bay Area.

As soon as Keri arrived, we stopped by my friend Nick Wilson's house, or rather, his parents' house. They lived in an attractive old neighborhood a few miles from Cal's campus. Instead of going away to college, Nick had stayed local and attended Cal. As one of my closest friends from high school I usually called him first whenever I came back into town.

Nick was a zealous liberal, prone to long-winded speeches on the merits of left-wing politics. Once he got started on political topics, no one could stop him. I'd learned to look instantly glassy-eyed and bored as soon as he mentioned public policy. That usually reminded him to talk about something else—*anything* besides political science, his academic major. Few things interested me less than long, drawn-out discussions about politicians.

Keri and I guzzled down fruit smoothies Nick made for us in his kitchen. Then we moved into his living room. Keri and Nick hit it off immediately. When he wasn't debating politics, his comedic side came out. He loved to crack slapstick jokes. Like us, he was always up for taking goofy pictures.

"Where's your camera?" Nick asked. He knew I rarely went anywhere without my camera.

"On the entry table near your front door," I replied. He disappeared around the corner and reappeared with the camera. He handed it to Keri.

"Keri, take a picture of this," he beamed. "Adele, let's see what you'd look like with my hair." During the past months, Nick had grown his short dark hair out to a neat shoulder length with clean, trimmed sideburns.

"I'll look like you," I quipped, knowing good and well that we'd never look alike. Nick had keen features and a trim athletic build from years of running on the cross-country team.

"Come sit in this chair," he said motioning to a formal, sky-colored armchair. Nick's parents' living room embodied elegance with its dark wood floors, enormous Oriental rug, and stately, antique-style European furnishings. The entire house emanated order and tradition, but it begged for disruption, and Nick knew it. Once, when his parents went out of town, Nick had bought crazy colored paints and reimagined his entire bedroom with funky patterns and clashing colors. Needless to say, Nick's mother had not been excited when she returned from vacation and discovered his newly repainted room.

Nick's living room was the perfect setting for a stodgy family portrait. Naturally, it inspired Nick to create his own series of slightly demented family portraits. I sat down in the chair as Nick instructed. Then he came behind the chair and leaned toward me so his hair flipped over the top of my head. Keri started cracking up as she fired off a shot. In the picture you couldn't see Nick at all, only me, sitting in the perfect setting for a formal portrait, except that I had long brown hair streaming all over my head.

"He's so funny," Keri giggled.

Then Nick and Keri took a turn. They sat in opposite, matching straight-back armchairs. Nick folded his hands properly in his lap and sat up straight in the chair, looking intensely serious. Keri crossed her legs and folded her hands properly, mimicking Nick. But then she leaned over to one side of the chair, rolled her eyes back in her head, and contorted her face into a look of sheer insanity, with a lopsided, lunatic grin. I took the shot and tried not to shake the camera as I laughed.

Keri and Nick reversed roles. She sat erect and proper in her seat, looking demure with her hands folded and legs crossed. Nick pulled all his hair over his face like Cousin Itt from *The Addams Family*. I snapped another photo. They were perfect for my junior-year photo album.

When we finally left Nick's house, Keri burst with giddiness.

"He's so cute," Keri grinned. "Do you know what he said to me when you went to the bathroom? He said, 'It's a good thing we're sitting here in the living room. I can think of a lot of other things we could be doing.'"

"Do you know what else he said?" Keri continued. "I told him I only dated Jewish guys, and he said 'My dad is Jewish.'"

Unbelievable—Nick had played the Jewish card! It was true: Nick's dad was Jewish—but he was a religiously nonobservant Jewish atheist. Nick had been raised Catholic, the faith of his mother. All the years I'd known Nick, he'd always referred to himself as just a white boy but never a Jewish boy.

Nick was like a cousin, and Keri was like a sister. But he was an incurable flirt. So, why was I surprised he had flirted with family? The thought that they might be attracted to each other never crossed my mind.

Even my parents considered Nick family. Christmas Day at the Moore household was never complete until Nick arrived. He spent the morning with his parents and the afternoon at our house. Every year my mom offered him the same thing—fruitcake. Every year, he replied the same way: "Do people really *eat* fruitcake?"

Every Christmas my mom said, "Oh, this is a special fruitcake. I order it from a wonderful bakery in Texas."

Nick's follow-up answer varied slightly each Christmas, but the end result was always the same: "Okay, Mrs. Moore, I'll have a piece of fruitcake, since you special-ordered it from Texas." Every Christmas, he looked forward to my mom's offer of the dreaded fruitcake. One year she forgot, and he asked, "Mrs. Moore, where's that fruitcake thingy that you usually have every holiday?"

Nick and I had been friends since I was sixteen. We met at a student council convention for the Catholic high schools in our region. Both of us were in student government at our respective high schools. I wasn't Catholic, but I went to a coed Catholic high school. Nick went to an all-boys Catholic high school. I think the absence of girls in the student body scarred him for life. He openly hit on every attractive woman that would talk to him. The only exceptions were a handful of longtime designated female friends, like me. We'd always been great friends, drawn together by a mutual love for nonconformity. But Nick was always on the lookout for more than "just friends."

I owed much of my worldly education about men to Nick. Since the beginning of our friendship, he'd patiently outlined the rules of the Playa's Game to me.

"I have two kinds of female friends," he explained to me when we were freshman in college. "I have friends like you . . . that are great, of course . . . I mean you're one of my favorite people . . . don't get me wrong. . . but I don't get any *benefits* from you."

"Benefits? What do you mean?" I asked naïvely.

"Well, I have 'friends' and I have 'friends with *benefits*,'" he explained. "I might give one of my friends with benefits a foot rub or a back massage, for example, and then she gives me *benefits*—if you know what I mean." He raised an eyebrow and smiled.

I started to get the picture, but I wanted to be sure we were on the same page. "So, what kind of benefits exactly?" I inquired hesitantly.

"Well, I get to stay over at her place for the night," he continued. "And she might give me . . ."

"Okay, okay, okay, I get it," I replied, quickly cutting him off. I didn't need a play-by-play. Vague clarification would suffice.

I first learned about the inner workings of hookups from Nick too. I don't remember exactly what we'd been doing that day, but we were hanging out in Berkeley, right off Cal's campus. I'd returned home for a school break. Nick and I had probably seen a movie or gone record shopping as we often did. But I remember that we were both famished and he took me to one of his favorite sandwich shops—a place on Telegraph Avenue.

Telegraph Avenue was the main retail artery for Cal, characterized by funky boutiques, eclectic eateries, and hordes of loitering oddballs—punks with brightly colored mohawks; white kids with dreadlocks, channeling their inner Bob Marley; neo-hippie teen junkies, and self-appointed prophets of recently fabricated schools of knowledge, touting their philosophies on tie-dyed T-shirts, homemade banners, and occasionally on a sandwich board heralding, "THE WORLD IS ENDING SOON!" Artisan philosophers lined the street selling jewelry and crafts and dispensing ideology for free.

I always looked for Hate Man. In high school, my friend Heather had affectionately nicknamed him Sparky the Transvestite Bum; at the time, we didn't know that Cal students all referred to the homeless guy as Hate Man. Hate Man was a famous Berzerkeley fixture. He often wore a raggedy dress along with improvised, long evening gloves (the kind you'd wear to a formal ball, but with no fingers and usually in a printed pattern) and a tight tank top—hot pink was his best color. You couldn't miss him, with his long, shaggy gray beard and assortment of discarded women's clothing. As long as he stayed across the street from me, I found him amusing as he spewed rhetoric from the sidewalk near Sproul Plaza on Berkeley's campus. "I HATE YOU!" he yelled regularly at strangers.

Nick told me that he wouldn't begin a conversation with anyone, unless you began with, "I hate you." If you didn't say those magic words, he wouldn't acknowledge you. According to Hate Man's philosophy, called oppositionality, all humans should be honest about the negative feelings they held toward each other. I never ventured close to the hate philosopher, though. A friend told me that he hated most people equally, but he especially hated Christians. I'm not even sure that was true, but my overactive imagination pictured Hate Man coming after me one day. I envisioned myself fleeing down Telegraph Avenue as he chased me in high heels, his boa and long gray hair blowing in the wind, yelling, "Die, Christian die! I HATE YOU!" Supposedly, he wasn't violent, but the angry curses he often hurled made me wonder.

Aside from his ill-tempered ranting, I liked seeing Hate Man as long as he remained at a safe distance. The peculiar characters that defined Telegraph made it one of my favorite Bay Area hangouts in high school and all through college. I never came home for break without grabbing a meal or going shopping on that colorful street.

But on that particular day, Nick and I had popped into a place on Telegraph famous for its fresh-baked bread, enormous salads, and homemade salad dressing. Students willingly stood in line for fifteen minutes just to order a turkey club. As we stood in the long line talking, Nick began to include the woman standing behind us in our conversation. He was often friendly to strangers, so I didn't think anything of it. After we ordered our sandwiches and sat down, the woman sat down at the table right next to us. Nick and I introduced ourselves.

"I'm Jasmine," she said.

The three of us chatted about how much we liked shopping at Rasputin's Records and some other unmemorable subjects. She seemed a little uptight—very proper and reserved—with tidy, medium-length light-brown hair and a frilly, conservative dress. She looked at least four or five years older than we were. In any case, I finished my lunch and took off for a dentist's appointment. I left Nick at the café, talking away with the prissy woman.

Several days later, Nick and I met up again. As we talked, he casually said, "When Jasmine left yesterday morning, I went for a short run."

Naturally, I was confused. We didn't have any mutual friends named Jasmine. "Who's Jasmine?" I asked.

"You know, the woman we met at lunch the other day," he smiled.

"Left? What do you mean? She stayed with you?"

"Uh-huh," he grinned. "She's been staying with me the past two days. My parents are out of town, you know." He smiled like the cat that ate the canary.

It turned out Jasmine wasn't so prissy after all. Nick never mentioned her again. He'd moved on to other women at other cafés, bars, clubs, political rallies, wherever. That was my first lesson in Hookup 101. Thanks to Nick, I wasn't completely clueless.

Many years later, long after Nick finished grad school, we reminisced about some of our adventures in college.

"Do you remember that girl you picked up in the café when we were freshman? She stayed with you for two days?" I asked.

Nick shrugged and laughed lightheartedly. "Who? Like I'd really remember someone from that long ago?" He didn't remember anything about her—not her face, her name, not a single thing. If she walked up to him on the street the next day and said, "Hi, Nick," there was a good chance he'd have no idea who she was.

But I remembered her; I even remembered her name. "Jasmine. Her name was Jasmine," I pressed. I remembered because it was an uncommon name, and recently I'd just met another woman with the same name.

"Jasmine?" He paused. "Oh yeah . . . from LA . . . I remember now," he said, grinning. "She was a few years older. Yeah, she came back for more . . . the next time she was in town."

At least now she was more than a forgotten conquest. Now she was a woman that had paid him a return visit—a detail worth recalling simply because it fueled his ego.

Shortly after Keri returned to the East Coast after visiting my family for Christmas junior year, I headed out to Atlanta to spend the remainder of winter break at the Impact conference. Impact '91 was the first large-scale student conference of its kind. Five hundred African American college students from all over the country assembled for several days of teaching, worship, fellowship, and a huge New Year's Eve party. The conference organizers brought in outstanding African American speakers and pastors from across the nation. Of all the talks I heard at the conference, one in particular stood out—the sex sermon. Hallelujah! Finally a pastor had the guts to break down Song of Solomon, the Bible's tribute to sensual pleasure in vivid, 3-D IMAX detail. Even the most unimaginative listener left with a lucid picture of God's vision for a mind-blowing experience.

It was the most memorable talk I'd ever heard. In all the years I'd been in church, no one—not a single pastor—had ever dared to broach that subject. This pastor had no such fear. I was forever grateful. During the talk, I sat in my seat, squirming and blushing alongside a host of other conference attendees with equally limited sensual vocabularies. When he finished, half the room was on the verge of cardiac arrest.

"He should give that talk to married people. Only married people!" the campus minister sitting next to me huffed. She fumed.

The speaker had given a descriptive talk on the joys of great married sex. Among the many details he revealed, he talked about his wife and how her scent intoxicated him when he held her. I'd never heard the terms "great" and "married sex" used in conjunction before. Those weren't his exact words, but that's what he implied. These were unchartered waters. God wanted people to have great sex! Why was that such a secret? Why didn't pastors preach that all the time? You could fill thousands of empty pews with that kind of message. College students hungered to hear this kind of authentic straight talk. We didn't live in a G-rated world. I rejoiced that we'd been spared from a watered-down,

G-rated *just wait* talk. I left the conference liberated. Finally, I had a goal to embrace enthusiastically at the end of my lifetime of abstinence.

In January, I returned to school after winter break with the memories of Keri's visit and Impact '91 fresh in my mind. Spring semester had barely begun when some chilling news came to my roommates and me via one of our friends from Bible study. The next day sketchy details of a harrowing event appeared in the student paper the *Daily Pennsylvanian*, "FEMALE STUDENTS ASSAULTED OFF CAMPUS."

Our friend Clare and her roommate Rhonda were in the headlines. I hadn't hung out with Clare often, but my sophomore year we'd orchestrated a magnificent prank together, along with Mandy, the often-absent V Society member. In the early hours of the morning, the three of us had armed ourselves with a wagonload of newspapers and tape. We built a newspaper wall that completely covered the doorway of our friend Brad's dorm door. Before we sealed off the top of the door, we stuffed the space between the indented door and the paper barricade with tons of crumpled newspapers. It was a birthday surprise. When Brad awoke in the morning and opened the door to go to class, a barrage of crumpled newspapers showered him, and an impenetrable newspaper wall blocked his exit. He couldn't go to class that morning without busting a Jackie Chan move and karate chopping or kicking his way through the newspaper.

The night before the paper reported the assaults, our friends Clare and Rhonda opened the front door of their apartment, several blocks off campus. Clare later told me in her own words exactly what happened next: "I felt like something was off . . . a little strange . . . but I put the thought out of my head. I thought I saw a weird shadow, but then I told myself, 'It's nothing.'" Seconds later Clare found herself face-to-face with an intruder—a strange man inside her apartment.

I didn't know how to comfort her or what to do. None of us did. I couldn't think of a single thing I could do to lift her from the depths of her sorrow, her anguish, or her nightmares. All the things I'd normally do to comfort a friend—visit, send a card or flowers, call her up and joke around until the laughter made her sides ache—seemed wrong and intrusive. If I called her, what would I say? We were friends, but not close friends. We saw each other in our weekly fellowship meetings, but we didn't hang out regularly. Would she want to hear from me? What could I possibly offer to ease the depths of her devastation? Every word I could think of was inappropriate, empty, and meaningless. I couldn't think of a single thing I could do to reach out to her. I felt powerless, and useless as a friend. Immediately after the incident, Clare withdrew from school to recover and heal. I didn't hear from her again for months.

Earlier in the semester, Clare had begun dating my friend Justin. Justin and I had been friends since freshman year. He was one of my closest guy friends in the Christian student group that Michelle, Mandy, and I attended. He was also my fraternity brother since I had pledged his coed fraternity sophomore year. I felt even worse about my inability to comfort Justin. Everything I could think to say sounded trite. Nothing could make up for what had happened to his girlfriend. I'm sure he wanted to kill the guy—literally tear him to shreds with his bare hands. What could I say to comfort that? Were his waking hours haunted by regret and rage? He probably wished he'd been with Clare when she had opened her front door that night so he could punch the intruder's face in. If I mentioned Clare, would it make him feel worse? Should I tell him I was praying for him? I didn't know, so I said nothing.

I bought a book to comfort myself. I hoped it would explain "why bad things happen to good people." It was the best I could do to reconcile the irreconcilable. But I couldn't settle it. I couldn't wrap my arms around Clare's fate. It wasn't right. The seriousness, the gravity. The injustice. Why her? Why anybody? But especially, why Clare, dear Clare?

Keri, Michelle, and I didn't know what to say among ourselves. It was the first and only time we didn't discuss a subject exhaustively. How could we address what had happened to Clare? Why hadn't it been me or any of the V Society members? What if it had been one of us? What would we do? It changed me. It changed us. I thought about Clare, but I was afraid to dwell on her fate. After a few weeks, I put it all out of my mind. That was the best I could do to cope. We received periodic updates on her status from our friends from Bible study.

I prayed for her and thought of her. I waited for her to return. It was all I knew how to do. In the end, Clare comforted me. After long weeks of mourning and recuperation, she returned to school and graduated. I saw her at a party several months later. I hugged her. I marveled at how boldly she referred to her attacker by name. She told me how she had learned about him and his background. She knew what had led him to the place in his life where he broke into her apartment and stole something deeply sacred from her. She talked about seeing him repeatedly in the trial.

"I looked him in the face," she said. "Shadows still freak me out. That's how I knew someone was in the apartment—I saw his shadow first. But I'm okay."

She spoke without hatred or bitterness. I wondered and stood in awe of her courage and honesty in referring to what had happened. I never would have brought it up—ever. She was still dealing with it. She'd never forget. Yet she was moving on and moving forward with her life. She seemed mobilized—propelled by a supernatural determination as she pushed, struggled, and fought for her healing and restoration. I listened to her with the deepest, quietest respect and awe. She amazed me.

Chapter Ten

───────────── ∽ ─────────────

THE BEST YEAR EVER

{May, Second Semester of Junior Year}

So much had happened that semester—the Elevator Society, Milan, making my first film, and, finally, random Sexy spottings. I found it hard to focus on final exams. Thankfully, Keri and Michelle were extremely studious. Their diligence helped me stay focused. I found most of my assigned communications reading dull. Unlike Keri, I never went searching for additional books in my major to read. I read some of the interesting assignments—everything on movies, filmmaking, and art—but usually waited until the last minute to read everything else.

With the last official day of classes behind us, Reading Week arrived—the designated time for around-the-clock cram sessions before exams began. I sat in my room, memorizing lecture notes, theories, and dates for hours at a time. I infused my study regime with varying decibels of energizing alternative music. It helped me stay awake as I memorized boring academic theories.

Keri, Michelle, Stephanie, and I managed to weasel out some fun during Reading Week by studying together. Milan joined the gang of us in our late-night study sessions upstairs in the sprawling, smoke-filled Hall of Flags balcony. The hall brimmed over with packs of students wired on free coffee served up by the university. Everyone camped out in the hall received free tokens good for coffee refills.

Our group study sessions were rarely productive. One of us would spot a friend studying nearby, and we'd get up to go talk to him. Then someone would get hungry, and we'd go searching for snacks. All five of us could never stay quiet and seated at the same time. Someone would start whispering, which would be followed by laughing, and then everyone else would want to know what was so funny. Everyone except Milan, that is.

"Do you mind?" he growled one night as he shot a dirty look at Stephanie and Keri, chatting in low voices and laughing on their side of the table. "*Some* people here are trying to study," he snapped.

When Milan looked back down at his study notes, Stephanie stuck out her tongue. A wave of muffled snickers erupted around the table. Milan grew more annoyed. Usually, he'd abandon the four of us sporadically, for fifteen-minute intervals, while he smoked and chatted with friends in the vicinity. But he always returned—grumpy, but still unwilling to trade us for better-behaved study partners.

V SOCIETY, MAY 5
Junior Year

LOVE POEMS TO KERI

Composed in the smoky love nest of the Hall of Flags during the all-the-bitter-poop-water-cofee-you-can-drink-free-tokens-at-11:30pm-growling-Milan night of finals.

BY STEPHANIE SCHWARTZBAUM

Soft of butt
Loud of laugh
Bright of eye
Keri carelessly klonks
with folklore cries
Down Locust Walk
Collecting spare change
For the Feeble-Minded Institute of Technology.

BY ADELE MOORE (REVISED VERSION)

So I was thinking
and I fell asleep
it is
and we are
what
inside myself
I crawl up in a knot
dreaming of Skeri Keri
sixty million wonderments
this class
this class
I fall asleep
slumber rises
in and out
of me
my head nods
and I fall
back to sleep.

With our schedules consumed by finals, Milan, Stephanie, and I hadn't completed our film.

"Hey, when are we going to edit the film?" Milan asked me as we packed up to leave the Hall of Flags.

"I don't know. That's going to take hours. I don't have time with exams and everything."

"I don't have time either," he replied.

"Stephanie mentioned that she could hire a professional editor to do it for us," I remembered. "She said she'd pay him. We just have to tell him what we want."

"That would be much faster," Milan admitted.

"Should we do that?" I asked.

"Sure, otherwise I don't see how we'll finish it before the summer."

"I'll find out when she's planning to schedule the editing session, then you and I can meet with the editor to do our sections."

"Yep, that's fine," Milan answered.

Stephanie took the reins and secured the editor. Several days later, I met her in the editing suite. She'd completed three-quarters of the film and saved the last bit for me to edit.

"This is Chris," she said introducing me to the editor. He worked for a video production team on campus. "I'm finished with my part, so I'll leave you here, and you can tell him what you want. Oh, but wait! Before I leave, let me show you what I've done so far."

"Great," I agreed. I was dying to see the culmination of our cinematic endeavor.

Chris queued up the completed section of the film and played it for me. As I watched the short film, I grew increasingly exasperated. Stephanie had used only about five seconds of the footage Milan and I had shot. It was interesting imagery—vibrant colorful shots with a witty, surreal feel. But it was all Stephanie's footage, with the exception of a few scenes we'd shot together. A big chunk of the footage had been filmed at Dartmouth while she was on spring break in Hanover, New Hampshire. It didn't take place anywhere near Penn. But the video was supposed to be a promotional short for *Penn* Film and Video, not Dartmouth Film and Video. On top of that, most of the soundtrack was country-western music—Johnny Cash. Aside from the Vivaldi *Four Seasons* clip, paired up with establishing shots of Penn's campus at the very beginning of the film, there wasn't a single note from the types of music Milan and I preferred.

To seal the deal on the botched mess, I opened the film with the worst delivery of a one-liner in human film history. The film began with my co-star (some golden-voiced pretty boy that Stephanie knew) walking through campus and then into my apartment. He grabs a drink out of my refrigerator, sits down, and enthusiastically says, "Adele, I just came from a Penn Film and Video meeting. I have so many ideas running through my head right now." I reply, "Let me see," and then rise and look into his ear—the secret passage leading to the brilliant film concepts whirling around inside his brain. My line sets the stage for the forthcoming montage of random images that spill out in a four-part dream sequence. It should have been an easy line to deliver. Unfortunately, I was the worst actress in the universe. I could have won the anti-Oscar for the most dreadful screen debut—ever.

C'est la vie. I could do nothing to salvage our creation. Most of the film was finished already. Stephanie had already edited three of the four dream sequences. She left the fourth and final one for me to complete. Milan was busy with exams and couldn't help me. Stephanie had already paid the editor. I had to finish the job. I dug through the footage Milan and I had filmed. I picked my favorite clips and asked the editor to lay down an ethereal-sounding electronic song as the soundtrack. Our film monstrosity was complete.

I didn't have a chance to show Milan the completed film until after we all returned in August after the summer. His sentiments closely echoed mine.

"I don't want my name associated with that film," he stated resolutely. "It's nothing like what I had in mind."

But he was too late. The film was a done deal.

Finals ended with the mad dash to pack up all our belongings. All students had to move out of the dorms for the summer. Shortly after completing my last exam, I hastily threw everything in my room into a dozen gigantic cardboard boxes.

"What are you doing this summer?" Stephanie asked.

"Going home. I have an internship at the Clorox Company head-quarters."

"That's cool. What are you doing for them?"

"I'm supposed to be in the corporate communications department, assisting the director of corporate communications. How about you? What are you doing?"

"I'm going to LA. I have an internship with one of the big film studios," she replied.

"No way! That sounds so fun. I'd love to intern with a fashion photographer in LA."

"You can come stay with me for the summer if you want," Stephanie offered.

"Thanks, but this is my fourth summer at Clorox. They're expecting me."

With that, I hugged Stephanie good-bye and wished her the best over the long break.

Milan stopped by and we exchanged addresses for the summer.

"You can reach me here," he said. He handed me a paper with his address scribbled on it.

"I'll write," I promised, as we parted.

Michelle planned to spend the summer in San Diego on a summer mission's project. Keri intended to take the summer off for some rest, relaxation, and vacation time with her parents.

My three roommates and I hauled all of our things out of the apartment and turned in our keys to the university housing department. Keri, Michelle, and I would move back into the same apartment in the fall. Allison had decided to room with some of her fellow nursing students the next year. I couldn't blame her. Michelle, Keri, Stephanie, and I were always yelling and causing a ruckus while she tried to sleep. We always forgot that she went to bed at a decent hour while we often stayed up much too late. My friend Amy, who was studying abroad in England, would replace Allison as our fourth roommate in the fall.

Before we left, Keri typed and distributed all of our remaining V Society notes, including our horrible attempts at poetry writing and all our peculiar musings. I compiled the list of our favorite things from junior year.

THE V SOCIETY NOTES
Junior Year
The following notes are the confidential property of the V Society registered members of the Virgin Association of America

V SOCIETY, MARCH 24
Junior Year

ANNOUNCEMENT V-FEST

V-Fest is a springtime commemoration of the untimely sacrificial death of Jephtah's virgin daughter. For approximately four days, members of the V Society (a not-for-profligate organization) mourn for our unlucky dead predecessor and celebrate the fact that we are live virgins. Often this celebration occurs during dead week or finals, but it has been suggested that this year's V-Fest be extended for several months possibly, and celebrated in Europe. (Judges 11:39–40)

Addendum: *Some commentaries indicate that Jephtah's daughter was not killed but committed to lifelong celibacy or solitary confinement. Ouch! Either way, we should still plan a European vacation.*

V Society, April 5
Junior Year

QUOTES OF THE DAY

Adele's resignation regarding sex and men: "She who dies with the most friends wins!" Upon deciding that the above game plan is still too messy and painful, she proclaims, "She wins who dies alone!"

V Society, May
Junior Year

NOTE FROM THE SECRET-KERI OF THE VIRGIN SOCIETY

Believe it or not, this is all I have that we've captured in writing.

If you are withholding any valuable information, documents, or drawings, please mail them to me, and I will enter them into the minutes. Stephanie, we would all like copies of your stories, and Michelle, try to write down those dreams!

In the fall, we will hold another recording session to get all of Stephanie's songs on tape. Let's all try to make an effort to recruit Margaret then, as well. I am missing the results of the end of the year V Society vote for best everything. As for Stephanie's color drawings, please see me in September to make color copies.

Thank you and remember, girls: Legs crossed, nothing lost!

V Society, Best of the Best List (Uncensored)
Junior Year

OUR NICKNAMES

Keri: *Bookwoman, Mom, Butt, Z, Slik, Kerril Zelsor*
Michelle: *Mich, Girl Boy, Smelly Shelly, Sexy*
Stephanie: *Homegirl, Rachel Lebowitz*
Adele: *Delie, Delmo, Adelaide, Weinerschnitzel*
Milan: *Don Juan Milan, Our Lover, Smelly Old Milan*
Allison: *Ally, Al, Little Lee, Weinerschnitzel*

BEST SONGS

"Used to Love Him" by V Society
*"Behind Black Eyes" by Stephanie Schwartzbaum and the V Society
(another song about Milan)*
"Trying to Throw Your Arms Around the World" by U2
"One" by U2
"Every Hour Here" by The Innocence Mission

RUNNERS-UP

"Nothing Is Alone" by Toad the Wet Sprocket
"This Woman's Work" by Kate Bush
"I Need Love" by Luka Bloom
"Like a Revelation" by Scaterd Few
"Girl of an Age" by EMF
"I Will Not Take These Things for Granted" by Toad the Wet Sprocket
"Androgynous" by Crash Test Dummies
"I'm Too Sexy" by Right Said Fred
"Superman's Song" by Crash Test Dummies

"This Is the Healing" by LSU
"G.G.G." by LSU
"Desperado" by Johnny Cash{Stephanie}
Star Trek theme song {Stephanie}

BEST MUSIC GROUPS
U2
Toad the Wet Sprocket
LSU (Lifesavers Underground)
Cocteau Twins
Enya
Yaz and Alison Moyet
Stephanie Schwartzbaum

RUNNERS-UP
Kate Bush
EMF
Scaterd Few
Luka Bloom
Crash Test Dummies
Primal Scream {Adele}
Boris {Michelle}
Marc Zola {Keri}
Elvis {Stephanie}
Johnny Cash {Stephanie}

BEST BOOKS
The Bible
The Gift of Sex: A Guide to Sexual Fulfillment by Clifford & Joyce Penner
Woman in the Bible by Mary J. Evans

Jesse James Was His Name; or Fact and Fiction concerning the Careers of the Notorious James Brothers of Missouri {Stephanie}

WEIRD HABITS
Farting Out the Window

RUNNERS-UP
Sniffing and Biting Milan {Stephanie}

FAVORITE THINGS TO DO
Pray
Adele's Photo Sessions
Make Films
Contemplate Milan
Dance
Discuss Sex
Shave Body Hairs

RUNNERS-UP
Bite People

FADS (AILNESSES)
Unshaved Armpits
Faded Levi's

RUNNERS-UP
Butt Cysts
Tadpole Raising
Greasies
Pants Hanging Off Your Butt

WORST SMELLS
Our Refrigerator
Michelle's Feet
Keri's Poop

FAVORITE PHRASES
"Up Keri's butt."
"It's your mom."
Milan: "K-I-D-ding (kidding)"
"Feeling a little bit verklempt." {Stephanie}

RUNNERS-UP
"Did you sleep with her?" "No." {Milan}

BEST CLASSES
Feminist Jewish Women's Folklore Literature
(not a real class unfortunately) {Keri}

MOST INTRIGUING PEOPLE
Milan
Sexy (aka Greasy I) {Adele}
Ken (aka Greasy II) {Stephanie}
Doug {Michelle}
Alan (Penn Film and Video guy that Keri thinks is fascinating. He likes Adele's sweater, so we decided he lives under Adele's bed and plays with her sweater all day.)
Noah (aka Boy-Girl, the androgynous pretty boy)

RUNNERS-UP
Actor-Boy Goodman (co-star of Stephanie and Adele's film short)
Jim (Michelle's ex, artsy English major)

Lee (Allison's friend and Adele's super-male-model)

Mert (Mich's Turkish friend, pronounced Matt)

Ari (Hot Israeli guy that Keri admires)

The guy in Michelle's dream

Tomato Cheeks aka Mark (cute redheaded guy with bright red cheeks) {Stephanie}

Kurt Cobain {Stephanie}

Mike Myers {Stephanie}

Chad Lowe {Stephanie}

Elvis {Stephanie}

Willie Nelson {Stephanie}

Act Two

summer

Chapter Eleven

LOS ANGELES

{June, Summer before Senior Year}

As the plane descended, I could see the island jutting out into the San Francisco Bay: Alameda, California. I was home—transported to the land of soccer moms and Volvos full of children on their way to swimming lessons and day camp—for summertime in suburbia. My quiet hometown, outlined by gentle ocean tides, seemed sedate. My neighborhood reminded me of a rest home with everything calmly scheduled and uneventfully orchestrated. I didn't realize how much I thrived in the anarchy and commotion of college life. In Philadelphia, anticipation of the unpredictable kept me engaged. Here, the tranquility made me restless.

My room in my parents' house remained exactly as I had left it. I settled in, surrounded by all my old things. My posters and paintings from high school still hung on the walls. My desk drawer contained the same dried-out pens and college-ruled notebook paper. The white eyelet bedspread and black blinds I'd selected when I turned sixteen remained. In many ways, returning home, where nothing ever changed, comforted me. My world transformed with each passing semester. Yet home sat frozen in time, like a ruler by which to measure each new stage of growth.

I rejoiced to see Mom and Dad; I enjoyed spending summer with them. They were good housemates—low-key and fun to talk with. They enjoyed listening to me ramble on about whatever new thing I'd discovered or done. I also loved that they kept the refrigerator stocked and the laundry machine didn't require cash. For three months, I wouldn't have to lug a stash of quarters as ransom for clean clothes.

I slept in and took it easy my first day back home. The next day, I got up and mailed a letter to Milan. On my way home from Philadelphia, I'd stopped over for a few days in Texas to visit my grandmother. I'd written Milan a short letter while I hibernated indoors, avoiding the roasting Texas summer heat. I figured it would take the letter weeks, if not months, to arrive on the other side of the world. Hopefully, it would get to Belgrade before summer ended.

I returned from the post office determined to call Clorox and confirm my start date. The receptionist put me through to Susan Tull, the director of the intern program at headquarters. Susan had been my ally and guide since my first summer at Clorox. She ran a tight ship; her program was a well-oiled machine. She determined the interns' host departments and assigned us to our summer supervisors. Clorox's substantial summer intern program usually boasted thirty interns from across the country—mostly undergrads and a few MBAs. Susan packed our summers with all kinds of perks, like luncheons on the company (my favorite) and face time with executives whom we'd never meet if we actually worked for the company after graduation.

"Hi, Susan. This is Adele Moore. How are you?" I began.

"Hello, Adele. It's good to hear from you. How was your school year?"

"It went well. How are things at Clorox?"

"It's been busy of course, getting ready for the summer interns to come onboard."

"That's great. Is it a large group this summer?"

"About the same as last year," Susan replied.

"Well, I was calling to check on my start date. When should I come into the office?"

"My plan was to place you in corporate communications this summer with the director of corporate communications, but it doesn't look that that is an option anymore."

"It isn't? What happened?" I asked, flabbergasted.

"You won the corporate communications photo contest last fall, didn't you?"

"Yes . . ."

"Well, the director of corporate communication oversaw that contest. She said she asked you to send in some information about your winning photo." Susan paused so I could respond.

"Yes."

"Well, she never received anything from you. As a result, she doesn't feel that this internship is a good fit for you this summer."

What could I say? The director of corporate communications had told me I *could* send in information about the photo if I'd *like* to. That sounded to me like a suggestion, not a mandatory requirement. I didn't have anything to say about my wining photo; I hadn't even given it a title. In the midst of returning to Philadelphia the previous fall, moving into a new dorm, squaring away my classes, and buying all my course materials, I had quickly dismissed the *suggestion* requested from three thousand miles away—to my detriment. But the director had felt snubbed: now I didn't have a summer job.

This became my first lesson in corporate office politics. It made no difference that I'd received glowing performance reviews my past three summers. All three of those summers, I'd worked in different departments under different managers. This manager hadn't read my previous reviews and didn't care.

"So, unless you can think of a way to sway her decision . . . I don't have a spot for you this summer," Susan explained.

"Okay, well thank you so much for the past three summers, Susan. I've really enjoyed my time with the company."

I hung up. Surprisingly, it didn't upset me. I'd blown it, and I was fine with that. Most college students were lucky to have two internships on their resume. I already had three. No one would miss my fourth summer. I'd spent every summer since high school graduation at Clorox headquarters, wearing a business suit and carrying an attaché case. I had relented to wearing a normal hairstyle and socially acceptable clothing for the sake of their corporate culture. But I felt like a fraud playing dress-up in grown-up land. I'd learned from my internship that I didn't want a corporate job in some office wearing a business suit after graduation. I'd suffocate. I needed something less structured and more chaotic and unpredictable. Being severed from Clorox freed me to pursue just that. For the first summer in years, I wouldn't have to spend my Saturdays in corporate etiquette classes, learning to pour soda into a cup instead of drinking it out of the can.

Watch out LA, I thought. *Here I come!*

I called Stephanie, "Hey, do you still want company this summer?"

"Are you coming?"

"Yeah!"

"What happened to your internship?"

"Long story—I'll tell you when I get there."

"Yippee! When are you coming?"

"I have to talk to my parents but hopefully soon. If it's okay with them, I'll fly into LAX at the end of the week. Is that cool?"

"Yeah, I arrive in four days. Maybe you can fly in at around the same time on the same day?"

"Sounds good. I'll talk to you soon," I replied.

I conferred with Mom.

"It didn't work out at Clorox this summer. I want go to LA for the summer—is that okay?"

"It didn't work out? What happened?" she asked.

I gave her the abbreviated version of my phone conversation and included some incentives for my new summer plans: "Stephanie said I can stay with her in LA all summer. You don't even have to pay for it. She said I can stay for free."

"Sure, you can go. But find out how much her rent is, so I can give you a check for half. You aren't going to stay there all summer and not pay your share."

"But she said I don't have to pay," I reminded Mom.

"Like I said, call Stephanie and find out how much she is paying for rent so I can give you a check for half of the amount," Mom restated in that firm tone that quietly stated, *Don't make me tell you twice.*

"Okay, Mom."

Four days later, I met Stephanie at LAX with Mom's check and a suitcase full of jeans, shorts, and T-shirts. I'd shed all but one business suit, which I brought just in case I had a dress-up emergency.

As Stephanie and I pulled off the freeway and drove on a scenic route through the surrounding neighborhoods, I thought it funny that we were spending the summer in a place called Westwood *Village.* Only in LA could a village be flanked by Beverly Hills and Bel Air. As Stephanie drove to our apartment, I realized that UCLA sat smack-dab in the middle of our village. This was great. I could use UCLA's library to research my three favorite photographers, and I would use UCLA's computers to type letters begging for a photography internship with one of the three living photography legends.

As a kid, I had always found LA too hot. I didn't like it when the temperature went above 72 degrees—perfect San Francisco Bay weather. But as we cruised through Westwood, I felt pretty sure this would be a fun summer. We pulled up in front of our apartment building, which sat on a quiet, sloping residential street, less than six blocks from the edge of UCLA's campus. The apartment building couldn't have been more than three years old. The modern, multilevel facade was painted in various shades of dark and light, pastel, peachy beiges. Lush bushes and trees sprouted everywhere. The thick, green grass out front had recently been mowed. Everything looked sparkling new.

A broad driveway led into what appeared to be a covered underground garage. Four wide, partially glassed-in balconies with double sliding glass doors, sat above the garage. The rest of the building was a sea of windows and stucco-covered private balconies, with each vertical row of apartments protruding out on a different pastel plane. A crisp coffee-colored awning and rows of giant, rectangular, flower boxes filled with colorful flowers and plants marked the entryway. A wall of floor-to-ceiling panes of glass stretched across the entire lobby.

Our completely furnished apartment boasted new appliances and all the standard furniture. We had one large bedroom and a spacious living room with high ceilings. A couple days after moving in, I purchased a double-sized futon from a student moving out. I placed it in the bedroom, under a window, a few feet away from Stephanie's queen-sized bed. I was set for the summer.

The building had an open, plaza-like floor plan and a large outdoor pool and hot tub. I couldn't tell how many units existed because each vertical row of apartments sat on a different plane as the buildings edifice protruded or receded. Balconies jutted out unevenly from each apartment. We were on the second floor. We could see our neighbors' units and balconies a hundred feet away across the ceramic-tiled courtyard, laden with large potted trees and wooden benches.

I spent my first few days in Los Angeles exploring Westwood Village and researching my three favorite photographers—Bruce Weber, Herb Ritts and Matthew Rolston—in the UCLA library. All three were world-famous celebrity photographers. *American Photo's* list of the Top 100 Most Influential People in Photography included each of them. I would willingly work for pennies. I would sweep the studio, be a gopher to carry lattes—whatever it took. A resume with any one of those three names on it was golden in the photography world. Once I worked for one of them, I could go just about anywhere.

Matthew Rolston and Herb Ritts were partially responsible for inspiring me to be a photographer. I had seen their work in a traveling photo exhibit and knew then that I wanted to do photography.

My research revealed that Matthew Rolston and Herb Ritts both had studio addresses in LA. Bruce Weber appeared to be based out of New York. I typed up the most convincing, flattering appeal that I could draft, requesting work as a summer servant. I mailed one copy of the letter to Matthew Rolston and the other to Herb Ritts. At the time, I had no clue that celebrity photographers generally didn't staff summer interns, especially not those with no formal photography training and no experience on commercial photo shoots. Photographers of that magnitude, who worked almost exclusively with A-list actors and rock stars, staffed experienced crews of highly skilled first and second assistants, usually photo school graduates, and then hired additional well-seasoned assistants, as the job demanded. I didn't have a sliver of a chance at a photo internship with either of them. But in my naïveté, I kept calling until I finally reached a receptionist at Matthew Rolston's studio.

"Hello, this is Adele Moore. I wrote a letter to Mr. Rolston requesting a photo internship."

"Yes, I read your letter. That was a very nice letter."

She knew who I was! She liked my letter. Maybe I had a chance.

"Well, yes, I'm here for the summer, and I would really love the opportunity to work with Mr. Rolston. I'm a huge admirer of his work."

"We don't have any positions like that at this time," she replied kindly. "But thank you for the letter. That was a really nice letter," she repeated before hanging up.

Several years later, I interviewed Matthew Rolston over the phone for an assignment. He was the nicest guy. He loaned me his promotional reel, which I watched over and over again, mesmerized by his genius. I never told him how I'd tried to get a job with him as an inexperienced, clueless photo intern.

With all possibilities of a photo internship off the table, I had to do *something* for the next three months. I called my mom.

"What should I do?" I asked.

"You should get a summer job somewhere else—that's what you should do," Mom replied.

The next day, I hit the ground running. Down the hill in Westwood Village, bunches of hip little restaurants and clothing stores abounded. Surely, someone needed summer help. I turned in an application at

Oaktree, a trendy men's clothing store. They were hiring. After a short interview, the store manager welcomed me aboard. I made several good acquaintances among the young and friendly summer staff at Oaktree. But most of the friends I made that summer were through Stephanie and her internship at the film studio. The studio had a handful of interns, college kids from across the country. None of us were from LA, so we quickly became summertime friends and stuck together.

All together there were eight of us—five guys and three girls. There was John, an unassuming, short, quiet guy who wore large wire-rimmed glasses. Then there was Julia, a pleasant, laid-back blonde student. Stephanie's favorite interns were identical twins: Derek and Thomas, both with curly light-brown hair.

Jayson—a warm-hearted, heavyset guy from the Midwest with prematurely thinning hair and a clever wit—was my favorite intern. He struck me as an old soul. Although the same age as the rest of us, he seemed to fit in a little less than the other interns. Maybe that's why I liked him best; he was the most atypical of the otherwise conventional band of college students, the least predictable of the gang. Jayson loved musicals. By the end of summer, he'd created his own film short highlighting the greatest Broadway musicals of the era. Jayson and I stayed in touch after the summer in LA. He was a sweetheart—every April for years afterward he sent me a birthday card.

George was the last of the interns and the only one I didn't enjoy getting to know that summer. I could never have a sensible conversation with him that didn't somehow end up in a discussion about his three great passions: pop diva Madonna, clubbing, and dance music. I wasn't fond of conversations that systematically ended up at the same destination time after time; and I didn't have a whole lot to say about Madonna or the latest rave music. George was a student from Texas and the only one in the gang besides me that wasn't Jewish. His goal for the summer was to dance at the Roxbury—Madonna's favorite and LA's hottest nightclub. Getting into the Roxbury wasn't an easy task since you had to be twenty-one to get inside. None of us, except Stephanie, was twenty-one, and most of us didn't own fake IDs.

Working in Westwood Village I quickly discovered a big advantage to working in a men's clothing store for the summer: men shopped there. Oaktree was probably the only clothing store in Westwood Village that catered exclusively to men, so guys came in all the time. Some came with their girlfriends, but most just wandered in off Westwood Boulevard, looking for a little fashion guidance. It was my job to help them pick out the right shirt or fit them in the right ninety-nine-dollar suit. Only Oaktree sold men's three-piece suits for ninety-nine dollars. There were two colors—a handsome, brown faux tweed and a fashion-forward emerald green. It wasn't Rodeo Drive, but it worked for the casual shopper and UCLA students.

An LA fashionista-guy stopped into the store shortly after I began working there. He looked just like an East Coast fashionista, but with a tan. To my dismay, my manager Scott helped him before I could offer, and the guy didn't stay long. Several weeks later, I noticed another interesting customer. I'd been on my shift about two hours when a cute, clean-cut black guy walked into the store. He looked about the same age as me. He milled around and browsed through the racks.

"Hello," I said. "May I help you?"

"Hello." He stopped, looked at me, and smiled. "I'm just looking around," he said pleasantly.

"Can I help you find anything specific?"

"No, not really. Thank you. I'm just browsing."

I moved a few feet away from him to give him room to shop, but stayed within earshot, in case he needed help finding a size.

"Are you a UCLA student?" he asked.

"No, I'm just here for the summer. I go to school on the East Coast."

"Oh, yeah? Which school?"

"Penn."

"Oh, really?" he said. "You go to the University of Pennsylvania in Philadelphia?"

He had my attention. Most people on the West Coast thought Penn was Penn State. They didn't know that Penn stood *only* for the University of Pennsylvania, which was a completely different school, in an entirely different part of Pennsylvania than Penn State, a public university famous for its football team. Always afraid of sounding like a little snot if I mentioned that Penn was an Ivy League school, I usually just said, "The University of Pennsylvania and Penn State are two different schools." But this West Coast guy didn't need an explanation. He knew the difference.

"So, how do you know about Penn?" I asked.

"Oh, I looked at schools on the East Coast too. I was accepted, but I deferred starting for a year."

"Really? What school?"

"Harvard," he said. Then he paused. "Sorry, I should have introduced myself—I'm August."

"I'm Adele. So, your parents named you after August Wilson?" I teased.

We both laughed.

He had the most appealing baby face with big, round, Charmin-squeezable cheeks.

We talked a little bit longer.

"Well, hey, I'd better let you get back to work," he finally said. "But, may I have your number?"

One of the skills I'd perfected during my short time in LA was the Thirty-Second Guy Assessment Test. When I met a guy in LA, I generally had thirty seconds to decide whether I would give him my phone number. I had to quickly conclude, using the available cues, whether or not he was a playa in the habit of collecting many women's numbers—and therefore someone who would not value my seven digits. In that small window of time, I also had to figure out if he was prone to drunken late-night phone calls, compulsive lying, or just plain weirdness.

The Thirty-Second Guy Assessment Test required that I listen very carefully to a guy's choice of words, how he looked at me, and his body language. August had passed the Thirty-Second Guy Assessment Test with flying colors. I gladly scrawled my number on a piece of paper for him. He called the next day, and we agreed to meet up at Café Miro, a cute eatery with prime real estate in Westwood Village. I passed Café Miro every day, walking to and from work. When I arrived, August was already inside the café sitting at a table.

"Hi," he said with a huge grin as he hopped up from his seat.

"Hi." I smiled back.

"Can I get you something?" he offered.

"Oh, no worries. I'll just get a drink. I'll be right back," I told him.

I ordered a drink at the counter and then returned to sit opposite him at the small café-style table.

"So, do you live in Westwood?" I asked.

"No. Beverly Hills."

"Really? Did you go to Beverly Hills high school?"

"Yes," he smiled.

"No way. I'm sure everyone asks you this stupid question, but . . . what's it like to go to the real *90210* high school?"

"Funny you should ask. People talked about that show all the time at school. Some kids hate the show. Other kids think it's cool. Beverly Hills High School is okay. I have my friends . . . and we just kind of do our own thing."

The V Society had voted *Beverly Hills 90210*—which took place at Beverly Hills High School—as one of our favorite sitcoms.

"So, do you watch the show?"

"Not regularly. It's okay." he smiled. "You know what's funny about the school? There are kids whose parents rent these tiny apartments just inside the city limits of Beverly Hills just so their kids can go to school there. Weird, huh?"

"That makes sense. It's probably an amazing education compared to other LA public schools. And it's free."

"I guess. But I wouldn't want to live in a little apartment just to go to that school. It's nothing special," he added casually, before asking, "So you go to Penn?"

"Yep."

"Do you like it?"

"I do. I have great friends there, so that makes it fun."

"That's cool. Are you from LA?"

"No, I'm just here for the summer. My summer internship didn't work out, so I just came down here to hang out with a friend from school."

"I see. Where was your internship?"

"With a company in Northern California."

"Well, LA isn't a bad place to be for the summer," he said cheerfully.

"Very true," I agreed, with a smile. "I do like LA. It's not bad at all. And Westwood isn't as smoggy as I'd expected."

He laughed. "Yeah, Westwood isn't a bad place to be."

"It's funny. I've been to LA several times before this summer but never to Westwood."

"Where did you visit before?" he asked.

"Oh, you know, the usual places—Disneyland . . ."

August laughed. He was such a cutie with his husky voice. "You *have* to go to Disneyland if you come to LA," he teased.

"Not just Disneyland. I've also visited Venice Beach, the Cheesecake Factory in Marina del Rey, Knott's Berry Farm. You know—all those great cultural icons of LA."

"Right, of course," he smiled.

"And Loyola Marymount University. I've visited there too."

"Why'd you go there?"

"Just for this conference in high school."

"Oh."

"So, you mentioned that you deferred going to Harvard . . . ?"

"Ahh," he sighed. "I'm not sure I *want* to go to Harvard."

I looked at him expectantly, waiting for an explanation. Who didn't want to go to Harvard if they'd already been accepted?

"It's my dad's school, that's all," he said wearily. "I think I want to go to Columbia or somewhere else. Somewhere that's not my dad's school."

"So, you're a legacy," I stated.

"Yep," he sighed.

Was he crazy? A person would sell his kidney for legacy status at Harvard. If one of your parents was an alumnus, you were a legacy. At Penn, legacies had a special admissions process.

They weren't grouped into the same pool as all the other general applicants. Your chances of being admitted were higher if you were a legacy and you were up against a nonlegacy of equal merit. During the first week of school, Penn had a special reception for legacies and their parents. The rest of us, nonlegacies, were herded into a mass reception without good food. I suspected that the legacies had tasty hors d'oeuvres and limitless, free-flowing drinks at their reception. Legacy status was a coveted privilege; affirmative action for the elite. But August acted as if it were an inconvenience.

"Yeah, it sounds like your life is really rough," I joked. "To Harvard or not to Harvard? That is the question."

He smiled again. "Don't you want anything to eat?" he asked. "Why don't you order something?"

"Are you going to eat?"

"Sure, if you do."

We ordered sandwiches and continued talking for a good hour and a half. He was a really nice guy—good-natured, polite, and fun to talk to. I was glad when he asked if I wanted to go out with him again later that week.

"Sure," I grinned. Then I walked happily home.

LA was a peculiar place. The longer I stayed, the more surreal my life became. I felt like I lived inside a television sitcom complete with a story line—college kids pursuing arts and entertainment careers in LA— but with no reality check. All summer, the interns and I met up after work at a handsome bungalow in Westwood. But none of us knew the homeowner, except Julia. I was told Julia's aunt, a movie studio executive, owned the place. But she was never home; according to Julia, she was traveling. On top of that, I never saw a picture of her or her family anywhere in the house. She was like *Sesame Street*'s Snuffleupagus, a make-believe person, that no one knew for sure existed.

We treated the bungalow like we owned it. We sprawled on the sofas, put our feet up on the coffee tables, and stored our drinks in the refrigerator. I did a couple photo shoots at the house. I even invited over a girl I had just met and had her model out by the pool. There were no real grown-ups in our lives all summer. Our existence was devoid of people who paid mortgages and utility bills. We were in and out of nice homes from June through August. Yet we were never accountable to the real grown-ups who made our lifestyles possible; they were always off set.

At some point later in the summer, after Keri had joined our LA crew, my parents would board the hour-long flight down to LA for a day, just to say hello, give me a hug, and make sure I was okay. They literally flew in, stopped by the apartment to take a look, took me out to lunch, and then returned home to Northern California. "We don't want to interfere with your schedule," they said. But no one else's parents came to visit all summer. The absence of real grown-ups seemed the norm in this town. When August took me by his house for a quick tour, there were no parents in sight.

One afternoon the interns and I visited a girl named Erin. She lived in a standard-looking Beverly Hills home. It would have been considered vast and impressive, if it had been in any other neighborhood, but it seemed extremely average for Beverly Hills. The neighbors' homes were almost identical in size. We played billiards in Erin's pool house, which overlooked a beautifully landscaped swimming pool. Someone cranked up the stereo, and we lounged around for a good while before moving on to another spot.

The studio did not pay any of the interns, but they all lived in nicely furnished apartments—mostly in Westwood. The twins lived in an attractive house in West Hollywood. I was the only person with a paycheck, and I made minimum wage. It didn't make sense that we were able to live that way all summer. Every other summer in college, I had worn bland business attire and carried my little briefcase to a rigorous but well-paid corporate gig. I had to complete a serious project by the end of the summer. I had to detail my weekly progress via typed weekly status reports to my boss, a midlevel corporate manager. At the end of the summer, I was expected to give a presentation on my project to the divisional vice president and the department directors. On weekends, I had to attend mandatory intern-training sessions. They drilled us on things like networking effectively and writing succinct business memos.

LA was completely different. Our lives were more detached and superficial than an episode of *Melrose Place*, the popular sitcom about twentysomethings in LA. The characters on *Melrose Place* had real jobs. They had responsibilities and obligations. We had none of those things. Every single one of us seemed to have invisible parents whose existence could only be verified by the checks they deposited into our bank accounts.

One day me and the interns were all hanging out at the bungalow. Our empty take-out boxes littered one of the tables, and leftover Chinese food filled the refrigerator. The phone rang. I sat closest to the receiver.

"Hey, can you get that?" John called over to me. I picked up the phone.

"Hello?"

"Yes, hello. Who is this?"

"Uhhh . . . this is Adele. I'm, uhh . . . a friend of Julia's—the homeowner's niece."

"Carol doesn't have a niece," the voice replied curtly. "Who is this? What did you say your name was?"

Bewildered, I quickly hung up the phone.

Up until then, I had never questioned my access to the homes of so many people I didn't know. Julia had a key, and always welcomed Stephanie and I. As far as I knew, Julia stayed at the house, and John had stayed with her the past couple of days.

"Hey, John . . . Julia," I said, crossing the family room to where they sat. John sat cross-legged on the floor while Julia gave him a shoulder massage. "Someone just called asking for . . . Carol—is that her name? I told the woman on the phone I was a friend of Carol's niece. The lady said Carol doesn't have a niece."

"Julia's her niece by marriage," John stated matter-of-factly. "Don't worry about it. I'll answer the phone next time."

In a few minutes, the phone rang again. John answered this time. He spoke into the receiver as though he owned the house. I could hear him in the next room, speaking firmly and confidently to the caller.

Like me, he had only met Julia a few weeks ago. He wasn't even officially her boyfriend. They had only decided a couple days before that they liked each other.

LA was a *very* peculiar place.

After my first month in Westwood Village, I began to recognize some of the same people. I noticed that the same two guys always drank espresso at separate tables outside Café Miro—a curly-haired blond guy and another guy with a black ponytail. But they never seemed to be working, reading, or studying. They just sat there—people watching, I guessed. I wondered how they each made a living warming a café chair all day. I'd also seen the same fashionista-guy who had come into Oaktree one day strolling around the area.

But most noticeably, I observed a big, beautiful, athletic-looking black guy striding through Westwood Village. I'd seen him several times, always half a block ahead of me or crossing to the other side of the street, usually dressed in athletic shorts and a sporty T-shirt like he was headed to the gym. I never passed him in close enough proximity to make eye contact. But I certainly noticed him. In fact, by the third time I saw him, I realized that I was getting in touch with my cheerleader side.

I didn't know I had a cheerleader side until right at that very moment. As much as I disliked watching sports, I suddenly became convinced I could become a fan of his team—whatever it was. Basketball, football, baseball—"Yay! Go team!" Yep, shouting, waving pompoms—I could do that for a hot second if it meant I'd get to watch him dribble, tackle, bat, or do *whatever* he did.

Midway through the summer, George, the Madonna-loving intern, figured out a way for all of us to get into the Roxbury despite the fact that we were underage. He'd devised a brilliant, nearly foolproof entry strategy. The Roxbury had a restaurant. If you ate at the restaurant, you automatically had access to the club. No one checked IDs once you were already inside the building. You could easily dine at the restaurant and then walk right into the club. It was the perfect plan.

Several nights later, George made dinner reservations for all of us at the Roxbury. We parked the cars and found a place in the long line of club-goers winding down Sunset Boulevard. George let a bouncer know that we had dinner reservations, and the bouncer quickly bumped us up to the front of the line as VIPs—sort of. Soon we snuggled comfortably around our table. We had done it! We were inside LA's hottest dance club. George beamed ecstatically.

The waitress came to take our order. She held her pen suspended in midair, waiting to scribble down our selections. Stephanie and George ordered. No one else said a word. The waitress looked up, making eye contact with the rest of us at the table.

She looked impatient. "What else?" she asked.

"Just water for me," I said.

"Nothing for me."

"I'm not hungry either."

"Nothing for me either, thank you."

"I'll have an order of fries."

She went around the table. Out of the seven of us, only three people had ordered.

"The majority of your party must order if you want to keep your table," the waitress snapped, clearly vexed.

Most of us had eaten already. We had come to dance, not eat.

The waitress began motioning to a guy on the other side of the room.

"We're here from a magazine," George lied. "We're reviewing your club."

The waitress wasn't convinced. The Roxbury didn't need a review. Madonna had already proclaimed it her favorite dance destination. That was all it needed to keep lines of people patiently queuing outside for hours.

In a matter of moments, some serious-looking guys greeted us then escorted us outside. Our night at the Roxbury ended.

I'd never been kicked out of a nightclub before—especially not Madonna's favorite hotspot.

Chapter Twelve

—— ❧ ——

VILLAGE PEOPLE

{July, Summer before Senior Year}

LIKE MANY AFTERNOONS BEFORE, STEPHANIE AND I ZIPPED through town on our usual route from the twins' house in West Hollywood, through Beverly Hills on Santa Monica Boulevard, to Westwood. I looked to my left as we pulled up to a stop sign in Beverly Hills. A black sports car stopped in the lane next to us. *I know that girl*, I thought as I peered inside. I'd seen that face before—long brown hair, the wide mouth. No way! I couldn't wait to call my mom. She'd die.

"Mom, you'll never guess who I saw today!"

"I have no idea," Mom laughed.

"One of your favorite actresses—*Pretty Woman!*"

"Pretty woman?"

"You love that movie, Mom. Julia Roberts! Julia Roberts was right next to us at a stop sign in Beverly Hills. She pulled up in a black Porsche—right at the stop sign. *Can you believe it?*"

"Really, Julia Roberts? Wow! That is something!"

"I know. I couldn't believe it. She was sitting right there. Right next to us."

"What did she look like?"

"Like Julia Roberts."

After the Julia Roberts sighting, I started imagining that I saw famous people everywhere. I sat inside Café Miro, and a guy that looked like

Billy from *Melrose Place* passed by the café window. It probably wasn't him; no paparazzi followed close behind. But it sure *looked* like him.

Days later, I relaxed in the apartment when Stephanie suddenly came bursting through the door after work, a bundle of cheerful energy.

"We're all going to dinner at Spago later this week. Do you want to come?"

"What's Spago?" I asked.

"It's the restaurant where you go to look for stars. Celebrities eat there."

"Cool, yeah, I'll go. What night are you going? I have to work Thursday night, but otherwise I can go."

"Oh," she sighed. "Our reservations are for Thursday night. It's already set. All the interns are going."

"That's cool. You'll have to tell me how it is."

"Can't you switch your work schedule?"

"No, it's my turn to stay until closing. No big deal. Really. Have fun. Tell me if I miss anything." I'd already seen one more celebrity than I had expected to see all summer. I didn't mind passing up Spago's.

Thursday night Stephanie came home late. She hadn't seen anyone famous—at least not for sure. Someone thought they had seen one of the Baldwin brothers. But no one else could verify it. Fake celebrity sightings didn't count. I hadn't missed anything.

The following afternoon, I finished my shift at Oaktree and craved a good sugar hit. Diddy Riese, the best place for freshly baked goodies in Westwood Village, would deliver. I stepped out onto the sidewalk and into the steady stream of leisurely, strolling walkers. I felt alive and content. I liked my summer job. I liked LA. Mild, sunny, dry Southern California weather characterized every day. I hardly noticed the thin layer of smog choking the atmosphere. I headed up the street in the direction of Diddy Riese. As I passed Café Miro, I observed Curly-Haired Blond Guy sitting outside in his usual chair, drinking an espresso concoction. Was he glued to that seat? I wondered if they paid him to sit there all day.

The seductive smell of freshly baked cookies greeted me as I stepped inside the bakery. I surveyed the abundant rows of cookies and muffins beneath the clear glass. So many choices: chocolate chip, white chocolate macadamia, M&M, peanut butter, chocolate chocolate chip. Oh, yeah—today it would be white chocolate chip and a regular chocolate chip, with a pint of milk. You couldn't get a better deal for one dollar. I paid and stepped back outside with the bag of cookies and milk carton in hand.

I couldn't believe my luck. Tan Fashionista-Guy was walking down the block twenty feet ahead of me. I decided to follow him. I stuffed the sealed milk carton into my backpack and pretended to search for something in my bag of cookies. I let him get farther ahead of me so he wouldn't notice me behind him. He crossed the street and continued down Broxton Avenue in the opposite direction of my apartment. I followed.

I'd been trailing him for about a minute. Halfway down the block, a paralyzing wave of panic overcame me. It hit me like a bucket of ice water on a scorching day. I was a stalker! I was stalking a random male-fashionista through the streets of Westwood Village. What was the matter with me? Thank goodness he hadn't seen me. Embarrassed, I crossed to the other side of the street and headed back in the direction of my apartment. What if I had been caught? I could see the headline, "PSYCHO MALE-FASHIONISTA STALKER APPREHENDED IN WESTWOOD VILLAGE CARRYING MILK AND COOKIES."

I needed to go back home and spend some time praying and reading my Bible. There had to be a verse: "Thou shall not stalk desirable men."

I was long past due to find a good church. I had stopped into a few Sunday services at different churches here and there in Westwood, but Mom told me about a church in South Central led by a longtime friend of my grandfather. My grandfather, Rev. Lee C. Phillip, was the first dean of the chapel at Prairie View A&M University, a historically black college in Texas. He led all the college's chapel services. Generations of Prairie View students knew my grandfather well for his thoughtful sermons and fearless ministry across racial lines. Few black spiritual leaders in the South, stepped outside the black community to build bridges of faith across color lines, a rarity in the 1950s. Jim Crow ruled, and a black man traveling and speaking out about anything, especially outside the safety of his community, was life-threatening business. But my grandfather, an avid globetrotter, who visited more than thirteen European countries, and many other places, marched to his own drummer. Through the Young Men's Christian Association (YMCA), he boldly reached out to blacks and whites for the sake of the Gospel.

I couldn't ask Stephanie to drive me all the way out to South Central early on a Sunday morning. It would be rude to ask her to sit through Sunday school and then a three-hour church service. That entire summer she had graciously driven me all over town in her rental car. Besides, she didn't have the right clothes to wear to an all-black church. You couldn't attend a traditional African American church and not wear a dress or suit. Stephanie only had jeans.

Sunday morning I set out early for church. Two bus transfers, and three buses later, I had finally made it from Westwood to South Central. The journey took an hour and a half. I hopped off the rumbling, dusty city bus, excited with the anticipation of *real* church. Bits of trash littered the streets, and untamed weeds poked through the sidewalk. An unkempt vacant lot and several small houses with dry, spotty lawns lined the urban intersection. I needed this. I longed to feel more grounded amidst my footloose and fancy-free summer. I wore my pants suit, the only one I'd brought with me to LA. It was tailored and conservative, probably the nicest item of clothing I owned. Mom had bought it for me to wear during my first summer as an intern. I always received compliments when I wore it at my church back home.

I double-checked the piece of paper on which I'd written down the church address. It was less than two blocks away from where the bus had dropped me off. I hurried down the block and approached an expansive off-white building. The large church took up a huge portion of the block where it sat. I walked inside. I approached the first person that I saw—a sharply dressed woman in a skirt, matching coat, and huge hat.

"Hello. Can you tell me where the young adult Sunday School meets?" I asked.

"Yes, dear," she replied. She directed me through the church lobby and up a flight of stairs to classrooms above. "Your classroom is through that door on that side," she said, pointing to a classroom several doors down. I was early. Sunday school started at 9:00 a.m., and I'd arrived at 8:30. The room was empty, but I didn't mind. I sat patiently waiting for the other students to arrive. Slowly, well-dressed young people in their Sunday suits began to trickle in.

The Sunday school teacher arrived and asked me to introduce myself.

"Hello. My name is Adele. I'm here in LA visiting for the summer."

"Where are you staying?" the teacher asked kindly.

"In Westwood."

"My, you've come quite a way from Westwood," she replied.

My fellow Sunday school classmates smiled welcomingly. The people sitting closest to me introduced themselves.

"How are you liking LA?" the girl on my right asked.

"I like it a lot," I said with a smile.

The Sunday school lesson began. It was right on point. We read some Bible verses and then discussed them and their application to our lives. We closed in prayer; and everyone poured out of the classroom and down into the lobby outside the church sanctuary. I disappeared into the bathroom and lost track of my classmates as they dispersed into the extensive rows of pews and seated themselves.

Swinging double doors separated the church lobby from the main sanctuary. I opened a door and walked in. The seats were filling up, but service hadn't started yet. No ushers stood nearby to show me to a seat, so I walked to the middle of the sanctuary and sat down near the aisle of one of the long pews.

The sanctuary looked the same as at most every other African American church I had attended in my lifetime. The stair-stepped choir loft rested in the front of the church, behind the pastor's decorated podium.

An organist sat off to the side, poised on the giant organ. Female ushers dressed in skirt suits, big hats, and white gloves stood positioned around the edges of the sanctuary. They held bulletins in their hands and handed them to people taking their seats.

I breathed a sigh of relief. I felt at home.

Long, drawn-out church services had tortured me throughout my childhood. Relief—in the form of benediction and coffee hour, with its promise of cookies, cake and fruit punch—never came quickly enough. At the church where I grew up, it took forever to read the announcements. And the choir always sang too many encores. But on that day in South Central, I wouldn't have minded if someone had read an encyclopedia-long list of announcements. I was pleasantly resolved to a litany of recurring choir encores. I was just glad to be there and prepared for a long afternoon.

When I entered the sanctuary, I had missed getting a bulletin from one of the ushers. But soon an usher approached me. I held out my hand expecting to receive a program for the service.

"Young lady," she said, "women are not allowed in the sanctuary wearing pants."

I was stunned—speechless.

"Please follow me," she said.

I got up dutifully and followed the usher. She escorted me out of the sanctuary and into a room in the church lobby. The room was directly connected to the sanctuary via a large, one-way glass window. I could see into the sanctuary, but the people inside could not see me.

"This is a room for nursing mothers," she informed me. "You can watch the service from here."

I sat down in the closest chair.

"Thank you," I said blindly, without thinking. The usher left.

It took me a moment to process what had just happened. I sat there, alone in the room. The insides of my nose began to tingle, and my eyes burned. A tear started to trickle down the side of my face. I stood up and sped out of the church before anyone could see me. I made it halfway down the block, before tears streamed everywhere and a soupy mixture trickled from my nose and ran down my face. My heart plunged straight through a crack in the sidewalk, past the cement and the hard layer of earth beneath to the dark, leaden, rocky abyss below. I had literally been kicked out of church. I stood on the side of the road, at a bus stop in South Central, bawling. Thankfully, the street was deserted. By the time the big, rickety city bus pulled up, I'd composed myself somewhat. I'd wiped my nose and cleaned my face with a Kleenex. I couldn't wait to get back to Westwood.

"How was church?" Stephanie asked, when I got home.

"Sunday School was good," I replied, before disappearing into the bedroom to change into cut-off jean shorts and my favorite T-shirt. Actually, it was Stephanie's T-shirt, but I wore it so often I sometimes forgot that. I closed the door to the room and called my mom.

Mom was comforting and indignant as I relayed the details of that morning.

"Why don't you write them a letter and tell them you're Rev. Phillip's granddaughter?" my mother retorted. "Let them know how you were treated. That is completely unacceptable!"

I planned to write a long letter, quoting a tirelessly long list of Scripture stating that everyone is welcome in the house of God. I intended to make a smart-mouthed comment about how they'd probably turn Jesus away because he'd show up dressed in sandals and needing a shower. I'd reprimand them up one side and down the other, using every Bible verse I could find to rain down the wrath of God on their heads. Who were they to turn me away because I hadn't complied with their little dress code? But I never did. What was the point? I would only be in LA another month and a half. I would never go back to that church.

If I went to church in Westwood, I could walk or ride a bus less than fifteen minutes. On top of that, I could wear jeans and a T-shirt, and I would be welcomed, not treated like a second-class citizen. Forget it. I'd wait until I returned to my parents' house at the end of the summer to hear hymns and enjoy worshipping in the tradition most familiar to me.

Anyway, I had better things to think about—like my upcoming dinner with August.

He picked me up at my apartment, dressed in jeans and a T-shirt. I wore a T-shirt too, but with a skirt.

"Are you hungry?" he asked.

"I'm always hungry," I joked. "Except when I'm asleep."

"Should we go back to Café Miro?" he asked.

"Sure. I don't know what the dinner menu is like, but I'm sure it's fine."

We found parking quickly, seated ourselves, and ordered.

"So, what are you going to do during your year off from school?" I asked.

"I feel like I need to find myself," he answered slowly.

"That's cool. How do you plan to do that?" I thought he'd have some sort of community service project lined up—maybe volunteering with Habitat for Humanity. Or maybe he was going to teach elementary school to underprivileged children in a remote village overseas.

"I'm not sure yet."

"Are you going to do community service or volunteer somewhere or something?"

August hesitated before answering, "I don't know."

"Well, how will you stay busy all year?"

"I haven't figured that out yet," he replied quietly.

I didn't want to press the issue, but I felt I must have missed something. Where was his plan of action? Who had ever heard of a man finding himself by loafing around in Beverly Hills for a year doing nothing—especially while he lived with his parents? My parents would have laughed out loud if I had told them I was skipping college to *find myself*. Mom would have said, "Go find yourself at college—then find yourself in grad school. Then find yourself a *job*. After that, you can go find whatever else your little heart desires." In my opinion, Harvard was a perfectly good place for a young black man to *find* himself. At Harvard he could find himself a college degree and stop freeloading off his parents for the rest of his life.

When we finished eating, he asked, "Would you like a little tour of LA?"

"Sure."

The night felt pleasantly warm compared to San Francisco's freezing summer nights. I slipped a light sweater over my T-shirt as we stepped outside. We cruised high up into the hills on Mulholland Drive. He pointed out the different neighborhoods down below. We laughed and talked easily. He listened attentively to every word I said. The night grew later, and as much fun as we were having, I needed to get some sleep.

"Well, let me take you home," he smiled. "I was thinking about something, though.""Oh, yeah?"

"I think you should marry me."

What! He did not just say that. Did I wash my ears when I showered last night? I can't remember. Marry him? He just met me. I could be a psychopath, a pyromaniac, or an axe murderer! Startled and unable to think of a single appropriate response, I resorted to my usual mode of handling awkward situations with guys: I pretended not hear him and changed the subject.

"I've had such a great time hanging out with you tonight. Whew, I'm beat," I said, feigning a yawn. "What's this road called again?"

"Uh . . . Mulholland Drive." Before he could turn the conversation back to the proposal, I chattered on, determined to permanently redirect our dialogue. Within twenty minutes we'd pulled up in front of my apartment. Almost before the engine cut off, I swung my door open and leapt out the car.

"Thanks so much for tonight. I had a great time. Okay, whew, I'm beat," I repeated. "I'm going to bed now. Okay, good night."

I barely gave him a second to say good night before I dashed into the lobby of my building, up the stairs, and out of sight.

The next morning I awoke convinced that, in the heady buzz of an enjoyable evening, August had simply lowered his defenses and forgotten to filter. In an unexpectedly relaxed moment, he'd accidentally blurted a bit of the illogical private inner dialogue we all have with ourselves, the sort that would cause others to question our sanity if they heard it. Occasionally, the same thing happened to me when I passed a bank. For a split second I'd wonder, "What if I robbed that bank?" I had no intention of robbing the bank, of course, but the fleeting notion crossed my mind. That kind of thought was never meant to be uttered aloud. Only a careless slip of the tongue disclosed such things. I felt at ease knowing August was a reasonable person; he wouldn't make the same mistake twice.

All summer, I was never at a loss for new photo subjects in LA, the Land of Beautiful People where half the town aspired to big-screen superstardom. From the intern group alone, I recruited three models. Early on, I took a good look at John and realized that he hid under a Clark Kent disguise.

"Hey, John, take off your glasses and stick your head in the pool," I told him before we began our photo shoot.

"Are you sure you want to photograph me?" he balked.

"Trust me on this one," I encouraged.

He stuck his head in the pool, and instantly his shaggy-dog haircut disappeared into slick, groomed perfection. With his hair out of his face and the glasses off—*Poof!*—the guy looked like Superman (minus the superhuman brawn). All this time John had been a model in hiding.

Several days later, I showed him the proof sheets from our shoot.

"I can't believe you made me look so good!" he exclaimed.

"It's all you," I said with a smile. I loved working with people who were completely unaware of their star power. It was refreshing.

Around that same time, I discovered that one of the twins already had a small portfolio of modeling jobs.

"Yeah, I did this car ad," Thomas said as he thumbed through his book, showing me his collection of advertising work.

"Nice, I'll have to photograph you and your brother together."

"No problem, but you aren't going to use the photos for anything are you? You aren't going to *sell* my picture to anyone are you? I'm not supposed to let anyone photograph me without my agent's permission."

"No, I'm not going to use them for anything or sell them," I assured him. I couldn't think of anyone who would want to buy his photograph besides Stephanie, and I'd give her all the pictures she wanted for free.

I photographed the twins later in the summer. Their pictures didn't turn out nearly as good as I had hoped. They were good lifestyle models but not the best fashion models. John's pictures had turned out far better.

Stephanie and my summer schedules each took on a comfortable routine. Every weekday she got up and headed out to the film studio. I usually slept in, always preferring to work in the afternoon rather than the morning. The Oaktree manager rarely scheduled me to come in before noon, and I never worked more than four or five days a week.

On one of my days off, I milled around in Westwood Village and then stepped into a small music store to shop for CDs. I found the soundtrack I wanted and had started on my way home when I remembered that the refrigerator back at our apartment was practically bare. One little convenience store stocked a decent selection of food a few blocks away, just off my usual route home. I hustled across the intersection, down the block, and into the store. I contemplated all my favorite foods as I meandered down the first short aisle and decided what I wanted for dinner.

All of a sudden, I saw him—Big Beautiful Black Athlete. He wore athletic shorts and a sleeveless T-shirt that exposed his bulging biceps. I'd never seen him this close before. He was about six foot three and 210 pounds of sheer, rippling, magnificent muscle—probably UCLA's star football player or something. I might have had a clue if I'd paid attention to sports. I ducked down the next aisle, afraid he'd catch me staring, but the little corner store only had three aisles. Soon he appeared at the far end of my aisle, striding rapidly toward me.

Ignore him, I thought. *Just act like you're looking for a can of soup or something on the shelf. Don't look, don't look. He'll know you're drooling.*

Soon he stood right in front of me in the aisle. I tried to look away, unsuccessfully.

"Hello," he said with a pleasant smile as he passed me and headed past me.

"Hi," I mumbled with a weak smile, trying to sound disinterested as though I hadn't even noticed him—as if you could overlook a six-foot-three man.

With that "hello," amnesia suddenly overcame me. The synapses in my brain stopped firing properly, and I short-circuited. *What did I come in the store for? I was supposed to buy something. What do I need to buy?* I couldn't remember a thing.

I turned down the last aisle only to find him standing in that aisle looking at items on a shelf. *If I pass him again I can't say hi. We already said hi. Should I smile? No, I already smiled—sort of. He might think I'm stalking him.* My heart started to race. *Get a grip, moron. He just said hello. Don't have a meltdown just because some big, beautiful man said hello to you. Pull it together, girl!*

Suddenly, the urge to flee to the cash register with whatever I held in my hand overcame me. I had to get out of there. I was completely irrational. *Is my face giving me away? Can he tell what I'm thinking? You're so hot! I'm such a dork. What is the matter with me?*

I couldn't concentrate. I hurried to the register in an addled state of mind, paid for whatever I was holding in my hand, and walked briskly out the door. For the life of me, I couldn't recall what I had gone into the store to buy in the first place.

The next day, August picked me up after work. We went to dinner and then hopped into his car to head back toward my side of town. Then, out of the blue, he pulled his car over and stopped the engine.

Trouble. If he tried to make a move, I was determined to let him down as gently as possible. After all, he didn't know about the V Society or anything about me, really.

He turned and looked at me earnestly. "I really think you should marry me . . . ," he started.

This time I couldn't change the subject. Playing deaf only worked the first time around. This direct proposition required a direct answer.

"August," I said, picking my words delicately as though I considered marriage to him a real possibility—which I didn't. "Where will we live if we get married? I'm moving back to Philadelphia next month. Are you moving to Philadelphia?" I hoped this line of questioning might help him realize that two underemployed people who barely knew each other should *not* discuss something so utterly preposterous. There was no way I was starting senior year with a husband.

"I would figure that out," he replied, trying to sound confident. He paused and then said, "I'll find an apartment in Philadelphia."

In his hesitation, I knew instantly that he hadn't thought of a single detail past the proposal. He'd probably never gone apartment hunting before. I'd bet he had never lived in an apartment—*ever*. More than likely, he didn't even have friends that lived in apartments.

These questions were just the tip of the iceberg. A hundred other questions to consider glared like, "Do you really want to be the only freshman, beginning college with a wife?" and "Who is going to pay for my last year of school, your four years of school, and then graduate school for both of us? Your parents?" I didn't expect my parents to pay if I did something as crazy as get married before graduation. In the nicest way I knew how, I screamed, "This is ridiculous!" You can't just ask someone to marry you and have no plan for the future— for your independence. On top of that, we weren't on the same page spiritually. But I wasn't going to bring that up and further prolong our futile discussion.

"Hey, August, I'm tired," I said. "Why don't you drop me off at home?" He sighed and started up the engine. "Okay."

I could hear the disappointed resolve in his voice as he started the car. I had tried my best not to hurt his feelings, but this was getting out of hand. There was no point talking about things that would never happen. He steered the car into the street, and we headed back to Westwood, barely saying a word.

Chapter Thirteen

BOYS of SUMMer

{July–August, Summer before Senior Year}

WE HAD EXACTLY FIVE WEEKS LEFT OF SOUTHERN CALIFORNIA sunshine, Hollywood glamour, and the boys of summer. After enjoying a Caribbean cruise with her parents, Keri hopped a flight to Los Angeles to join Stephanie and me during our last month in La-La Land. She had already seen her fair share of palm trees, but four weeks of everything else LA had to offer gave her reason enough to make the cross-country trip.

"How do you like my new hairstyle?" Keri asked.

"Whoa—I didn't know your hair could do that!" I exclaimed. Some-one had transformed Keri's dark locks into rows of long cornrows. I'd grown up believing that, aside from Bo Derek in the 1979 movie *Ten* (the actress became world famous for her scenes running on the beach with blonde cornrows), people of non-African descent couldn't wear cornrows. Keri proved me wrong—the girl was full of surprises.

"That's pretty wild," I said, carefully looking over the tiny sprouts of identical braids.

"I had it done on one of the islands while we were on vacation," Keri said, smiling.

"That must have taken a long time," I remarked.

Keri wouldn't be in LA long enough to hold down a job, so she joined the café dwellers—Curly-Haired Blond Guy and Ponytail Guy— warming up a seat at Café Miro. All day, Keri sat reading *The Brothers Karamazov* and the Bible.

"I met the café owner, Isaac," she reported after her first week. Isaac was a striking Persian in his early forties. Every day, he pulled up in a big luxury sedan, dressed in neat slacks and a relaxed but tidy shirt. His black hair perfectly framed his always-tan face.

"He always talks to me whenever I come into the café," she said. "Somehow, we started discussing spiritual topics, so he's been telling me all about Kabbalah, Jewish mysticism. He said, 'It will make you crazy if you get involved in Kabbalah before you're forty.'"

In the following weeks, Isaac invited Keri with him a couple times on Friday before the Sabbath to meet his gang of well-heeled Persian Israeli Jewish male friends. I met Isaac once. He struck me as a smooth-talking charmer.

"He's slick," Keri agreed, "and *very* friendly, if you know what I mean."

After her second week on the job as a café dweller, Keri delivered the scoop on Curly-Haired Blond Guy and Ponytail Guy.

"Curly-Haired Blond Guy is Daniel. He's the son of a Croatian mafioso. He only works when he needs to. When he does work, he earns enough to live off for months, so he quits working until he needs to work again," Keri explained.

"What kind of work does he do?" I asked.

"Good question," Keri replied. "He was rather vague about that part. But he wasn't vague about some other things. Do you know what he told me?" Keri asked.

"No. What?"

"He said he's loved 150 women in his life."

"Really?" I laughed

"Yeah, and he told me, 'I loved every woman with my heart and soul. I did everything to please them.'"

"That's the biggest load of crap I've ever heard," I returned. "Like he can even remember all their names—please.'"

"I know, seriously," Keri laughed. "Hey, I met that other guy too."

"Ponytail Guy?"

"Yep."

"So, what's his deal?"

"His name is Ramon. He's from Central America and completely against marriage. His mother divorced his father in his home country, and she was ostracized. So he doesn't see the point. He said he's had two hundred lovers," Keri continued.

It never occurred to me to ask Keri why these guys divulged this information. I'm sure she didn't ask for a detailed resume of their past encounters. Obviously, the favorite topic of conversation—from the V Society dorm room to the cafés of LA—was the same. Everyone wanted to talk about sex. It was impossible to ignore it and impossible to pretend it didn't affect every living, breathing, able-bodied man and woman. It was wired into our DNA, like eating and sleeping.

While at sea in the Caribbean, Keri must have overdosed on the extravagant varieties of food offered onboard. Apparently, her palette needed to detoxify with simpler comfort foods. Since arriving in LA, she'd adopted a new diet centered entirely around chocolate chip cookie dough. She ate it as an appetizer, an entrée, and a side dish. Like salt and pepper, cookie dough went with everything.

During the one visit my parents made to LA that summer, my dad had noticed Keri's cookie dough addiction. "What's the matter with your roommate?" he'd asked.

"Nothing," I'd replied. Eating cookie dough was the least of the strange things I'd seen Keri do over the years.

The week that Keri arrived, the two of us stood out on our balcony, facing the wide, tiled courtyard that separated us from the neighbors.

The sun lit up the apartments across from us but cast a heavy shadow of shade over our side of the building, keeping us cool at that time of day. One story above us, three people suddenly appeared on the opposite-facing balcony. They looked to be in their mid-twenties, just a few years older than us. The bright sunlight streamed across their faces, casting strong, well-defined shadows beneath their noses and chins. The couple on the right of the balcony looked picture perfect—a dark-haired, handsome woman with a strong, square jawline, and her boyfriend, with equally long blond hair and an even stronger, squarer, more masculine lower jaw. The sun rippled across the boyfriend's bare, toned chest.

"I've got to photograph them," I whispered to Keri. "They're perfect together."

"Well, go ask them."

"Very funny."

"Hey, look! They're waving at us," she whispered.

"Hi," the third person on the balcony, a guy with curly, light-brown, blondish hair, called out.

"Hi," Keri called back with a wave.

"Hi," I followed.

"What are you two doing down there?" the guy called out pleasantly.

"Nothing," Keri called back, smiling. Inside Stephanie heard the back-and-forth exchange and soon came to join us.

"Hi," the guy called down, greeting Stephanie.

"Hi." She squinted as she looked up at the three figures glowing in the sunlight.

"She wants to photograph them," Keri whispered to Stephanie.

"Not all three of them. Just the couple," I whispered back.

"She's too chicken to ask them, though," Keri added.

"I'll ask them," Stephanie shrugged. I had always admired Stephanie's boldness. She was fearless when it came to asking for what she wanted. "All they can say is no," she said with a smile. "But you won't know until you ask."

"Hey, why don't you come up here?" the friendly guy yelled down. "Come on up," he encouraged again with a welcoming wave of his arm.

"Let's go," Stephanie said and put her arm in Keri's.

"I'm not going up there," I protested.

"That's okay. Keri and I will go, and we'll ask them to model for you," Stephanie called over her shoulder as she whisked Keri out the door and up the elevator.

A few minutes later, Keri and Stephanie appeared on the balcony with the three figures and waved down.

"Come on up!" Stephanie yelled. "Bring your camera. They said they'll pose for you."

I was such a wimp. I had to be the only fashion photographer in the world too chicken to ask strangers to model. Embarrassed that I hadn't asked the couple myself, I slowly gathered up my camera gear and headed upstairs at the speed of molasses.

"It took you long enough," Stephanie called. Her head poked out of the neighbor's front door as she looked for me to appear around the corner in the hallway.

"This is Adele," Keri announced, introducing me to the three. "This is Eran, and this is his apartment," Keri said, gesturing toward the smiling guy who had invited us up.

"These are my friends Katherine and Hubert," Eran said, nodding toward the couple. "They're visiting from Europe."

"Nice to meet you," I said, shaking all three of their hands.

"You are a photographer?" Hubert asked.

"Yep," I answered.

"You want to take our picture?" Katherine chimed in with a smile. "No problem."

All eyes in the room were on me—waiting.

"Okay." I hopped into action. "The light was perfect on you out on the balcony, so let's go out there," I said to Katherine and Hubert. The three of us migrated onto the balcony, and I backed against the railing farthest from them.

"Just pretend I'm not here and you're just enjoying a moment alone on the balcony," I coached. "But make sure you're both looking in the same direction." I fired off several frames, but the shot wasn't quite right. I was too close to them on the balcony with the lens I'd brought with me. I couldn't fit their heads and torsos into the shot without a wider-angle lens.

"Hey, I think the best angle was actually shooting up at you from my balcony," I said. I'll go back downstairs and photograph you from there, okay?"

"You don't want to photograph us from here?" Hubert asked.

"I took a few, but the composition isn't right. It was better from downstairs. The light hit you at the right angle, and I could frame the picture better. Also, I can move around more from down there. I don't have enough room to move around up here on the balcony with you."

"Okay," they agreed.

Keri and Stephanie sat comfortably in the living room, chatting away with Eran.

"That was quick," Keri commented as the three of us came in off the balcony.

"I'm not finished yet," I replied. "I was at a better angle from our floor, so I'm going to go photograph them from the courtyard. I'll be down there in two minutes," I told the couple.

"Okay, we'll be out on the balcony," they agreed.

"Nice meeting you," I called to Eran before I disappeared through his door.

Downstairs, I climbed over the short wall of my balcony and into the open courtyard. Though we were on the second floor, our apartment sat on the same level as the courtyard. The courtyard sat above the enclosed downstairs level, which had no apartments just mailboxes, the huge lobby, and an entrance to the underground parking garage. From the courtyard, I composed exactly the architectural type of picture I wanted, with stark shadows separating the balcony from the light-colored wall and the couple's strong features illuminated in the contrasting tones of my black-and-white film. I finished off a couple rolls and then yelled a thank you up to the balcony before I disappeared back inside. I put a CD on the stereo and settled down across the sofa, waiting for Stephanie and Keri to return.

I must have fallen asleep because the sun had sunk much lower in the sky by the time Keri and Stephanie came home.

"Hey, what happened to you?" Keri grinned. "Why didn't you come back up?"

"I fell asleep, I guess," I replied.

Keri came and squeezed next to me, reclined on the sofa.

"Eran's Israeli," she beamed.

"He is?"

"Yes," Keri smiled, her face lit up—radiant.

"He asked us to come out with him and some of his friends later in the week," she continued.

"Oh, really," I grinned back. "Look who's smiling now," I teased.

"Guess what?" Keri continued. "Eran thought I was black."

"What?" I asked.

"When I got up to his apartment, he looked at me funny and said, 'You're white?' in a surprised voice. I had no idea what he was talking about, so I said, 'Excuse me?' Then he said, 'When I saw you two downstairs . . . you were in the shade, I guess . . . I thought you were both African American.'"

"Well, who can blame him?" I laughed. "You're the first nonblack person I've ever seen with that hairdo." Keri kept the cornrows for a few more days before she undid the tiny braids and returned to her usual hairstyle. It was hard to shampoo her hair easily and keep the cornrows intact.

Several days later, Keri, Stephanie, and I awoke to the sound of a Kate Bush song blaring loudly.

"Ughhhh, who's playing music?" I grumbled.

"I don't know," Keri groaned from somewhere in the room. I pulled the covers over my head, dreaming that somehow the sheets would magically block out the sound. I could hear Keri rustling around in the room. She peeked out the window through the blinds.

"The music is coming from outside," she announced.

"What time is it?" I moaned.

"Seven in the morning," Stephanie retorted.

"I think it's coming from Eran's apartment," Keri decided.

"Tell him to quit that, would you?" I mumbled from beneath my blanket wall. I loved Kate Bush but not before ten in the morning. Eran's stereo stayed cranked up for the entire song before he finally acknowledged the need for volume control.

"Ugggh, that's not cute. You should really tell him it's not cool to wake up his neighbors this early in the morning," I moaned before slipping back to sleep in the restored silence.

The following night Keri and I met up with Eran for a night out on the town. Stephanie bailed on us, preferring to spend the evening with the twins. I sat in the back of Eran's car, attempting to politely avoid conversation with his friend sitting in the seat next to me. I was not excited about the semblance of a double date. Keri sat directly in front of me, in the passenger seat next to Eran. She might have been on a date with Eran, but I was not on a date with the random guy in the backseat. Eran sped his black convertible down Santa Monica Boulevard heading toward Third Street Promenade. He gunned the engine and then raced between the stoplights. *Was that supposed to impress us?* I thought. I could tell this was the beginning of a very long night.

"I have quite a few traffic violations," Eran had admitted to Keri earlier. *Duh—no kidding.* All of them were probably from racing his stupid sports car through town trying to impress girls.

We pulled into a parking lot. A second car full of Eran's friends pulled up nearby. The group of us unloaded and spilled through the front door of a bar and grill. Everyone took seats around a long table. I sat in the seat closest to Keri so there would only be one of Eran's friends, instead of two, within conversation distance. I ordered my usual soda and tried not to look bored. An hour passed. I halfheartedly engaged in small talk with the guy sitting on my left. Eran sat on the other side of Keri, talking about himself.

"I really think I'm so much better than most of the girls I go out with. I want to date someone honorable for a change. You know—have a respectable relationship," he told Keri. "I come to New York pretty often for business. Maybe you could meet me in New York—you know, for dinner or something?"

I didn't see what Keri saw in this guy. As always, my thoughts must have flashed like a neon sign across my face. Keri shot me a "You're a big whiny brat" look, but I didn't care. If only Eran would stop talking about himself and take us home! Finally, after an eternity, we piled back into Eran's car and returned home. I couldn't wait to wish him and his friend goodnight—for good.

By the end of Keri's second week in Westwood, we had again fallen into a steady routine. Stephanie went to the film studio. Keri and I slept late. I went to work. Keri went to Café Miro. It ran like clockwork. In the late afternoon, the three of us reconvened at the apartment and decided what we'd do for the evening. Usually, we met up with the interns. Like us, their numbers had multiplied in the last month. Derek and Thomas's friend, an aspiring actor named Matt, now crashed at their place. Blake, a classmate of Julia's from out of town, also joined the gang for a week or two.

With Matt's arrival, I now had the perfect model to pair with Keri. The two looked fabulous together. One of the images from their photo shoot became my favorite image of the entire summer. I'd copied the pose from a black-and-white fashion advertisement I had torn from *Vogue* magazine. Keri looked down at Matt's head cradled in her arms, while he rested his head on her chest, his eyes closed in peaceful resolve. The final image consisted of a closely cropped black-and-white shot of his head and hers nestled together.

Later that week, Keri, Stephanie, and I lounged around the bungalow with the interns. The group of us spread around the house. A few people

lay out by the pool. Some goofed off in the kitchen, while the rest of
the gang milled around between the living room, kitchen, and outside.

I stood outside blabbering away with Keri when suddenly Stephanie
flew past us in tears, bawling as she dashed to her car. Keri caught her,
and from a distance I could see her attempt to comfort Stephanie before
she peeled out of the driveway.

"Is she okay? What's the matter?" I asked Keri as Stephanie zoomed
down the street.

"George told her he doesn't think she's pretty."

"George! Why would he say that? That's so insensitive. What does he
know anyway? He's in love with Madonna."

"Stephanie is totally cute. What's his problem?" Keri asked.

"I have no idea."

Stephanie was a genuine sweetheart. She'd been nice to George all
summer—not an easy task. She didn't deserve to have her self-esteem
stomped on by the likes of him. A couple hours later, Stephanie returned, collected but clearly lacking her usually bubbly disposition.

"We're ready to go if you are," Keri assured her. Keri and I called out
our good-byes and then zipped home with Stephanie.

Days later, I came home late from work, after my closing shift.
Stephanie's eyes were puffy and red.

"What's the matter?" I asked Keri. Keri always seemed to have the
pulse on everyone's emotional state.

"She's just upset about Matt," Keri relayed.

"But I thought they were friends and everything was cool."

"Well, that's just it. I don't think she wants to be *just* friends with
Matt."

"Oh, I see." I wished I could do something to make Stephanie feel
better. But the whole Friend Zone was touchy. Sometimes you wanted
to be just friends and sometimes you wanted to be a lot more than friends.

"I'm going over to Eran's," Keri beamed, early Saturday morning.
"He invited me over for breakfast."

I waited for her to invite me. She didn't.

She dressed hurriedly and then flew out the door like lightning. I couldn't believe her. She had personally authored V Society Unwritten Rule Number One: If you are going to the apartment of a guy you want to hook up with, you shouldn't go alone. You were supposed to take a fellow V Society member with you. She had made me promise not to go to Milan's room by myself at night, and I had abided by that rule all semester. Now, at the first opportunity, she was running to Eran's room—alone. Talk about a double standard! I simmered with irritation.

Forty-five minutes later, Keri's key turned in the door. I pretended to be reading and completely disinterested in her excursion.

"Hi, Delie," she sighed as she plopped down on the floor next to where I lay on the sofa.

"Hey," I replied nonchalantly, still pretending to be preoccupied.

"Eran tried to kiss me," she sighed.

Duh—of course he did. What did you expect? "And . . . you were surprised?" I returned.

"Well, no . . . but I don't know . . . I guess . . . I guess I don't need to go up to his apartment anymore," she conceded.

"Um, yeah, that would be wise."

"You're being judgmental—I don't appreciate it!" Keri shot back.

"I'm judgmental? Whatever," I snapped.

The whole Girl-Scout-buddy-system thing was her idea. She was the one who had made up the rule and then didn't follow it. Why was she wasting her time with a guy who wasn't Messianic anyway? He was Jewish but didn't hold to her Messianic Jewish beliefs that Jesus was the Jewish Messiah. She would never consider him for a serious relationship. She was just stringing him along, allowing him to dote on her. Annoyed with me, Keri rose from the floor and went to the refrigerator in search of her daily dose of cookie dough.

It never occurred to me that I was doing the exact same thing to August that Keri was doing to Eran—allowing him to pursue me, knowing good and well that I wasn't serious about him. But somehow, I rationalized my outings with August. August and I were just hanging out; we weren't even dating. Unlike Eran, August hadn't tried to kiss me. He hadn't even tried to hold my hand, or do anything—except get me to marry him. August was a gentleman. I couldn't say that about many guys I knew. So I told myself that was okay. He was safe, so I could hang out with him as often as I liked. Nothing was going to happen. At the end of every outing with him, I always wanted to hug him—squeeze him tight like a teddy bear. Nothing more.

Besides, I suspected that August was on the rebound, which made it all the easier for me to dismiss his hasty marriage proposal and romantic intentions. One night while we were hanging out he had said, "There's only one other person that I've ever really cared about. And you make me forget all about her."

Summer ended in a month. Soon I'd be three thousand miles away on the other side of the country. Why should I forfeit the delights of my final college summer? August was fun and unsullied by the hubris and cynicism that characterized so many guys back at school. One day, after he figured out what he wanted to do with himself, he'd be the ideal husband for some lucky woman—just not me.

Right before my last week in LA, August and I drove out to Santa Monica Pier to spend the afternoon on the beach. In a picturesque throwback to times long past, Santa Monica Pier emulated an old school boardwalk, with a giant carousel, amusement park rides, and rows of little shops and eateries. Tourists swarmed everywhere in the temperate afternoon warmth, clamoring on rides and gorging themselves on fast food. We found a spot to sit and talk as we looked back toward the pier and gazed upon the giant Ferris wheel.

"I'm running away," August announced.

Aren't you a little old for that? I thought. In my book, if you left your parents' house after the age of eighteen, that was called "moving out," not running away.

"Running away to where?" I asked.

"I haven't decided," he replied.

"Hmmm . . . why?"

"What?"

"Why are you running away?"

Silence followed. I don't think he'd pinpointed the impetus for his decision to take flight.

Months later, August would come to visit me at Penn. I think he was still living with his parents; he hadn't run away. I hoped his short visit would help him understand the point I had tried to make that summer. At Penn, he had little to add to the discussions taking place all around him. Keri frequently extolled the merits of feminism and Zionism, sighting obscure passages from her latest reading. Meanwhile, Milan confidently rattled off his personal thesis about the economic consequences of sociopolitical forces shredding Yugoslavia into angry, murderous separatist regions. August was in over his head. He hadn't formulated his own opinions about life and discovered his passions yet. He needed to get out of Beverly Hills and do something that would result in genuine self-discovery. We lost touch shortly after he visited me at school.

That summer, my final week in Westwood ended perfectly, with a boisterous V Society reunion. Michelle finished her summer mission project in San Diego and made the trip north to cram into our now busting-at-the-seams one-bedroom apartment. After a purposeful summer doing missionary work, she was the only one among us not swept up in the idle thrills of a long, lazy, boy-crazy summer.

"So, were there any interesting guys on your mission team?" I asked.

"Did you meet anyone?" Keri interjected excitedly.

"No, not really," Michelle answered, smiling.

"Really? Not even *one* interesting guy?" Stephanie pressed.

"No," Michelle assured us. "I made a couple friends, but you know— that's it. How about you guys?"

Stephanie, Keri, and I sighed, looked at each other, and laughed. Where should we start—Eran, August, Matt, Keri's Café Miro crew, me stalking the fashionista-guy, or my meltdown in the convenience store stoked by the Big Beautiful Black Athlete?

"Not much to tell," Keri laughed. For all our drama, dates, and non-dates, none of us had a single juicy story to detail. What could we say about all the guys we hadn't kissed that summer?

The next morning a familiar noise jolted all four of us awake.

"Why is the stereo on?" Michelle moaned.

"It's not on," Stephanie replied.

"That's Keri's boyfriend," I joked. "Yeah, he thinks it's cute to blast his stereo at SEVEN IN THE MORING!"

I wished I knew where the circuit breaker for Eran's apartment was located. If I could have magically switched off his power without getting up off my futon, I'd have done it. More moans and groans echoed around the room as the four of us tried to sleep despite the vocals penetrating every corner of our slumbering space. Finally, the song ended, shrill and unexpected, like the rooster's morning crow. I rolled over and went back to sleep.

Sometime before noon, we all got up and tossed around plans for the day. We decided to head toward the beach and follow whatever whim moved us. En route to Venice Beach we stopped at a makeshift garage sale on the side of the road. Stephanie, Mich, and Keri tried on vintage dresses that they forced, to my amusement, over bulky cut-off jean shorts and T-shirts. Stephanie and Michelle paraded around in a slew of assorted vintage clogs and stilettos. They stood still just long enough for me to snap pictures.

We arrived at Venice Beach, greeted by an endless flow of colorful characters. I covertly photographed a handful of the most original passersby. I fired off a shot of a long-haired, bearded old hippie guy wearing white sneakers, black socks, and black running shorts and waving a huge American flag overlay by a hand-drawn illustration. He looked like he might be on something, despite the fact that his black T-shirt read "D.A.R.E. TO KEEP KIDS OFF DRUGS." I quietly snapped another photo of a heavyset African American woman wearing a large, bejeweled straw sombrero that she'd retrofitted with a Cat in the Hat–style hat covered in rainbow and polka-dot cloth. She wore hoop earrings the size of small pizzas. A middle-aged white guy with a 1970s moustache and a small beer belly zipped past us on old-school roller skates, wearing tiny yellow jogging shorts and aviator sunglasses. I snapped a shot of an ancient-looking man with long white hair and a wild white beard. He looked like Santa Claus after a long journey at sea without sunscreen. His skin shone, weathered and bronzed in the glowing ambient light. Venice Beach was one of my favorite places in LA. It reminded me of Telegraph Avenue in Berkeley—a carnival sideshow, but on the beach.

The four of us whipped through some of the old storefront shops. We bumbled around a thrift store where we tried on outfits and photographed each other in contorted poses with mischievous grins.

"Hey, we've got to buy a pair of these," I exclaimed. Mich and I stood in front of a mirror outside the dressing rooms, wearing matching over-size denim overalls.

"Here's five bucks toward the overalls," Mich smiled.

"Here," Keri beamed, handing me several more dollar bills.

I paid the difference, and we walked out with our collective purchase. Overalls were in fashion at the time; and the three of us shared the pair throughout the following school year. We halted our thrift store raid just long enough to enjoy a meal at an outdoor restaurant near the beach. Then we headed back to Westwood for a final hurrah at the bungalow with the interns. In the next few days, we ran wild, throwing ourselves headfirst into a whirlwind summer finale.

I sold my futon to a new student moving into our apartment building just before Keri, Michelle, and I packed our bags and caught a flight up to the San Francisco Bay area. Stephanie stayed in LA a few days longer, wrapping up her internship, before she headed back to the East Coast. We would meet up with her at school in the next week or so.

Meanwhile, Keri and Michelle visited with me and my family for a few days in Northern California.

The day after we arrived, Mich, Keri, and I took off on a road trip to Santa Cruz Beach Boardwalk, accompanied by Nick, my old friend from high school. On the drive down, we found inspiration in a large gray rock quarry on the roadside. We pulled over, spontaneously invigorated to pose as abstract rock sculptures sprouting from the ocean of stones. As always, I documented it on film—more quirky pictures for my ever-growing college photo album. The four of us spent the early part of the day mulling around Santa Cruz's boardwalk. Eventually, we settled down on the beach, amidst the other sunbathers, in a patch of gently sloping sand. We stripped down to our swimsuits and lay sprawled side by side on our bright, oversized beach towels. Sun-drenched and content, I dozed off in a light sleep in the midday warmth while Nick chatted away with Keri and Michelle.

Hours later, we roused from the beach, stirred by hunger. As the sun sank lower in the clear summer sky, we meandered slowly past the shops and storefronts before wandering into a small Mexican restaurant. After eating, we emerged to the sun setting and the sky aflame in a kaleidoscope of scarlet and orange. The four of us cruised home along the dark highway, humming loudly and singing off key to the sounds of our favorite tunes.

I spent the remaining days playing tour guide to Keri and Michelle, ferrying them to all my favorite spots and the best tourist places in San Francisco. Just days before move-in day at school, Keri and Michelle returned home to the East Coast, ending our perfect summer.

V Society, Best of Los Angeles
Summer before Senior Year

OUR FAVORITE THINGS DURING THE SUMMER BEFORE SENIOR YEAR

SUMMER HOME
Midvale Avenue

Westwood Village

SUMMER NICKNAMES
Stephanie: Fannie

Adele: Slappy (Ugly)

Keri: Skeri

Michelle: (S)melly

Nick: Nickster the Trickster

SUMMER HANGOUTS (AND PLACES WE WISHED WE HUNG OUT BUT DIDN'T)
Café Miro {every single day}

Diddy Riese

Sunset Boulevard

Melrose Avenue

Third Street Promenade

Westside Pavilion

Venice Beach

Alice's Restaurant

West & North Hollywood

Manning Avenue Bungalow
The Roxbury
The Whiskey
The Living Room

FAVORITE MUSIC

"D__ I Wish I Was Your Lover" by Sophie B. Hawkins
"Stay" by Shakespeare's Sister
"A Letter to Elise" by the Cure
"Remedy" by the Black Crowes
Thirtysomething soundtrack

SUMMER JOBS

Paramount {Stephanie}
Oaktree {Adele}
Hanging out at Café Miro {Keri}
CCC mission project {Michelle}

MEMORABLE MOMENTS

Getting Kicked out of the Roxbury
Adventures in Beverly Hills
*Waking up at 7:00 a.m., Eran (our neighbor)
is playing Kate Bush way too loud AGAIN!*

SUMMER TRIPS

San Francisco
Santa Cruz

Act Three

senior year

————— ✍ —————

Chapter Fourteen

SEXY AND THE "NUNS FROM HELL"

{August–September, First Semester of Senior Year}

"I CAN'T BELIEVE IT. THIS IS GOING TO BE THE WORST SEMESTER EVER! My new roommates suck. I'm rooming with the Nuns from HELL!" Noel hissed into the phone receiver.

Thanks to the university housing department, Noel was our new randomly assigned roommate. She didn't think anyone could hear her from behind the closed door of her room, but Keri heard. Keri had just explained to her the only two rules that we had in the apartment.

Rule #1: No smoking inside the apartment.

Rule #2: No guys sleeping over, unless he's a friend from out of town.

Noel hated us, but I didn't care. She rarely came home the first week of school. When she did come home, she retreated immediately into her room and closed the door. I paid her no attention. It was senior year, and I planned to have the best year of my life.

Unfortunately, our intended roommate, my friend Amy had backed out on us a couple weeks before school started. After returning from a semester abroad, she decided to live off campus senior year.

"Maybe we won't get a replacement roommate," I suggested in an attempt to console Keri and Michelle after we received the news from Amy toward the end of summer.

"That's really lame that she bailed at the last minute," Keri remarked.

"I know—I'm sorry," I apologized.

Keri and Michelle didn't know Amy. I'd met Amy during my Habitat for Humanity stint during spring break junior year. Michelle and Keri had taken my word that she would be a great roommate, and now she'd left us in the lurch.

"There's a good chance the housing department won't assign anyone to our room. We're seniors. They would only assign another upperclassman. I doubt any seniors will suddenly need housing at the last minute . . . right?" Michelle surmised.

"Right!" I agreed heartily.

We weren't so lucky. Just before move-in, a letter arrived from the university housing department. Four people were assigned to 2110 High Rise South: me, Keri, Michelle, and a fourth person named Noel Jean-Baptiste—a fellow senior and a complete stranger. With over two thousand students in the senior class, most of our classmates were strangers.

On move-in day, Keri and Michelle had arrived on campus before me. They were already unpacking their boxes when I shoved a mail cart full of my luggage up to our apartment door. The university housing department graciously provided an army of large rolling mail carts on move-in days. The deep bucket-shaped canvas carts could carry huge loads in a single trip.

"Hey, hey, hey!" I yelled as I turned my key in the lock of our apartment—the same one we'd occupied all last year.

"Hi!" Keri and Michelle hollered back before we tackled each other and fell on the sofa in a big group hug.

Home sweet home.

"Milan left us a note," Keri recalled as she untangled herself. She rose and handed me a slip of paper. "He left it under the door."

The note read, "Where are you guys? I stopped by, but you weren't home. Call me as soon as you get in." It was signed Milan and dated yesterday. He'd scribbled his new phone number at the bottom.

"That's a surprise," I remarked.

"I know. I guess he missed us this summer," Michelle joked.

"Yeah, maybe so," Keri chuckled.

"Did you call him?" I asked.

"No," Keri replied. "You can call him."

"Let me unpack some things, then I'll call."

I dragged my two enormous overstuffed suitcases and bulging carry-ons into the double bedroom that Keri and I would share for the semester. Michelle and Noel would occupy the single rooms that term.

Within the hour, the phone rang. Michelle answered. It was Milan.

"He's coming over," she said after a short conversation.

Within the hour, Milan arrived. He looked great. Amidst all the sunny diversions of Los Angeles, I'd forgotten all the details that made his presence so pleasing.

"Hey, what's up?" He smiled. Milan hugged each of us and sat down on the sofa. Three months had passed since I last saw that familiar face—with its dark features, smug and sublime. I took one look at Milan and all the boys of summer vanished like erased chalk sketches—forgotten. It was as though summer had never happened.

"How was your summer?" he asked.

"Great," I replied. "LA was a blast."

"We had a great time," Keri added.

"San Diego was nice too," Mich answered.

"How was your summer?" I asked.

"Good," he grinned. He seemed refreshed—all his surly grouchiness evaporated in the prolonged absence. Maybe he really had missed us.

"Where are you living this year?" I asked.

"Off campus." His new apartment was several blocks away in the surrounding West Philadelphia neighborhood.

Milan stayed for a couple hours before he left to let us finish unpacking.

Our new roommate Noel arrived the following day. Before I observed anything else about her, I noticed her hair. It was huge—a full forest of marvelous, naturally flowing black waves. It almost swallowed up the keen, attractive features of her face. She was brown-skinned, about a shade darker than me, and petite in build. We were about the same height.

"Hi, I'm Adele," I said with a smile.

"Hi. Noel," she replied evenly.

Noel regarded me with suspicion the first few weeks of school. She couldn't seem to figure out Michelle, Keri, and me. What was the matter with us? We looked like regular college students. Our friends seemed normal enough. But what kind of normal college students banned overnight male guests? It didn't add up. There had to be something wrong with us. Throughout the first few weeks of school, she kept her distance and tried to figure out what was amiss beneath our guise of normalcy.

Noel held no affinity for us, but she quickly recognized the benefits of civility toward Keri. Keri was a marvelous ally in screening unwanted phone calls. Soon after we moved in, Noel started receiving phone calls from some guy she had dated the previous semester—usually late at night. One evening around ten o'clock, the phone rang. Keri answered.

"Is Noel there?" the male caller asked.

Keri looked at Noel, who occasionally popped out of her room to speak to Keri, though she said little to Michelle or me.

"Who is it? Find out if it's *him*," Noel implored.

"Who's calling?" Keri replied.

"CJ."

"It's *him*," Keri mouthed to Noel.

"No, I'm not here," Noel whispered back.

"Sorry, she's not available. May I take a message?"

"Tell her CJ called. You know when she'll be back?"

"Well, I'll certainly give her the message, CJ," Keri answered sweetly before hanging up.

CJ called again several days later. Again, Keri answered the phone.

"Hey, whassup—is Noel there?" he asked.

"Sorry, she's not available," Keri replied.

"And you don't know when she'll be back, right?"

"No, I can't say for sure."

"Hmm," CJ sighed. "Seems like I talk to you everyday. What's your name, anyway?"

"Keri."

"Hi, Keri. I'm CJ." Then he laughed. "But you already knew that."

"Indeed I did," Keri laughed back.

"So, what's going on over there? I mean what are you up to—besides never knowing when your roommate is coming home?" he asked.

"Well, actually, I'm getting ready for a sushi party tomorrow night."

"You're going to a sushi party?"

"No, my roommates and I are throwing a sushi party tomorrow night. You should come by," Keri invited. "I'm making the sushi."

"Really? That's pretty cool. Seriously, you're making the sushi?"

"Yes—seriously. It's all vegetarian, but I'm making the sticky rice right now."

"So, what time is the party?"

"Around seven tomorrow evening."

"Where?"

"2110 High Rise South."

"I might just have to come check it out. Really, you're making the sushi yourself?"

"Yep," Keri assured him.

"2110 High Rise South. Cool. I guess I may see you in person to-morrow."

"Okay, bye."

"Bye."

Keri walked into the room we shared, where I lay on my upper bunk, reading a book and listening to music.

"Hey, I think Sexy might be coming to our party tomorrow," she called up at me.

I sat up quickly, suddenly filled with disbelief and nervous excite-ment. I leaned over the bunk to look down at Keri.

"*What?* Sexy? Here? You're kidding."

"No, I'm serious. This guy CJ keeps calling for Noel, and I invited him to our party. I didn't know what he looked like, so just now I asked Noel to describe him. He sounds like Sexy."

"No way!" I couldn't believe my good fortune. Of the hundreds of random hot guys roaming campus, was it really possible that Sexy was coming to our apartment?

"Ask Noel to describe him," Keri encouraged.

I climbed down out of my bunk quickly.

"Noel doesn't exactly talk to me," I said.

"Well, you want to know if it's him, don't you?"

"Yeah!" Of course, I wanted to know if it was him. I'd have to look super cute at the party if Sexy planned to come.

I followed Keri back into the living room, pretending to be interested only in talking to her.

"Hey," I said to Noel, who sat on the sofa in a red one-piece pajama jumpsuit.

"Hey," she replied.

"Noel, CJ has sideburns and longish dark curly hair, right?" Keri asked.

"Yep," she replied.

"Does he wear motorcycle boots?" I asked.

"All the time."

"And does he have a nice tan-colored suede jacket? And he always carries a brown, leather European-style schoolbag?"

"Uh-huh," Noel replied. She looked amused. "You know him?" she asked.

"Nope." She waited for me to give some sort of explanation for my list of questions. "I've just seen him around," I replied indifferently. I didn't want her to know about my secret Sexy infatuation. Inside I did backflips. I couldn't believe that at the same time the very next night he might be sitting in my living room.

The sushi party couldn't arrive soon enough. Had it not been for the pure unadulterated satisfaction of wrapping Milan in Saran wrap earlier that day, the time between Thursday evening and Friday night might have been the longest day of the year. Why was I getting so excited? Sexy probably wouldn't even show up. *Don't get all worked up over nothing*, I told myself. *He's just a guy* . . . Just the sexiest guy in the entire school!

Finally, Friday arrived. The last hour of daylight slipped away quickly while Keri rolled and sliced the final sushi rolls. We scrambled to straighten the room, leaving no stray books or study notes in sight. I straightened the abstract poster framed on pink poster board hanging on the living room wall. My reproduction of a colorful Romare Bearden collage, black ladies in fancy hats accompanied by brown-skinned men in dark suits, hung evenly on the opposite wall.

We'd arranged an assortment of red paper plates, soft drinks, plastic cups, and vegetable appetizers on the portable table in the front of the room. A tablecloth lay draped over the table, forcing elegance into our tidy but unspectacular dorm room. Michelle tucked the large, ivory-colored, flora-and-fauna-decorated piece of fabric covering the sofa snugly into the sofa's seams and draped the overhanging edges neatly over the armrests. The fabric served as a makeshift slipcover to hide the standard-issue dorm couch.

Soon we were dressed and ready. Within thirty minutes, our place buzzed, full of cheerful friends chowing down on Keri's sushi rolls, laughing and telling us about their summers. Even Noel decided to stick around. She chatted with Milan, while I showed a few guests the photos I'd taken in LA over the summer. Our place was packed, but Sexy still hadn't arrived. I was simultaneously disappointed and relieved.

"I can't believe you made sushi from scratch," Marko declared, upon arriving with several other of our Balkan guy friends. They ran in a loose clan of Bulgarian, Macedonian, and Serbian students.

"It's only vegetarian sushi," Keri replied modestly.

Milan sat in our big red canvas chair. "Zdravo," he called out, greeting the Balkan crew. Translation: "Hello."

"Did you bring the rakija?" Marko joked with Milan, referring to the Balkan moonshine they drank during their late-night, chain-smoking, male-bonding sessions.

Darian and his roommate Barry, two friendly black students down the hall, soon followed the Balkan boys.

"Hello, ladies," Darian greeted us warmly.

"Hi, Darian," Keri and I replied in unison.

Stephanie's friend Jenn arrived right behind Darian and Barry. She reminded me of a night-light. Her dyed platinum-blonde bob glowed electric, making her easy to follow wherever she moved in the room. The door swung open again and again in quick succession. No one bothered to knock. Our laughter and muffled voices were audible in the hallway outside; everyone knew the party was in full swing behind the door. Stephanie returned with her acoustic guitar and her cousin Sandra. Julie, a friend from the eighteenth floor, followed them. Viktor, a Russian friend of ours, strolled in immediately afterward.

"Hello, Me-shell," Viktor said with a thick Russian accent before kissing Michelle on the cheek.

"Privyet. Kak dyela?" she replied. She sounded each syllable out clearly, pree-vyet, kahk dee-lah. Translation: "Hello. How are you?" in Russian.

"Your accent is getting very good," Viktor smiled. "Not bad for—what?—your second year of Russian."

Just as I'd convinced myself that my crush was a no-show, our door swung open again. Two guys stood in the doorway—one with a crazy white-boy Afro—and *Sexy*. They entered. Keri greeted them, and she stood talking to Sexy CJ nearby in the kitchen area. CJ looked perfect, like he'd just stepped off a New York runway. Somehow, he married American grunge fashion with European style so his look appeared sophisticated, but earthy. He was just unkempt enough to give the impression that he didn't *try* to look good. But his all-black outfit—fine-knit long-sleeved shirt, jeans, and leather boots—probably came with a hefty price tag. It was difficult not to stare. His entire being exuded raw, grungy, masculine sensuality.

"Are you the host?" Sexy asked Keri.

"Yes," she replied. "I'm Keri."

"Hi, I'm CJ," he replied before stuffing a sushi roll in his mouth.

Keri looked at me seated on the sofa nearby and smiled.

"So, what are you studying?" she asked him.

"I'm in Wharton." Wharton was the university's business school. "And you? What are you studying?"

"Folklore."

"Folklore?" CJ asked, surprised. "I didn't know there *was* a folklore major."

"There are only two folklore majors in our entire class," Keri returned proudly.

"That's cool. So, what else are you into besides folklore?"

"Well, I'm studying feminism." That year Keri would investigate Jewish and Christian patriarchal interpretations of Scripture. "If God made man—male and female—in his image, then there has got to be more in the Scriptures to nurture strong, healthy women. That's what I'm interested in—finding the ways in which God sees women, in contrast to the messed-up, patriarchal reality that we know today."

She failed to mention the habit that had become the largest outward signifier, in my mind, of her feminism: she loved to crank up Ani Di-Franco, the angry, feminist folk singer with the shaved head.

"Feminism—that's cool. Yeah, haven't read much of the Torah since my bar mitzvah," CJ smirked. He surveyed the small room full of partygoers. "Looks like you have a nice little party going on here," he remarked.

"Yeah, it seems to have turned out okay," Keri smiled.

"When I heard you girls were having a sushi party, I thought I'd better come check it out," CJ said.

"So, where are you from?" Keri asked.

"Brazil originally, but I moved around a bit growing up. Mostly, I grew up just outside Chicago."

"Your family is from Brazil?" Keri asked.

"Uh, yeah, sort of. They lived there awhile, but that's not where they're originally from. Anyway . . . long story, not worth getting into right now. They're pretty cool though, my parents—good people."

"How about you? Where are you from?"

"Philadelphia."

"That's cool," CJ said, downing another sushi roll.

"So, how do like Wharton?"

"It's all right. I mean, you know—I always knew I'd end up here."

"It was your first-choice school?"

"Duh—yeah," CJ returned.

At that point, I lost track of the conversation. The music playing on our stereo hit a particularly loud note and drowned out Keri's reply.

I didn't want to appear eager, so I decided to wait half an hour before I introduced myself to him. I couldn't believe it. After an entire semester of admiring him from afar, Sexy was in my apartment, eating sushi and talking to Keri. This *was* going to be a good school year.

As I turned my attention away from them and back to my own neglected conversation, I couldn't help thinking that everything about CJ intrigued me. And later, when I had the chance to speak with him myself, I quickly realized that everything about him exuded deviousness as well. He was a gifted prodigy of guile.

On the other side of the room, near our small television set, Michelle chatted with Ethan, a friend of hers from high school who now studied nearby at Haverford College. Doug Chan stood beside Michelle, towering over her like a gentle giant.

"Organic chemistry is pretty tough this semester," Michelle remarked.

"Somehow, I doubt that it's getting the best of you," Ethan reassured her.

"Professor Dunn?" Doug inquired. "Oh, no, isn't Bannor teaching this term? He *is* rough."

"Not too rough for Michelle," Ethan interjected. "The girl was valedictorian of our high school class. There were over seven hundred students in our class. Trust me, if anyone can ace advanced organic chem, it's Michelle."

"You were valedictorian, Michelle?" Doug replied, surprised. "You have never, *ever* mentioned that."

"It's no big deal," Michelle shrugged. "That's not something I usually tell people."

Noel stood toward the back of the room, talking to Milan. Her marvelous, streaming black hair framed her silhouette.

"So, did you know Michelle, Adele, and Keri already?" Milan asked.

"No. I was assigned to their room at the last minute. I guess their fourth roommate came back from a semester in England and decided she'd rather live off campus senior year—so I got assigned to her spot."

"They're cool girls, no?"

"I don't know. They're kind of conservative."

"Conservative?"

"Yeah, they have a no-guys-sleeping-over rule, unless he's a friend from out of town."

"That's not such a bad rule," Milan chuckled.

"Well, I don't think I'm going to stay *here*," Noel retorted.

"Give them a chance. Just get to know them."

"So, where are you from?" she asked, changing the subject.

"Yugoslavia. And you?"

"Miami."

"You're *originally* from Miami?"

"No, I'm originally from Haiti. But my uncle and his wife—they live in Miami. They raised me from about the time I was five.

"You like them?"

"My uncle is great. His wife—not so great. We don't really get along."

"Hmmm. Yeah. Family is always interesting," Milan admitted.

Our party was a perfect blend of Keri, Michelle, and my multicultural, multifaceted, intersecting worlds: friends from Penn Film and Video

Club, our mutual friends from Bible study, and a random assortment of allies we'd made along the way. I sat amidst them all, thoroughly enjoying myself.

As the party rolled into the evening, Keri introduced herself to the guy with the wiry Afro who had come in with CJ. His name was Jesse, and he downloaded his entire life story to Keri as she listened politely and attentively.

"Yeah, I still have LSD flashbacks," Jesse mused, his face serious and pensive. "I never know when one is coming. They just happen sometimes for no reason."

"What do you mean? You can just be walking down the street, and all of a sudden you'll have an LSD flashback from a couple years ago?" Keri asked quietly.

"Yeah, something like that," Jesse replied. "Flashbacks can recur in our system for years. But, I was always totally in control when I used LSD. I was aware of everything that was going on around me. I was looking for clarity—a clearer picture of reality." Then Jesse paused, as though he were deep in thought. "But CJ, *he's* out of control."

Jesse leaned in close to Keri as though he were sharing information from a top-secret FBI file. "I think CJ may be *crazy!*" he said in a low voice. Then he nodded his head in a display of self-assurance and leaned back into the chair, looking reflective.

While I waited for the right opportunity to approach CJ, I sat on the sofa, flanked by a handful of guests who had asked to see my photography portfolio. Some were seated, and some stood in order to peer over the heads of those seated as I thumbed through images. I stopped to explain a black-and-white fashion portrait I'd taken over the summer. From out of the corner of my eye, I noticed Keri snapping pictures of me. We always liked to document our social successes.

Finally, enough time had passed for me to safely approach the object of my long-distance affections. "Hey," I said. "Welcome. I'm Adele. I live here."

"Hi," he replied. "You're Keri's roommate?"

"Right."

"Are you friends with Latonya?" he sneered.

"No." Surprisingly, I knew whom he referred to. Latonya was one of the most glamorous undergraduates in the entire school. She looked dead-on like supermodel Naomi Campbell; everything—from her long, straight black hair to her deep chocolate skin tone—was identical. The only difference between Naomi Campbell and Latonya was that Latonya was about five feet tall, much shorter than the world-famous model. It should have been obvious that Latonya and I weren't friends. She didn't run with ordinary people. She moved in a posse of glamorous, stylish black girls. Once, when she said hi to me, I was pleasantly shocked and awed that she'd acknowledged my existence. Truthfully, I wouldn't dare stand next to her. On my best day, I'd be an ugly duckling in comparison to her.

"You don't know her?" CJ repeated.

"I know who she is. But we aren't friends. I don't hang out with her," I retorted, trying not to sound defensive.

He looked unconvinced. Clearly, he had some sort of serious beef with her. When he mentioned her name, the contempt spewed like a gushing fire hose. His lip curled, and his eyes squinted in scorn. Any normal person would have let the unpleasant dialogue go after I denied association with her. Any other student would have moved on to more polite, superficial conversation. But not CJ. He seemed bent on needling me. Since Latonya wasn't the expected point of contention, he struck out in another direction.

"So, are you a wannabe?" he asked.

This guy had some nerve! He was trying hard to offend me and get me ticked off. Somewhere, he'd learned that this line of questioning was a hot button for light-skinned black girls, and he was preying on me.

Wannabe referred to "wanting to be white," when you were biracial—a white parent and a black parent. Or was it the other way around—wannabes wanted to be 100 percent black when in fact they had inherited a mixed ancestry? But CJ wasn't going to get a rise out of me with

that one. My personal identity wasn't laced with minefields, waiting to
be tripped by an insensitive provocateur. I was black, my parents were
black, and I liked being black. I had always felt good about being me.
A lack of love for my African American heritage was not one of my
problems.

When I was five years old, I attended a summer camp hosted by
my predominantly white private school. A boy called me "blackface." I
wasn't filled with shame or hurt. I knew he was going to be in trouble
because I held the power. I was going to tell on him, and the teachers
would punish him publicly and immediately. I told on him, and like
a SWAT team, the forces dispersed to track down the perpetrator and
bring him to justice.

In third grade, Darin, a gangly, unpopular white fourth grader called
me "blackface" again. I resolved the situation quickly and neatly. I was
at the same small school I'd attended since age three, and I knew the
all-white teaching staff would come to my aid. All I had to do was tell
on Darin and immediately he'd be punished. But that day, there was no
need to involve teachers. Darin was two years older than me and several inches taller, but he was a wimp—and desperately in need of some
ethnic sensitivity lessons. I decided to school him.

"Come here," I said, luring him around the corner, behind the sec-
ond-grade classroom. Every recess, the teachers stood in the middle
of the three-pronged playground. From this position, they had a 270-
degree view of the kids to the north, south, and west. But, in the field
to the south, we students knew we could step just behind the classroom
buildings and be hidden from the teachers' sight. (Years later, in fifth
grade, this spot would be immortalized as I received my first, quick on-
the-lips kiss from my "boyfriend" Todd.)

"What did you say to me?" I asked Darin, giving him the chance to
retract his statement. Before he could answer, he made the mistake of
stepping behind the building, closer to me and out of the teacher's sight.

Wham! My fist hit the side of his jaw with full force. Like a leaf,
his skinny body teetered, and he swayed left, in the direction in which

I had propelled him. Time stopped just long enough for Darin to realize he'd been hit. *Bam!* My other fist delivered a swift uppercut into his gut. Darin fell down for the count. The ethnic sensitivity lesson had been delivered articulately.

Before sending me off to school, my father had ensured that his tiny girl possessed basic self-defense skills. He taught me to box. As a child, he showed me how to make a good fist and deliver a whopping punch. Darin became the beneficiary of my well-learned instruction.

So, fifteen years later, as this ill-mannered boy, CJ, sat as a guest in my living room and attempted to disrespect me, the host of the sushi party, he could make no headway. He was like a guest passing gas at the table in the middle of dinner. His lack of propriety was uncivil, and he had embarrassed himself—not me. I cut the conversation short and moved on. He was so obnoxious.

Later that evening, our sushi party wound down. Aside from my conversation with CJ, it had been a great night.

"Great party!" Michelle exclaimed.

"Keri, your sushi is now legendary! I think congratulations are in order," I beamed.

"Indeed!"

We laughed and fell back on the sofa next to each other, exhausted.

Michelle squeezed me. Keri wrapped her arms around Michelle. I hugged both of them. Soon we were all entangled, piled on top of each other, with arms and legs overlapped and intertwined around each other in a messy group hug.

"So, you finally met Greasy—I mean, Sexy," Michelle teased.

"Yuck. I'm *so* over him," I replied, disgusted. "What a disappointment."

"He's interesting, though," Keri added.

"Yeah, interesting—until he opened his mouth," I shot back. "A man can be so beautiful and perfect until he starts talking and ruins everything."

Michelle and Keri sighed knowingly in agreement. "So true."

"Delie, I got great pictures of you," Keri exclaimed.

"Yeah, I saw you taking my picture."

"Are you kidding? I couldn't miss that for anything."

"What?"

"What do you mean *what*? You! You surrounded by all those guys, totally enthralled in your photographs."

"Guys?" I asked.

"Like you weren't paying attention! There were five guys gathered all around you at the same time," Keri explained.

"Really?" I honestly hadn't noticed that the group was all guys. I was so focused on answering the slew of questions about the photographs.

"Hello—*clueless*," Michelle laughed.

"Well, what about you and Sexy?" I asked Keri. "You looked like you were having a good conversation."

"You mean CJ? We can't call him Greasy or Sexy now that we know his real name. He said he's going to come back and fix us all crepes."

"That's nice," Michelle remarked. "I think we should still call him Greasy, though. I *still* don't think he washes his hair."

"Whatever—I guess," I replied in reference to CJ's crepe-making promise. Who cared if he fixed crepes? My infatuation was cured.

"So, Mich, what about you and your Russian fan club?" I laughed.

"Up Keri's butt," she returned. "What do you know?"

I don't remember how it came to be, but whenever anything was lost or someone referred to something fictitious, its origins were ascribed to a black hole. We referred to that place as "up Keri's butt."

"Actually, I think Doug is her secret admirer," Keri grinned.

"He is not," Michelle sassed back. "He's a really great guy and a good friend. I like him a lot, but he doesn't think of me that way."

"Okay, whatever you say—*more* clueless." I laughed.

After the party, I planned never to talk to CJ again. But a few days later, he returned to the apartment to cook us crepes as he'd promised. Keri, Michelle, and Stephanie made him feel welcome. They didn't know about our sushi-party conversation; I hadn't mentioned the details. The episode seemed trivial in light of an otherwise wonderful party.

CJ's hair covered his entire face as he hunched over, fervently mixing the crepe batter. Noel mocked him as he sat in our wooden kitchen chair bent over one of our pink plastic mixing bowls.

"Here's CJ making crepes," she teased. She took the bowl from him and then pulled all her hair over her face and leaned over the pink bowl, stirring like a mad man. She looked just like CJ. We couldn't help but laugh.

CJ hadn't brought any of his own ingredients for the crepes. He used our flour, eggs, and everything else that he needed. But, despite mooching our ingredients, he behaved himself the entire visit. He was pleasant to me the whole time. Perhaps he had realized that Michelle, Keri, and Stephanie were my partners in crime, not Latonya. Maybe he'd decided I was okay, now that he'd disassociated me from the hated girl group. Who knew?

Either way, I was cured of my infatuation with him. But after a whole semester of admiring him from afar, I still liked gazing at the sexy boy. I didn't mind watching him flip crepes in a skillet over my stove. Homemade crepes seemed an acceptable peace offering. I ate one of the skinny pancakes and tried to forget that he'd gotten off to such a bad start.

It turned out to be a good thing that I didn't hold a grudge, because CJ kept coming back to our apartment. Soon he camped out in the living room regularly, talking to Keri or Stephanie or whoever was home.

And that's how fall semester of my senior year began. I was cured of my crush on Sexy Greasy. He assumed his real name—CJ—and became the newest addition to the circle of misfits gathering in 2110 High Rise South.

Chapter Fifteen

BOY FRIENDS

{September–October, Senior Year}

THAT AUTUMN THE ACTIVITIES IN OUR APARTMENT UNFOLDED to a new tune as old habits reinvented themselves in tandem with new-fangled developments. Stephanie reclaimed her position as our honorary fifth roommate. Keri added vegetarian sushi recipes and new books to her ever-expanding library of feminist folklore literature. Michelle spent hours studying behind her closed door with the latest Sade album blaring. CJ parked regularly on our sofa, adding to the overall aesthetic appeal of the living room. Milan dropped in unannounced for impromptu visits and stimulating conversation. I continued recruiting new subjects for photo shoots. And Noel begrudgingly settled in as our new roommate, silently loathing the whole gang of us.

That semester, more students fell into orbit around our apartment. Keri and Stephanie hit it off with Jesse, CJ's friend with the wiry Afro. For some reason, both of them found his LSD tales intriguing. I wasn't all that interested in his high-minded philosophical discourse on recreational drugs. But he'd found an audience in Stephanie and Keri. The three of them also shared the same Jewish heritage. In return for Keri's objective listening ear on his latest drug use observations, Jesse readily engaged Keri in conversation about her latest Jewish feminist discoveries.

Ethan and Craig, a couple of Michelle's high school friends studying at nearby colleges, also drove out to our place periodically. I never had much to say to either of them. Ethan was a little too cerebral for me. I'm sure his IQ scored off the charts. I usually had no idea what he was talking about. If I had paid more attention to what he said, I could probably have followed him. Most of the time, however, my mind wandered to more compelling topics whenever we spoke. But Michelle and Keri seemed to enjoy his intellectual analyses of Japanese culture and whatever else interested him. Ethan was leaving for Japan during the coming semester and had plenty of advice for Keri's latest sushi recipes. Personally, I wouldn't take sushi advice from someone who wasn't Japanese, but that was my own cultural bias. Ethan was a tall, average-looking white guy; I was sure that when he returned from Japan he'd have some interesting experiences to share about his attempts to assimilate into Japanese culture.

One of the more interesting guests to appear in our living room that fall was a guy named Jonathan—a fresh-faced, blond WASP fashionista-guy from the Deep South. Jonathan was shamelessly enamored with Keri. In general, he tried to hide behind a show of callous aloofness, in his stylish jeans and expensive leather boots, but Keri turned him to pure Jell-O. Jonathan was about as un-Jewish and unhairy as a guy could be. He hardly embodied the Sasquatch of Keri's dreams, but her face lit up every time she saw him.

He'd self-consciously confessed to Keri, "I can't grow hair on my chest, no matter what I do." Jonathan hated his scrawny, pale hairless chest.

Keri and Jonathan had nothing in common except that both their fathers were ophthalmologists. But Jonathan was smitten. He didn't even mind that Keri's legs were hairier than his. That semester Keri had revived her revolt against razors. Her antishaving campaign rose like a phoenix from the flames of junior year. Unbeknown to Jonathan, she had also launched a private "burn the bra" campaign and stopped wearing a bra regularly.

"Hmmm . . . Why are your legs, um . . . well . . ." Jonathan hesitated. He struggled to politely formulate the question lingering in his mind.

"Hairy? I know," Keri told him. "I won't shave. It's unnatural."

"That's cool," Jonathan replied. She could be as hairy as a bear; he didn't care.

"He's a really nice guy," Keri told me.

I liked him. I believed a number of skeletons he kept locked away in his closet tempered his pretention. He disclosed his secrets to Keri. Naturally, she told them to me.

"He wants to be a landscape architect and start his own company."

"What's the matter with that?" I asked.

"Well, he's working for an urban planner right now, but he's embarrassed about working."

"Why?"

"Because he wants to fit in with his rich friends. They don't work."

"Oh."

"Yeah, his family is a little different. They're middle class, but they aspire to high society. They're into coming-out parties for girls, and belong to a country club."

"Coming-out parties aren't a big deal. They're kind of lame. I was a debutante in high school—it wasn't fun. I had to learn all these old-school waltzes. Then, on the big night—the cotillion—they held a huge black-tie gala, and I had to wear a big, puffy white dress. They wouldn't let me wear my hair spiked up—I hated that."

"I didn't know you were a debutante."

"Sad but true. My mom was in the cotillion, and my grandmother. I don't tell people about it—*ever*. Anyway, that's not important. What about Jonathan?"

"Well, his father's kind of . . . I don't know . . . different too."

"Different how?"

"He's a super pedantic type. He throws these huge parties and takes out his collection of expensive china pieces—hundreds of pieces—and serves weird, fancily decorated appetizers. He makes the appetizers himself."

"Like what?"

"Pâté garnished with oxtail pesto sauce."

"That's vile! " I exclaimed.

"His father thinks he's some sort of nouveau Southern fusion chef. It's embarrassing."

Keri, the Jewish Northerner, didn't fit any of Jonathan's Southern, familial, high-society WASP aspirations. And Jonathan certainly didn't fit the bill for Keri's Zionist, Hebrew-speaking, Israel-dwelling agenda. Gradually, their flirtation fizzled out. Keri wouldn't budge on her Qualities of an Ideal Husband list, which dictated her boyfriend requirements.

Michelle had a new admirer that fall too—David from Georgia (not the state of Georgia, but rather the recently independent former Soviet state). He was a good-looking, rugged blond guy. I'm not sure how she met him. He didn't attend Penn, but I think he'd befriended some Russian friends of ours. David had applied to the university, but he worked as a cab driver while he waited for his application to be accepted. He asked Michelle out several times and came by the room once or twice.

"He took me out to dinner, and I almost vomited," Michelle complained. Her nose squinched up in disgust.

"Why? What did he do?" I asked.

"He has the worst table manners of anyone I've ever met in my life. Seriously, I couldn't eat. Watching him eat made me ill," she continued.

"Really?" I laughed. "That's so gross. Did he talk with his mouth full?"

"All the time! And that wasn't even the worst part. He kept spitting stuff when he talked, and he had food dribbling out of the corner of his mouth. Uggh!" She shivered with the memory of his food-decorated lips.

It was too bad for David. He seemed nice, but Michelle blew him off. Since he wasn't a student, he couldn't just drop by our apartment whenever he pleased. Someone had to go down to the lobby and sign him into the dorm. Michelle didn't invite him up more than a couple times. She was probably afraid he'd eat a snack in our apartment and then she'd watch him and puke all over the apartment floor.

I enjoyed the new faces and impromptu gatherings that sprung up in our living room. But I always liked it best when Milan or CJ stopped by.

Milan emerged from the cocoon of summer, a magician. He'd suddenly appear at our front door and then disappear for a couple days into thin air. Then he'd reappear, only to vanish all over again. I never knew for sure when I'd see him. We didn't have cell phones, so I couldn't text him or get an instant update on his whereabouts. His new apartment off campus sat on a poorly lit street set back in a dark alcove, on a stretch of block with little student traffic. At night, it was a little scary to drop by without several friends for backup. In the daytime, he rarely seemed to be home. He was almost impossible to track down.

Milan's sporadic, unannounced visits—and my inability to control them—drove me a little crazy. Sometimes he'd call the room, but one of my roommates would answer the phone and talk to him indefinitely. By the time Michelle or Keri finished talking to him, he was usually too conversation-weary to talk to anyone else in the apartment. He'd just have to repeat the entire conversation all over again with a different roommate. I found it unsettling.

But I never spent much time dwelling on Milan's exasperating behavior, because as soon as he disappeared, CJ would appear. One mellow afternoon, CJ came over and sat in the red canvas chair talking to Keri and me. Michelle was home, but she was reading in her room. Once in a while she'd pop out to get a drink out of the fridge and add something funny to our ongoing chatter.

Michelle had just walked back into the kitchen when CJ announced, "I need to do my laundry. Can one of you help me? I don't know how to use those laundry machines."

Instinctively, I played deaf. There was no way I was helping some guy do his laundry. I didn't like doing my own laundry, much less someone else's. Besides, he was an upperclassman. Learning to do your own laundry was a lesson from Freshman Year 101. Michelle quickly disappeared back into her room. I guess she wasn't volunteering for laundry duty either.

That left Keri. "What do you need help with?" she asked. "Just stick in your clothes, pour in the detergent, and put the quarters in the slot. Then choose the temperature. But make sure you separate out the whites and darks. It's pretty simple."

"Can you just help me?" CJ begged. "I really need someone to *show* me."

"Okay," Keri agreed. The girl was a saint. CJ was enrolled in one of the most competitive academic programs in the country, but he couldn't figure out how to work a washing machine? *Please.* Keri knew that. She was just too nice to let him suffer alone.

Before he left, CJ suggested to me, "Hey, let's get coffee or something tomorrow."

"Sure," I replied casually. I couldn't believe it. All last semester I'd been dying to have coffee with him. Now it was actually going to happen.

The next day, I met CJ at Beanie's Coffeehouse. He arrived about five minutes after I did and joined me at the tiny café table. He sat close enough that I had to strategically rearrange my legs so my knees didn't bump into his underneath the table.

"Well, you wanted to have coffee with me," said CJ, smiling smugly, "so here we are."

Thank goodness my skin tone hid the usual red-face effects of a blush. Inside I blushed bright red, but outwardly I played it off like coffee with CJ was an ordinary occurrence, not the coveted prize of a longtime wish fulfilled. At last, I sat across the table from Mr. Sexy. Obviously, some-one had tipped him off that I wanted to have coffee with him. I couldn't be sure who the guilty culprit was—Stephanie, Michelle, or Keri. One of them had also leaked the existence of the V Society to him. Aside from Milan, he was the only other person in the world that knew of our secret sisterhood.

"So, what's the deal with you? What are you about?" I blurted.

My words spilled out involuntarily, like an accusation. Apparently, I'd checked my sense of reason and all of my manners at the front door of the café. I couldn't seem to reign in, much less process, the flood of conflicting emotions filling me—attraction and repulsion, hostility and admiration. In many ways, I felt overwhelmingly satisfied to be there, with *him*, the object of junior year's misplaced affection. But a sneaking sense of unease curled up next to my satisfaction. The uncomfortable residue of our very first conversation at the sushi party still hovered in my memory. He'd behaved pleasantly after that ugly conversation, but I couldn't reconcile the well-mannered CJ sitting in front of me with the malicious CJ that lurked somewhere under the surface.

"That's no way to get to know someone," he retorted, obviously taken aback by my abrupt, aggressive questioning.

"Um, yeah, uhhh . . . sorry," I mumbled, embarrassed by my behavior but still trying to act as though I had everything under control. I hoped he couldn't read my discomfort as I struggled to appear cool and indifferent.

"I have to get some water," I said, rising from the table. I needed a moment to pull myself together so I could act normal.

I meandered past two nearby café tables to the small counter and requested a glass of water from the server before returning to the table and CJ. I'd gotten a grip on myself. My initial blunder and his terse response had placed a damper on the enthusiasm I'd felt just ten minutes earlier, but there was no point in wallowing in my deflation. After all, I was on a friendly coffee outing with CJ. We could finally have a real conversation. I should find some pleasure in that. But for whatever reason, I found it hard to really enjoy myself. I was glad to be out with him, but at the same time I couldn't wait to shed his company and return home to the safety and familiarity of my apartment.

Michelle, Mandy, and I all began leading Bible studies that fall. We all took part in the student leadership team of our college fellowship. Each of us led separate weekly Bible studies made up of five or six sophomore and junior women. The girls in my Bible study were pretty cool—we usually had a good time together. In addition to delving into Scripture with them each week, I also met with each person one-on-one to chat about whatever issues she wanted to discuss relating to her spiritual growth.

At the same time, Mandy, Michelle, and I all attended a weekly women's Bible study for student leaders. Three other students besides us met weekly with Kathy, our small group leader making six of us in all. Kathy served as one of the staff members of the fellowship group we attended each week. Kathy made herself available to each of us to chat one-on-one about all our spiritual questions and dilemmas. I rarely had any deep, penetrating questions to ask her; Michelle and Keri usually helped me resolve my inquiries as soon as they popped out of my mouth.

Despite Kathy and all the other people dropping by our place, we managed to keep the V Society a guarded secret. Besides Milan and CJ, no one knew the V Society existed all school year.

A couple days after Kathy stopped by to meet with me one week, Milan stopped by for a midafternoon visit. He, Michelle, Keri, and I kicked it in the usual spot.

"Cigarettes are bad for you," Milan mused as he leaned back, relaxing comfortably into the sofa. His head tilted backward against the wall, and he gazed at the ceiling. His face turned back toward me. "I shouldn't smoke."

"I've never smoked," I returned.

"Really?" he replied. "Never?"

"Never," I restated matter-of-factly.

Keri got up to go to the bathroom, and Michelle went to retrieve a new CD from her room. Milan and I sat alone in the living room.

"Want to teach me to smoke?" I asked, half joking.

"Of course," he smiled slyly, not joking.

"I'll just try it once to see . . . you know, since I've never tried . . . ,"
I said. The thought of him as professor and me as his pupil—it was too
tempting. I consented without a second thought.

Michelle returned to the living room with a new CD in hand. Keri
remained in the bathroom as Milan and I got up and headed out of the
front door to the stairwell just outside. The concrete, fire-safe stairwell
provided the perfect place to light up without filling the entire dorm
hallway with the smell of smoke.

"Where are you going?" Michelle asked, surprised.

"I'm teaching Adele to smoke," Milan replied.

Michelle frowned ever so slightly and said nothing. Once in the stairwell, Milan pulled out a pack of cigarettes from his pocket and removed
one. He handed it to me. It felt awkward in my hand. I didn't know
what to do with it or how to hold it. I tried hard to look sophisticated,
like it was no big deal. It wasn't a big deal, really—it was just a cigarette.
I was twenty years old. It's not like I was ten and trying some intended-
for-adults-only mischief at an early age. I struggled to mask the secret
excitement that enveloped the idea of his tutelage.

In the movies, the woman always held the cigarette in her mouth,
and the guy lit it for her. But I had no idea if I was supposed to inhale or
exhale or what I was supposed to do. So I held the cigarette in my hand
and let him light it as I pinched it clumsily between my index finger
and thumb. Sensing that I had no idea what I was doing, he took out
another cigarette and held it in his hand.

"Hold it like this," he said in a low voice, instructing me reassuringly.

He let the cigarette rest gently at the intersection of his index and
middle fingers, with his palm open. I copied him and then hesitated,
waiting for further instruction.

"Okay, now inhale and then blow the smoke out through your
mouth," Milan said.

I lifted the cigarette to my lips as he watched me expectantly. I sucked in gently and felt my nostrils and mouth fill with the taste of burning trash.

"Ewwww," I exclaimed and coughed. I looked at him, disappointed.

"Nasty, huh?" he said knowingly. He took the cigarette out of my hand and put it out for me.

We returned to the apartment and made no mention of my anticlimactic smoking lesson. For a brief moment, a window had cracked into Milan, revealing a layer of warmth beneath the dispassionate facade. It was a rare occasion when Milan openly displayed sensitivity. Once, I'd run into him on Locust Walk just after Keri and I had a small disagreement.

"Hey, what's the matter?" Milan asked tenderly, as he peered into my face.

"Nothing," I snapped.

"Nothing?" he inquired gently. "Then why is your face all frowned up?"

"It is?" I replied.

"You know, you can tell me if anything is bothering you," he assured me. His eyes softened as a look of genuine concern swept across his face.

But as soon as he shared those brief words of comfort, his guard went back up. I could never be sure about anything with Milan. His mood swung by the hour. Often he acted like he didn't care about anything or anyone. He'd stay away for a day or two, but he always returned. He seemed incapable of disappearing for long periods. Something always drew him back and drew him in.

Maybe he felt safe in 2110 High Rise South. Maybe it was the same sanctuary for him that it was for the V Society—a place where he could be himself and be free from all the clamor that waited to gobble him up in the competitive environment outside our dorm door. In our apartment, you were free to voice any ridiculous thing that came to mind, and someone would laugh with you. Someone would entertain any crazy, ridiculous idea with you and you could run with it as far as it would take you. You were accepted, and no one judged you for all the ways you already knew you were imperfect. Could it be that he was inextricably drawn to the simple comfort our room offered? Like a moth to light, was he attracted to the invisible glow emanating from our apartment?

Several days later, Michelle, Keri, Milan, and I returned to the apartment after a night out. The four of us poured into the room and stood bunched on the small, tiled floor space that comprised the kitchen. I turned to check the answering machine nearby to see if I'd missed any messages. Just as I turned, Milan placed his hand gently on Michelle's smooth, flat belly and whispered something in her ear, inaudible to the rest of us. I missed the gesture all together, but Keri noticed. Little slipped past her.

Soon after he left, Michelle commented, "Milan looks better this year."

"Better? What do you mean he looks better?" Keri asked.

"I don't know. Cuter, I guess. He's kind of hot."

"Uh, hello—where were you all last year? He's *always* been hot," I countered.

"Maybe so," Michelle stated off-handedly.

In that moment, a feverish murmur, which had pulsed in the shadows undetected for months, surfaced. But I didn't notice. My quiet best friend gave no hint that she was just like me—kindling and coals placed too close to fire. In the swirl of my own tossing and turning restlessness, I missed the subtle signs. Michelle's heart remained a mystery to me, as mine was to her. We were often sloppy in our observations—oblivious to the seeds sown by a stray thought or an acknowledgement or a rising sensation. We didn't notice that Milan blew over both of us like a hurricane wind, sweeping up everything—and every*one* in his path. At the time, I thought nothing about Michelle's comment. And I didn't give Milan's action a second thought when Keri told me about it later. None of us had noticed early the previous spring that a Pandora's box had cracked open right in front of us.

That fall, I began a class called Surrealism and Artistic Movements, a small seminar with only fifteen students. We read things like the *Surrealist Manifesto* and *The Futurist Cookbook*, and played Mad Libs, exchanging sensible nouns for random, nonsensical ones. It was good fun. In class, we watched meaningless, grainy old avant-garde films. My fellow liberal arts classmates and I enjoyed contemplating the virtues of the absurd and randomness along with our young and witty professor.

Several weeks after starting the class, Milan and I sat in Le Bus at a small table tucked into a corner. I finished my tea and gathered my things to head to my afternoon seminar.

"What class are you going to?" he asked.

"Surrealism and Artistic Movements," I replied.

"What's that?" he asked curiously.

"Just like the course title. We're reading the *Surrealist Manifesto*. We're supposed to get into Dada and Russian constructivism soon. Sometimes we watch old surrealist films. It's pretty cool."

"Can I come?" he asked.

"Sure," I said, masking my excitement with measured nonchalance.

We left Le Bus by the back door, cut through the nearby food court, and headed across the street onto Locust Walk. Milan walked next to me, and we chatted a bit more about surrealism and my humorous young professor.

"He started class the other day and started talking about the painter Manet. Then he says, 'Manet-aise.' You know—mayonnaise. Totally random," I laughed.

When we got to class, I introduced Milan to my professor and asked if it was okay for him to sit in on the class. The professor readily agreed, and Milan sat down in the chair next to mine. The seminar lasted only fifty minutes, and we watched some peculiar, unmemorable film. I couldn't concentrate on the movie or take decent notes the entire class. I felt so deeply satisfied to be in the small classroom, learning about art movements with Milan. He came to my class every week for the next couple of months and sat slouched in the chair next to me. Sometimes he walked with me to class. Other times he arrived a few minutes late and met me there. My professor named him "the guest."

"Ah, our guest has arrived," the professor would say when Milan was tardy to class. It was one of the few times in the week that I could count on seeing Milan and not share him with my roommates. It was blissful.

———— ❧ ————

Chapter Sixteen

CJ

{October–November, Senior Year}

WHILE MILAN REVEALED LITTLE ABOUT HIMSELF, CJ SHARED almost everything. All we had to do was sit and listen while he poured out his life story. Over a series of afternoons, Keri, Stephanie, and I sat in the living room, as CJ unfolded before us.

"When I was kid, girls were always mean to me." He snickered with a mischievous laugh that bottled up in his nostrils before forcing itself out of his mouth. "Now those same girls—they all want to go out with me." I could see the boy inside him shrieking with glee as the turning of the tables weighted the odds heavily in his favor. The same sort of popular, attractive girls who had mocked him in elementary school now flocked to him.

"Why were they mean?" Keri asked.

"'Cause I came here from Brazil. Things were different there. When I came here I didn't have the right American clothes, and I didn't speak English very well. So they made fun of me all the time."

"How old were you?" I asked.

"Eleven."

But now, a decade later, the awkwardness of CJ's foreign roots had distilled into an international savvy. He'd mastered the English language;

and, decked out in clothing his father sent from New York, his wardrobe garnered the envy of fashionistas, male and female.

"CJ Knowlan doesn't sound very Brazilian," Keri commented.

"My parents aren't *from* Brazil originally. We just lived there when I was a kid. My life was crazy then . . ."

We were quiet, as we waited for him to elaborate.

"Abuse and stuff . . . anyway . . ." His voice trailed off. "It's fine. I'm cool now," he stated lightly. He mentioned all this casually. There was no sadness in his voice. Yet he'd told us; it must have been important to him that we know. Perhaps he'd made his peace with the demons of his past and just wanted someone to acknowledge the burden he carried with him.

Before silence could settle, he changed the subject. "People at this school are funny, you know. This girl wanted to go out with me. So, we went to dinner, and she picked some pricey place downtown. She ordered all kinds of stuff and charged up a huge bill. Whatever. So I ordered a bunch of things too. Then when the bill came, she looked at me—like I was supposed to pay it. I told her, 'Why do you think I'm paying for it? I don't have the money for this.'"

"So, what happened?" Keri asked.

"Well, she paid, of course. She just assumed I could afford that place." CJ didn't appear in the least bit embarrassed or apologetic. He seemed to think she owed him redress for wrongly expecting him to pick up the tab.

His date had probably assumed he could afford the overpriced restaurant because CJ looked like a trust-fund boy, with his leather book bag instead of the standard canvas backpack. Everything about his wardrobe indicated an endowed bank account. No wonder the social elite believed him to be one of their own.

"Hey, do you ever go to services at Hillel?" CJ asked Keri. Hillel was the on-campus Jewish center.

"No, I usually go home Fridays for service with my parents," Keri answered.

"I haven't been to synagogue in ages. I was thinking about stopping into a Hillel service on campus . . . but I don't know," CJ continued.

"I'll go with you one Friday," Keri offered.

"How about this Friday?" CJ asked.

"Sure," Keri agreed.

Friday evening, Keri borrowed a flattering wrap-around skirt from Michelle and dressed up in a cute top. She met CJ, and they headed out to the Friday Shabbat service. Keri returned in high spirits.

"Everyone there thought we were married grad students! He wore a suit," she sighed in satisfied exuberance. CJ made a fabulous looking date. No wonder they caught the eye of the others in attendance.

As October hummed to its end, Halloween arrived. In college I always greeted October 31 with indifferent laziness. I disliked wearing costumes that required effort. My fail-safe Halloween getup was usually a bathrobe and shower cap. It took five seconds to assemble and required no special purchases or planning. In junior high, I had planned my costumes a month in advance. In sixth grade, I transformed a giant cardboard box with colored poster board and black tape into an enormous Rubik's Cube costume. But after high school, I lost interest. I'd become too old to load up on free candy, so I didn't see the point. I hadn't done much of anything for Halloween in college. This year was no different.

My roommates and I, with the exception of Noel, were all home Halloween night, each of us busy doing our own thing. Around nine o'clock, we heard knocking on our door. Milan and our friend Marko had dropped by.

"Hey, a friend of mine is having a Halloween party tonight," Marko relayed. "It should be fun. Do you want to come?" he asked us.

"That means we need costumes," I reminded everyone. "I don't have one."

"Me neither," Marko replied. "What should we do?"

"We can find something," Michelle replied. "Let's look through our closets."

"I'm pretty sure I don't have anything good," I answered.

"I'm wearing my costume," Milan replied.

"What are you supposed to be?" Keri asked as she looked him over. He was smartly dressed in a black turtleneck, black pants, black shoes, and a black beret. He hadn't shaved in several days, so dark, even stubble decorated his jaw.

"I'm a Yugoslav resistance fighter," he replied.

He looked more like a beatnik poet than a resistance fighter—whatever they looked like—but no one criticized. At least he had a costume. The remaining four of us needed to dream up decent costumes within the next ten minutes. I didn't have a bathrobe and neither did any of my roommates.

"Let's start with your closet," Keri suggested.

Marko, Michelle, Keri, and I proceeded to my closet where I pointed out the most unusual pieces in my wardrobe.

"How about these overalls?" I said, pulling out the pair we'd bought during our summer in LA.

"I know. You can be a farmer," Michelle suggested to Marko. "Those overalls are long, so they'll fit you. You're already wearing a plaid shirt— it works with the overalls. Does someone have a bandana? He can tie a bandana around his neck, and he's done."

Keri snatched a yellow and orange bandana from her room, and Marko was good to go.

"Any other ideas?" I asked as I continued flipping through my closet.

"What about that suit?" Keri suggested as my hand rested on a brown faux-tweed men's suit. When I worked at Oaktree over the summer, I had bought one of their ninety-nine-dollar men's suits. A tailor had altered it to fit me perfectly.

"I know—I can be a guy," I joked.

"That'll work," Michelle replied.

"You can use eyeliner pencil to draw facial hair," Keri chuckled.

"I'll give you a goatee," Michelle offered.

"That's cool," I agreed. One more costume down. Just two more to go.

"What about those 1950s dresses we bought at the thrift store?" Keri remembered.

"Oh, yeah," said Michelle.

"We can be women from that era," Keri continued.

"I have some vintage accessories—sunglasses and scarves we can use to dress ourselves up," Michelle declared.

Marko took the overalls into our bathroom to change while Milan waited in the living room. The three of us hastily assembled our costumes and then regrouped. Michelle quickly drew a goatee around my mouth with my eyeliner pencil. Presto. We were ready to party.

"Pictures. We should take pictures," Keri reminded us.

Michelle snapped Marko dressed in his hillbilly farmer garb. Then Marko snapped Keri, Michelle, and me. Then he snapped Milan and me together—the guerilla fighter and the girly man in suit and tie. When Michelle received the prints of her pictures back, I couldn't believe what a great shot Marko had taken of Milan. He had his arm around my shoulders and looked amazing; his dark eyes stared, intense and smoldering, into the camera. Neither of us smiled as we looked steely and aloof. I had several pictures of us together, but we were often goofing off—posing like an obscure Balkan statue as we stood with my tripod hoisted like a torch in the air between us or huddling together on the sofa, pretending to cry on each other's shoulders. I could kick myself for choosing that stupid costume in the Halloween photo. It was the best picture I had of Milan and me together, but instead of looking feminine and cute under his arm, I looked like an uppity cross-dresser with a bad shave.

The five of us left for the party, and I enjoyed Halloween for the first time in years. My head didn't hit my pillow until sometime after two in the morning.

Every year, Parents Weekend rolled around in November. My dad always attended. My mom had accompanied him freshman year, but usually it was a fun father-and-daughter weekend with just me and Dad. Senior year, both my parents planned to come for the three-day event; it was my final Parents Weekend before graduation.

"My parents are coming into town," I told Keri and Michelle as the three of us and CJ sat in the living room. "We should get all our parents together for dinner."

"That's a great idea," Michelle agreed.

"My parents would love that," Keri added.

"My parents will be here that weekend too," CJ chimed in. "It's my birthday. I'm turning twenty-one."

"Invite them," Michelle suggested.

"I'll ask them," he replied.

We set the date and called our parents. They all agreed to dinner together.

Parents Weekend arrived quickly. On Saturday afternoon, my parents and I strolled through campus.

"Should I wear a tie to dinner tonight?" my father asked. He often wore a tie. The few times I'd seen Keri and Michelle's fathers, they had dressed casually. Neither wore a tie.

"No, Dad, you don't need to wear a tie to dinner tonight. It's casual," I assured him. I wanted him to fit in with the other fathers.

My dad was a spectroscopist—a scientist, more simply put. With his rimless glasses and salt-and-pepper beard, he looked like a dapper college professor. For the past twenty-seven years, my dad had shopped at one place—Brooks Brothers. Up until its rebranding, Brooks Brothers was a stodgy, pompous old-school clothier, with proper-looking, somber salespeople. I found it a dreadful, intimating place. In high school, I had always thought the sales associates would throw me out if I ever walked in without my father, wearing my punk-inspired wardrobe. But Dad loved that store.

Criss, the tailor, took my father's measurements on each visit and always greeted him, "Hello, Mr. Moore. It's good to see you again."

Every day, my dad wore the same ensemble to work, a conservative pair of Brooks Brothers slacks and a sports coat. On Sundays, he switched it up and wore custom Brooks Brothers suits to church.

The night of the dinner, CJ, Michelle, Keri, our families, and I assembled at the Palladium, an upscale bar and restaurant on campus. To my surprise, all three of my friends' fathers wore blazers and ties. Thankfully, my dad remained unruffled. He didn't seem annoyed at my ill-advised fashion directive. Dad wore a handsome heavy-gauge wool cardigan, a pale-blue dress shirt, and a conventional blue and maroon woolen winter scarf. He simply buttoned his sweater up and tucked his scarf snugly around his neckline, making it less apparent in the low-lit restaurant that his tie was absent.

We stood making small talk in the bar area, and the four of us introduced our parents to each other. CJ's little brother had come along as well. We lingered there about fifteen minutes before the hostess came to seat us at a long table in the stately dining room. The room buzzed, each table full of lively groupings. The din of scholarly prattle—debate and rebuttals coupled with merriment—whirred in the ample room.

CJ's father, Mr. Knowlan, began chitchatting with my parents and me as we scanned the menu and discussed the items that looked most appetizing. Everyone ordered, and our meals were served. Halfway through the meal, Mr. Knowlan called for everyone's attention.

"Today is my son's birthday," he announced proudly, smiling at CJ. Mr. Knowlan leaned in toward CJ and rested his hand on his son's back, in a gesture of approval and recognition.

"CJ, I'd like to present you with this gift." He handed CJ a good-sized jewelry box. CJ beamed with his usual broad, sly, squinty-eyed grin.

"Thanks, man," he replied gratefully to his father.

All eyes at the table fixed on CJ and his father. CJ lifted the lid, and his smile spread full and appreciative across his mouth. He lifted a sleek metal watch out of the box.

"It's a Rolex," CJ announced. Then he passed it around the table so we all could have a look.

My father took the watch box in his hand. "It's an authentic Rolex," Dad whispered in a low voice so that I alone could hear him. "See how the hand moves smoothly." My dad angled the watch face so I could see it. "On the fake replicas, the second hand jerks."

CJ and his parents smiled warmly and spoke softly among themselves as the rest of us took turns admiring the new watch. Everyone wished CJ happy birthday, and we resumed eating.

Just as I finished my entree, Mr. Knowlan addressed me.

"Adele, that's not a name that you hear often," he began. "There is a great love story—one of the greatest romances of all time—about a woman named Adele."

"Really?" I replied, greatly interested. My parents listened quietly without comment.

"Yes," he smiled charmingly. CJ's father was engaging. He wasn't particularly striking, with his dark, receding hairline, but there was something appealing about him for a man his age. He exuded a worldly sophistication, but unlike his son, who remained rough around the edges, he seemed refined—polished.

"Do you know this story?" he asked.

"No, I've never heard it," I replied.

"Well . . . many years ago, the heir to the British throne gave up his crown, his future—everything—for the love of a woman." Mr. Knowlan paused for effect before continuing.

"The British king fell in love with a divorcée named Adele. Not only was she a divorcée, but she was also a foreigner. The law stated that a British monarch could not marry a divorcée. But he loved her. He refused to live without her." The words rolled off Mr. Knowlan's tongue smoothly, punctuated by practiced dramatic inflections.

"Finally, he informed his family and all of England that he would abdicate the throne. He had to marry the love of his life. It's a beautiful story," he concluded with finality.

"Wow, I never heard that before," I replied. "Very interesting."

My parents remained quiet. It was unusual for my dad not to participate in a friendly chat. Normally, he might have contributed the name of the monarch or the time frame in which the abdication occurred. My father always claimed that he wasn't a people person, but he was surprisingly adept at these types of dinner conversations. Though he was an introvert, he was extremely personable. He flourished in social situations because he knew enough about history, politics, and current events to comfortably discuss most topics with just about anyone. "I try to know a little bit about everything," he told me whenever I shared something I'd newly learned, only to discover, to my surprise, that he already had a working knowledge of the subject.

As we finished dinner, everyone appeared to be enjoying themselves. Conversation and lighthearted discussion flowed easily. Laughter and voices reverberated around us. Mr. Knowlan continued to engage us. He had begun to talk about his profession. He worked as a freelance writer for several big fashion magazines and was telling us about his experiences in the industry.

"The female models make out with each other after the fashion shows. It's disgusting," he said with obvious insincerity. He couldn't conceal the glint in his eye, hinting at secret fascination.

"Really," I replied flatly.

"Yes, can you believe that?" he continued. "It happens all the time."

Soon we'd all finished our meals and polished off the last crumbs of dessert. The bill was paid without incident, and we all began to gather our belongings. Our families made their way through the dining room to the exit. I was cheerful from the stimulating evening and lethargic from the filling meal. I loved the first-rate dining that always accompanied Parents Weekend.

Just before CJ and his father stepped outside, Mr. Knowlan lowered his smooth baritone voice and whispered to CJ, just within my earshot, "This is for you." He placed a rumpled-looking bag discreetly into CJ's open palm. Mr. Knowlan grinned the same devious smile I'd seen on

CJ's face repeatedly. As far as I could tell, I was the only one who caught the quick exchange.

"What did your dad give you?" I asked CJ as we streamed outside onto Locust Walk.

"Nothing for you," he retorted naughtily, like a badly behaved child.

The large group of us congregated just outside the entrance as our parents shook hands and exchanged parting pleasantries. I couldn't press CJ for an answer now that everyone was busy milling around saying good-bye. Soon each family broke off into its own group, so our parents could chat briefly with each of us before leaving campus for their homes or hotels.

"The king of England did give up the throne, but not for a woman named Adele," my father stated quietly. Only my mother and I could hear him. "I can't recall her name at the moment . . . Simpson. I believe her last name was Simpson."

My father was right. King Edward VIII abdicated the British throne for the American divorcée Wallis Simpson. She was divorced once, and currently married, when she became the king's mistress. The name Wallis wasn't even close to Adele.

Before CJ left with his family, he invited my roommates and me over to his friend's place for a small birthday gathering later that night.

"Here's the address," he said, giving a slip of paper to Michelle. "I'll be there in about an hour."

"We'll stop by," Keri assured him.

Finally, my parents said good night, along with Michelle and Keri's.

Since we had lacked privacy at that moment, my parents didn't share their impression of the evening until the next day.

"There were some interesting dynamics with CJ's family," my father observed. "They completely ignored their younger son throughout dinner and focused entirely on the older boy."

I hadn't paid much attention, but my father was right—again. I didn't remember anyone acknowledging CJ's brother all evening. He sat throughout most of dinner without saying a word. I didn't recall CJ or his parents speaking to the little guy.

"Could you tell that his parents are divorced?" I asked.

"They are?" my mother replied.

"I never would have guessed that," my father agreed. The entire night, CJ's parents appeared exactly the same as all the married couples at the table. I'd never seen divorced parents behave so amiably toward each other. They had sat side by side rather than opposite each other across the table. One of them could have easily switched places with CJ's brother and put some distance between them.

But as Keri, Michelle, and I strolled home from the Palladium that night, I had yet to hear my parent's perspective on the issue. I did, however, want to check in with my friends about their thoughts.

"Did you two talk to CJ's father?" I asked.

"Yep, I talked to him when we all arrived at the Palladium," Keri answered.

"Me too," Michelle replied.

"What did you think of him?" I asked.

"I wouldn't trust him further than I could throw him," Michelle retorted.

"Yeah, no kidding," I agreed.

"He spends a lot of time consorting with models half his age," Keri added.

"I know. What's his deal with the models making out?" I inquired. "He kept mentioning it."

"It's that whole male-fantasy-lipstick-lesbian thing," Keri replied.

"I don't get that," Michelle stated flatly.

"Me neither," I said.

"I don't know. Some men are into that," Keri shrugged.

Back at the apartment, we changed into casual clothes and freshened up before heading off campus to CJ's friend's place.

When we arrived at the house, CJ was on the phone.

"No way, man. Yeah, that's cool. Yeah, man, all right," he said into the receiver before hanging up.

"Heeeeey-hee-ehh," he chortled. "That was my dad." I must have looked surprised, because CJ added, "I know it sounded like I was talking to one of my friends, huh?"

"Yeah," I agreed.

"Hey, these are my friends," CJ said, introducing us to the three guys present, a couple of Norwegian guys and a Brazilian. "This is Magnus, Sebastian, and Gil." Sebastian was the most striking of the three, with clean-cut light-brown hair and a chiseled, model-perfect, symmetrical face. Something about him made me uneasy. A calculated coldness in his manner kind of scared me. Gil, the Brazilian, was noticeably shorter than the other two, but impeccably dressed in a blue blazer, hip jeans, a pressed shirt, and stylish leather shoes. His eyes burned the clearest, brightest green I'd ever seen, shining out from a handsome, manly face. Like most fashionista-guys, he sported the signature neatly clipped sideburns. His hair was short and neatly tousled. The other guy, Magnus, the tallest of the three, seemed the friendliest and most pleasant. He smiled kindly and shook our hands. Sebastian and Gil seemed a bit more reserved. I got the feeling they were checking us out.

CJ's friends began talking to Michelle and Keri, while I sat down with CJ.

"My dad really liked your parents," CJ said. "He liked your mom's style—very Jackie O., with the single string of pearls and all."

"Thanks," I replied. "I didn't really get to talk to your mom, but she seemed nice. Your dad had some interesting stories. Did your mom enjoy talking to Keri's mom?"

"They're very different personality types," CJ replied. "I'm not sure they really hit it off."

I could see why. CJ's mom came across as quiet and demure. Keri's mom, on the other hand, was a riot. Keri's mother was the funniest parent I'd ever met. Junior year, the V Society had voted her one of the funniest people on our Favorites list. Keri's mother was a jovial, prank-prone elementary school teacher. The first time I went home with Keri to have dinner with her family, her mother forgot to clean up a small pile of dog poop sitting on their pink living room carpet. At least that's what Mrs. Zelman wanted me to think. She didn't know that Keri had already relayed her mother's best pranks to me well before I arrived at the Zelman home.

Years ago, Mrs. Zelman had come across a bag of plastic poop in some random discount clearance store. The poop was an exact replica of what you might expect a small housedog to leave behind. I could imagine Mrs. Zelman wandering into the discount store and digging in a bottomless cardboard clearance bin like a pirate seeking hidden treasure, determined to find something magnificent in the ninety-nine-cent trove.

"Ah, ah . . . ah-ha!" she exclaimed to herself. "This is it!"

I could see Mrs. Zelman's eyes flashing with joy, lighting up like those of a child who had just discovered the prized giant chocolate egg during an Easter egg hunt. Her cheerful, lopsided smile broke out across her naturally pink cheeks, and she reveled in the thought of all the houseguests she would alarm with this poopy surprise.

I had never met a parent as mischievous and hilarious as Mrs. Zelman. My parents were great, but far more serious. Never in a million years would my parents think of buying fake plastic poop. And never in a million years would they put it on the floor to trick guests into thinking they were poor housekeepers.

I smiled at the memory of Mrs. Zelman's antics and then asked CJ, "But your parents had a good time, right?"

"Yeah, they did," he replied.

"Mine too. It was nice that they could all meet each other."

"Definitely. By the way, it was pot," CJ smirked.

"What was pot?"

"The bag my dad gave me. He gave me a bag of pot for my birthday."

"Oh. I was wondering why you were so secretive," I remarked.

I'm sure CJ was later glad that he had received more than one present for his birthday, as the watch didn't last long. Four months later, CJ lost the Rolex during a barbiturate-filled spring break in Miami's South Beach. I asked him what happened to the watch after we all returned from spring break. "Someone stole it," CJ replied with little emotion. "I don't remember what happened exactly. I fell asleep on the beach. When I woke up, it was gone." But later, Keri said, "CJ told me his watch got stolen when some guys followed him into an alley, beat him up, and stole it." Who really knew what happened to his watch? Only one thing was certain—it disappeared.

Keri, Michelle, and I hung out with CJ and his friends for another half hour. The vibe was a little strange with CJ's buddies. Maybe they were anxious for us to leave so they could smoke CJ's birthday pot. CJ had probably told them we didn't smoke. Or maybe they'd tried flirting with Keri and Michelle and received the brush-off. In any case, I was glad to leave. We took off and headed home.

A couple days later, CJ paid us a visit. Keri, Stephanie, and I were there.

"Man, my foot is killing me. Tough-actin' Tinactin time," CJ announced.

"What's tough-actin' Tinactin?" Keri asked.

CJ crowed his gruff, nasal laugh. "It's for my foot fungus."

"Gross," I murmured. "That's WTMI." Way too much information. He should have kept that a secret.

"Well, maybe if you took your boots off more than once a week," Keri mumbled under her breath.

"You don't have any tough-actin' Tinactin, do you?" he asked.

"No," Keri and I replied in unison.

"Oh, well," he replied. Unable to resolve the athlete's foot issue, he moved on to the other irritating topic spinning in his head. "Man, this girl on my hall is all mad at me," he complained.

"Why?" Stephanie asked.

"I don't know. We were just fooling around. I told her we were just messing around. I don't know what she was expecting," he said indignantly. "You know . . . that girl Julie."

I knew her. CJ had introduced me to the cute, likable girl. She lived in his dorm. She was an underclassman—a sophomore, maybe even a freshman—I wasn't sure. I wondered if this was her initiation into the college hook-up scene. Maybe she didn't know that once you hooked up with a guy he might only be interested in you for future hook-ups, nothing more. Or he might cut you off completely and never talk to you again. You might pass him on Locust Walk, and he might act like he didn't even know you. If he had been drunk or high, depending on how drunk or how high, he *actually* might not remember you at all. Poor girl. She'd been played, and now she was ticked.

"I dated this girl a couple years ago . . . We were together for a while," CJ reflected. "She'd yell and scream at me. She'd get all mad and try to hit me. But she couldn't hurt me. No matter what she did, she couldn't hurt me."

CJ mentioned that particular ex-girlfriend more than once. Their relationship never sounded healthy or happy. But, of all the women he dated, he seemed to care the most about her. In his own convoluted way, he seemed to love her—the best way he knew how. Not until many seasons later, did I make some sense of why CJ treasured her memory.

Heartbreak. That was the big, scary, lurking monster that frightened him most. I suspected that CJ's deepest, darkest fear was the woman that would trample on his heart if he let her in. Why else would he go on and on about that ex-girlfriend? Maybe he wasn't afraid to love her because she could never hurt him. Perhaps he felt invincible with her. That was the only reasoning that made any sense to me.

Chapter Seventeen

RANDOM NOVEMBER STUFF

{November–December, Senior Year}

ALL OF A SUDDEN, MY ROOMMATE NOEL'S SILENT TREATMENT ended. She began speaking to me regularly. Out of the blue, she stopped calling us the nuns from hell behind our back. Keri had won her over. By association, Noel decided Michelle and I weren't so bad. Sure, we didn't have guys sleeping over—still a little strange by all modern norms. But we weren't unbearably weird.

"Noel and I are going to lunch," Keri called down the hall to me.

"Do you want to come?" Noel asked, suddenly appearing at the door of my room.

"Sure," I replied.

I pulled on my long winter coat and quickly draped a thick scarf around my neck. I hurried after them into the hallway outside and pulled on my gloves as we stood waiting for the elevator.

"Which restaurant are you going to?" I asked.

"I know this couple that's from Haiti—that's where I'm from—they own a little place a few blocks from here. I eat there all the time," Noel replied.

"They're really great," Keri added. "And the food is good."

"Perfect. I'm there," I said.

"Do you go back to Haiti often?" I asked.

"No," she answered. "My brother and I came here to stay with my uncle. My parents wanted us to move to the US with him and his wife so we could grow up here and get an American education. After college, they expect us to go back and visit and help them out."

"Do you have a lot of family there?"

"Tons," she replied. "I have a bunch of brothers and sisters back home. My parents are still there too."

"That's cool," I replied. We loaded onto the elevator, hurried through Superblock, and crossed the street into the surrounding West Philadelphia neighborhood. It was a cloudless, sunny autumn day. The air bristled with a settling chill that caused my ears to prickle in the cold.

"There's a new sorority starting up this year," Noel said. "I'm in the first pledge class they're going to initiate."

"Really," I replied dryly. I couldn't think of anything pleasant to say about pledging. I'd pledged a coed fraternity sophomore year, only to resign the following year. I disliked the formality of the mandatory meetings, and the predetermined circle of friends.

We arrived at the little eatery, and the owners, a friendly Haitian couple, came out from behind the counter to greet Noel. The place smelled of rich spices. Decadent buttery flavors wafted in rolling, scented waves from the small kitchen. We sat and ordered. The server brought our food quickly, and we chowed down on the delicious, steaming meal. The portions were enormous. While we ate, Noel gave us the full scoop on her new sorority, including an elaborate description of her fellow pledges, the sorority's history, and the reasons they'd chosen to establish a chapter at our university that year.

"It's kind of neat to be one of the founding members of the chapter," she continued.

As we trudged home after lunch, each of us carried a Styrofoam carton packed with leftovers. Keri's thin plastic bag, containing her takeout box, swung back and forth at her side as she relayed the highlights of our summer in LA to Noel.

"Stephanie, Adele, and I were there in Westwood for a month. Michelle came during the last week," said Keri. "Stephanie had an internship with a movie studio. She let all of us stay with her—"

"We took some hilarious pictures," I interjected. "I'll show them to you when we get home."

Back at the apartment, I pulled out my big photo album from junior year and the new album I'd started over the summer for senior year. I seated myself on the sofa next to Noel.

"Here are our pictures from the summer," I said, flipping the second book open.

"That's nothing like you two!" Noel balked as her eyes rested on the first page.

The picture showed Michelle and me dressed in our matching pairs of giant-sized overalls, posing outside the dressing rooms of the Venice Beach thrift store. Both of us stood smiling with huge grins. It was a cute picture except for one detail that Noel found disturbing. Before snapping the picture, I had suggested to Michelle that she stick one hand out of her giant overalls through the button-up crotch. I did the same. So there the two of us stood in our overalls, each of us with a disembodied hand protruding from between our legs. Michelle and I thought it was hilarious. But Noel couldn't reconcile our twisted sense of humor with our conservative-seeming morals.

"We were just joking around," I said dismissively.

Noel looked unsettled. I turned quickly through the next few pages, which were less startling.

"That's it," I declared as we reached the last picture. Most of the book was still empty since it awaited photos for the remainder of senior year. I decided not to share my junior year photo album with her. Noel might find many of the photos disquieting.

As much as my roommates and I liked taking glamorous photos of ourselves, we liked taking ugly photos of ourselves even more. For some reason, I loved photos that made us look hideous. In the junior-year album there was a fabulous shot of Michelle, Mandy, and me looking horrendously unattractive. Two little zits on my face had inspired me to whip out a package of Band-Aids. I'd ceremoniously placed two medium-sized Band-Aids over the blemishes—one on my forehead and another on the side of my mouth. I wore my big brown-framed eyeglasses to enhance the look. Michelle joined me in the anti-makeover by parting her hair down the middle and pulling it back in an unruly ponytail. Mandy messed up her hair, and the three of us stood in front of the camera making the most homely expressions we could muster—three Ugly Betties.

We'd built an entire collection of ugly roommate photos. My favorites were of Keri posing as a deranged barefoot-and-pregnant woman. She tied her hair back with a green bandana, put on one of her muumuu tank tops, and stuffed pillows underneath, giving her the appearance of a woman pregnant with a small automobile. Then she bugged her eyes out and smiled with a broad, crazed grin. Then a photo showed Michelle masquerading as a feeble-minded redneck. She braided her hair in two messy braids on either side and then ratted the back out like week-old bedhead. She wore an enormous pair of faded jeans with a huge hole torn in the knee and an old maroon T-shirt. She stood awkwardly, smiling with an expression of pure idiocy. Another great picture of Michelle depicted her fully dressed, sitting on the floor pretending to give birth to Keri. Keri screamed like a newborn baby as she pretended to emerge from Michelle's womb. Mandy played the role of midwife, pretending to deliver Keri.

But of the three of us, I had the ugliest pictures of all. There was an entire series of contrived bad-hair pictures: my hair parted down the middle and flattened across the top, my hair wet and spiking in fifty different directions, my hair tied up in a red bandana while I stuck out my tongue at the camera and donned my big glasses. I juxtaposed all these pictures in my photo album next to the fashion photos of my roommates and me. I enjoyed the contrasting extremes.

I returned the photo albums to my room and then settled down at the living room table to skim the J. Crew catalog I'd picked up with my mail. The postal service delivered the catalogs in stacks and piled them several layers deep on tables near our mailboxes.

Keri left to check out some books from the library. Noel lounged nearby. As of late, Noel habitually parked on the sofa and prank-called her friends on the phone.

Noel picked up the phone and dialed.

"Hi, this is Noey Knott," she said into the receiver. "Did you call me?"

The person on the other end answered, perplexed, "No, I didn't call."

"Yes, you did," Noel insisted. "Why did you call?" After she'd thoroughly confused the person on the other end of the line, she cracked up and identified herself.

"Hey, it's me—Noel. Noel Jean-Baptiste," she finally admitted to her bewildered friend.

Five minutes later, Noel wrapped up her call and curled up on the sofa with a can of Pringles to watch TV.

"Who's Noey Knott?" I asked.

"Me," she replied. "My boyfriend's last name is Knott. So that's the nickname I made up."

I finished perusing the J. Crew catalog and migrated to my room to review some assigned reading. I walked past Michelle's door but changed my mind and doubled back. Since it was closed, I knew she was reading or doing her daily devotions. She must have come home while we were out for lunch. Michelle was incredibly self-disciplined. Somehow, she achieved an enviable balance in her spiritual, academic, and social lives. She did it easily. She rarely missed out on a coffeehouse run or random late-night chat, yet her grades and pursuit of God soared along at a steady pace.

Often in the evening, she'd disappear into her room for hours in deliberate, focused study sessions. She studied her Bible and studied for exams with the same quiet, steady commitment. I always knew she was studying for a test when I heard the latest Sade album, melodic and soulful, crooning from her stereo. Sade's smooth jazz vocals aided Mich in the supernatural absorption of chemistry formulas and all kinds of

academic mumbo-jumbo that made about as much sense to me as a
poem recited backwards in Latin. I could hardly sit in my room and
study for more than forty-five minutes before I craved some sort of in-
teractive diversion.

"Hey, whatcha doing in there?" I yelled over Michelle's stereo
as I knocked out a loud rhythm—*bap-ratta-bap-boom-boom*—on her
closed door. I knew good and well that she was preparing for a test.

The door swung open, and Michelle looked at me with one of her
wonderfully endearing goofy looks.

"What are you doing . . . ," I repeated, ". . . having a prom in there?"

A smile spread across her lips as she squeezed me in sloppy hug. She
didn't mind that I'd interrupted her cram session in order to lure her
away to some distraction I'd yet to dream up.

"Reading," she replied. "What are you doing, Delmo?"

"Nothing. Let's go do something," I implored.

"Okay," she agreed. "Like what?"

"I don't know."

"I think Keri mentioned something about Stephanie wanting to go
somewhere to some *thing* tonight," Michelle recalled.

"Oh, yeah? Where?" I asked curiously.

"I don't know. Some friends of hers invited us somewhere," Michelle
continued.

"Who?" I asked, my interest rising.

"I don't know—ask Keri. Oh, I don't know if she knows either.
Ask Stephanie. I think Stephanie said they're in one of her classes
or something."

"Hmmm," I replied. "Okay." Meeting up with some random friends
of Stephanie's sounded promising—just the distraction I craved.

Keri returned home a couple hours later. Stephanie picked us up
around nine o'clock and steered her car into the heart of downtown.
We parked and filed into the designated meeting spot, one of the small
microbreweries that were suddenly springing up across town. Inside, an
assembly of male-fashionistas buzzed around like bees in a hive. I recog-

nized a couple of the guys from around campus—all Castle-party types in overpriced shirts and jeans. The tribe of wild boys consisted of an assorted mix of Pakistani students and South American Jewish guys—Stephanie's Wharton classmates.

Apparently, one of them had invited us, but the boys barely turned to pay us a bit of attention as they caroused nosily back and forth between the nearby pool tables and the long bar table already overflowing with empty shot glasses and beer mugs. A tall, chubby guy with slicked-back hair and a silky accent greeted Stephanie like he was the king of the brewery. I'd seen him before. He always ignored me, but that only bothered me a little bit.

The bar area was loud, and I couldn't hear a word spoken by anyone more than three feet away. The self-important guy with slicked-back hair said something to Stephanie, inviting the four of us to join several stragglers amidst the swirling pack of boys at the long table. As it turned out, both Michelle and Keri simultaneously intrigued one of the guys somewhere in the mix. He'd passed on that interesting bit of information to Stephanie and encouraged her to bring her friends to the tavern that night. I guess he figured that if he struck out with one, he might get lucky with the other one.

The four of us sat at the table for ten minutes. That's about how long it took before it became crystal-clear to the interested guy that he wasn't going to make headway with Michelle or Keri. Neither of them shared my affection for international male-fashionistas. Soon, their suitor lost interest. I was already disinterested since none of the guys seemed very friendly. I was happy to move on elsewhere for the evening. The four of us drifted toward the exit just as a slender, rambunctious Pakistani guy announced to the other guys, "I'm outta here. I'm going to get my car." As he abandoned his collection of empty beer mugs, I could tell he was on his way to a whopping DUI. A few of his friends and the four of us poured out of the entrance as he hopped into a fancy red sports car—a rare model I'd never seen before and couldn't name—revved the engine, and sped down the narrow street. We gladly headed to Stephanie's car in the opposite direction and zipped away before anyone noticed we were gone.

A few days later, Milan and I met up before my surrealism class. He seemed more grim than usual as we walked to class. Like most Americans, I was blindly unaware of the political upheaval taking place in the rest of the world. I never asked if the violent military conflicts shredding Yugoslavia had anything to do with his disposition. The other students I knew from his region of the world didn't respond with drastic mood swings as he did—rapidly vacillating from mellow to sullen. Maybe he was hypersensitive and felt isolated—alone, in his unfamiliar American surroundings, while his homeland collapsed into savage tumult. Who knew? I could never be certain what tides turned Milan's emotional state.

"What's your favorite book?" I asked in an attempt to lift his thoughts.

"*The Little Prince*," he smiled.

"I've never heard of it. Who's it by?"

"No way! You've never read *The Little Prince* by Antoine de Saint-Exupéry?" he asked in disbelief.

"Nope. What's it about?"

"A little prince," he returned. "You have to read it. Promise me you'll read it."

"Okay," I promised. Eventually I bought the book. I barely got through the first few chapters. I couldn't get into the storyline—a fable of love and loneliness and a little prince that traveled from planet to planet.

We arrived at our classroom and took seats next to each other. Fifty minutes later, my professor wrapped up his lecture on Russian constructivism. I said bye to Milan and trekked home through the graying winter day.

I bustled through my front door. Michelle sat at the kitchen table.

"Hi, Mom," I greeted her.

"Hi, Butthead," she replied sweetly.

"I saw Milan today. He's getting more cynical by the moment." I sat down at the table across from her.

"I noticed that," she replied. "We should tell him to read Ecclesiastes."

"That's a great idea." The book of Ecclesiastes was perfect for our pessimistic friend. It began:

The words of the Teacher, son of David, king in Jerusalem:

"Meaningless! Meaningless!" says the Teacher.

"Utterly meaningless! Everything is meaningless."

Ecclesiastes reigned as one of the Bible's great wisdom books, penned by King Solomon—one of the wisest men to walk the earth. King Solomon had three hundred concubines and seven hundred wives—all unbelievably beautiful. Milan would surely appreciate that detail. Michelle and I hoped Solomon's poetic discourse on the futility of a life lived without God might resonate with Milan.

"Do you have an extra Bible?" Michelle asked.

"No, I loaned the extra one that Kathy gave me to someone."

"I'll get an extra one from her at our next Bible study," Michelle replied.

Days later, Michelle and I presented Milan with a paperback New International Version translation of the Bible. The thick but compact book was covered with a computerized detail of Michelangelo's Sistine Chapel painting. The Bible cover carried a close-up image of the hand of God reaching down to the hand of man. The book looked more like an art guide than the standard gigantic Bible.

"Read Ecclesiastes," Michelle told him.

"Why?" he asked.

"We think you'll like it," I encouraged.

"Okay," Milan replied and stuffed the Bible into his backpack.

Several days later, I followed up.

"So, what did you think of Ecclesiastes?" I asked.

"I agree, everything seems pretty meaningless," he said evenly.

"Well, keep reading. There's more good stuff in there."

A couple days after our Ecclesiastes discussion, Milan appeared at our front door. He sauntered into the room wearing a broad grin. Keri, Michelle, and I took notice immediately to the contrast from the brooding grouchiness that had colored his demeanor as of late.

"You'll never guess what I just read," he stated enthusiastically.

"What?" Michelle asked.

"I just read an article that says men can have more than one orgasm—in a row," he announced. He looked pleased as pie.

"And I'm interested in that information because . . .?" Keri replied sassily.

"Well, it would be nice to have more than one in a row," he continued.

"That's nice. Knock yourself out," I replied sarcastically. While gratification ranked in our top five favorite V Society discussions, we were entirely interested in the female side of the equation. If he'd mentioned an article on the same topic related to women, we might have snatched the article from his hand, expelled him from the apartment, and called an emergency V Society meeting to engage, uncensored, in a spirited debate about the merits of the new medical findings. But we had no interest in his male-centered scientific revelation. I yawned and moved on to a mutually more interesting subject.

"Hey, when are you going to model for me?" I asked Milan.

My most recent male supermodel discovery had turned down a photo shoot with me. He hadn't actually turned *me* down—he didn't know me. But he'd turned down the friend I'd sent out via my stealth model recruiting network. "He's not interested in modeling," my contact reported back. It was such a shame. He was a splendid-looking brown-skinned Indian student. I could practically close my eyes and snap a good picture of this guy. Oh, well. I won some, and I lost some—thus was the life of an aspiring fashion photographer.

"I can model for you anytime," Milan replied.

"Okay, next week then?" I asked.

"No problem. Just tell me when and where."

"Hey, check this out." I showed Milan the black-and-white photograph on the cover of a recently published student magazine. "That's my shot on the front cover."

"Nice," he said. He took the magazine from me and carefully examined the image. "Nice shot."

"Thanks."

Photography had begun to take off for me that semester. Two of my photographs appeared in a group exhibit that had opened that November at the nearby Institute of Contemporary Art. Some student magazines published a couple of my other photographs. I'd also received an invitation to step in as the art editor of the *Penn Review*, one of the student literary magazines. I'd accepted the position.

I photographed Milan the following week. Before the shoot, Keri listened while I laid out my plan for Milan's photo session.

"I just read in a photo magazine that male models wear makeup on photo shoots. Can you put some of your makeup on Milan before I photograph him?"

"Sure," Keri agreed. "What kind of makeup should I put on him?"

"I have no idea. What do you think?"

"I haven't the slightest idea. Didn't the article say what kind of makeup?"

"No. It just said that professional makeup artist's work on male and female models. Hmm . . . let's try powder and eyeliner. Probably not lipstick, do you think?"

"I don't know. We can try it and see how it looks."

Milan arrived for the photo shoot wearing a blousy white button-up poet's shirt that I'd picked out of his closet and dark jeans.

"Keri is going to put makeup on you. I just read that professional male models wear makeup," I told him.

"Really?" He looked skeptical, but agreed.

Keri powdered Milan's face and drew a thin black line beneath each eye.

"How do I look?" Milan asked.

"I don't know," I replied. Keri and I stood back and looked at him. I couldn't be sure if the eyeliner improved anything. Was it too much? Too little? I wouldn't know until I got the proofs from the photo shoot back.

Milan posed while I fired off several black-and-white rolls of film. He sat outside, lounging on some concrete stairs, while I directed him to turn his head this way, then that way. The next afternoon I developed the film and printed the contact sheets in the darkroom. Keri and I had completely overdone it. We'd put way too much makeup on him. Only one or two pictures were worth printing. He looked funny in all the others.

In my ignorance of fashion photography intricacies, I didn't know that male models rarely wore more than light powder to eliminate shine on their skin. I brought the proof sheets and prints home. Milan stopped by to see his pictures.

"I look like a girl," he said with a grimace. He took a ballpoint pen and marked big *X*'s across his face on the rows of tiny headshots.

"Sorry," I apologized. I thought of telling him he didn't look like a girl but more like a very pretty guy. But I wasn't sure he'd find that description comforting.

"I guess male models aren't supposed to wear that much makeup," I said in an effort to console him. "Now I know."

The next day was Thursday. Early that evening, CJ came over. He turned the floor lamp down to the lowest setting. Then he sat smiling at us, with a big, cheesy grin and squinting eyes. CJ officially ranked at the top of my Most Obnoxious Penn Men list. When he arrived, it was obvious that Keri and I were reading in the living room. Each of us held a book—*Clue Number One*; and the room lights were turned up bright—*Clue Number Two*. Usually, CJ asked our permission before turning the lights down. But today he didn't bother to ask. He had just walked into the apartment, used the bathroom, and then returned to the living room where he sat down, leaned over, and turned the light down. The boy lived on his own planet. He stayed a couple hours before he finally left.

"Do you notice that every time CJ comes over here, he goes into the bathroom shortly after he arrives?" Michelle asked.

"No, I never noticed that," I replied.

"You're right," Keri reflected. "He does go to the bathroom almost every time he comes over."

"You're not thinking . . . what I *think* you're thinking . . . No way!" I exclaimed.

"You've got to be kidding!" Keri cried.

"You think he's getting high in our bathroom?" I screeched.

"Uh, yeah," Michelle stated flatly.

"The *nerve* of that guy," I huffed.

"So, what are we going to do?" Keri asked.

"Well, he can't get high in our bathroom—that's for sure!" Michelle asserted.

"Is he smoking pot in there?" I wondered out loud.

"I never smell anything, though. It never *smells* like marijuana," Michelle remarked.

"Maybe he's figured out a way to camouflage the smell. He's pretty sneaky," Keri suggested.

Was it possible to smoke pot and completely camouflage the smell? We didn't know. But CJ was doing *something* in our bathroom that made the light hurt his eyes and made him grin like the Cheshire cat. Something had to be done. He was getting way too comfortable in our space. Not to mention that illegal drug possession was grounds to get us all expelled from our dorm—and probably expelled from school.

There was just one small problem: we weren't quite sure how to broach the subject. We hadn't actually seen him do drugs, so he could deny it if we confronted him. Addressing CJ required some creativity. The next time he came over and went to the bathroom, I met him as he came out into the hall.

"You know those fumes killed my goldfish the last time you did that," I stated seriously.

"Really? No, they didn't," he replied guiltily, in disbelief.

"Don't let it happen again," I warned.

"Yeah, sorry," he agreed, his head hanging. Guilt-laden by the memory of my deceased goldfish, CJ stopped his extracurricular activities in our bathroom.

One of my goldfish *had* died, but not because of CJ. The goldfish had committed suicide. He jumped to his death in a daring fatal leap out of the tank. I'd found my goldfish a week after he killed himself. He was dried up, like beef jerky, lying behind the giant dictionary that sat on the shelf next to my fish tank.

"Oh, look," I told Michelle. "I found my dead fish."

"How sad. What happened?"

"I think he jumped out of the tank."

"What are you going to do with it—flush it down the toilet?" Michelle asked.

"Yeah, I guess so." I thought about it for a minute. Suddenly, I had a brilliant idea. "Let's mail it to Milan—anonymously."

"Oh, that's perfect," she giggled.

My dried-up goldfish was the ideal gift for a guy who found cinematic inspiration in bloody chickens. We were sending him a dead animal—bloodless, but nonetheless dead. Maybe it would inspire a new film—*Gruesome Goldfish Suicide*.

Weeks later, Milan stood near the desk in my room, looking at my fish tank. "Didn't there used to be another fish in there?" he asked.

"Yep. One killed itself. Didn't you receive something *special* in the mail?" I asked innocently.

Milan looked bewildered. "*You* did that? I was wondering who would do a sick thing like that. Disgusting! You girls were the ones that mailed me that dead thing?"

"We thought you could make a film about it. It's not a bloody chicken, but it's interesting, right?" I couldn't stop laughing. His look of sheer revulsion was priceless.

"I can't believe you girls would do something like that," he replied, disgusted.

Apparently, Milan didn't find dead animals truly inspirational. It seemed that his repeated ramblings about splattered patterns of red on snow was all huff and puff. He was just blowing smoke in a show of male bravado meant to shock and awe. Maybe we'd been wrong about Milan. Perhaps he only pretended to be preoccupied with blood, gore, and twisted tales. Maybe he was far less shallow and cocky than he let on.

Friday afternoon, I sat alone in my room, pondering Milan and CJ, and the revelations that school year had brought about both of them. I couldn't help but wonder how much time we spent—each of us—masking and hiding our insecurities from the opposite sex. We all seemed to abide by that age-old adage, "Never let 'em see you sweat." In a show of manufactured confidence, I always pretended to be indifferent toward guys, as though they had no effect on me. I pretended to barely notice them, like faded old wallpaper, when in fact, they colored, confused, and swirled my world in a hundred brilliant shades and hues.

Was it possible that Milan and CJ were actors too? They always pretended to know everything about women. But they were twenty-one years old—what could they possibly know? Why did they carelessly and purposefully mention their past lovers and conquests as though we needed proof of their virility? Why did Milan always hide his feelings? Why did CJ act like he was immune to heartbreak? Were they boys trying to prove their manhood? Or men attempting to shed the bewildered, uncertain feelings of boys? What did any of us know? About men or women, love, or sex? We'd barely left our parents' homes to live on our own. We hardly knew ourselves.

Underneath, we knew we were vulnerable. That's what scared us. Who of us didn't want someone, that right *someone*, to see us, accept us, and love us? Instead, we all pretended—at least, across gender lines—to hardly need each other. And yet, somehow we all found ourselves most at home, most delighted, and most comforted in the presence of one another inside the walls of the apartment.

If I were a deeper thinker—which I wasn't—I might have contemplated this realization about Milan, CJ, and myself for more than a split second. But I didn't give a whole lot of thought to my relationships with the opposite sex—or to my thought processes. Keri and Michelle liked to analyze ideas—pull apart concepts and abstractions and then reexamine them. Keri would ask a question like "How does God intend men and women to interact with each other?" Then she'd go look up every reference and Bible verse she could find to answer her question. I rarely did that. Ideas and concepts beyond art and the visual world didn't particularly interest me. I spent little time evaluating bad relational habits I'd developed.

As a kid, I was a tomboy, always preferring a game of dodgeball or kickball to standing around chatting with girls. As a result, I had as many boy friends as I had girl friends throughout primary school. But physical affection was rarely part of the equation with boys. Most of the time, I didn't even hug my guy friends. That changed during the later years of high school and the beginning of college. Out of the blue, one of my high school friends started to hold my hand when we went out. We were purely platonic, but I loved it when he'd catch my hand in his—such a warm, easy, natural feeling. Our friends knew we weren't dating. There was nothing implied, and no hidden agenda, in our hand holding. Rather, it was a sweet gesture; he affirmed me. In a very public way, he seemed to say, "I appreciate you as a woman. I'm proud to hold your hand in public." I have no idea if that's what holding my hand meant to him, but that's what it meant to me.

Since my experiences with my male friends were generally positive, I never asked whether my *thinking* about my male friends was positive—or right. It never occurred to me that I objectified men. My friend from high school was a pretty nice-looking guy. Would I have let him hold my hand if he hadn't been cute? Probably not. Would I have become friends with him if he hadn't been attractive? I'd like to think so—but I can't say yes for sure.

I evaluated my morality primarily by what I *didn't* do. I didn't steal, and I didn't lie (often). But I never looked critically at what I *did* do—like deciding if I'd pursue friendship with a guy based on what he looked like. That wasn't right or fair, but shallow and self-serving.

I can trace the origins of my wrong thinking back to a single moment in high school. I went to the junior prom that year with a longtime friend of mine who attended a different high school. The Monday after prom, a couple of students asked me about him. "Who was that? He was hot." In that moment, my ego blew up like an overfilled blimp as they prodded me for more details about my mysterious prom date. I hadn't intended to use my friend, but unknowingly I did. I took immense pleasure in the admiration I received from other students. My thinking was a serious problem—but I didn't recognize it. After that, I started collecting nice-looking guy friends the way little boys collected trading cards or comic books.

In the same vein, I defined my chastity by what I *didn't* do. I didn't lust (often)—so I considered myself pretty good. But I missed the root of chastity—purity of mind. I didn't criticize my internal rating system, which automatically scored guys on a scale of one to ten by hotness. If someone had confronted me on my objectification, I might have blamed it on my influences—overexposure to twisted, hypersexualized art films and my love of the fashion industry—an industry founded on objectifying people. But the blame lay with me and my way of thinking.

But, like I said, I didn't ponder any of these things at the time—especially not my love of the superficial. I admitted I was flawed; but so was everyone else. I never made the connection that I thought about men in exactly the way I hated for men to think about women. I didn't like it when a guy called a woman a babe or ignored a woman because she wasn't hot. But I did the same thing, always referring to CJ as Sexy. In my own messed-up thinking, I didn't recognize that objectification—mine and everyone else's—lay at the root of the entire college hookup culture that was so prevalent. At one level or another, friends, acquaintances, and even strangers had grown accustomed to using each other, as objects, to satisfy selfish needs. No wonder we were all so guarded and cautious across gender lines. We were all afraid of being objectified and used, the same way we subconsciously knew we used others.

Chapter Eighteen

winter escapades

{December–January, Winter of Senior Year}

A BRUTAL COLD SHROUDED THE UNIVERSITY IN AN ENVELOPE of ice and chill. We cranked up the apartment heater and never turned it off. Every hot meal that I didn't have to cook was a blessing directly from heaven. I treasured my supply of prepackaged bags of Swiss Miss hot cocoa like a newfound friend. To our delight, Keri whipped up a couple batches of cookies from scratch, filling our apartment with the smell of Christmas and home. She placed a small menorah in the living room, and we celebrated Hanukkah, the Festival of Lights, with her.

Keri invited over a Jewish guy that she thought was cute to light the Hanukkah candles with us. He was a little younger than my roommates and me. For some reason, he'd decided to test himself by going all winter without a coat. "I think it's some sort of mind-over-matter thing," Keri explained. As far as I knew, no one could *will* hypothermia away. I hoped he didn't end up with pneumonia.

After we lit the candles, Keri told him, "It's our family custom for everyone to kiss and wish each other a happy Hanukkah." Keri had told him the truth—that *was* the custom in her family. But she had ulterior motives. The two exchanged kisses on the cheek—very benign—but funny nonetheless. Keri cracked me up.

The door closed on my final fall semester. Finals loomed, and I spent much of my time preparing for exams in my room. It was much too cold to trek unnecessarily to the library or elsewhere to study once I was comfortably tucked in my cozy bedroom.

"I'm going to Prague next semester," Noel told me.

"No way—I'm dying to go to Prague."

"Yep, I'm doing a semester abroad."

"You're going to have so much fun," I replied enthusiastically.

With the fall of Communism, Eastern Europe had opened up to the West. American students rushed to the Czech Republic in droves. "It's what Paris used to be back in the day," a classmate told me. Prague was the "it" destination for a semester abroad—full of fresh possibilities and ripe opportunity for young innovators and dreamers. I had just read an article about some American students who had started a new English language magazine there.

"You're going in the middle of winter, though," I reminded her. "It's going to be freezing."

"I know," she replied. "That's the part I'm not looking forward to."

"It's supposed to be beautiful, though—the architecture, the art . . . You have to send me a postcard."

"Definitely," she returned. "Don't worry—you'll hear from me, for sure."

"Are you going after Christmas?" I asked.

"Yep. I'll go home for Christmas break. Then I'll leave after New Year's."

"That's so cool," I replied.

The day after my last final, I crammed stacks of clothes into my largest suitcase and hugged our gang good-bye. I wished everyone merry Christmas and happy Hanukkah and then fled the biting Philadelphia frost for a mild Christmas in California.

Back home, I enjoyed a relaxing two weeks with my parents and younger brother. My brother and I slept in just about every day during the break and watched lots of movies. On Christmas Day, we ate too much and sat around the dining table, as we did each year, telling stories about the silly things my brother and I did growing up. As always,

Nick Wilson came over Christmas Day and graciously accepted a slice of Mom's feared and beloved fruitcake. A couple days after New Year's, I returned to school—for my grand finale.

Keri moved out of the room we shared and into Noel's old room as soon as she returned from Christmas break. I would have the entire double bedroom to myself that semester. Michelle stayed in her single room. Each of us would enjoy our own bedrooms for the rest of the year.

The day after I returned from break, Milan came over.

"Hey, how was Christmas?" he asked.

"Good," I answered. "How was yours?"

"It was nice to get away from here for a while."

"Hey, I got you something," I replied, handing him a box wrapped in colorful Christmas paper.

"Really?" he asked curiously as he untied the ribbon and tore the wrapping paper from the box.

He lifted the black leather book out of the box. "Thank you," he stated quietly.

"Really?" I asked. "I had your name engraved on the front. Did you see it?"

"Yes," he said appreciatively. "Really, I mean it. Thank you," he repeated genuinely.

He placed the lid back on the Bible's box and tucked it under his arm before he departed. I knew he'd probably dispose of the Bible that Michelle and I had given him earlier. He didn't have any personal attachment to it. But I figured he'd keep this one; it was leather bound with his name in silver on the front. You couldn't very well throw something away, or give it away, if your name was engraved on it.

A new year and a new semester rolled in. It was only fitting that my roommates and I throw a party—in honor of Michelle's twenty-first birthday. We celebrated with a rip-roaring seventies costume disco party in our apartment, the fourth party we'd thrown senior year. Keri's first sushi party was so successful that we had hosted two more.

Guests packed the living room for Michelle's birthday, rocking polyester bell-bottoms, wide collars, fringed suede jackets, and groovy shades. We snapped the usual tell-all pictures: Milan dancing with a giant aluminum-foil disco ball around his neck, and the sisterhood, lined up, triumphantly flashing our two-finger *V* pose. We got down to the Bee Gees and used a broomstick to bust open a crazy-looking, homemade puppy-dog piñata that Keri had created. As always, the party wound down late. It was the perfect beginning to our last semester.

That semester, I successfully locked down the ideal schedule for a graduating senior. I had no classes before noon, and all day Wednesday was free. Once a week on Monday nights, I showed up for a basic art history course. Tuesday night, I mixed it up with a creative writing class. We wrote poetry and short stories and then read them aloud to the class. Every Friday afternoon, I dropped in for my jazz and blues class. My assignments included listening to recordings by jazz legends Oscar Peterson and Thelonious Monk. I only had one class that met more than once a week—Knowledge and Social Structure. I had no idea what that course was about, but it fulfilled a course requirement and sounded interesting.

Each academic year, students were allowed to take a course pass/fail. I'd saved up all my pass/fails for my final semester. That meant that I only had to put forth minimal effort toward exams and papers. If I showed up for lectures and took good notes, I was sure to pass all my classes and sail through to graduation with ease.

With such a light course load, I could devote the semester almost exclusively to photography. I made a short list of professional commercial photographers in Philadelphia and went knocking door to door, looking for an internship to fill up each Wednesday. I made appointments and met with photographers at two commercial studios before I walked into Joseph Andris's studio. Like most professional studios dedicated to advertising, it was a decent-sized industrial space with high ceilings, multiple cameras mounted on large metal stands, and thousands of dollars' worth of lights, stands, and equipment everywhere. Joe, a pleasant, slight man in his late thirties or early forties, specialized in product photography for print advertising. He photographed the types of everyday household items you'd buy at your neighborhood Target. You might see his photographs in a newspaper insert or a magazine.

"Sure, you can intern with me," he offered. "It won't be paid, but you can come in whenever you want and observe our photo shoots."

"Thank you. Thank you," I beamed, pumping his hand. I'd never been on a professional photo shoot or worked in a commercial studio before.

All semester, I spent every Wednesday at Joe's studio, working alongside him and his studio manager, Mike. I literally hung out and watched, while they explained the entire commercial photography process to me. They were great guys; they never asked me to do grunt work like sweeping the studio or running out for lattes. Instead, they taught me to refer to the pieces of photo equipment by their proper names. Lights weren't just lights; they were "softboxes" and "strobes" powered by "power packs." I learned that in addition to 35-milimeter cameras there were large- and medium-format cameras. Joe used a large-format 4 x 5 camera to shoot most of his advertising work.

I sat through my first food photo shoot at Joe's studio. Actually, it was an advertisement for paper towels, but the food stylist—who had a job I didn't even know existed—brought in two-dozen homemade muffins. Only one of those muffins, the most beautiful and perfect one, would sit on the paper towel in the advertisement. I couldn't believe it—a beauty pageant for muffins. The food stylist spent thirty minutes selecting which muffin would appear in the image. She and the photographer examined the runner-up muffins together and discussed the muffins' best attributes before they finally agreed which won the pageant. After that, the food stylist spent another forty-five minutes preparing the special chosen muffin for its cameo. The muffin couldn't have a single stray crumb or any knicks or imperfections anywhere. In the event that the photograph was blown up to billboard size, the gigantic muffin would need to appear flawless in every regard.

I wasn't allowed near the paper towel or the muffin during the shoot. A simple accidental bump of a light or the muffin could result in the need for painstaking relighting. Hours of time and effort could be lost if a single item shifted on the set.

However, the following week I *was* allowed to roll up my sleeves and help with an advertisement for Maalox. Joe frequently shot Maalox boxes. It was my job to use a can of air to blow off the table where the box sat, just before Joe fired off the power packs. Every speck of dust showed up in the giant negative produced by the large-format camera, so before each exposure, every microscopic bit of dust had to be eliminated. I was the official DustBuster. I became quite skilled at wielding my little aerosol can of air and blasting every speck of unwanted dust.

Through Joe, I met a Philadelphia-based fashion photographer named Greg, an easygoing middle-aged guy who often rode his Harley-Davidson to work. The two had been friends for years. I had learned volumes from the Maalox photo shoots, but I really wanted to assist on fashion photo shoots. One day, I arranged to go visit Greg for a tour of his fashion studio.

"Do you need an intern?" I asked.

"No, I already have someone that helps out around the studio," he answered. I'd met his assistant earlier. She looked about my age. She confidently moved around Greg's workspace doing official-looking things. She looked to be far more knowledgeable of the inner workings of a professional studio than I.

"Well, if you do need an intern—later," I continued, "here's my contact information."

I continued working with Joe all semester but stayed in touch with Greg, the only real fashion photographer I'd personally met. I wasn't about to lose that connection.

Not long after my visit to Greg's studio, I bumped into CJ walking through campus.

"Ehh-hey-eh. Whassup?" he called out.

"Nada. What's going on?" I replied.

"Nothing," he answered. "Where are you headed?"

"Home. Hey, let me snap your picture really quick," I suggested as I stood looking up at him. CJ looked even more delicious than usual today.

"Let's get a picture of us together," he replied.

We stood right in the heart of campus, near the intersection of the Palladium patio and just a ways up from the Castle house. CJ flagged down a student.

"Hey, will you take our picture?" he asked the girl.

"Yeah. No problem," she agreed. I showed her how to focus my camera and handed it over.

"Hey, let's make this a good one," CJ said with a grin. "I'm going to put you on my shoulders."

CJ bent down so I could straddle his neck. He stood and lifted me easily onto his shoulders. Suddenly I was high in the air; he locked his arms around my legs to hold me steady. He yelped a wild yawp just as the camera shutter released. The shot turned out great. CJ stood in his sunglasses, legs slightly apart as he flashed a broad, contagious smile for the camera. I sat on his shoulders, wearing a suede jacket just a shade darker than his, grinning like a mad fool—me and Sexy immortalized on film forever.

Several days later, I came home from the library late in the afternoon. I'd been settled down at my desk with my art history book for a while when a knock on the door interrupted me. Keri let Stephanie in. I joined them in the living room. Soon CJ arrived.

"Hey, when are you going to the darkroom again?" he asked.

"Tomorrow probably."

"Can I come? I have some pictures I want to develop."

"Sure," I replied.

The darkroom was my personal clubhouse. The year before, my photography professor had given me my own darkroom key. I had a locker where I stored my boxes of light-sensitive photo paper and darkroom chemicals. Often I spent hours alone in the place, printing images for my portfolio. Usually, I was the only person in the darkroom. It belonged to the Fine Arts Department but fine arts students rarely used the facility. Dark and isolated, it smelled pungently acidic with the vapors emitted by the photo chemicals. The darkroom resided inside a remote facility on the outskirts of campus. A large drawing and painting studio, littered with easels and spilled paint, occupied most of the building. The darkroom seemed like an afterthought, stuffed into an empty quadrant that lay off the art studio.

Keri, Michelle, and Stephanie never came to the darkroom with me. Occasionally, some of my models asked to join me—Milan and a few others. They were curious about the black-and-white printing process. Once in the darkroom, illuminated by the low-wattage safelight and surrounded by the large metal photo enlargers that transferred the image from the negative to paper, the magical process that transformed a blank piece of light-sensitive paper into an irresistibly rich photographic canvas enraptured my darkroom guests. I appreciated the company. Once in a while, it was pleasant to have someone to talk to while holed up in the dim cavern.

I would be nice to have CJ along. Since the darkroom was my domain, it was the one place where even the most beautiful male super-model didn't intimidate me. He was my pupil as I guided him through the process of making an exposure and then placing the paper in the chemicals and timing the image's development.

The next afternoon, CJ met me at my apartment, and we walked across campus toward the easternmost part of the school.

"Here it is," I said as I let us into the locked building and walked through the dark painting studio into the small anteroom just outside the darkroom. "The darkroom is through that door. Let me grab my trays and some things from my locker. You can have a seat inside while I mix some fresh chemicals and get everything set up."

I guided CJ into the pitch-black darkroom, and we stood momentarily, waiting until our eyes adjusted to the dim safelight.

"These are the enlargers," I said, pointing out the several large structures mounted at individual stations with black partitions between each. "This is the sink where we'll develop everything," I explained. The long, waist-high rectangular sink filled up most of the small room. "Pick an enlarger to work at," I advised. "I usually work at that one, so you can get situated at the one right next to me."

CJ grabbed a seat while I laid out the trays and prepared the chemicals.

"It's dark in here," he remarked.

"Uh, yeah," I replied with a chuckle. "That's why it's called a *dark-room.*"

"Right," he replied. "What is that? It smells funny."

I named off the trays of chemicals. "Developer, stop bath, fixer. Yeah, they don't smell so great. But I love that smell—that's the smell of photography!" I explained enthusiastically.

"Where's your negative?" I asked him. "Let me see the negative you want to print."

He handed it to me. Then I walked him through the process of loading the negative into the negative carrier, focusing the image, and then making test strips to determine the proper exposure. Once I got him settled in, I set up my own negative in the enlarger next to him.

"Can you believe it?" CJ huffed. "I took these images to the photo place to process, and they wouldn't print them. They said the images were *inappropriate.* Can you believe that?"

"You're kidding, right?" I retorted.

"No. I'm so sure. Inappropriate!" he scoffed.

"Who took the photos?"

"I did," he answered.

I couldn't believe him. CJ was UNBELIEVABLE! In an instant I just *knew* the crazy boy was printing porn—his own homemade porn.

"Don't look at the pictures," he warned me.

I wanted to clock him. Hard! I should have known better than to think we'd have a pleasant, uneventful evening printing nice pictures in the darkroom. *Don't look at them? Was he high? I had every right to look at the pictures. He was using my paper, my chemicals, and MY TIME—for SMUTTY PICTURES!* I was just about to blast him when I caught myself. What was the point of yelling at him? He didn't think anything was the matter with his photos. He was surprised, even appalled, that the photo processing lab disapproved of his pictures.

I was tempted to flip over the picture he'd just dropped into the developer, with the image facedown, just to prove to him that he couldn't tell me what to do. But I thought about it for another moment. Did I really want to see some raunchy pictures he'd taken? Chances were he'd photographed one of the girls he'd hooked up with. She was probably scantily clad or topless or posing provocatively—just indecent enough that the photo lab wouldn't print the images, but not pornographic enough that he'd expected their refusal of service. There was a very good chance that I knew the girl. I'd probably met her through CJ—which would explain why he didn't want me to see the photos. CJ had a tendency to introduce all his friends to each other, including hookup buddies and friends with benefits.

But that was just my best guess about what the photos contained. I really had no idea. The subject matter could have been far more risqué. They could have been pictures with CJ *in* them. Did I really want explicit pictures of CJ emblazoned in my mind for the rest of senior year?

In the end, I decided not to look at the photos and not to say anything. If I looked at the photos and saw a student I knew, I'd forever think of her as the girl who posed for CJ's personal porn library. She deserved more than that. She was more than just the object of his inappropriate pictures. Later, she'd probably regret the decision herself. Who knew who he'd show the pictures to or where they'd resurface after college? I didn't need to know what she and CJ had done. I didn't *want* to know. I saw no point in giving CJ a lecture about how his photos devalued her as a person. He'd simply argue that she was a consenting adult and say that he'd taken the pictures with her permission. It would be a fruitless battle of opposing moral values. He'd feel unfairly judged by his preachy friend (me), and I'd just be angry. Nothing would be resolved.

Without the same point of reference guiding his moral compass, we'd always be on antagonistic ends of the values spectrum.

I didn't object to all images containing nudity—on the contrary—some of my favorite works of art showed a lot of skin. But those works honored the body as a beautiful and divine creation. You had to consider the artist's intention as well as the image. Was the image meant to portray the beauty of form in a way that brought respect and dignity to the subject? Or did the image degrade the subject by objectifying her? There was a very fine line—and a very subjective one at that. The photo lab might deem CJ's images pornographic, but he might argue that they were art.

That evening CJ printed several four-by-six-inch pictures before he left the darkroom. I let him go without looking at any of them. I stayed in the darkroom for a couple more hours, printing the images from my most recent photo shoot.

The following day, I was at home when the phone rang.

"Hello."

"Hey, it's me. It's freezing here. I bought a coat that covers my entire body. I look like the Michelin Man. How are you?" a women's voice exclaimed.

I didn't recognize the cheerful greeting.

"I have a collect call from Noey Knott in Prague," an operator interrupted.

"I accept," I chirped.

"You're not supposed to accept!" Noel exclaimed. "Ask Keri. She knows the drill. When I call, there's just enough time before the operator interrupts for me to say hi. It's just to let you know I'm okay."

The collect call was Noel's way of sending a postcard-sized sound bite, free of charge over the phone line. Skype and the other low-cost Internet communication services didn't exist yet.

"So next time, don't accept. Okay?" she implored.

"Got it."

"How are you by the way?" she asked.

"Good. I have the perfect schedule this semester."

"Nice. Okay, I'm getting off. This call is going to cost you a fortune! Bye." Noel hung up. I was glad she'd called. I could picture her bundled up like the bulbous Michelin tire man, in a giant Arctic-style coat that swallowed up her hair and her slim little body.

A couple days later, when I arrived home after class, CJ sat in the living room, visiting with Keri.

"Hey, what's up?" I greeted them both.

"Hey, Delie," Keri replied.

"What's going on?" CJ answered.

Just then, the phone rang. I picked it up. It was my mom. I pulled our single landline, with its extra long extension cord, into my room and closed the door to block out Keri and CJ's discussion in the living room. As I jabbered away with my mom, I remembered that I'd left my day planner in the living room. I'd written down some information in there that I needed to give her.

"Hey, Mom, hold on a minute. I need to get my planner," I said before scurrying to retrieve it from the living room. As I searched hurriedly for the date book, I listened in on Keri and CJ's discussion.

"That was you knocking on my door, wasn't it?" CJ asked Keri.

"Yeah, I was knocking forever. I almost opened it and came in," Keri replied.

He snickered. "It's a good thing you didn't. You might have seen my butt. I was messin' around with Maya—you know, that girl down the hall."

"Yuck," Keri retorted. "You're lucky. I almost walked in on you."

"Eh-hey-heee," CJ laughed with his big, bad Brutus cackle. Recently he'd begun referring to himself, quite fittingly, as Brutus. I had assumed this was a reference to the Brutus villain from the Popeye cartoon, not the noble, moralizing Brutus of Shakespeare's *Julius Caesar*.

I found the planner and jetted back down the hall to wrap up my conversation with Mom. After a few more minutes, we hung up. I headed back into the living room to join CJ and Keri. Stephanie and

LSD Jesse stopped by. Eventually Michelle joined us. The six of us sat around joking and talking for the rest of the evening.

Several days later, early Friday evening, my friend Justin Greco dropped by the apartment to say hello. He'd come down from New York for a quick visit to his alma mater. Justin had graduated the year before us. That year, he'd been dating Clare when the intruder broke into her apartment and assaulted her. After graduation, Justin had accepted a sweet job in New York. I always stayed with him whenever I visited Manhattan. He was a great friend and a fabulous host—always in the know on the hippest new restaurant or lounge we should check out whenever I came into town.

Justin had saved my hide when I pledged his coed fraternity sophomore year. I was a rotten pledge. I didn't bother to memorize the fraternity's history or learn anything in my pledge handbook. Truthfully, I didn't even know where my pledge handbook was—buried under a pile of course packets and old lecture notes, most likely.

"Pledge, recite the Greek alphabet," one of my fraternity sisters barked as I stood blindfolded and fully clothed in a shower stall on initiation night.

"Uh, alpha, beta, gamma, uh . . . gamma, delta . . . ah, hmmm . . . phi?"

Fortunately, the pledge next to me in the shower was more diligent. "Delta, epsilon, zeta, eta, theta . . . ," my fellow pledge rattled off uninterrupted.

"You lucked out pledge night," Justin warned me. "They were going to turn the shower on you."

I knew he had gone to bat for me. Had it not been for Justin, I probably would have walked home through West Philadelphia that evening soaking wet, each of my shoes squishing in its own personal puddle and my clothes thoroughly drenched from the outside in. It would not have been a pleasant walk, with the autumn temperatures giving way to a wintery forty degrees at night. I was forever grateful to Justin for getting me through initiation night unscathed, with minimal hazing.

All through college, I had believed the Greek system was inherently lame. I didn't see the point of submitting myself to torture throughout the pledge process for the right to belong to a predetermined circle of friends. But as an outsider to the Greek system, it was easy to criticize. To objectively confirm that the Greek system was bogus, I had to be a part of it. So I pledged Phi Sigma Pi. I wasn't about to pledge a sorority—I wouldn't meet any interesting guys there. I joined to find out from the inside, whether or not Greek life had any meaningful purpose.

Most of the people in my fraternity were okay, but I rarely hung out with them, except Justin. I stuck with the fraternity through sophomore year, but junior year marked the invention of the Elevator Society. I resigned from the fraternity junior year, my true allegiance pledged to the V Society sisterhood. I might have stayed in Phi Sigma Pi if I hadn't been required to attend the dull, mandatory, monthly two-hour Parliamentary-procedure-guided meetings on Sunday afternoons. Parliamentary procedure, with all its formal motions and seconds, bored me to tears. Meetings with agendas and outlines, by the sheer fact that they enlisted agendas and outlines, weren't fun and usually weren't very interesting. The V Society would never bow to such rigorous order and formal controls. The natural anarchy and spontaneity of Elevator Society gatherings suited me far better.

As a freshman, I'd had a crush on Justin for two whole days. He was cute. But one of my friends had a long-standing crush on him, so my late-to-the-party crush seemed a bit of a betrayal. I had to keep my infatuation under lock and key for the entire forty-eight hours. Fortunately, summer break was a mere four days away, and I wasn't one to drag the baggage of the past school year into a fresh, new summer, with its endless possibilities of newborn romantic interests.

When he had been in school with us, Justin had led a Bible study. He knew Scripture the way I knew f-stops on my camera. He was a straight shooter—trustworthy and honest, the kind of friend you could depend on. Some people, like Justin, didn't understand why Keri, Michelle, and I were friends with CJ and Milan. He'd met Milan the previous year and, on the night of his visit, spoke briefly with CJ, who was on his way out, as Justin arrived.

"Why do you, Keri, and Michelle hang out with those guys?" Justin asked me. He didn't care much for either of them.

We hung out with them because we liked them; they were our friends. Despite all of our differences, they were people that we enjoyed talking to. They challenged our beliefs, and that helped us grow. They forced us to clearly articulate what we believed and why. I couldn't give CJ or Milan a pat Sunday School answer for my reverence for purity, righteousness, and holiness—they were too smart to accept that. There would always be a deeper "Why?" What good was my faith if it was never challenged?

I didn't see the point of surrounding myself with people that believed only as I did and acted as I did. It was imperative that my innermost circle of friends—Keri and Michelle—shared my core beliefs, because they held me accountable. They helped me stay the spiritual course that I had chosen. But how could I be a light in the world, if I shunned everyone *in* the world? I couldn't share the love I'd found in Jesus with people other than Michelle and Keri, if I was unwilling to be a friend to anyone else.

Not a single guy in our Christian fellowship student group was interested in making films with me. The term *avant-garde* didn't exist in their vocabulary. A lot of the guys there were business majors and on their way to running Fortune 500 companies. I didn't see how hanging out with tomorrow's Wall Street tycoons would help me develop my talent as a photographer and filmmaker. Milan was ingeniously creative and instinctively gravitated toward film and the arts. CJ was a business guy, but he was interested in the film business; he wanted to produce films and run film festivals.

Also, I didn't think it was immoral to laugh and have fun. Some Christian students seemed way too serious all the time—like they had missed the roll call when God handed out senses of humor. Jesus hung out with prostitutes and tax collectors. They loved being with him. Their lives were already humorless and probably pretty depressing. I couldn't imagine that they loved hanging out with a guy who never laughed. Jesus was probably fun.

Some people acted like Satan conceived and birthed the art world. Every spark of creativity, innovation, and breaking with tradition was assumed to have sprung straight from the pit of hell. But I loved art and everything related to it. The absence of people of faith from the art world was precisely why the arts—film, modern art, performing art, and music—had evolved as they had. Everyone seemed to have forgotten that during the Renaissance the Church was the largest patron of the arts. Michelangelo and Leonardo da Vinci were the rock stars of their day. The Church largely funded their paintings. Michelangelo created the famed frescoes on the ceiling of the Sistine Chapel. Michelangelo's *David* was King David of the Bible. Leonardo da Vinci painted more images of Jesus, Mary, saints, and angels than I could count. One of his most famous paintings was of Jesus's last supper with the twelve disciples.

Why was I friends with CJ and Milan? One of the biggest reasons was the simplest. Their presence awed me. Regardless of how much they exasperated me, whenever I spent time with either of them, I never noticed the other cute guys in my peripheral vision. They both captured my full attention. That was rare for me.

But I didn't tell Justin any of that. I just shrugged his question off with, "I don't know. They're our friends because they're our friends." Then I changed the subject. Justin stayed another hour.

"I'll see you next time I'm in New York," I told him as he left to visit some other friends in our building.

Chapter Nineteen

february adventures

{February, Winter of Senior Year}

AMIDST ALL THE BURGEONING ACTIVITIES REGULARLY TRANS-
piring in our world, Michelle and I recognized that some neglected old
business needed resolution.

"We really have to do something about Keri's underwear," I told her.

"I know. It's getting really bad," Michelle agreed.

"No kidding. I told her those panties were sad. She just laughed."

"Sometimes it takes a good friend to expose the ugly truth,"
Michelle replied.

"I think it's time we orchestrated an underwear intervention on Keri's
behalf," I agreed.

All through junior year and into senior year, Keri had held hostage
some extremely unsavory panties that were past due for replacement.
It was cruel and wrong for her to wear the current stash that she had
brought in from the laundry room. Those things piled up in her laundry
basket offended both Michelle and me. Keri had stacks of giant, saggy
once-white and now dingy-off-white-from-too-many-no-bleach-wash-
ings cotton panties that she could practically pull up to her chin. She
was a beautiful twenty-year-old, not someone's grandmother! The panties were like a bad omen; they screamed, "Virgin forever!" We couldn't

have that. The goal was to become a V Society alumna, not a permanent member.

Keri needed to go shopping. We weren't suggesting anything fancy— just some new, don't-hit-the-chin bikinis from a generic department store. It was wrong for someone in the prime of her life to wear those alarming things. Once or twice, Michelle and I had made wisecracks directly to Keri about the frightening panties. She hadn't taken the hint, so we crafted a plan to make sure she got the message.

One day, while Keri was out, Michelle and I went into Keri's underwear drawer and found the biggest, saggiest, saddest pairs of panties. We hung them all over the walls of Keri's room. Keri came home, walked into her room, and screamed in horror. She told her mom on us the next Friday when she went home for Shabbat service. Her mom was equally horrified.

"I can't believe Michelle and Adele would do something so naughty. They seem like such nice girls," Mrs. Zelman scolded. Nonetheless, Mrs. Zelman took Keri underwear shopping, and the scary granny-panties became a sad memory of the past.

The week after the panty revolt, my roommates and I sat around speculating on *what if* and *when* questions. At some point in the evening our conversation turned to honeymoons:

"When you get married, where do you think you'll go on your honeymoon?" Michelle asked.

"Hmmm . . . good question. Somewhere quiet and relaxing, like . . ." Keri paused. She was probably reviewing a mental list of faraway romantic destinations.

"Who cares where you go for the first few days," I interjected.

"What do you mean? Don't you want to go somewhere nice for your honeymoon?" Keri asked.

"Of course. But I'm not leaving the hotel room for at least the first four days. I've been waiting *forever*. Do you have any idea how much catching up I have to do?"

Like little volcanoes, Keri and Michelle erupted into thunder-like peals of room-shaking laughter. I thought they were going to fall off their seats.

"Speaking of honeymoons," I continued, "I can't remember who, but someone told me, 'When you go Victoria's Secret don't even bother trying on the lingerie. Just ball it up and throw it on the floor.'"

"What?" Michelle asked.

"Well, on your wedding night, you're only going to have lingerie on for what—like five seconds? It's just going to end up in a ball on the floor, so why bother trying it on? You're never going to wear it—not really. Instead, pick a bunch of cute things and just throw them on the floor. If they look good *there*—buy them!"

Keri and Michelle howled with laughter. Their faces flushed pink. Keri roared so loudly, her eyes started to tear.

"Even better, just throw it up in the air and see how it looks hanging off the light fixtures. Dangling from the chandeliers . . ." I couldn't finish the sentence; my whole body shook with infectious giggles. When I finally caught my breath, I continued. "Too bad we're not all engaged, we could have the perfect V Society field trip—lingerie shopping. We wouldn't try things on, we'd just go and throw things all over the floor. Could you imagine? Then we'd get arrested for disorderly conduct, and the headline would say, 'VIRGINS GO WILD IN VICTORIA'S SECRET.'"

The three of us were laughing so loudly now, I was sure all our neighbors could hear us. Once or twice, one of our neighbors had actually *asked* me why there was always such a ruckus in our apartment. I had shrugged and played innocent, hoping they'd think Keri or Michelle caused all the commotion.

"I think I'm going to choke," Keri gasped between chortles.

"Ughh, my stomach hurts," Michelle groaned, doubled over. She laughed so hard it was a wonder her sides didn't split. It took us five whole minutes before one of us could speak again.

"I think I'm going to be sick," I said as I lay down on the floor, aching from my laugh attack.

That spurred more chuckling, and soon we were all cracking up again.

"I think I wet my pants," Michelle jested.

Days later, the phone rang. I answered.

"Hi! I'm in Poland. I'm seeing someone new—he's Polish. I'm fine," a familiar voice exclaimed.

"I have a collect call from Noey Knott in Poland. Will you accept?" the operator spoke over Noel.

"Bye, Noel. Have fun!" I cried. "No, I won't accept the charges," I replied to the operator.

"Bye, Adele."

"Bye!"

Later that evening, CJ popped in.

"I'm growing cannabis in my room," he smirked.

"Yeah, right," I dismissed him. I didn't believe a word he said. I wasn't wasting time talking to him about nonsense. "In your opinion, what's the greatest film ever made?" I asked, changing the subject.

"Seriously, I'm growing pot in my room," he redirected.

"Whatever," I sighed.

"You don't believe me?"

"No."

"I'll show you," CJ insisted. "I built a whole greenhouse setup. Come to my room, and I'll show you. It's really nice. I set up lights and everything."

"When?"

"Today. We can leave in about thirty minutes—'cause I'm comfortable *here* right now," he said, relaxing in his favorite spot. "But I'll show you later."

"Whatever—if it makes you happy."

An hour later, CJ rose to leave. I remained seated.

"Are you coming?"

"Where?"

"To see my cannabis plants."

"Do I have to?" I replied lazily. Truthfully, I *was* curious. But I was 99 percent sure he was making it up. He stood looking at me, willing me to get up and look at his little greenhouse concoction.

"Fine, fine, I'm coming," I agreed.

We plodded through the cold to his dorm. CJ opened the door to his dorm room. In all the time I had known him, I'd never been to his place. We entered, and he strode toward his closet. I was surprised that he didn't have a single bit of artwork on his walls. Not a poster, or even pages torn out of a magazine. Nothing. The room was stark and minimal. He'd hardly done anything with the space to make it feel like more than a basic dorm room. CJ slid the closet door open and stood looking at me, his face awash with self-satisfied delight. Several rows of plants sat in containers under an extensive rig of lights.

He turned toward the closet. "These are the lights I installed to help the plants grow," he said pointing to the long, thin bulbs in plastic casing hanging down over the plants. I wondered what he'd done with his clothes. The whole upper portion of the closet housed the cannabis nursery. There were no clothes in sight.

"Now do you believe me?"

"Yes." I replied evenly. "Fine—let's go."

CJ's room smelled foul—like musty gym socks comingled with a damp greenhouse aroma. I couldn't believe anyone could hook up in the midst of that smell. At any moment, my dinner was sure to rush up out of my stomach and spill all over CJ's industrial dorm room carpet. It sickened me; I couldn't wait to get out of there. How could the university's sexiest guy have the rankest smelling room in the entire school?

Several weeks after my visit, two uniformed police officers knocked on CJ's door.

"Are you CJ Knowlan?" the first officer asked.

"Yeah," CJ returned.

"You have the right to remain silent," the officer stated sternly. "Anything you say can and will be used against you in a court of law . . ."

Suddenly, CJ's college career flashed before his eyes like a near-death flashback. His Penn days were over. CJ wasn't graduating from Wharton; he was going to jail for growing contraband.

CJ began to cry. Tears streamed down his face.

"Please don't take me to jail," he wailed. He was beside himself. "Please, please . . . ," he begged.

Just as the officers proceeded to cuff him, Gabrielle, one of the girls in CJ's dorm appeared in the doorway laughing her head off.

"Gotcha!" she howled. CJ, the playa, had been played. Finally, one of the girls in CJ's dorm had decided to turn the tables and wreak a little havoc in his world.

"Those are my friends—in costume," Gabrielle laughed, pointing at the officers.

CJ sat in my living room, retelling the story in detail. "Man, I was crying and crying," he said. "I really thought I was going to jail."

"Gabrielle rocks," I commended her.

"Whatever," CJ replied. "I'm going to get her back. Don't worry," he said ominously. I could only imagine what he'd do to her as payback. The idea of being on his vendetta list scared me a little. CJ's creativity had no limit.

By now, the semester had advanced deep into February. In a matter of weeks, winter would lose its grip. I continued to exile myself to the lonely darkroom on a weekly basis. One day, I arrived in the midafternoon—earlier than usual. I entered the large art studio adjacent to the darkroom. To my surprise, a drawing class was in session.

All the times I'd been to the darkroom, I'd never actually seen a class in the studio. I usually went to the darkroom in the evening after classes had adjourned. But that afternoon the studio brimmed with students, each with charcoal in hand and sitting at large easels arranged in the back portion of the room. They paid me no mind as I walked across the room behind a small wooden platform positioned in front of all the students. A male student removed his T-shirt near the small platform about fifteen feet from me. *Interesting,* I thought as I headed into the darkroom to mix my chemicals and set up my printing trays.

I let myself into the darkroom and dropped off my backpack along with a fresh box of photo paper. I exited the darkroom, en route to the bathroom. I crossed back through the art class again. The male student had removed all of his clothing except for a pair of boxers. *Very interesting,* I thought. I went to the bathroom and then passed back through the studio for the final time. The student was now naked, standing frozen on the small platform while the art students drew him. I felt my face flush, as I quickly sized up the back of his muscular form.

I spent the next several hours printing images in the darkroom. When I finally finished, it was late. I walked through the empty art studio and caught a ride on the shuttle to the other side of campus. I thought about the art studio class on the way home. Every great artist that I could think of from the Renaissance to modern times—Michelangelo, da Vinci, Picasso, Dalí, Matisse—every one of them depicted nudes. All my favorite photographers photographed the naked human body. My photography professor was practically obsessed with photographing naked people. She had entire bodies of work featuring people in their birthday suits.

"I saw a naked guy today," I told Keri and Michelle as soon as I hit the living room.

"What?" Keri replied.

"There was a naked guy outside the darkroom," I repeated.

"What do you mean, 'There was a naked guy outside the darkroom'?" Michelle asked, slightly alarmed.

"The art class was doing an exercise—drawing the human form. So when I went to the bathroom, Naked Guy was standing there in his birthday suit," I explained.

"Oh," Keri laughed. "You had me worried there for a second, like suddenly random naked guys hang out outside the darkroom."

I sat down next to Michelle on the sofa. "All great artists explore the human form. Painters, photographers, everyone," I stated.

"That's true—the human form is amazing," Michelle agreed.

"The human body is one of God's most beautiful creations," Keri added.

"My photography professor—she's always photographing naked women," I laughed.

We all looked at each other and chuckled.

"Anyway, maybe I should explore the human form. What do you guys think?"

"Sure, why not?" Keri replied.

"Sure," Michelle shrugged.

"We read this book in one of my communications classes last year," I began, "that talked about the fact that in Western art, all the way from the Renaissance up until modern advertising, women are depicted in a manner to please male viewers. Think about it, women always look sensual and sexy in paintings, in advertising, in everything. They don't look that way to make other women happy. I mean really—like I care about a picture of a sexy woman—who cares? They're shown that way—all the time—to make men happy."

In the class, my communications professor had showed image after image of women as depicted over centuries in Western paintings and modern advertising. Every single woman wore an inviting or enticing expression. Victoria's Secret ads were the perfect example. The model in the ad always looked hypersexy. Wasn't Victoria's Secret supposed to be selling underwear to women? So, why would the main audience—straight women—want to look at page after page of vampy, skinny lingerie models in sexy poses? Most women found it irritating to look at models with perfect bodies, knowing good and well that none of us looked that good in our undies. But that was the point: the models weren't posing for the women shoppers; they were all posing for a male lover off camera somewhere. It was ridiculous.

"No one would sell straight men underwear by filling up a whole catalog with images of sexy men in provocative poses," I concluded. "Are you kidding? Not a single straight guy would look at that catalog without feeling the need to drink a beer and chest bump his friend."

"Good point," Keri said thoughtfully.

"So, my question is, *Can I take a picture of the human form that is purely to show the beauty of the figure?* You know a picture that is simply a gorgeous, nonerotic, nonsexy image?" I contemplated aloud.

"That brings up the whole question of whether or not our society makes it possible to appreciate the body purely as a work of art," Michelle asserted.

"Right, 'cause we're all so hung up on sex in this society. You see a naked body and automatically you think—sex. Not 'Oh, didn't God make the human body beautiful?,'" I said.

"So, I guess that's your challenge," Keri asserted.

"Right. Do you think I can take a beautiful picture of the human body that makes you say, 'Wow, God's creation is magnificent'?" I asked.

"You should certainly try," Michelle challenged.

"Where can I find a model?" I asked.

"I'll do it," Keri volunteered.

"I don't have a problem with it either," Michelle stated nonchalantly.

"I only need one model," I replied.

"You should photograph whoever looks better nude," Keri replied.

"Who's that?" I asked.

"I don't know," Michelle shrugged. "It's not like we walk around here without our clothes."

"Well, let's see then," Keri suggested. The three of us relocated to my room and locked the door in case one of our usual guests came knocking at the front door unannounced.

Keri undressed down to her bikini.

"Keri looks pretty good," Michelle said.

"Yeah, she does," I agreed.

Keri got dressed, and Mich undressed.

"Mich looks really good," Keri stated objectively.

"Yep, she does," I agreed.

"I think Michelle is more symmetrical than I am," Keri observed.

Michelle looked amazing. Her baggy jeans masked her ideal proportions, her flat stomach, and her stately torso. I'd never looked at my roommates that closely before. Keri also had a great figure. Both their husbands would be happy campers.

"I think Michelle is better," Keri decided.

"Okay, then Michelle it is," I said.

Michelle dressed, and the three of us migrated back into the living room.

"So, that takes care of the female model, but shouldn't I photograph a guy too?"

"You're going to photograph a guy, too?" Michelle asked, surprised.

"Not *with* you, silly. I mean separately. I'll photograph you by yourself. Then in a separate session, I'll photograph him. Do you think that's a good idea?" I asked.

"I think it's okay," Michelle answered.

"I think it's fine. You just have to be careful who you pick for a model," Keri warned. "But it shouldn't be hard to find someone. We know lots of guys."

"Yeah, but it has to be someone that isn't too cute—someone I'm *not* attracted to. So I won't lust after him," I added.

"Well, that's not so easy," Keri joked.

"We must know some unattractive guys," Michelle asserted.

"Not completely *un*attractive; he's modeling. Just someone that isn't attractive to *me*," I relayed.

The three of us sat there, mentally running through the names and faces of all our guy friends and drawing blanks.

"All our guy friends are pretty nice looking," Michelle finally concluded.

"That's true," I reflected.

"Come on, we have to know at least one guy that isn't cute, but isn't totally ugly either," I encouraged. "And someone who isn't going to try anything funny if I photograph him naked."

"I know—Ethan!" Michelle exclaimed.

"Oh, yeah. He would be great," Keri chimed in.

"Ethan? Right—Ethan! You mean Ethan from Haverford? Oh yeah, he's perfect," I exclaimed.

Cerebral Ethan, with the high IQ and affinity for all things Japanese, was perfect. I wasn't in danger of lusting after him. Ethan was pleasant enough, but I had absolutely nothing in common with him. After we greeted each other and exchanged salutations like "Nice weather we're having, isn't it?," we were usually at a loss for anything else to say to each other. He wasn't my type. Ethan was tall and pale, like he rarely spent a day in direct sun. He had an average build and short, clean-cut dirty-blond hair and blue eyes.

"I'll call Ethan and see if he's into it," Michelle offered.

The next day Michelle reported back. "Ethan's totally into it. He wants to set up a date for his photo session. Let him know as soon as you have the details."

The following week, I photographed Michelle. My double bedroom was big enough that I could easily set up a backdrop and use it as a studio. Enough natural light trickled into the room that I didn't need lights. The session with Michelle went smoothly. I wasn't so sure about the photo shoot with Ethan.

A few days later, I photographed Ethan. After Ethan's photo session, I processed all his images, and he came by later to review the contact sheets. Michelle, Keri, and I had kept the double photo sessions under wraps. Ethan didn't know that Michelle had modeled for me. No one outside our room knew. I stored her images in a secret location, separate from all of my other photo work.

Ethan arrived, and Michelle, Keri, and I lounged around the living room as he looked through his photos. Ethan began describing his photo session with me.

"Adele was so funny. Whenever I felt bold enough to turn around and face forward, she looked away."

"I know! I couldn't help it. It was a bit much—seeing all of you," I confessed, "It was a little too *personal* looking at you directly from the front. I don't know. I felt like I got great pictures from the back."

"Less is more?" Michelle asked.

"Right, exactly," I concurred.

The final picture that I printed of Ethan was a serene study of light and soft shadows. The image was almost completely white, the background, the foreground, his skin—everything, except for subtle gray shadows that outlined his form, the curves of his back and backside. It was lovely and tranquil, not in the least bit provocative or erotic.

The final picture that I selected of Michelle was also taken from the back. She was seated, her hair pulled up in a loose bun. All the pictures of her that I had taken from the front conjured up notions of more than just art. I had photographed her in color, rather than black and white, but used a special process that made her skin translucent white and all the shadows around her, pale sky blue. She was a peaceful portrait of a noble hourglass figure, still and at rest.

I felt like I'd accomplished the assignment I'd set out for myself. Both images depicted the beauty of the human form without a hint of eroticism.

Later that week, early on a Thursday evening, Milan lounged around with Michelle and me at our place.

"We're going to our weekly fellowship. Do you want to come?" I asked him.

"What do you do there?"

"It's just our weekly meeting. We sing songs and usually someone does a funny skit or something. Then we listen to a talk," Michelle explained.

"A talk on what?"

"I don't know, it depends. Maybe on God's plan for our lives," Michelle continued.

"Or faith," I added. "Or, you know, something interesting and relevant. It varies. Come see for yourself."

"This is the thing you guys go to every week, right?"

"Yep," Michelle confirmed.

Milan looked at his watch. "How long is it?"

"Just an hour and a half," I replied.

"Starts at 7 p.m. and ends at 8:30," Michelle added.

"Okay, I'll check it out," Milan agreed.

We arrived at Bennet Hall and entered the large library-style classroom. We took our place among the sixty or seventy other chattering, boisterous students gathered for praise and worship.

The worship leaders started strumming away on their acoustic guitars, and we all joined in unison, glancing at the lyrics projected high on the wall.

"As the deer pants for the water . . . ," we sang. "So my soul longs after you . . . You alone are my heart's desire, and I long to worship you . . ."

Michelle and I, and all the other students, sang along enthusiastically as Milan looked on. The guitar players took a seat, and several students did a *Saturday Night Live*–inspired skit.

"This is *Saturday Night Live*—for Jesus. I'm the Church Lady . . ." Laughter, applause, and then a brief talk on "why bad things happen to good people."

"God is just, but is God fair?" the speaker began. He made his point quickly, sighted his three real-life examples, and wrapped up in twenty minutes.

"So, what did you think?" Michelle asked Milan as the meeting concluded and we left.

He looked at us blankly. "You go to that *every* week? . . . Why?"

"Why?" I asked. "So we can know God better."

"So we can learn more and grow spiritually," Michelle added.

"Okay," Milan replied, unimpressed. His face said it all. Our worship made no sense to him. Our reverence for God was hocus-pocus. We

might as well have been wearing kilts, beating African drums, and singing Native American songs in Vietnamese—he could not see the logic.

"Well, at least you came," Michelle said with a smile as the three of
us stood just outside the entrance to Bennet Hall.

"Yeah, now you know where we go every Thursday night," I said.

"Well, I'll talk to you later," Milan replied before he turned and
disappeared into the night.

Michelle and I walked home through campus, chatting lightheartedly, our spirits lifted by the thoughtful talk and time of praise. Soon
after we rolled through the front door, the phone rang. I answered it.

"Hey, whassup? It's CJ," he said.

"Hi, CJ. I know it's *you*. I recognize your voice, you know."

He laughed. "What are you doing?"

"Hanging out with Michelle. What are you doing?"

"Just going to this thing in a bit. But hey, I was calling 'cause there's a
Wharton Film meeting coming up. I'm going to check it out. I thought
you might want to go. Do you want to come with me?"

"Yeah. Of course," I replied. I had heard about Wharton Film from
Stephanie and was curious about the club. But apparently, only Wharton students were invited to the meetings. I didn't know where they met
or who was in it, so I couldn't just show up. Stephanie wasn't interested
and hadn't gone to any of the meetings, so I couldn't tag along with her.
I appreciated CJs thoughtful invitation.

A couple days later, CJ met me downstairs in my dorm lobby, and
we walked to the dorm where the meeting would be held. We stepped
off the elevator into the enormous rooftop lounge. Each high-rise dorm
possessed a rooftop lounge that took up the entire top floor. The lounge
boasted banks of windows on all four sides, which provided spectacular
panoramic views of the landscape below. We'd arrived late. The Wharton Film meeting was in full swing.

All the students in attendance, about twenty people, sat in various
sizes and shapes of chairs and sofas arranged in a large semicircle. Only
one seat remained, a single large couch-like chair, ample and comfort-

able for one person, but extremely snug for two. CJ strode through the room. I followed at his side. I hated arriving late to functions and calling attention to myself. Everyone watched as CJ walked through the center of the circle and took the last seat. Seeing nowhere else to sit, I squished down next to him in the chair.

As soon as we'd entered the room, two female students eyed CJ. I pretended not to notice them staring at him thirstily with overt pining. I'd never seen women look so *obvious* before, with the same kind of parched longing look that I imagined professional male athletes received from admiring women whenever they went out in public.

I settled in next to CJ and tried to appear relaxed. I wasn't used to sitting so close to him, with my side and leg pressed against his. I felt like a rock star sitting there—all those eyes fixed on him with interest. I probably appeared to be CJ's girl of the moment—I didn't mind one bit, especially with those two girls looking like they wanted to switch places with me.

We'd arrived just in time for introductions. Students began stating their names and a little about themselves. The introductions traveled counterclockwise. My turn came before CJ's.

"Hi, I'm Adele. I'm a huge fan of independent film. I'm here to connect with other filmmakers and people interested in the film industry."

CJ went next. "I'm CJ. Adele and I have been working on a film together. We've developed a strong screenplay. We're in the process of putting together our film crew and production team. We'll start filming soon."

It was an impressive lie. A couple of students nodded and smiled in quiet admiration. The person next to CJ began introducing himself; there was no time to amend the disclosure of our feigned accomplishments.

CJ's tall tale garnered the attention of Penn-Film-and-Video Josh who also attended. At the next Film Club meeting, he initiated a conversation with me—something he never did.

"That guy you were with seemed awfully sure of himself. What's your film about?" he prodded.

I quickly looked for a way to exit the conversation without lying and without telling Mr. Penn-Film-and-Video that CJ had difficulty discerning truth from fiction.

"That was a bit of an exaggeration," I remarked offhandedly. Then I moved away before he could press me for more information.

Chapter Twenty

SPRINGING INTO ACTION

{March–April, Second Semester of Senior Year}

I DIDN'T GO ANYWHERE DURING SPRING BREAK. I SAT PEERING out of my frosted windows for days on end. Outside, twenty-one stories below, I gazed down at a city frozen still—trapped. Below, snow— waist-deep in places—buried cars, streets, everything. Weather forecasters called it the storm of the century, the greatest blizzard in modern Philadelphia history. On Friday, the snow began falling gently, lightly coating the sidewalks and tree branches, like a passing fog. But it never stopped. The snow flurries rained tirelessly until every dirty street and grimy curb awoke whitewashed, immaculate, a city transformed into an Arctic urban landscape. The neglected West Philadelphia streets, usually littered with fast-food wrappers and discarded bits of trash, received a facelift. The snow covered it all, painting the town pristine.

City officials spent sleepless nights mobilizing an army of snowplows and workers to dig the metropolis out from beneath the ice and slush. The airport closed. For days, buses didn't run, and no one drove. I didn't mind. From my toasty apartment, I watched the silent white glove swallow up the land and then slowly recede in the coming days as the sun melted away the layers of snowfall.

The storm had begun in the Gulf of Mexico and rushed up the Eastern seaboard in a fearsome tempest, immobilizing New York,

Massachusetts, Delaware, New Jersey, Connecticut, Rhode Island, Tennessee, and Georgia. Floods and winds of up to one hundred miles per hour battered the East. Eight states declared a state of emergency. All the while I sat peacefully perched, a willing captive. I'd stocked the refrigerator and cabinets days before the storm descended. I read. I rested. I waited until snowplows finally cleared the streets and sidewalks and forced the sludge into four-foot-tall snow barricades along the edges of the cleared roadways. Then I ventured outside for ten minutes, just long enough to stand and look up at the newly bulldozed snow walls and to feel the chill, before I returned indoors.

Philadelphia recovered from the blizzard, and everyone returned from spring break. Classes resumed on schedule.

One evening shortly after break, the phone rang.

"Hey, do you want to come to dinner with me at the dining hall?" CJ asked. I have an extra pass so I can bring a friend."

"Yeah, sure. When?"

"In twenty minutes. I'll meet you in front of 1920 Commons." 1920 Commons was the main dining hall that served all of Superblock.

"Okay."

Fifteen minutes later, I pulled on my coat and headed downstairs to meet CJ. As I approached the Commons, I could see CJ standing just outside the dining hall entrance.

"Ehhhh," he greeted me in his strange but amusing CJ-speak. "Here's the pass. Just take it to *that* window." He pointed to the cafeteria turnstile and entrance on the right.

"Okay," I said.

I went to the window on the right and handed my pass to the woman working behind the counter. She released the turnstile, and I passed through. CJ went to the opposite turnstile on the other side of the small lobby. I stood at the top of the cafeteria steps waiting for him to pass through and ascend the stairs. He swiped his student ID card in the card reader attached to the turnstile and pushed. The turnstile didn't budge. Supposedly, anyone with a paid meal plan could swipe their

ID in the card reader and it would automatically admit that student into the dining hall. CJ swiped his card again and shoved the turnstile. It held fast.

The woman behind the counter on my side eyed CJ suspiciously. CJ hurried to swipe his card again in a last-ditch effort to make it work. I doubled back to CJ's side.

"What's the matter?" I asked.

"Nothing," he mumbled.

The cafeteria worker, a robust black woman in her thirties, barreled out from behind her counter, a fierce look burned across her face She wore a short Jheri curl and a serious no-nonsense attitude. I remembered her from sophomore year. She didn't smile at the students—ever—with one exception. I saw her flash a little grin once when a cute male student called her by name and said hello. She was there to do her job; she wasn't taking mess from nobody. She walked deliberately toward us, glaring. I started to get nervous. Both of her hands rested on her hips—locked and loaded—a bad sign. When a sistah put her hands on her hips, it meant war. Her eyes flashed with anger.

"You gave *her* your pass . . . *didn't you?*" she snarled at CJ. Her finger pointed at me. I knew what was coming next. I began inching toward the exit. I didn't know if CJ knew, but if he were smart, he'd ease out the door right behind me. We were about to get a full-on, neck-rolling, black-auntie dressing-down. She wasn't holding back just because we weren't kin to her.

The woman's head began to roll around on her neck. Steam came out of her nose, and fire shot from her eyes.

She lit into us.

"You just tried to use your card over there," she snapped and motioned toward the turnstile where CJ had attempted entry. "But you took the pass you were *supposed* to use for *yourself* . . . because your ID is temporarily deactivated . . . and you gave it to *her*. Didn't you?" she exclaimed. "You tried to sneak *her*"—she pointed at me again—"into the dining hall!"

By that time, I was at the front door. I opened it and slipped outside, away from Hopping-Mad Auntie. I felt safe out there. She was still at work and wouldn't chase me outdoors. I moved away from the main entrance and waited for CJ to resurface after his beatdown. Fortunately, the dining hall lobby was empty with no eyewitnesses to attest to our berating.

"Thanks," I snapped, when he finally appeared.

"She should have let you use the pass," he mumbled. "Let's go to a different dining hall," he suggested.

"I don't think so," I replied.

I should have been suspicious as soon as CJ beelined to the opposite turnstile. He had no reason to send me through the manned entry while he went through the unmanned one, unless he was up to something.

We stood there negotiating a less illicit plan for dinner. Finally, we both agreed to grab a bite to eat elsewhere, and I returned home.

The next day, I was out and about around campus on a fine spring afternoon. Locust Walk glowed in the sun-streaked copper light. I had just passed the Palladium and the St. A's fraternity house when I saw Milan walking down Locust Walk in my direction with Zoe. Of the twenty thousand students on campus, Zoe physically resembled me the most. She had the same light-brown skin and short black hair. We were about the same height and weight. The freckles on her nose were more pronounced than mine, but otherwise looking at her was a bit like looking at a reflection of myself. *Is he sleeping with her?* Suddenly, unexpectedly, I became agitated.

I told myself I wasn't jealous. Flames weren't shooting from my eyes and impaling him with daggers through the heart. What did I care who he slept with? He could sleep with half the school—it didn't bother me.

"Hey," Milan called out, as they stopped to chat with me.

"Hey, what's going on?" I forced a smile. "Hey, Zoe, I haven't seen you in ages. What's new?" I said with strained cheerfulness. I'd met Zoe freshman year but hadn't seen her much since then.

"Not much," she replied.

"Well, hey, great to see you two. I'll catch you later," I said, looking down at my watch and pretending to be in a hurry.

"Okay, I'll talk to you soon." Milan smiled.

Not if you get run over by a bus first, I thought. "Yep, I'll talk to you soon," I replied and picked up my pace back to West campus.

Back at the apartment, I dumped my frustration on the first roommate I saw—Keri.

"I just saw Milan on Locust walk with Zoe. Do you know her?"

"No," Keri replied.

"Well, she looks just like me," I grumbled.

Keri didn't take the bait and engage me in my grumblefest. She squelched my "Death to Milan" soliloquy before I could deliver it. Keri just shrugged and went about her business, washing up the dishes she'd piled up in our sink.

Two weeks later, Milan told me he was dating Zoe's roommate, Denise. He still popped in sporadically for late-afternoon visits, but I saw less of him in the evenings. I felt silly for having felt so irritated when I saw him with Zoe. It wasn't likely that he was sleeping with both of them. What was the matter with me? Why was I even thinking about him and his stupid sleepover buddies? He was just my friend. I didn't care.

The following week, I ran into Milan and Denise, walking together as I returned home from class. I sat in the living room, recounting my impression to Michelle.

"They don't look like they're together. They look like friends."

"What do you mean?"

"Well, if I had a boyfriend, you'd know. We'd be holding hands or something. They weren't holding hands or doing anything affectionate. They didn't even look happy."

"He said she wants to keep their relationship on the down low," Michelle replied.

"Why? If I had a boyfriend, no way would I keep it on the down low! I'd let the whole planet know."

"He said she isn't into excessive PDA."

"That's cool. I get that. I'm not saying they should make out in the middle of Locust Walk. I'm just saying that if *I* had a boyfriend, you wouldn't confuse him with one of my friends—there would be a difference. If you saw us together, you'd say 'Oh, that's her boyfriend,' that's all," I rambled.

If I found a guy that I could actually consider for a serious relationship, my joy would read like a flashing neon sign across my entire face. My friends would get tired of my 24/7 stupid-happy grin. I definitely wouldn't be walking around like it was just another ordinary day.

"She's not exactly what I expected," I continued.

"What do you mean?"

"Milan said he likes 'Latino, black, Persian women and all beautiful women,' right? Well she doesn't fit into any of those categories. I mean she seems cool and all. But, you know . . ."

Michelle looked at me blankly.

His girlfriend was short, stout, and Korean. She had a cool edginess to her—but she wouldn't stand out in a crowd. *Shut up. Shut up. What is the matter with me? Why am I obsessing, like an idiot? Why can't I shut up?* It was none of my business. *Turn your brain off. Think about something else. Anything else.*

"Anyway, I hope they're happy," I told Michelle before heading to my room.

The following afternoon, the phone rang in our apartment.

"Hey, it's for you," Mich called.

"Who is it?" I asked.

"Your mom. Just kidding. Some guy named Scott," Mich answered.

Scott? I drew a blank.

"Hello," I spoke into the phone.

"Hey, this is Scott from Penn Film and Video. We met at one of the meetings a couple weeks ago."

"Right! Scott. How are you?" I remembered him: tall—over six feet—clean-cut, dark hair, all-American, pretty cute. Not the kind of guy I was likely to have a crush on, but definitely cute.

"Yeah, I have a film idea I want to run by you. Can we get together?" he asked.

"Sure. When?"

"How about Thursday?"

"That's cool. What time?"

"How about in the afternoon—like around two?"

"Perfect. My class ends at 1:30 on Thursday. Where should we meet?"

"Do you want to meet just inside Steinberg Dietrich Hall, then we can walk somewhere from there?"

"Sure."

"I'll see you then."

I hung up the phone.

Thursday, after Knowledge and Social Structure, I walked up to Steinberg Dietrich Hall to meet Scott. He was already standing on the steps of the modern red-brick building when I arrived.

"Hi," he said with a good-natured smile.

"Hey," I greeted him. I'd forgotten how tall he was. I felt tiny as he looked down at me.

"How about if we head over to the food court and grab something? I want to tell you about this film I have in mind."

"Sure, sounds good."

We walked through the center of campus, past the main library and toward the food court near the Le Bus café.

Scott chattered in a friendly manner. "I was home over the break, and I crashed my dad's Lexus. I was really worried. But it worked out. I didn't get in too much trouble. The car was under lease, and they covered the entire thing," he sighed with relief.

"Lucky for you," I replied. "Car wrecks are the worst—thank goodness for insurance."

"Definitely," he agreed.

We reached the food court and grabbed seats.

"So, I've been thinking about this film for a while," Scott began. "I'm doing a semester abroad this coming fall, but I wanted to see if you might be interested in working on it with me when I return in the spring."

Scott continued to lay out the storyline and plans for his film concept. His ideas were coherent and interesting. I let him finish before I made any comment.

"Scott, that sounds awesome. I'd love to work with you, but I'm graduating this semester."

"You are?" he asked, surprised.

"Yeah, I'm a senior."

"Oh well," he replied nonchalantly.

If I had been a junior, I would have jumped at the opportunity to work with him. At the same time I was glad we'd never get to collaborate. Strangely, I was pleased that my roommates would never get to meet him. It could be another Milan situation all over again. Scott was no Milan—he was straightforward and easygoing—but the same roommate dynamics might come into play. I could picture it. Scott would call to meet up and work on film plots. Then Keri or Michelle would answer the phone and talk to him forever. Or if he came over to hang out, we wouldn't be able to talk about film because my roommates would talk to him half the night. I loved Keri and Michelle, but sometimes I wondered why they didn't join their own clubs and meet people with similar extracurricular interests. Keri needed to start her own feminist, Zionist, Messianic Judaism club. Michelle should create the Ambivalent Supermodels Foregoing Fame and Fortune for Phi Beta Kappa in the Natural Sciences Club.

After my meeting with Scott, I stopped by the library to do some research for one of my papers. I stayed there, bent over reference books and taking notes, for several hours before I returned home.

Back at the apartment, it was a full house. Stephanie buzzed around the living room as Keri and Michelle sat listening to her. As usual, they were embroiled in a lively whirlwind of a conversation, and Stephanie's face lit up pink with laughter. I joined in the fun, listening to the tail end of Stephanie's description of a film she wanted to make starring Keri, Michelle, and me. Just as Stephanie wrapped up her animated explanation, the phone rang. Stephanie answered it.

"It's CJ," she said. "Something is the matter. He wants to speak to Keri—only Keri," she stated, looking perplexed. Her face became suddenly somber. We knew something serious was up.

Stephanie and I gathered around Keri and the phone.

"What's the matter with him?" I whispered.

"I don't know," Stephanie shrugged.

"He's crying," Keri whispered.

"Crying? Why's he crying?" I asked.

"Shhhh," Keri hushed our banter.

We listened quietly. We couldn't hear, but on the other end of the phone CJ bawled loudly with abandon.

"It's going to be okay, CJ. It's okay. Take a deep breath. You're going to be okay," Keri said gently.

"What's the matter?" Stephanie pressed.

"He smoked some bad hashish," Keri whispered. "He's hallucinating. He says something bad is trying to get him," she said in a low, concerned voice.

At eleven o'clock at night, CJ was somewhere tripping hard. I'm not sure what he'd smoked or taken, hashish alone or hashish in combination with something else, but he was freaking out—really losing it.

"CJ, calm down. I want you to sit down and listen to me. They are not going to *get* you. Take a deep breath with me. Listen. Breathe in. I want to hear you—take a deep breath with me. You're going to be okay," Keri spoke reassuringly.

"What's happening? *What's happening?*" we pestered.

"He isn't crying as hard," Keri whispered as she covered the mouthpiece. CJ had stopped wailing. The volume of his sobs dropped down a notch.

"CJ, are you okay? You're going to be okay," Keri repeated.

"What did he say?" Stephanie asked.

"He said he doesn't feel good," Keri relayed.

"CJ, no more hashish, okay? That stuff isn't good for you," Keri told him, her voice soothing but firm.

On the other end of the phone, CJ whimpered an exhausted, "Okay."

Keri stayed on the phone, gently calming him for another ten minutes. She practically soothed him to sleep before he felt pacified enough to hang up.

"Is he okay?" I asked.

"I think so. He was really scared," Keri answered.

CJ had made a wise choice. Even in the midst of a drug-induced panic attack, he knew to ask for Keri. Of the four of us, she was the most naturally endowed with maternal instincts and best able to provide the sanity he needed.

Days later, I prepared to hang my first big photography exhibit. Several weeks before the exhibit, I had run into my freshman-year roommate on campus. I hadn't seen her all senior year, so we had stopped to talk.

"Hey, how are you?" she'd asked.

"I'm great. You?" I'd replied. "How're your parents?" Freshman year I'd gone home with her for Thanksgiving and stayed with her family.

"They're well," she'd replied. "I saw one of your photos on the cover of a magazine."

"Oh, yeah," I'd said with a smile.

"You know I'm in the Philomathean Society, and we have a gallery in College Hall. We might be interested in exhibiting your work."

"*Really?*" I'd exclaimed. "I can bring my portfolio by or drop it off so you guys can take a look."

"Cool."

We'd exchanged numbers and promised to be in touch. I didn't know much about the Philomathean Society. I knew that it was the oldest collegiate literary society in the country. A guy in my photography class had ranted for five whole minutes about its members. "They are so pretentious," he'd whined. "They wouldn't let me join. They rejected me." I'd seen the guy's photography and didn't think their rejection was indicative of pretention, but rather discernment. His photography wasn't very interesting in my opinion, and he liked to spout off in dry, self-important monologues. He'd probably tried to pass himself off as a photographic genius, and they'd called his bluff. In any case, I was thrilled that the esteemed society would consider me for an exhibit.

I had touched base with my old roommate the following week.

"I gave your name to the student who oversees the gallery," she said. "I think she's going to call you."

The gallery manager called me. We met, and a few days later, she called me back.

"Hey, we'd like to give you a solo exhibit. You can have the entire gallery," she told me.

"No way!" I exclaimed.

"Yes, your exhibit will open on Friday, March 26. We'll host the reception. You can design the invitations. We'll cover the cost. We'll promote the event and advertise in the *Daily Pennsylvanian* and take care of all that," she continued. "Does March 26 work for you?"

Does March 26 work for me? Is the earth round? "Absolutely! March 26 is great," I replied.

"Well, let's set up a date for you to come see the gallery so you can get an idea of how you'd like to hang your show."

I'd spent the next several weeks cutting mats and mounting photographs in preparation for the exhibit. The work represented a culmination of all my photography endeavors over the past three years. It featured fashion portraits from Los Angeles and Philadelphia, documentary images from New York and North Philadelphia, fashion-inspired portraits and documentary portraits from a visit to Mississippi. There were several eerie, abstract surreal images, in color and black and white. I also selected several of the nude portraits I'd created. All together, I gathered approximately fifty photographs, all eight inches by ten inches, grouped in sections by similar themes. I named the show *Live Stock* and hung it a couple days before the opening.

I was pleasantly surprised the night that the show opened. I wasn't
sure what to expect—would people show up? Fortunately for me, the
Philomathean Society *knew* how to open an art exhibit. Their gallery, located in the same magnificent Gothic building as the university's president's office, drew a good-size crowd. All night a steady flow of people—
Philomathean Society members and supporters, along with my friends
from Penn Film and Video, Bible study, and elsewhere—kept the place
whirring with activity. Everyone came—all four of my V Society sisters,
Milan, and CJ, wearing a suit and tie. Many acquaintances I'd made
over the past four years of college turned up as well. The gallery had
an adjacent room set up with comfortable chairs, so people came, sat,
and just hung out half the evening. I loved milling around, answering
questions about the photographs all night and talking to my classmates
about the creative process that so thrilled me. It was an immensely satisfying night—one of the highlights of senior year.

THE PHILOMATHEAN SOCIETY
ART GALLERY

presents

"LIVE STOCK"

An Exhibition of Photographs by

Adele C. Moore

Opening Reception
Friday, March 26
6 to 8 pm

Fourth Floor, College Hall

Wine and cheese

INVITATION (FRONT)

Why "Live Stock"

So why did I call this collection of photographs "Live Stock"?
Well, I have two reasons.

Reason number one: Stock is paper. In this case it is photographic paper or photographic stock. And it is *live* because
most of the people in the photographs are people that I know.
None of them are paid models who spent hours in make-up
or anything like that. But they are everyday people portrayed
as they are. So "Live Stock" means real, live people and places
jumping out at you from the paper or photography stock.

Reason number two: There are two kinds of people in this
world—sheep and goats. I hope you are a sheep. If you don't
know what I mean, ask me about it later. We'll have coffee,
hang out, and I'll explain.

Thanks for coming,

INVITATION (BACK)

At the same time that I'd been scurrying to put together the photo exhibit, Michelle and I had begun working on a film together at the request of Kathy, our Bible study leader. The thirty-minute film entitled *Express Yourself* probed deep into the meaning of life. It featured short candid interviews with students answering questions on spiritual topics. We asked questions such as, "What does love mean to you?" and "What do you think is the meaning of life?" The answers were as diverse and interesting as the students we polled. In response to "Do you believe in a personal creator?" one girl answered, "I believe in a universal overseer." Another answered, "No. I'm an atheist." One guy shrugged and said, "I'm pretty sure there's *someone* up there." After six or seven students answered each question, the segment concluded with a Bible verse that addressed the question we'd just posed.

Mich and I filmed most of the interviews in one dorm, Kings Court English House. It was smaller than the gigantic High Rise dorms where you might not know your neighbors. Kings Court English House was community oriented, so residents were likely to know each other and be interested in each other's opinions. After I edited the film, with the help of a professional editor, Michelle, Kathy, and I showed the film to a gathering of Kings Court English House residents. A lively discussion ensued afterward. The objective was to create dialogue and discussion about spirituality. That's exactly what happened. The students that showed up for the screening readily shared their perspectives. After the discussion, we invited all interested students to a Bible study that met regularly in Kings Court English House. My favorite part of the whole project was working with Michelle. We'd never collaborated on an artistic project together.

Stephanie began working on a new film that spring too. She assumed her alias, Rachel Lebowitz, a make-believe Jewish American Princess (inspired by Mike Myers's *Saturday Night Live* impersonation of a Jewish American Princess in the "Coffee Talk" skit), and produced an autobiographical faux-documentary exploring, "Who is Rachel Lebowitz?" Keri, Michelle, and I served as the panel of close friends who spoke on camera about all the wonderful, quirky characteristics of our fabulous friend Rachel. We praised her and told anecdotes about her many fictitious but noteworthy accomplishments.

Unfortunately, Stephanie filmed us hastily, in harsh light with little makeup. Keri, Michelle, and I looked horrible in the final cut. Stephanie should have renamed her film, *Rachel Lebowitz, as Seen Through the Eyes of Her Three Ugly Friends.*

Warhol Says:
You'll Have Your Fifteen Minutes of Fame. . .

see a free showing of

"EXPRESS YOURSELF"

the film short

"What does love mean to you?"

"Do you believe in a personal creator?"

"What do you think is the meaning of life?"

Find out what Penn students think about these questions and more!
(featuring more than 40 Kings Court / English House Residents)

Duncan Lounge
Wednesday, April 7th
9:00 PM

refreshments and discussion after the film

sponsored by 4th floor Kings Court and Campus Crusade for Christ

⁓

TWENTY-ONE

{April–August, End of Senior Year}

LATE SPRING ARRIVED, HURLING ME TOWARD GRADUATION AND my fast-approaching twenty-first birthday. The season filled me with yearning to simultaneously savor and devour the moment like a delicious morsel. Everything—the little shrubs along the perimeter of Locust Walk, the giant bowed gingko trees, the air itself—felt reborn, emanating a contagious new warmth. All signs of the crippling blizzard weeks ago had vanished. College Green swarmed with life, the lawns full of lounging and rollicking students. The sky was perfect—clear and azure. I'd shoved my gloves and heavy coat far back into the depths of my closet, to be forgotten until the next winter.

We congregated after classes on the flourishing greens, in front of the peace sign to the left of Van Pelt Library. The V Society sprawled in a comfortable circle, surrounded by identical bunches of students reclined in clusters nearby. Keri sat cross-legged while Stephanie lay on her back with her head resting on Keri's knee. Michelle and I sat close by. I felt invigorated, simultaneously grown-up, in my final year as an undergraduate, and green, on the cusp of yet another great journey at the end of the semester. I lay on the grass, filled with satisfaction, my shoes kicked off and my backpack tossed carelessly on the thick green lawn.

"What's the worst pickup line you've ever heard?" Stephanie asked, giggling, with her hair overflowing around her, swallowing up most of Keri's left knee.

"The worst was what's-his-name—you know, the one who's always throwing those big parties at other people's houses," Keri started.

"Oh yeah, what's-his-name—the one who thinks he's all that?" Michelle asked.

"Right. What's his name? I think he's Australian or something. Anyway, he came up to me and said, 'So, what's your art?'" Keri continued.

"'What's your art?' What's that supposed to mean?" Stephanie balked.

"That's so random—how are you supposed to answer that? I would have said photography, but obviously everyone doesn't do art," I quipped.

"Well, I told him *food* was my art," Keri replied saucily.

"Oh, that's good," Michelle laughed.

"I love that. I love food!" I exclaimed.

"Yeah, so what did he say?" Stephanie sat straight up now, anticipating the details.

"He didn't say anything. He just disappeared back into the crowd at the party." Keri shrugged and laughed.

"That's too funny," I said, cracking up.

"I mean, ask a random question, and you're bound to get a random answer," Michelle snickered.

"Did I ever tell you guys about the professor that hit on me sophomore year?" Keri asked.

"No way!" Stephanie exclaimed.

"Oh, yeah. He was something else," Keri laughed.

"Was he cute? Or was he some crusty old guy?" I asked.

"He was okay, not super old. It was when I worked in the anthropology library at the museum. He came in, and I was so excited because he was a visiting professor from Israel. Of course I wanted any connection I could make with Israel."

"So, what happened?" Stephanie pressed.

"Well, he came into the library that evening, and it was really slow and quiet. He was meeting an Israeli. We chatted for a few minutes in Hebrew, and then he invited me for coffee in his office during office hours. I thought it was the coolest thing; I was so clueless. I had no idea that inviting a woman for coffee is like saying you want to sleep with her in Israel."

"Did you have coffee with him?" Michelle asked.

"I went to his office, and it was kind of strange. It was during office hours, but he sent his actual students away that needed help and just sat there talking to me," Keri continued.

"No way! I'd be so annoyed if I went in for office hours and my professor wouldn't see me because he was hitting on some student," I added.

"Then what happened?" Stephanie urged.

"He asked where I lived and told me where he lived. Then he asked if he could come by and we could go for a walk together. I don't remember if I gave him my phone number or not. I guess that I was rather elusive, or maybe he figured out that I was a totally naïve idiot, and he never came by."

"Was he married, or just some single guy that liked to date students?" Michelle asked.

"I found out later that he was married. He was on sabbatical—without his wife and family."

We mulled over Keri's lecherous professor with the misappropriated office hours for a split second.

"It wasn't a pickup line, but freshman year I met that guy that told me, 'I want to date you, not your religion.' I'll never forget that. I told him I believed Yeshua was Messiah, and he told me that. He was half Jewish," Keri continued.

"'I want to date you, not your religion.' That's a loaded one," I remarked.

"No kidding," Michelle agreed.

"Oh. Oh! I just remembered the worst pickup line ever. It was that guy at Café Miro," Keri exclaimed.

"Ewwww, that slimy guy with the ponytail?" Stephanie asked, her nose wrinkled up in repulsion. "Ewwwww, he made me want to barf!"

"The one with two hundred lovers? That guy?" I asked.

"He had two hundred lovers?" Michelle asked in disbelief.

"Not all at once. But, yeah he said he'd had at least two hundred lovers, probably more."

"Wait, how old is that guy?" I asked.

"I don't know—like twenty-four or twenty-five," Keri answered.

"Okay, so let's do the math. Say he started getting busy at fourteen, how many hookups is that a year?" I asked the group.

"Twenty-five minus fourteen. That's eleven years. So divide two hundred by eleven . . . That's eighteen or nineteen hookups a year!" Michelle exclaimed.

"No way!" Stephanie cried.

"That's one busy boy," I responded.

"Okay, like I was saying . . . ," Keri started again.

"Oh, right, what did he say?" Stephanie asked excitedly.

"He said, 'You know, Keri, you're an animal!'"

"Grrrr," I roared like a tiger, and we all fell over laughing our heads off.

"Right, like that was supposed to make me feel sexy," Keri scoffed.

"Grrrrrrrrrrrr," Stephanie repeated, making claws with her hands and amping up the sexy tiger imitation one more notch. We couldn't stop laughing.

"So, what did you say?" Michelle asked between guffaws.

"I didn't know what to say. I told him we're all animals—mammals, humans. Whatever. He finally gave up on me," Keri smiled.

A settling briskness interrupted our chatter and joking. Late afternoon fell upon us. The sun lowered over the blooming trees on the walk, casting warm, glowing afternoon light and long shadows on the red brick and gray stone. We gathered our things, still growling and laughing at each other.

"I have to go use the flat-art copy station in Furness," I said, turning left toward the big, red fine arts library.

"What's that?" Keri asked.

"It's just two lights hanging equal distances from the table so you can copy photographs and stuff onto slides," I explained. "I'll be home in a little bit."

Michelle, Stephanie, and Keri headed in the opposite direction toward West campus. The yellow glow of the sinking sun created a wash of glowing amber on the crowns of their heads. Their long shadows trailed behind them, animated by the variances in shifting light as they ambled slowly home.

Years later, long after I left Philadelphia and college far behind, I still remembered—still tasted—the radiant freshness of an East Coast spring. Nothing felt quite like it. The wafting, pulsing breaths of copper sunlight as they burst through gray tree branches, summoning them back to life—like an ephemeral aria, a vibrant promise of vitality, the season renewed. I always associate that feeling and its quiet exhilaration as the essence that encircled my entire existence as a college student.

I had no idea what I'd do the day after graduation. As if with the wave of a magic wand, my grad school dreams exploded in a puff of fairy dust. Months ago, I had applied to the graduate photography program at two schools. I'd decided that pursuing a career as a filmmaker was too expensive. I already had a bunch of student loans to repay. I didn't want to charge up more debt making film shorts funded by my credit card. But as it turned out, Rhode Island School of Design and Pratt Institute would both tell me to take a hike. I couldn't wrap my mind around it. I'd never received a rejection letter from a school before—not when

I had applied to my high school or to colleges. And this wasn't law school or med school. *Art* school had rejected me! It never occurred to me that the measure of my ego and hubris might exceed the measure of my talent.

Both schools gave the same reason for their decision. I didn't have an undergraduate degree in fine art. My degree was in communications. My photography portfolio didn't reflect the depth of someone who had studied fine art for four years and majored in it. I should have anticipated my rejection when I spoke to the graduate admissions office at Art Center College of Design—one of the schools I most wanted to attend. Their admissions officer was a sweetheart; we conversed for twenty minutes about Philadelphia and Penn. Her nephew had attended Penn but didn't like it.

"I'm glad you enjoyed your time there. My nephew transferred schools—Penn wasn't the right environment for him. It's a fine school. But at Art Center we won't consider you for a master's in fine arts without a bachelor of fine arts degree—no matter what," she stated with finality.

Nonetheless, when I received the rejections from RISD and Pratt, I simmered with anger—unconvinced—and deaf to their reasoning. I lit the rejection letters on fire and cried alone in my room.

Weeks later, I sprang into action with Plan B—Brooks Institute of Photography in Santa Barbara. Brooks had a pre-grad photography program. If you already had a college degree, you could take undergraduate photo classes for a year and a half to get up to speed on the technical aspects of photography. After that, you could go directly into the one-year master's program. I could have a master's degree after two and a half short years in sunny Santa Barbara.

As I waited anxiously for my post-graduation plans to unfold, Nick Wilson, my good friend from high school, stayed true to his word. He joined us for a few days of fun in Philadelphia. "I promised I'd come visit you before you graduated," he said as he hopped off the airport shuttle that morning and grabbed me in a giant bear hug. Then he squeezed Keri and Michelle with near-crushing embraces. I was elated. He'd arrived just in time for my big birthday party.

Nick looked good with his neatly trimmed sideburns and dark shoulder-length hair. He almost looked like a male-fashionista, except for his grunge-inspired Berkeley outfit. He wore off-white converse high tops (a fashion no-no for male-fashionistas), khaki shorts, and a fire-colored, plaid button-down shirt.

Nick hauled his bag up to our apartment and freshened up. Then Keri, Michelle, and I rushed to class, leaving Nick sitting on a bench in Superblock. When I met up with him later that afternoon, he was all smiles.

"I love this school," he exclaimed. "It's so great!"

"Oh yeah?"

"Yeah. I was sitting there in Superblock, and this totally friendly girl starts talking to me. She gave me a tour of the school, and we hung out all afternoon. She was totally cool."

I knew Nick all to well—he was an unapologetic bundle of exploding male libido. I knew he was leaving out part of the story because he was grinning like a lottery winner. He wanted me to ask him the next obvious question.

"Nick, you slept with her, didn't you?" I asked, rolling my eyes. I felt like his mother.

"No," he lied, grinning even more. He wanted me to know. He was bragging without overtly bragging—by alluding to his enjoyable afternoon.

"I really love this school," he repeated.

Unbelievable. He'd arrived on campus less than twenty-four hours ago, and he'd already hooked up. He wasn't even a student at Penn.

"She thought I was cute," he added, still grinning.

Keri and Michelle prepared a fancy, sit-down dorm-room dinner for my twenty-first birthday. My eight favorite people—Keri, Michelle, Nick, Milan, CJ, and a few others—received invitations to the dinner party. Afterward, we pulled apart the portable tables that had formed one long makeshift dining table under the tablecloth, and made room for mixing and mingling. The rest of our friends came to join us during the after-party, enjoying yet another V Society social extravaganza.

Finally, I was of legal drinking age and could get into the bar at the Palladium, which, I happily knew, the school's finest male-fashionistas frequented. I'd only been inside the Palladium once—during Parents Weekend—but that didn't count since my parents had been there and we had spent most of our visit in the dining room, not in the bar and not on the outdoor terrace where the school's socialites gathered.

I was the final V Society member to turn twenty-one. At last, the entire V Society could legally descend upon a bar together. The micro-brewery we'd visited earlier in the year hadn't required an ID to enter—I'm not sure why—maybe it doubled as a restaurant. Most students had been frequenting local bars since freshman year. Bars didn't particularly interest me; the simple fact that I'd been kept out of them for most of college made me curious.

"What are you going to order?" Nick asked as he, Michelle, Keri, and I took a seat at a small bar table inside the Palladium. I didn't know the name of a single grown-up cocktail. Did Shirley Temples count?

"I have no idea. What should I get?" I asked Nick.

"Order a Midori sour," he suggested. "It's a good drink for little light-weights like you," he laughed.

"Lightweight?" I chuckled. "Just because I only drink things that taste like Kool-Aid, I'm a lightweight?"

"Exactly. A Midori sour tastes a little like Kool-Aid. Perfect for you."

I laughed at myself. Nick was right. Keri, Michelle, and I were novices when it came to drinking. Once or twice Keri had brought home a bottle of kosher wine from Passover. We gathered around the apartment sampling it in paper cups. It tasted like grape juice.

Finally, I stood inside the place I had passed countless Friday nights for the past four years, unable to peek inside. I felt oh-so mature and in the know. By senior year, we'd studied enough of the Castle clan's fashion scene that we accessorized skillfully. I didn't wear a Gap shirt this time. Provided you didn't look at the labels inside our clothing, we almost blended in at the Palladium among the sophisticated crowd that usually congregated there. It made no difference that the Palladium was practically empty that night. I was inside the university's hippest tavern.

I took a few sips of my Midori sour. Nick finished it off for me.

"Can't even hold your liquor," he teased.

A couple days after my birthday, Nick bid us farewell and returned home.

May slipped onto the calendar with the blink of an eye. Final exams loomed just around the corner. Late-night cram sessions, loud music, and Ben and Jerry's ice cream binges ruled my world. Suddenly, I had to catch up on all the reading I'd neglected most of the semester.

"Ehhh—it's Brutus!" a muffled voice called, punctuated by rhythmic tapping on the door. Michelle opened the door for CJ.

"Hey, what's going on?" he asked, sauntering in and making himself comfortable in the red chair.

"Studying," Michelle replied before disappearing into her room and closing the door.

". . . and more studying," I replied. "Really exciting," I added sarcastically.

"When is your first final?"

"Next Monday in art history."

"When's yours?"

"I have a couple at the beginning of next week, and a makeup final later."

"A makeup final? Why are you taking a makeup final?"

The familiar sly grin inched across CJ's mouth, "'Cause I am."

"What do you mean? No one gets to take a makeup final. If you miss your final exam you automatically fail. You have to have open-heart surgery or something to miss an exam and retake it."

"That's what *you* think." He paused. "I always take makeup exams," he remarked confidently. "I tell the professor what he needs to hear, and I get to take the makeup exam."

"You lost me . . ."

"I pay someone who goes to the regular exam to get the exam questions. The makeup is usually about the same as the original exam. So I take the makeup a couple days later."

"No way!"

I was flabbergasted. How did he come up with these things? He was smart enough that he'd probably get a decent score without cheating. Why not just study and earn the grade?

"Wow," I said, shocked. "I don't even know what to say."

"How do you think I maintain an almost-perfect GPA in Wharton?" he asked.

"Unbelievable," I remarked, shaking my head.

Hours later, Keri sat in the living room when the phone rang. "I have a collect call from Prague from Noey Knott," the operator said.

"I'm coming back to Philadelphia for graduation," Noel blurted out over the operator. "Can I stay with you guys?"

"Of course," Keri cried back before denying the collect call.

A few days later, Noel resettled herself back in the apartment, just like old times, except she no longer referred to us as the nuns from hell, and no longer laughed when people called us the holy trinity.

"Want some Pringles?" Noel offered me the red potato chip can as she looked up from watching a talk show. She was back in her spot, snuggled up on the sofa in her red one-piece pajamas.

While Noel assumed the role of a fairly pleasant roommate, I transformed into a complete jerk toward Keri the last few weeks of school. I didn't know why, and I couldn't seem to control myself. My natural tendency toward passive-aggressive behavior possessed me. In retrospect, I can see that separation anxiety probably caused me to ignore Keri during the weeks leading up to graduation. Deep down I knew that as soon as we all graduated, I'd be separated from my dearest friend.

The sorrow was too deep. I was incapable of telling her, "You're the best friend I've ever had. The loss of you makes my heart ache." So instead, I pulled away.

I retreated into moody detachment. I brooded and simmered with listlessness. I was mildly emotionally retarded through most of my early twenties. I was well aware of my shallow longings but removed from my deeper feelings. Keri took it all in stride. She never confronted me about my unexplained indifference. She treated me as kindly as she always had.

"Hey, Delie, Noel and I are going to my parents' house for the night. We're going to have dinner there and stay over. Do you want to come?" she asked.

"Not really. I mean, I don't care. Whatever. If I can't find anything better to do, I'll go with you," I grumbled.

I didn't have anything better to do that afternoon, so I went with Keri and Noel. We caught the bus and train out to Keri's parents' place. Keri and Noel sat next to each other chatting up a storm, while I sat several seats away, barely saying a word the entire trip. The next day, I returned to school in time to cram for several more days before wrapping up all my exams.

I needed to forget about my impending departure from college and the apartment that had been my home for the past two years. Michelle and I fled to the New Jersey shore for a couple days before graduation. Justin Greco and a few of our friends who had graduated the year before joined us. Someone had offered the bunch of us the use of a beach house for a few days, free of charge. We lounged on the sandy shore, comforted by the scents of sunblock and wet, salty air.

Days later, Michelle, Keri, Mandy, Noel, and I joined the excited frenzy amassing in West Campus. We took our place in the crowd of jesting, unruly graduates from the College of Arts and Sciences. Everywhere, students fired off snapshots of each other and mugged with arms around one other for innumerable graduation photos. Milan showed up, handsomely dressed in a blue blazer and khaki slacks, just in time to pose in a picture with Keri, Michelle, and me. Then he excused himself to join his girlfriend and her family for the graduation procession.

On cue, the sea of robes and tassels flowed down the sun-drenched walk, beneath the arc of trees bidding farewell. We marched in the half-mile procession into the university's enormous stadium. First Lady Hillary Rodham Clinton and hordes of Secret Service men led the parade. I might not have slept through most of the ceremony if I hadn't been out all night with my roommates at a huge outdoor block party until five in the morning. It didn't help that First Lady Clinton didn't say anything particularly funny. If she'd cracked some good jokes, I might have stayed awake. Or if Mrs. Clinton had given us some real advice like "Don't take out any more student loans; and pay off the ones you already have as quickly as possible. They'll strap you to a life of debt before you can get a leg up in your career. Sallie Mae (the largest lender of student loans) is a monster. She'll eat you alive if you default." That's the speech people should make at college graduations. That's useful life information. Spare me the stuff about my great potential and changing the world. It's hard to reach your full potential and change the world when a fortune in student loans weighed you down.

Michelle or Keri—I'm not sure who—took a picture of me snoozing through most of the congratulatory speeches. Thankfully, I didn't drool on my robe while I nodded off. More than once before, I'd awakened to little dribble spots on my top after falling asleep sitting upright in a chair.

About six thousand students graduated from Penn that afternoon, hordes of graduate students from every college—medical students, dental students, Whartonites—and us, the puny undergrads. The senior class filled up row after row of folding chairs, covering the football field. Philadelphia's skyline towered above us against the pristine aqua-blue sky. The sun beat down, roasting us in our seats, at the school's 237th commencement, flush with an impressive show of academic tradition and stands filled with rowdy, cheering, gleeful families.

"I could see you and Michelle!" my mom exclaimed.

She even had pictures of us to prove it. Among the six thousand identically dressed cap-and-gown-clad graduates, she'd identified Michelle and me by the giant bright yellow ichthys fish symbols we'd taped on top of our graduation caps. The ichthys bore testimony to our graduation proclamation: "Jesus Christ, Son of God, Savior!"

Just before graduation, I went hunting for new digs off campus. I wasn't ready to return to California and sit around at my parents' house all summer. I found a cheap sublet across the street from my dorm, on the third floor of a four-story house. I rented the huge studio room, and Michelle rented the second floor room directly beneath me. All the students in the house shared a filthy, disheveled kitchen on the fourth floor. By the end of the summer, the flies and stench were so bad that I resorted to eating two-dollar Whoppers at Burger King, and random things that fit in the tiny, portable refrigerator in my studio.

All summer, a handful of our friends and acquaintances lingered around campus, working odd jobs or milling around idly in the musty, humid city. A slick, streetwise, boyish-looking skater caught Michelle's attention as soon as the mild warmth of May relented to the long, hot days of June.

"This is Jude," she said as she introduced me for the first time. She had met him at the all-night block party the day before graduation.

"I like your overalls," he complimented her as she danced in the pair we'd shared throughout the school year.

Slender twenty-two-year-old Jude wasn't a typical college guy. In fact, I don't think he was a student at all—anywhere. He hung out in skate parks and slept on sofas and did whatever it took to get by. He wore long, baggy cut-off shorts and ratty old T-shirts, and traveled across the country on a skateboard.

I couldn't place his straight jet-black hair and brown skin undertones and asked Michelle about his background.

"He's half Jamaican and half white, I think."

"He'd be a good model."

"I'll ask him. I'm sure he'd be glad to model for you."

Jude and Michelle hung out on and off all summer. She liked him—a lot, though she never said so outright. She just hinted at it by talking about him nonstop. I only saw him a couple more times, when he modeled for me. He didn't say much, so he didn't make an impression on me one way or the other. I worked most of the day and usually didn't meet up with Michelle until the evening, when Jude was long gone.

Keri met him later and told Michelle frankly, "I don't trust him. He seems dangerous."

In the end, Keri was right. Jude turned out to be bad news. Michelle found him a comfortable apartment to sublet from one of our college friends who had graduated with us and then landed a great job and was traveling on business that summer. Jude stayed at our friend's place for months and then skipped out on the bills he'd accrued on the sublet. He left Michelle to settle his tab.

Michelle and I both seemed drawn to our polar opposites. Nature propelled us toward men who embodied our antithesis. While spiritually and intellectually we wanted one sort of man, chemistry and physics stirred us in another direction.

Immediately after graduation, Keri moved home with her parents, cashing in on their offer of free room and board. Then she hit the ground running, trying to unearth that perfect job she was sure existed somewhere in a tall, luxurious office building in Center City. Well before graduation, she had mapped out a carefully crafted strategic plan to work with Jewish immigrants from the former Soviet Union. But as soon as we graduated, the US government cut all immigrant absorption program budgets in half. They had nothing to offer Keri. According to Plan B, she would travel to Russia and work with Messianic Jewish organizations or do a stint in the Peace Corps. But, since Russian communism had crashed to its demise two years earlier, the entire country lay crippled, engulfed in a mad tempest of social and economic upheaval. Seventy years of failed utopian idealism whirled out of control like a drunken, spinning top. As Russia hobbled toward embracing capitalism, its greatest capitalists—the mafia—quickly developed a chokehold on burgeoning businesses. The upheaval reverberated throughout the country, forcing both Keri and Michelle, who had hoped to use her Russian language skills, to abandon all hopes of working in the former USSR.

Near the end of senior year, Keri devised a three-tier potential-job chart for herself. Tier one: Job Heaven. Tier one remained empty all spring semester and throughout the early part of summer. Not a single offer came her way. Tier two: Job Purgatory. Tier two was reserved for all the job applications and resumes that went unanswered. Waiting was torture. Tier three: Job Hell—set aside for rejection letters. Tier three grew rapidly during the first few weeks of summer.

One day Keri downloaded her frustrations: "I leave the house in my rotten business suit, heading off to some interview, only to get rejected. Every day my mom looks at me disapprovingly and asks, 'Nothing yet?' 'No, Mom,' I tell her. Then she says, 'Well, why don't you use the university computer? They'll find you the perfect position.' My mother has this crazy idea that the school has a magical computer for all graduates. All I have to do is put in my personal information, and it will match me with the perfect job. She seems to think that I'm simply too lazy to use it," Keri lamented.

Finally, Keri went to a temp agency and dazzled them with her nimble ability to master Word and Excel in one day using on-site tutorials. "Very impressive," commented the interviewing manger, grinning in generous praise. But Keri had had enough.

"I've been duped by the whole lofty liberal arts promise of enlightenment," she moaned before fleeing Philadelphia with Noel. They escaped to Mexico—a temporary reprieve from the monotonous, disheartening hours spent sending out countless crisp resumes and neatly typed cover letters in heavy-stock envelopes.

The job market during that summer was bruised and drowsy; good jobs were hard to come by in the slow economy. Just before graduation, I sent a resume to a Jewish magazine, along with a cover letter detailing my chutzpah. I didn't get an interview. Some of our classmates, like Jim (an English major), opted out of trying to work up the corporate ladder from an obscure entry-level job. Instead, he chose to devote himself to the intricacies of bartending knowledge; he became a professor of mixed drinks. Even with a college degree, you were lucky to get a minimum-wage job at a retail store.

"You're hired," the J. Crew store manager told me. "You get 50 percent off your wardrobe, and you start next week."

I was happy. Fifty percent off everything at J. Crew was a nice perk. I folded shirts and arranged dress slacks on hangers for three weeks before my phone rang with a better offer.

"Hey, this is Greg, the photographer; I could use a hand around the studio. Are you available? I'll pay you whatever J. Crew is paying you."

I put in my notice at J. Crew the next day and went to work for Greg the following week.

"Here's a key to the studio," he said in his laid-back drawl. Then he hesitated and looked at me sideways. "You aren't going to steal anything, are you?"

"No," I promised.

His last assistant had let herself into the studio while Greg was gone, ransacked his photo archives, and run off with all the prints and negatives from her nude photo shoot. I'd seen some of the pictures. The ones I saw were clean, well-lit photos—nothing X-rated or weird. As far as I knew, she had volunteered to be photographed and then had second thoughts after the photo shoot. What were they thinking? Photographing your employee naked and modeling for your employer in the nude were bound to make things a little funky at work. It was a sexual harassment suit just waiting to happen—not the smartest professional move for either one of them. But their misadventures didn't faze me. I wasn't confused about my role in the photo studio. As a photographer, I belonged behind the camera. I had no interest in modeling.

Working with a fashion photographer all summer was a dream come true. Before the photo studio and J. Crew, I had interviewed for a minimum-wage temp job as a telemarketer and was turned down before I could even finish reading the script. "That's all, thank you," the interviewer said before pointing me toward the door.

I had better luck in sales—sort of. I trained to be a low-level sales associate, hustling advertising from small businesses for a fly-by-night magazine targeting students. But dressing up, walking all day in scorching heat, knocking on doors, and sweet-talking business owners into spending hard-earned money wasn't for me. I quit after a three-day trial. The company never paid me, and the manager stopped returning my phone calls asking about my check. I worked another temp job with Michelle and one of her teaching assistants, a Penn graduate student, stuffing envelopes in an office downtown. At least they paid me for my efforts. I raked in a whopping $5.25 an hour.

Working for Greg, the photographer, was a godsend. He was a master photographer and a fine teacher. I learned to manipulate his heavy, clunky large-format cameras and load large single sheets of film into the removable camera backs. Best of all, he showed me how to line up two cameras on two different sets and create eye-popping surrealist effects using multiple exposures.

Greg only came into the studio a few days a week. On the days when he didn't come in, I was free to blast his stereo and use his pricey photo equipment to work on my personal projects. By the end of the summer, I had several impressive new images for my portfolio. Weeks earlier, I had received my acceptance letter to Brooks Institute of Photography. I used the new portfolio images, along with some of Greg's techniques that I had mastered, to bypass the first-term class at photo school.

I savored the days in the photo studio. But aside from photography, summer slow boiled on a hot plate, restless and uneventful. No marriage proposals. No serious conversations with a cute guy in a dark car on a Los Angeles night. The thrill-loving, boy-crazy part of me grew bored. With Milan and CJ long gone since graduation, I missed my daily dose of raw male intensity. No electricity filled the air. As summer languished into the last sizzling weeks, I picked up my address book, thumbed past all the nice, safe guys and called CJ's friend Gil. I had first met Gil back in November on the night of CJ's birthday celebration. Since then, we'd run into each other several times around campus. During one of those chance encounters, we'd exchanged phone numbers. I'd last seen Gil at the beginning of summer; he'd said he would be here in Philadelphia. Dark-haired, well-dressed Gil, with his mesmerizing clear green eyes and lovely Brazilian accent, was bound to prod my sleepy summer wide awake. He was just a little taller than me, but he oozed with sensuality. He was intense. He always looked at me like I was lunch and he hadn't eaten in a week.

"Let's see the new John Grisham film," Gil suggested.

We set a time to meet in the early evening and met up the next day. We sat through the film quietly and then chatted casually as he walked me home.

"Are you still doing photography?" Gil asked.

"Yep, I have a bunch of new shots."

"I'd like to see your latest photos."

We ascended the three flights up to my room, and I flipped on the lights, illuminating the dark studio. I opened the large windows, but felt no breeze. The old house didn't have air-conditioning. Indoors and out-doors, it was a hundred degrees, and the air felt as thick and hot as lava. It was the kind of muggy, stifling humidity that made you want to peel off every stitch of sticky clothing and lie down in front of a giant fan.

I looked around my room for somewhere to sit. I didn't have any chairs. My red milk crates sat lined up as shelves, full of books. I couldn't even grab a couple of them and flip them over to sit on. *Why didn't I have a single chair?* The carpet probably hadn't been shampooed since the first student rented the room a hundred years ago. The idea of sitting on it grossed me out. There was nowhere to sit except on my bed—my gigantic, expansive bed. It rose like a centerpiece, protruding from the wall into the middle of my room. My enormous fan aimed directly at my sheets. I was dying to turn the fan on.

How could I play this one off? I couldn't ask him to sit on the bed. That would be a deliberate and careless lead-on. I grabbed my box of new photographs and laid them out across the edge of the bed as we stood looking at them. He looked through the photos quickly, without asking questions. Then his calculated, even gaze rested easily on me. It was the look I remembered when I first met him—cool and hungry. I imagined he gave all women that look.

The game had begun. Was the night ending or just beginning? He waited for me to call the next play. After all, he wasn't in my room at 9:30 at night, on a blazing summer evening, to chat about photography. Outside, the city melted, slowly cooking away in a giant Crock-Pot. I knew I was handling live coals, juggling the smoldering embers and trying not to get smoked out.

I met his silent inquiry: *What's it going to be?*

"Yeah, well, thanks for the movie," I said. "It was good."

"It was," he agreed. His eyes remained fixed on me, burning through me like X-ray vision.

"So . . . ," I started. I didn't know what to say. He was waiting for something, but he wasn't saying anything. I didn't want to ask him what he thought of my pictures. They seemed to bore him.

"Well, I guess I'll be talking to you," I said.

"So, good night?" he asked.

"Yeah, it's getting kind of late."

I had slipped through the noose. I could get away with it this one time and not be considered a tease. We were just hanging out; it wasn't even a real date. I had played my not-a-slut card. Guys like Gil would let you off the hook if you didn't give it up the first time you went out. You were basically saying, "I'm not a slut." But with the second outing, the stakes became higher. I'd be expected to deliver *something*.

His look made it clear; he didn't want to be friends. He wasn't hanging out because he wanted someone to watch movies with him and listen to his thoughts over a latte at a café. He left, and I decided to embrace my quiet summer for the next few weeks before I left for Santa Barbara. I vowed never to call him again. Now was not the time to be prowling for trouble, regardless of how alive it made me feel.

The countdown was on—two weeks until I'd move to a strange town on the other side of the country. I didn't think twice about whether or not I'd like Santa Barbara. It would be fine. I'd make new friends. I'd have a good time—I always did. I bumped around in the disarray of my half-packed, tornado-struck room. I spent my last week tossing books, clothing, and photo equipment into mismatched boxes and stepping over piles of things littering the floor on their way to designated containers.

Before my final departure, I took the train up to New York to hang out with my old classmate Justin Greco. Justin had accepted a job offer in New York shortly after his graduation a year earlier. He lived just across the river from Manhattan in a small Jersey City apartment.

Manhattan exhilarated me. The city never stopped its mad churn forward at light speed. Everything whizzed by in a mad dash—people, taxis, the subway. Only the street-side hot dog stands and outdoor magazine vendors stood still. When I walked through the city, I delighted in passing lone New York moms, meandering past the rows of brownstones and steely commercial edifices with their children. They always walked a little more slowly than the rest of the mad dashers. It was hard to propel yourself like a rocket, from destination to destination, with a toddler in tow. I imagined they were the only ones moving slowly enough to enjoy the city.

Soho, Noho, the Village, Washington Square, Chinatown, Little Italy, South Street Seaport, Midtown, Uptown—Justin and I spun through all of them in two days. I needed a New York fix before the tide swept me away to the distant shores of Southern California.

When I returned to Philadelphia, Michelle threw an amazing going-away party for me downstairs in her studio. She hosted an indulgent sugarfest, a dessert party jam-packed with fresh cakes and cookies and all the sweets I needed to sail away on an artificial, tooth-rotting high. Keri, Mandy, Noel, and all our friends who still lived in the Philadelphia area piled into Michelle's room—a whole slew of people, including Milan's ex-girlfriend Denise and our junior-year roommate, Allison. Michelle had furniture, chairs, a little sofa, even a table to serve food. Thank goodness we didn't have to throw the party in my room, with everyone cavorting on my bed.

My friend Patrick, who had graduated a year ahead of me, brought a present.

"Here you go," he said, handing me a small, neatly wrapped box.

"What is it?" I grinned, shaking it like a little kid to see if anything rattled inside.

"Oh, it's something very special," he stated with a big smile. "It will remind you of all the fun we had in the dining hall a couple years back." Patrick and I had hung out my sophomore year, when he was a junior. We often met up to go to the dining hall together, where we speculated about the main ingredient in all the food.

I tore open the package to reveal a simple green and white box that resembled the packaging for butter. "Lard," the label read. That night we retold the story of our scientific discovery: "Did you know all the food served on campus is made from one secret ingredient? Lard! It doesn't matter what you eat or what you order from the cooks, everything is 100 percent artificially colored, artificially flavored LARD." We all talked late into the night.

"Do you know how many recipes there are for lard?"

"Yes, pig fat is like tofu. It takes on the flavor of whatever you cook it in."

"No, of course it's not kosher."

Chapter Twenty-Two

santa barbara

{August, Summer after Graduation}

My plane touched down in the smallest airport in the whole world—at least, it appeared the smallest airport I'd ever seen. If it weren't for the runway, you'd completely miss it. The combined square footage of the bathroom stalls at most airports was bigger than the square footage of the entire Santa Barbara airport.

It had only one baggage claim. Not one baggage-claim *building*; I mean one baggage-claim *belt*. Supposedly, a second baggage claim existed, but I never saw it. As far as I was concerned, its existence was a myth. The entire airport fit into a single-level Spanish-style bungalow with a red-tile roof. Many people in the town had homes bigger than the airport.

I'd arrived in Santa Barbara. Welcome to graduate school.

Santa Barbara possessed all that was good about LA but shed all the Hollywood hype and pretension. Kevin Costner occasionally strode into the local Starbucks. "Steve Martin rides his bike through town," someone told me. "I saw David Bowie and Iman at the gas station up the street," another friend said. No one paid celebrities a bit of attention in Santa Barbara. Santa Barbara was mellow like that.

Santa Barbara had perfect Southern California weather, but no smog and no traffic. I'd disembarked in the land of palm trees and never-ending beaches. This was California's Riviera, surrounded by miles of coastline and nestled beneath a string of mountains. Tourists flocked to Santa Barbara like children to Disneyland. Rumor had it that Jackie O. and JFK spent their honeymoon there.

It was the most cosmopolitan small town I'd ever visited. Oprah and Rob Lowe owned homes in a part of town called Montecito. Montecito drove me crazy at night. Driving there could be a nightmare. The roads were narrow, and the driveways were enormous. More than once, I turned up a giant driveway in the pitch-dark evening, thinking it was a street. I'd drive down the street only to be blocked by an enormous, ornate steel gate and a call box. Apparently, I'd missed my turn and driven to the home of some famous film producer.

Santa Barbara was beautiful—but woefully homogeneous. Were it not for the four colleges there, the entire ethnic population of Santa Barbara would have fit into a teaspoon. My first few days there, I was sure Oprah and I were the only two black people in the entire population of eighty-five thousand.

"This is the land of the newly wed and the nearly dead," locals joked. Santa Barbara residents consisted of carefree, transient young people and an ample population of old, moneyed Republicans. Few people existed in between. Just like with my apartment in LA, I suspected that the management of my Santa Barbara apartment complex enforced undisclosed age restrictions. Every renter appeared younger than thirty. My apartment manager, Joan; Alberto, the handyman; and parents visiting from out of town were the only exceptions.

I only had three friends my first six months in Santa Barbara. When I first arrived, I shared a room on Brooks's Montecito campus with a gifted fashion photography student from Hungary. We roomed together for about two weeks before I moved into my own apartment. She graduated soon after I began classes, but before she left to launch her career in New York, I hung out with her and her boyfriend. At school, Jeff from Minneapolis became my photo partner. All my photo assignments had to be completed by a team of two, so Jeff and I did all our assignments together. My only other friend was my oddball neighbor, Trevor, a young schoolteacher who lived in the apartment next to me. I had him model for me for one of my photo projects. He was cute, but peculiar. He stopped by once for a friendly visit, and we sat around talking as we often did.

"The weather's been really nice lately," Trevor remarked.

"Yep. Great for going to the beach," I replied.

"Which beach do you go to?" he asked.

"I usually go to the one up the street by the Biltmore."

"Oh, right. Butterfly Beach."

"Is that what it's called? I thought it was called the Biltmore Beach."

"Yeah, people call it the Biltmore Beach. But that's not the real name."

"Well, you learn something new every day, don't you?" I replied, laughing at myself. "Speaking of learning, how's teaching going?"

"Okay." Then he paused in thought. "Except a few problems with some parents. I don't like emailing the students their homework assignments at the end of each day. I think they should write it down in class. I shouldn't have to give them the homework twice," he complained.

"I think it's a good idea to email it. That way your students can look it up at home if they forget something."

"Well, I don't want to do it, and the kids' parents are giving me a hard time."

"Well, yeah. If you're the only teacher in the whole school that won't email homework, of course the parents are going to give you a hard time."

"Hmmm. I guess." Trevor paused as though he was weighing the merits of complying with the parents' request. "Hey, I have a question for you."

"Yep, what?" I asked, expecting a request for additional advice on his school situation.

"Can I kiss you?" he asked.

He made the request the same way you'd ask for a glass of water.

"What? . . . *No.*"

What was the matter with him? There wasn't even a remote spark of romance anywhere in our neighborly interactions. At least *I* wasn't feeling starry-eyed. We'd gone to lunch a couple times and hung out here and there. But really, he couldn't be serious. Maybe I should have hesitated more as if I was considering the possibility before delivering my emphatic no. I might not have sounded so appalled. But I wasn't considering the possibility. One minute we're talking about homework, and then he comes up with something totally random like that.

"Hmm, let's dance," he suggested.

"Dance?" I asked, amused. *I don't hear any music. Do you hear music? Okay, Mr. One Flew Over the Cuckoo's Nest*, I thought.

I stopped hanging out with Trevor shortly after I rode with him to the beach one night and he showed me a gun he kept in the trunk of his car.

"That's for protection," he explained.

Why did he need protection in Santa Barbara? Was he afraid of getting assaulted by one of the little blue-haired, Jaguar-driving grandmas as she left the country club? Maybe he thought one of his elementary school students would mug him.

Michelle comforted me the most during my first six months in Santa Barbara. We talked every weekend. I rarely talked to Keri, though she was back in Philadelphia living at her parents' house. Her Spanish-speaking abilities had landed her an administrative assistant job at Chiquita's corporate offices. She worked for the banana empire for five months and mastered Chilean slang. Michelle and Mandy lived a short drive from Keri's job, in the historic part of downtown. Keri crashed at their pad often—keeping the V Society adventures and endeavors alive.

A fat envelope from Philadelphia arrived in the mail one day. Michelle sent me a quirky photo essay—starring her. It was a virtual tour of her new flat in downtown Philadelphia, combined with cheerful tidings. In the first photo, Mich stood in her kitchen, engulfed in a domestic swirl of pots, a spice rack, and a dining table littered with a newspaper, an empty bowl, and a juice glass. She wore a pair of giant jeans and a dark gray cardigan. A lined, white binder-paper sign exclaiming, "HELLO DELMO" covered her face. In the next photo, she stood against her bedroom wall with three of my black-and-white photographs mounted triptych-style. A sign called out, "HELLO ADELE." In the next photograph Michelle sat on a wide white window ledge, looking pensively down at the floor as if an ant moving slowly across the room hypnotized her. The words on the sign she held spelled out, "HELLO STINKY'S SISTER." (I had occasionally called my brother Stinky when we were little. I had also published a portrait of my grandmother, in a magazine at Penn under the pseudonym Stinky's Sister.) The next sign cried, "HELLO MOM" as Mich stood with her head tilted sideways, expressionless and lovely, in typical kooky Michelle style. She had positioned herself upstairs, standing in a doorway by a wooden stair banister, at the end of a clean white hallway. Another photo exclaimed, "HELLO ADELAIDE." Michelle looked directly at the camera, her pouting lips slightly parted and her hair flowing around her cardigan. She stood in her bedroom, next to a painted green chest of drawers covered with random bedroom knickknacks—makeup, lotion, a large colorful vase, dried flowers, and jewelry in a low, flat basket.

She had photographed herself in just about every room of her new pad. Five more signs called out cheerful greetings using my various given names and V Society nicknames: Adele C. Moore, Butthead, My Little Friend, Sexy, and Slappy. In the second-to-last photo, Mandy wore a comical, goofball expression and held up a sign that read, "HOLA ADELE." Amy, Michelle's new roommate, held up the closing sign, inquiring, "HEY ADELE. WHEN YA GONNA COME VISIT?"

I really needed and appreciated the reminder of Philadelphia and all our times together. Even in the temperate Santa Barbara climate, where winter never dipped below fifty degrees, I still delighted in the sensations and smells of East Coast seasons. I remembered the newness and excitement of the new school year and imagined autumn's cool settling quietly on Locust Walk. New kids had moved into 2110 High Rise South, and a new graduating class rejoiced in its final year.

Mich thrilled me when she decided to come visit me some time later. We took a road trip down to Los Angeles before continuing on to San Diego. Michelle itched to show me all of her favorite San Diego hangouts from the previous summer.

"Should we make a reservation at a hotel in LA?" Michelle asked before we shoved our bags and snacks into my new compact car.

"I don't have the cash for a nice hotel," I laughed. "I'm still on a student budget."

"I'm not trying to spend a lot either," she agreed. Her new job didn't pay much.

"I think there are a bunch of inexpensive but decent motels just south of LA. We'll just stop off in some little suburb off the highway and stay at a Motel 6 or something," I replied.

"Okay," she agreed.

Off we went—headed south down the scenic Highway 101 along the coast to Los Angeles. Just before Sherman Oaks, we swung onto the 405 freeway and cruised into Westwood. There we visited all our old hangouts from the previous summer. Naturally, things had changed. New people loitered outside Café Miro. No one looked familiar. But our morning in Westwood flew by as we revisited our old stomping grounds and reminisced about the previous year.

We left Westwood and zipped out to Santa Monica to bum around near the pier. Just as the sun sank low into the horizon, we pulled back onto the highway, in search of a quaint roadside motel. We drove a good half hour without seeing a decent-looking place to stop.

"Let's check a phone book," Mich suggested. We pulled into a gas station and dug through a tattered Yellow Pages. There wasn't a single Motel 6 in the vicinity. We called the first couple of places listed under motels.

"Hey, this one is about fifty-five dollars a night. And it's less than five miles away!" Mich exclaimed as she hung up the phone.

"Sounds good to me," I replied, exhausted. The long miles of driving, combined with the unflinching rays of constant direct sunlight, had depleted every ounce of my energy. Michelle read the directions as I steered us to the inn.

"Is this it?" I exclaimed as we pulled up to an unimpressive, dingy-white two-story building. It looked like a poorly maintained apartment complex.

"It doesn't look so hot," Michelle commented.

"How bad can it be?" I laughed.

We parked the car in the small, unkempt parking lot.

"Where's the lobby?" I asked.

We looked around for a clearly marked entrance, but saw none. Instead, we saw a small window, sort of like the drive-through window for a bank attached to a small office.

"I guess that's it," Mich surmised.

We approached the window. Thick glass separated us from the man inside the office. A small mail slot positioned at waist level allowed for money exchanges at the base of the window.

"Your rooms are fifty-five dollars a night, right?" I asked.

"Yep," the crusty-looking guy in the office replied.

"I'll put it on my card," Mich said. "You can pay me back later."

"Okay," I agreed.

She paid, and the man gave us the key. We unloaded our bags from the car and walked in the direction he'd indicated.

"Look at that!" Michelle exclaimed as her gaze fell on a weathered metal sign posted above two pay phones. It read, "No DRUG-RELATED TRANSACTIONS PERMITTED ON THESE PHONES."

We turned and looked at each other.

"Are you sure you want to stay here?" Mich asked.

"No. But I'm tired. If I drive any farther, I may fall asleep at the wheel. Let's just look at the room," I replied hesitantly.

Michelle bravely proceeded toward our dwelling and unlocked the door. She swung it open and flipped on the lights. We entered. Thank goodness the carpet was deep brown. That made it difficult to distinguish the stains plaguing the floor space. Two rickety double beds with dark, patterned, decades-old bedspreads greeted us. It looked like a scene from a bad retro B movie. I half expected some joker named Super-Fly Pimp Daddy to jump out of the closet, decked out in a baby-blue bell-bottom polyester suit.

Michelle strode boldly into the bathroom. "You've got to see this," she stated evenly.

Cigarette burns dotted the countertop around the sink. I stuck my head into the shower to make sure there wasn't a dead body or something hiding in there. There wasn't. But one thing was certain; I wouldn't be taking a shower in there—*ever*.

"We can leave if you want," I offered hopefully.

"It's just one night. I'll survive." She smiled. Mich was a brave soul.

"We're getting out of here at the crack of dawn—right?" I inquired.

"Definitely," she agreed.

The next morning, we awoke, speedily brushed our teeth, and checked out.

"I'm proud of you," Michelle said with a smile.

"Why?"

"I was sure you wouldn't spend the night there," she said with a laugh.

I smiled back. "I have to save my money for all my photo supplies," I explained. She was right. If I hadn't been so tired, I would have insisted that we keep driving until we found somewhere better to stay.

We hopped into my car and shot off. Within a couple of hours, we arrived in San Diego. There we went to Michelle's favorite coffeehouse, just a few blocks from the beach. "Last summer, I came by here just about every day," she gushed.

After we left the café, we spent the afternoon perusing some of the local shops and kicked it on the beach. That night we stayed with one of our classmate's parents. We'd never met them, but our classmate had called ahead and made the arrangements. His parents welcomed us into their spotless, sprawling house. I'd never been so glad to see a clean shower in my life.

The next day, we hit the road again and jetted back to Santa Barbara. Michelle and I goofed around town for a couple more days before I dropped her off at Santa Barbara's tiny airport.

"Which terminal are you leaving from?" I asked as I pulled up to the airport.

"I'm not sure," she said, fumbling through the narrow envelope that held her itinerary and plane ticket.

"I'm just kidding. There's only one terminal," I teased.

"Bye, Delmo." She smiled as she leaned across her seat and squeezed me.

"Bye, Mom." I grinned and returned the hug. "I'll talk to you this weekend."

She stepped out of the car, grabbed her bags, and disappeared into the little white building.

After arriving in Santa Barbara, I had dropped into a couple of churches before I stumbled upon Calvary Chapel. The church met inside a big old-fashioned movie theater on State Street, the main street downtown. Calvary Chapel churches sprung up during the sixties to offer hippies a place to worship. Most mainstream Protestant churches frowned on the free-spirited, barefoot kids that showed up underdressed for services. Calvary Chapel didn't have a dress code. As you long as you didn't show up naked, you were welcome. They didn't care what kind of clothes you wore to church. At Calvary Chapel Santa Barbara, the hippies of the sixties had long been replaced by long-haired, sun-loving surfers. Surfers populated the place like sand on a beach. The pastor for Reality, the college group, was a blond die-hard surfer from Hawaii. Calvary Chapel's senior pastor, a jolly portly fortysomething, was a surfing legend. Supposedly, he'd won a bunch of awards in international surf competitions.

Surfers were like Martians to me. They used the words *dude* and *rad* and never wore socks. Most surfer guys owned less than five pairs of

long pants. None of those pants were dress slacks. Ownership of a suit
and tie—forget about it.

Reality quickly became the pipeline for filling my social calendar.
Reality met Friday nights for worship and Waxer, the young pastor, gave
a talk. His nickname derived from the process of waxing a surfboard.
Surfers applied wax to their boards to make them wave ready.

"When I looked for a wife, I hoped God would give me someone as
sweet as Mother Teresa, but that looked like Barbie," Waxer told several
of us one day. God answered Waxer's prayers down to the last detail;
his wife Cindy was the perfect embodiment of that request. She was as
sweet as could be and looked dead-on Barbie.

My newfound friends at Reality were a mixture of students from all
four Santa Barbara schools: UCSB, Westmont College, Santa Barbara
City College, and Brooks Institute of Photography. Most of us were in
our early twenties, with a couple of eighteen- and nineteen-year-olds
sometimes tagging along. We traveled in a group of eight to ten. Every
Friday night after Reality, our gang descended on a café, taking up the
large tables for a couple of hours while we drank lattes and kicked it.
Every Sunday, after morning church service, our pack swooped in on
one of our three favorite restaurants for brunch.

All of us in Reality were expected to practice abstinence. Waxer
encouraged sexual purity, as did all the pastors at Calvary Chapel.
As always, it was a struggle. Most of us were abstinent. But a couple of
girls in the group turned up pregnant. Abstinence was less of a struggle
for me in Santa Barbara. Fashionista-guys with sideburns and charming
accents didn't flock to lazy surf towns. There were a lot of international
students at photo school, but none quite as tempting as East Coast collegiate guys. The surfers and preppy, clean-cut all-American types that
populated Santa Barbara didn't fascinate me. Santa Barbara was like
a convent. Trouble rarely appeared out of nowhere and knocked on my
apartment door, as it had back at High Rise South.

I learned to surf with my friends from Reality. One weekend about
twenty of us, including Waxer and his wife Cindy, headed down to San

Onofre, a beach just north of San Diego. The waves there were small and regular, perfect for beginning surfers. We camped overnight near the beach, and Waxer gave the nonsurfers, including me, surf lessons. He was an excellent teacher. Someone loaned me a wet suit and a surfboard. By the end of my first surf lesson, I could ride a wave standing up on a long board. I was beside myself with glee. Maybe I would be in the *Guinness Book of World Records* as the only black surfer in all of Santa Barbara. Did Oprah surf? She was the only contender who might challenge me.

I finally understood why surfers lived to catch the next big wave. Riding waves felt unreal, a perfect communion with nature. When I sailed on that wave, surrounded by the vast depths of the ocean, the salty spritz spraying my face, it was like prayer—an up-close personal conversation with God. I couldn't imagine how you could be a surfer and be an atheist. The ocean was God's giant playground.

Throughout those lackadaisical Santa Barbara days, I still spoke to Michelle regularly. We talked every weekend and shared all the latest adventures in our post-college lives. Stephanie lived in LA, and Mandy had enrolled in extra classes to prepare for medical school acceptance. Milan and I spoke periodically. He still lived on the East Coast.

And then there was the biggest news of all: Keri was engaged. The V Society was about to have its first alum.

Chapter Twenty-Three

─────── ∽ ───────

THE WEDDING

{October, One Year after College Graduation}

WHITE STEAM ROSE FROM THE THICK, BLACK SIDEWALK GRATE, spiraling in a dance. I stepped through the wisps and felt the heat from the subway far below rush up the leg of my pants. The city hummed with the chorus of whirling tires against asphalt, and reeked of grit. I had forgotten what it smelled like, grungy and neglected, like it needed to be hosed off and aired out. For a split second, I loved that smell, as every familiar memory from my years there washed over me. Oh, my city of brotherly love—Philadelphia.

Here I could trade in my shorts and flip-flops for leather boots, jeans, and a long-sleeve silk shirt. Three thousand miles erased every hint of the long-haired surfer culture that engulfed me in Santa Barbara. I was transported back into my urban element, my hunger abated. It was October, sun-drenched and crisp, one of my favorite times of year on the East Coast.

I was returning for the first time, after more than a year, for Keri's wedding. She'd found her hairy, Zionist, Hebrew-speaking, Messianic Jewish man. Erez, Keri's husband-to-be, was a musically gifted West Point graduate. He was nine years older than she and struck me as very serious. I couldn't imagine that he'd find any of our V Society songs amusing. I certainly couldn't envision him doing the Elevator Dance.

He and Keri had written to each other for years, pen pals introduced by Keri's Hebrew teacher. All through college, Keri had dismissed Erez's quiet, earnest pursuit of her.

"I went out with Erez," she had said after meeting him for dinner junior year. "I'm just not into him—at all." The outing had been a complete disaster.

But that had been over two years ago, when the V Society romped and played in High Rise South and pretty, charming boy-men enthralled its members.

While talking to one of her coworkers in the Chiquita office, just four months after joining the company, Keri had a revelation. "I'm going to marry Erez," her inner voice stated calmly, decidedly. "I just knew it," she relayed. "I went over to Mandy and Michelle's and told them that afternoon."

Not long afterward, Erez flew in from Israel for a friend's wedding. "We dated five days, if you can even call it that. I mean we never left each other's side, practically," Keri explained matter-of-factly. "When Erez returned to Israel, I called him ten days later to say that I was immigrating in a month and a half—much earlier than I had planned."

The V Society was about to have its very first alumna—an amazing triumph since Keri's list of requirements for a husband had always seemed the hardest out of all of ours to satisfy. My husband-to-be list seemed much simpler. I just wanted a hot guy that walked the same spiritual path as me and wanted to make wildly creative, brilliant art films. Not a tall order. He only had to speak one language (English), and I didn't have any particular body-hair requirements. I didn't have any ethnic parameters either. He didn't even have to be a male-fashionista.

Now that I was back on my old stomping grounds, I was ecstatic to see Michelle and share all the new details of our lives face to face.

"Hi, Mom," she grinned.

"Hi, Petunia Mom," I beamed back at her as we squeezed each other in a full embrace at the baggage claim. Late senior year, I'd added the Petunia Pig reference to "Mom." Michelle was the exact opposite of the cartoon piggy, so the name seemed humorously fitting. We tumbled into a cab and sped from the airport toward Center City and downtown Philly. I settled in at Mich's flat, a brownstone several blocks off a busy boulevard in the heart of the city.

"Your place is great, Mich," I commented, taking in the spacious, welcoming rooms with honey-colored hardwood floors and high ceilings.

Soon, someone rang the doorbell. As Michelle opened the door, I could hear the thud of heavy boots in the entryway broadcasting his arrival—CJ.

"Hey, Brutus." I smiled.

"Hey, Adele." He grinned, strolling into the room with that ever-so-familiar confident, sauntering gait. "Whasuuuuup?" he greeted me, drawing out the "ah" sound like a car screeching around an incredibly long hairpin curve. CJ and I hugged, and he plopped down in the chair across from me at Michelle's kitchen table. The three of us pigged out on Mich's cooking, laughing and stuffing our faces as if it were still senior year. I downed part of a pint of Ben and Jerry's ice cream while CJ re-layed the events of the past year.

"Yeah, Michelle was always the quiet one, studying all the time when we were in school. She never said much. I never really got to know her until this year," he confessed. "She's really cool."

CJ and Michelle had become close friends in the past year, spending lots of time together. I could see how her gentle sweetness and simple steadfastness brought out the best in him. She was a true friend; she didn't judge him. She was trustworthy and diplomatic—he could let his guard down with her. Around her, he acted less like a big, bad Brutus and more like a man in search of himself.

We goofed around at Michelle's place for a couple of hours. The contradictory sensations of fascination and annoyance filled me, as they always did when I hung out with CJ. He sprawled across Michelle's sofa in his black jeans and black sweater, taking up the whole sofa so I couldn't sit down.

"Fine," I said indignantly. I sat down on top of him, squashing his midsection like a pancake. Michelle photographed me sitting on his stomach, while he laughed at the camera and I exposed a mouthful of partially chewed food.

"Hey, you haven't seen the whole place yet," Michelle reminded me.

"Well, take me on the grand tour," I replied.

We stepped onto the deck momentarily and then peeked quickly into Mandy and Amy's rooms. The tour ended in Michelle's room, where we retreated to continue our antics. Like the rest of the rooms in the apartment, hers was a good size, with fresh ivory walls and the same hardwood floor that extended throughout the flat. Mich's room was well furnished and neat. It felt comfortable, with small pockets of contained disarray that created a familiar, lived-in feeling. Her personal belongings lay everywhere—books, CDs in a wooden case, and a large pastel-green chest of drawers, covered with keepsakes and an assortment of scented lotions and fragrances. A decent-sized desk, with a wooden chair painted purple, sat against a wall, looking out a huge paned window.

An eclectic collection of artwork from college classmates adorned the walls: a sketch by Doug Chan and a colorful self-portrait collage that Keri had created. Three of my matted black-and-white photographs hung on the adjacent wall. The first photograph was a documentary-style close-up I had taken of a New York phone booth where someone had pasted a handwritten "BELIEVE IN JESUS" sign over a Camel cigarette advertisement. The second photo depicted bare-chested Jude, the skateboarder, crouching and covered in metallic body paint. His dark body glistened against the black background. His eyes were closed, as he appeared suspended, his body twisted in a stress position, in the balance between agony and ecstasy. The final photograph was a simple, witty portrait of my grandmother. I had asked her to sit in the metal chair on her porch. She sat in the chair, in her neat white dress, and set her black purse in the identical chair next to her. It was a lovely image of my petite, tidy grandmother and her petite, tidy black purse.

"That's a cute dress!" I exclaimed to Michelle, noticing a tapered, sleeveless sixties-style mod dress with a bright floral print hanging on a hook from her open closet door.

"Ehhhh—that *is* a nice dress. Lemme see it," CJ requested with an impish smile, his eyes squinted up. Michelle took the dress down from where it hung and handed it to CJ. He swept it up and disappeared into the bathroom. Moments later, he reappeared, decked out in his white undershirt, big clomping boots with black socks peeking over the top, and paraded in Michelle's floral dress. His wide shoulders prevented him from completely zipping up the dress in the back, but otherwise the dress fit him well. Michelle and I fell over laughing. He was hysterical, as he tried to look prim and feminine in Michelle's frock.

"Ehhh, heh–ehhhh. How do I look?" he asked in a high-pitched, girly voice, snickering like the cat that ate the canary.

"You're off your rocker," I choked, giggling. "You've got really nice legs, though." CJ's legs *were* nice. Even though they were hairy and sticking out of a floral dress, he had the best-looking legs of any guy I'd ever seen. Who else could don a yellow dress and still brim over with earthy, masculine appeal?

"You do have nice legs," Michelle agreed, laughing.

"Why, thank you," CJ said with feigned modesty, using a high-pitched voice again. "You're embarrassing me," he squeaked, pretending to be bashful.

"I've got to get a picture of you," I proclaimed. I handed Michelle my camera. *Snap.* She captured me standing next to CJ in the dress. CJ curtsied clumsily, beaming with a magnificent, playful grin.

"That was a terrible curtsy," Michelle teased.

"Well, how am I supposed to curtsey?" he retorted in jest.

"Like this." Michelle pantomimed a careless but dainty curtsey. CJ tried to follow her lead, succeeding only in looking even more preposterous as his manly frame tried to force itself into ladylike obedience.

"Oh, forget it!" CJ exclaimed. He gave up after several botched attempts and disappeared back into the bathroom. He reappeared in his own clothes just before Keri and Erez arrived.

Keri had asked me to take a cool portrait of her and Erez together.

"I picked out these black jeans for Erez," Keri explained, giddy and head over heels for her fiancée. "I thought he'd look really good in them for the photo shoot."

"Good choice," I agreed. "Everyone looks good in black jeans."

We went outside into the alleyway, and I fired off frame after frame of the adoring couple. The images had an edgy, lyrical, urban *West Side Story* feel, as the two of them stared into each other's eyes dreamily, sometimes oblivious to me. Walls of nearby buildings and brownstones created the background canvas. I took several shots of Erez wearing a black beret, his arms wrapped lovingly around Keri. I doubted he'd ever worn a black beret and a fashionable all-black outfit before. I'm sure beatnik attire was banned at West Point.

After about the third roll, I felt pretty good.

"I think I got it," I declared. "How do you guys feel?"

"You think you got some good pictures of us?" Keri asked, a little concerned. They were leaving for the honeymoon and then returning to Israel after the wedding. It would be a long time before I would see them again to take more pictures.

"Yep, I'm sure I got some really good shots of both of you," I assured her.

"Okay, then," Erez stated with confidence.

Erez was a real *mensch* (Yiddish for "a real man"). He emanated self-assurance and maturity, the kind of guy you imagined would be a good father and a reliable husband. He wasn't one of the pretty, vain schoolboys who had sent us into hormone-driven tizzy fits all through our Penn days.

"We'd better get going then," Erez said, gently taking Keri's hand in his. The gesture struck me like a stomach cramp, and I tried to ignore the feeling that the V Society would never be the same. Keri no longer belonged to us. After the exchanging of vows tomorrow, she would be

Erez's. All of our late-night, naïve conversations about men and sex were over. I couldn't lean over the edge of my bunk and share my random thoughts with her in the bed below me. She would no longer participate in our foolish girlish speculations, fantasies, and what-if discussions. We were no longer the confidants of her secrets and dreams; Erez was. I felt overwhelmingly happy for her, yet I had the sinking feeling that I'd lost my best friend again—for good—to a faraway country and some strait-laced guy that I hardly knew.

"We still have some last-minute things to do before the wedding," Keri explained.

"No problem. Nice meeting you again, Erez," I said before reaching out to shake his hand. I probably should have hugged him, but this was only the second time I'd ever laid eyes on him. I hoped he had a sense of humor. I couldn't imagine Keri spending the rest of her life eight thousand miles away in a humorless household. They seemed so grown-up. I could see them buying a house and raising children together. They were undeniably full-fledged adults, while I still walked a tightrope between adulthood and the last remnants of prolonged adolescence.

Keri squeezed me tightly, and they left. I spent the rest of the day reveling in my reconnection with Michelle and our perpetual unattached states. I was glad Michelle had a flat with roommates and a futon bed. I told myself that discussions about mortgages and children's names and picking out real furniture—the kind you expect to keep a lifetime—was boring. Yet, deep down, I wanted to settle down with a real man and have mundane conversations about buying appliances and all those banal domestic things.

The next day disappeared in the whirlwind flurry of Keri's wedding. Michelle, Mandy, and I arrived several hours early to the wedding hall, an elegant building that accommodated the ceremony in one wing and the large sit-down dinner in an adjoining ballroom. We dressed in our long, midnight-blue bridesmaids' evening gowns. A hairstylist fussed with the other bridesmaids' hair. I wouldn't let him near my black girl's hair, though. No way. I would do my own hair, with my own hair products. Stephanie arrived later than the rest of us and seemed distracted most of the wedding. She wore dark purple lipstick, so dark it almost looked black. It mortified Keri and her parents but they said nothing.

Everything flew by at light speed. Keri and Erez stood under the *chuppah*, the traditional Jewish wedding canopy. The rabbi read the vows. Before I knew it, they had stepped on the wine glass that lay at their feet wrapped in a napkin. "Mazel tov!" I blinked my eyes, and the wedding reception was in full swing. Milan, CJ, Noel, and a sea of guests from Keri's family's synagogue celebrated noisily in high-spirited merriment. Keri and Erez cut the cake, and guests made speeches and shed tears as they exchanged joyful good-byes. The wedding swept by in such a blur that I didn't have time to absorb the cherished reunion of the Elevator Society.

"I hate your old roommate," Milan grumbled angrily as the reception wound down. "How can you even be friends with her?" he groused between curses flung in Noel's direction. Apparently, he and Noel had had it out in a disagreement about their collaboration to purchase Keri a wedding present. There was some misunderstanding about who was paying for what or what was actually purchased or some other vexing point that had ticked Milan off.

By early evening, Michelle, Mandy, and I were piling into a car speeding back to Center City. "Let's meet up tonight," Milan had suggested, before Michelle and I left the reception. Mich and I returned to her place and changed into casual clothes. CJ and Milan met us, still dressed in their wedding outfits.

Everything magical and visceral about college rushed back in new incarnations. The budding excitement of sitting across a table from Milan or CJ returned with the same force and familiarity. All through school, I'd only hung out with them separately, never both at once. The sight of the two of them together, in sharply tailored suits and fashionable neckties, was utterly breathtaking. I was underdressed in jeans and a long-sleeve shirt, but I didn't care. That night a raging flood or blazing inferno could have destroyed the entire city, and I wouldn't have noticed. I was the one place I most wanted to be, with the three people I most wanted to be with.

The sun had set hours ago, cloaking downtown in damp nightfall. Rain had fallen in torrents all day. The Philadelphia streets still looked and smelled wet. As we stepped out into the cool night, I looked cautiously for puddles of water to avoid, but there were none. The nippy air encircled us, and I buttoned up my long trench coat and tightened the belt to hold in the warmth. Cars skidded and bumped over potholes as they barreled past us. Taxis and city buses raced forward, disappearing under distant yellow streetlights. While the city lurched ahead, I burned to slow the evening down, like a film played in slow motion.

The four of us walked down a narrow cobblestone street until it opened onto a busy roadway. We hailed a cab and piled out a few moments later at a handsome brick building on a corner downtown. Soft incandescent light poured out of the windows above our heads. We walked up a short flight of stairs and into an upscale, candle-lit neighborhood tavern. I was completely unaware of everyone else inside the bar, apart from Milan, CJ, and Michelle. Did heads turn to look at the two beautiful men in smart, conservative suits and the tall, comely woman as we made our way through the bar to an isolated table? Probably, but I didn't notice.

"How's this?" Milan asked as he and CJ led us to a table on the far side of the low-lit room.

"Fine," Michelle said.

"Good," I agreed as we took our seats in rich, dark wooden chairs, around a small, dark round table. I didn't see the people at other tables. I didn't see the server when he took our order and brought our drinks. I don't even remember what I ordered—mineral water or cranberry juice. Every part of me felt deeply satisfied and wholeheartedly engaged. In this context, in this circle of friends, a freedom existed that I didn't have in Santa Barbara or anywhere else. We challenged and recognized each other at every level. We silently acknowledged one another as complex beings—intellectually, spiritually, and carnally motivated. I felt strangely at home.

My life in Santa Barbara richly nurtured my spiritual side and rendered the rest of me half asleep in a sort of provocation-free coma. There, I rarely had interactions with men in which I felt attractive or desirable; Santa Barbara guys seemed to view me as asexual. Truthfully, that was probably the best environment for me. I was better off with my mind focused on all things spiritual in my temptation-free Santa Barbara existence. But I never felt as content in spotless, virtue-filled Santa Barbara, as I did in the begrimed city, with these three. I felt relieved and awake. All of me was present, for better or worse. Among these friends, it was only a lightly veiled secret that we were all interwoven messes of tangled, conflicting desires and intentions.

Our drinks arrived, and I settled comfortably into my seat. I found myself wishing I could stay right there in that particular moment, forever. I studied each face at the table—blissful. CJ had cut his hair shorter than it had been in school. It was still longish, but neatly trimmed, hanging just below his ears. Michelle appeared unchanged, the same porcelain complexion and ambivalent sweet smile. Her long, wavy light-brown hair streamed down liberally and rested well below her shoulders.

My eyes found their final resting place in the same direction they always did—toward Milan. He still looked as physically striking as I remembered. It was that same strong face that had delighted and tormented me all of junior and senior year—the dark eyes and thick black hair. That same irresistible accent. He was a delectable portrait, dressed in his dark gray suit and crisp blue tie with a subtle, stylish pattern. He'd added a few pounds of weight, and no longer appeared to be a boy-man. The year had transformed him into an exquisitely filled-out man. He had not only matured physically, but his countenance had greatly altered. There was no trace of his boyish exuberance, and no absurd ranting. All expressions of delight and enthusiasm were gone. Everything about him appeared gloomier—disappointed. He was the same age as me, twenty-two, but he seemed to have supernaturally aged in spirit.

"Americans have it so easy," he said cynically.

"What do you mean?" I asked.

"I mean everything is handed to you on a silver platter. You have no idea what it's like for everyone else," he stated matter-of-factly. His voice dripped acidic with bitterness.

He'd become jaded. Invisible weights pressed down on him, anchoring him to an unseen abyss. He no longer flowed and sailed on the vitality of his youthful hubris. Milan never explained the events or circumstances that had changed him so radically. But their effects were evident. The four of us sat there deep in conversation. Milan listened and commented as Michelle, CJ, and I recounted all we'd seen and done in the past year.

"We're closing in a few minutes," the bartender finally told us. "But there's no rush. Take your time."

It was late, around one or two in the morning. I couldn't be sure. We'd been there talking for a couple of hours. Milan and CJ picked up the tab, and we walked several long blocks through the unusually quiet streets to Michelle's flat. Warm-colored streetlights and flashing traffic lights illuminated the empty sidewalks. We passed long rows of urban residences. Their windows twinkled in the darkness, where lamps had been left on.

Michelle's roommates were asleep, and the four of us slipped quietly into her room and closed the door. Michelle and I sat down on the full-sized futon on her floor. Both of us took our shoes off and slouched back on the futon mattress. I rearranged the pillow behind me and made myself comfortable while CJ sat in the wooden desk chair across from us, by the window. Milan sat down in the red canvas chair, the same Ikea chair we'd had in our dorm living room, junior and senior years.

Michelle reached over and popped a soulful blues CD into the little gray boom box on the dresser.

A deep, melodic, sultry female voice filled the room, crooning:
You don't know what love is . . .

Until you learn the meaning of the blues,
Until you've lost a love you had to lose. . .

Our conversation picked up where we had left off in the tavern.

"So, are you still a virgin?" CJ asked.

"Why wouldn't I be?" I shot back with a grin. "Do you think I am?"

It was none of his business, so I left it at that and let him wonder. Yes, I was still a virgin. My fellow V society members knew; there was no need to broadcast my status to the world.

The jazz vocalist continued in the background.

You don't know how lips hurt,
Until you've kissed and had to pay the cost.
Until you've flipped your heart and you have lost. . .
And how lips that taste of tears.
Ooh, they lose their taste for kissing
You don't know how hearts burn,
For love that cannot live yet never dies,
Until you've faced each dawn with sleepless eyes. . .
You don't know what love is . . .

"Hey, who is this?" CJ asked. "I'm diggin' this."

"Cassandra Wilson," Michelle replied. "It's her album, *Blue Light 'til Dawn*."

She passed him the CD cover, and he examined it closely, looking over the list of songs.

"This is really cool," I chimed in. I purchased the CD for my own music library several weeks later after returning to Santa Barbara.

"So, are you still into that spiritual stuff?" CJ asked me.

"You mean, do I still believe in a holy and righteous God and a risen Savior?" I said with a sly smile, though I was completely serious.

"Yeah," CJ replied.

"Yep," I answered.

"So, how can you be so sure that what you believe is true?" Milan asked.

"It's like anything you believe in that's intangible," I replied.

"Like what?" CJ asked.

"Do you believe in justice? Or love? Are those real concepts?" I probed.

"Yes," Milan replied. CJ nodded in agreement.

"Well, how do you know they exist? Have you ever seen them or touched them?"

"No, of course not," Milan replied.

"You believe in them because of the evidence of their existence. My belief is based in the evidence of God's existence," I explained. "Do you believe in wind?"

"What?" CJ returned.

"Do you believe that there is a force called wind?" I repeated.

"Yes," Milan answered.

"Why?" I asked.

"Because you can see it doing stuff—blowing things around," Milan answered. "In other words, you see the evidence of wind?" I clarified.

"Yes," Milan answered.

"Well, prove to me that wind exists. Show it to me," I replied lightly. "You can't show it to me, can you? You can't put it a bottle or put in under a microscope and show me—here is wind. You can't map it on a periodic chart. You can only show me the evidence of its force and power. You can show me trees blowing and leaves flying through the air and blowing across a street. It's the same with God. I see the evidence of his existence in my life every day. He is an undeniable force."

"But why believe in that one point of view?" Milan questioned.

"I believe in Jesus out of faith. But his existence—the fact that he actually walked on earth is documented historically. Historians in that time period like Pliny the Younger and Josephus actually document historically the existence of a rabbi named Yeshua, Jesus in Hebrew," I continued.

"Yes, but how are you so sure?" Milan pressed.

"Look, at the most basic level it's like this," I began. "If you take a dog with a bunch of fleas, and then ask the fleas, 'Hey, what does the dog look like?' The flea on the dog's nose says, 'Well, the dog is shiny, black, and wet.' Then you ask the flea inside his ear, and that flea says,

'Well, the dog is soft and smooth and pink.' Then you ask the flea on his tail. That flea says, 'Well, the dog is furry and long and skinny.' Are you following me so far?" I paused.

"Yeah," Milan replied.

"We're all like fleas on a dog," I continued. "The dog is life. Each one of us has a different opinion of life and who God is based on our individual experiences. None of us is capable of painting an accurate picture of the dog—that is life—from where we sit. Basically, none of us has a clue, about anything, unless someone comes from outside and says, 'Hey, this is what the dog looks like.'" I paused again. "Does that make sense?"

"I see what you're saying," Milan answered.

"The point is that Jesus is the one person who came from the outside. He's not on the dog. He's coming from outside—out here," I said, balling up my left fist to symbolize the dog and then showing my right hand hovering in the realm above the dog. "Jesus is coming from outside this world. He's coming directly from the creator of the dog—God—to tell us what the dog is. Jesus came directly from God to give us the scoop on life. He came as God, in human form, to show us the way and explain the point of life. Do you see what I mean?" I asked.

Milan nodded a yes, and I felt emboldened to continue. "We're all separated from God because he's perfect, and we're not. We're innately flawed—that's what's called sin. Sin simply means 'missing the mark'. Missing God's mark of perfection. So, by accepting Jesus as personal Savior, our broken relationship with God is restored. Jesus was perfect, so we don't have to be perfect."

"Hmmm—I see what you're saying," Milan answered. "And what about the Bible?"

"It's God's instruction manual," Michelle replied.

Milan and CJ were listening, doubtful, but nonetheless paying close attention.

The room was quiet as the guys looked contemplative.

At that moment, I realized that for the entire past year, bits and pieces of my mind had lain dormant. I hadn't had a single conversation with anyone that fully engaged me at every level, intellectually, spiritually, and as a woman. No one had insisted that I articulate my beliefs and explain the intangible. No one engaged me in a thoughtful dialogue on the merits and weightiness of faith. It felt good to talk honestly, plainly, with good friends about what I knew to be the Truth. We didn't have to agree, but we could listen to each other and respect one another.

No night was as memorable to me as that evening with Milan, CJ, and Michelle. Our time together was burned in my mind on a carefully archived mental filmstrip—one of the absolutely perfect nights in my V Society memories. I could have talked to the three of them forever. There was always something interesting to discuss and some other perspective to explore. College wouldn't have been the same—life wouldn't have been so vivid and colorful—without the three of them. How different, how much more shallow I would have been without Milan and CJ to challenge me to dig deeper.

It was well past three in the morning. We all felt exhausted.

"We better get going," CJ remarked, uncoiling his arms and legs in a full-body stretch. He yawned, stood up, and stretched again, temporarily forcing the sleepiness out of his fatigued limbs.

"Yeah," Milan agreed, slowly pushing himself up out of his seat.

"Um, yeah," Michelle smiled in agreement.

"What time is it?" I mumbled, covering my mouth as I yawned.

"I have no idea," Michelle answered.

Michelle and I stood up. Milan and I hugged, while CJ and Michelle embraced. Then we switched partners; I embraced CJ, and Michelle wrapped her arms around Milan. Seconds later, the guys disappeared down the stairs into the black morning. It was the last time the four of us were all together.

The next day, Michelle and I hopped a train to New York for a quick romp in the big city. I never traveled to the East Coast without a side trip to Manhattan. Too cash-strapped for a cab, Michelle and I lugged our luggage onto a subway and headed uptown. I should have brought a small overnight bag for the short trip, but instead I'd dragged my entire suitcase with me, pulling the bulky wheeled bag by a strap. We headed to the Upper West Side.

None of our college friends had enough room to accommodate both of us in their tiny studio apartments. My mom had called a childhood friend of hers and asked that he put us up for the night. He had grown up down the street from her in Prairie View, Texas, and was now a Wall Street tycoon, a partner at one of the major investment banks. He was out of town and apparently had a couple of homes dotted around the world. His personal assistant, a casually dressed middle-aged black man, greeted us.

"I was expecting a cab," the personal assistant said as he looked up and down the street, wondering how we had arrived on the doorstep, luggage in tow.

"Uh, we took the subway," I said in a low voice.

"Oh, the subway?" he asked, surprised. He gave us a quick tour of the neat, handsomely decorated three-story brownstone, including the walk-in sauna, before showing us to our room. "Mr. Woods' daughter will be home shortly," he informed us. "Make yourselves at home."

Apparently, Mr. Woods didn't live at this residence, at least not for extended periods. His grown daughter, who was a few years older than we were, came home within the hour and greeted us. We clearly didn't shop on Fifth Avenue, dressed sloppily as we were in loose-fitting jeans and ordinary long-sleeve shirts. She looked us up and down.

"Where did you say you went to school?" she asked curiously.

We spent the night, and the next morning we walked down the street to meet a photographer who lived in the same neighborhood. He was a friend of Tony's, a college friend who had graduated a year ahead of us.

"This friend of mine, John, does some pretty unusual work," Tony had told me. "You should definitely look him up the next time you're in New York. I think the two of you would get along well."

"Your work is really cool," I remarked as John showed Michelle and I stark black-and-white headshots of people with unusually interesting faces.

From there we headed to the Upper East Side to meet our old classmate and my former fraternity brother Justin Greco.

"Have you been to Central Park?" Justin asked.

"Not in ages," I replied.

Michelle, Justin, and I caught a cab to the outskirts of Central Park and bought hot dogs and pretzels from a stand on the sidewalk. We photographed each other in weird, abstract poses, skipping around and climbing on top of giant rocks in the park. That evening we dined at a trendy little restaurant in the Village before Michelle and I returned to Philadelphia. I bid my Philly friends good-bye and caught a flight back to California the next day.

Several months later, I picked up the phone and dialed Michelle for one of our weekend chats.

"Hello?"

"Hi, Petunia Mom—what's up?" I asked her cheerily.

"Hi, Delmo! What're you doing, butthead?" she giggled using a funny, nasal-sounding voice.

"Nothing—what are you doing?" I laughed. "You're eating poop-on-a-stick, aren't you?"

I could hear her laughing on the other end of the phone.

"So, how's Philadelphia?" I asked.

"The same."

"How life's and everything else?"

"Okay."

"So, what have you been doing with yourself?"

"Working."

We chatted for a few more minutes about the mundane things of our daily routines—her work in Philadelphia, my work and Santa Barbara, the weather, our brothers, our parents.

"I have something to tell you," she said. Her tone was flat and emotionless. "I saw Milan several weeks ago. We went out. I spent the night at his place."

Then she paused. I listened quietly.

"I'm still in the V Society, though," she added, almost as an afterthought. I knew she was telling the truth.

"I told him I loved him." Another long pause. "He said, 'You just *think* you love me. I don't love you.'"

Pause.

I remained quiet. He'd broken her heart.

There was nothing I could say to comfort her. What was done was done. I wished Keri, Michelle, and I were all still roommates—or at least that we all still lived in the same city. For Michelle's sake, Keri and I would have tracked Milan's raggedy butt down, and tarred and feathered him, before tying him to the train tracks. But I lived three thousand miles away, and Keri was in Israel, living a new life with her husband.

Milan tried to make amends with Michelle. But she was through. I tried never to mention his name to her again.

Chapter Twenty-Four

SUN -N- SURF POSSE

{Three Years after College Graduation}

MY THIRD ANNIVERSARY IN SANTA BARBARA PASSED LIKE A whisper—inaudible and barely noticed. Long ago, I had embraced the seductive leisure that thwarted all attempts at productivity. The constantly beckoning ocean, only five minutes away, hypnotized me with a resurging, careless song. My stint in Southern California was all about the journey, not the goal. Life didn't hurry itself in Santa Barbara. I found no reason to rush my thesis to completion.

Old friends liked to visit. Justin came out from New York for a long weekend. He rented a convertible, and we drove down the coast to the Getty Museum in LA. I tied a long scarf around my neck, hoping it would blow behind me in the wind—the same way scarves blew glamorously in the movies. Instead, the scarf slapped me in the face repeatedly and blocked my view of the ocean. Nick came down from San Francisco for several days. We had a good time together, and he managed not to hit on any of my friends. At least, no one reported back to me that he'd tried to score. My senior-year roommate Noel came and brought a girlfriend of hers. They stayed a few days to lounge on the beach.

The Riviera Theatre and El Encanto Hotel, my royal retreat perched high in the hills overlooking the shoreline, commanded my undying affection. The grand old Riviera Theatre, devoted exclusively to showing independent films, summoned me as soon as the latest art or foreign film rode into town. I practically had a reserved seat on my favorite row in the vast, historic auditorium. Tourists rarely trekked up the steep hillside to the isolated single-screen theater. The place was usually empty. I felt like the movie review team of Siskel and Ebert, enjoying an exclusive, midafternoon private screening amidst the vacant rows of old-fashioned seats.

The long outdoor balcony at the El Encanto Hotel restaurant, just across the way from the theater, lured me to its majestic panoramic views. The lone friendly server at the bar was always happy to whip up a hot chocolate on cool evenings. The hotel staff seemed glad that someone, anyone, would take the time to loiter at the tables on the solitary balcony and marvel at the breathtaking sunsets, swirling in fiery crimson, scarlet, and purple shades above the glassy hues of the tide.

Santa Barbara's year-round superb weather, miles of voluptuous coastline, and cheerful palm trees reminded me to keep pace with the local schedule. My weekly routine meandered around the same pastimes— the beach, helping out at church, playing tennis on the courts across the street from my apartment, and warming a chair at the Santa Barbara Roasting Company, a favorite café and meeting place for me and my like-minded friends.

Students didn't race to graduate in Santa Barbara. In fact, I'm not sure when anyone went to class. Most of my friends were undergraduates, but we were the same age since most of my friends prescribed to a loose six-year commencement plan that allowed far more time for surfing and snowboarding than an ambitious four-year graduation schedule would have. There were less than a dozen graduate students at Brooks. Most lived out of town and only commuted in for classes. I rarely saw any of my Brooks grad program classmates outside of school.

I plugged away at a snail's pace on my master's thesis, sporadically orchestrating photo shoots, whenever creative inspiration struck. According to plan, I had wrapped up all my coursework in two and a half years. But I had five years to complete the thesis. That translated into an endless vacation to chill with my sun-n-surf-loving posse: Ryan, Tori, and Arlené.

I had met all three through Reality. Tori and I became friends first. She was one of the City College students among the bunch of us that went out to brunch after church every week and met up regularly for sugary espresso drinks. Tori and Santa Barbara went together like bikinis and sand. She hailed from Japan but embodied the essence of the Santa Barbara vibe—a surfer-girl hipster, always dressed in cute cut-off shorts and some edgy, tiny T-shirt. She sported a small nose ring and loved to snowboard. Tori was almost as infatuated with snowboarding as she was with a chubby surfer who worked downstairs in the building adjacent to her apartment. We dropped in at each other's places regularly en route to some outdoor, sun-related activity. One particular afternoon, I stopped by the apartment she shared with her brother, and she showed off her latest snowboarding moves.

"Watch this," she called out with a smile.

She pantomimed riding her snowboard down a powdery mountain. Tori stuck her arms out, both hovering above her sides, her knees bent as she crouched down, and her feet pointed sideways, parallel to each other.

"Check out this move!" she exclaimed as she flew, like lightning, down the imaginary ski slope, pretending to catch air on the moguls. Her medium-length black hair swished around her, appearing to take flight with the rest of her, as she mimicked an airborne descent, her knees fluxing in an exaggerated bend and then straightening ever so slightly as she landed her jump and coasted down the hill.

"Nice move," I applauded.

I'd met Arlené the previous year. She was a Santa Barbara native who had spent a stint managing an apartment in New York. She had fled the sunny shores of Santa Barbara, at the tender age of seventeen, for a storied life in the Big Apple. She dropped back by Santa Barbara for a few weeks—that's when I met her—before leaving town abruptly again and then suddenly reappearing a year later, out of the blue.

"I always wanted to live in New York, for as long as I could remember," she told me. "I was homeless on the streets for a while until I hooked up a gig managing an apartment building, in exchange for free rent."

Arlené aspired to be an actress. She hadn't bothered to earn her high school diploma before rushing to New York. But the difference in our backgrounds seemed irrelevant. We were never at a loss for engaging conversation. She was incredibly smart and could disagree with me, with as much fire and information to support her points as Michelle or Keri. Arlené was one cool and interesting girl—I naturally gravitated toward her. Tori and Arlené had become my new girl crew.

Like Tori, I met Ryan through our brunch-n-latte gang. He was 100 percent surfer—long, sun-bleached brown hair and a uniform of shorts and faded T-shirts, always paired with worn out flip-flops. I would bet fifty bucks that he owned less than three pairs of socks. But, uncharacteristic of most surfers, Ryan was ripped—with a broad chest, big shoulders, and the bulging muscular biceps you'd expect on a rugby player. No one who sat behind Ryan in a worship service could help but marvel at his apparent athleticism. Recently, he'd started wearing his hair shorter, clean and preppy from his last visit to the barber, but he remained a purebred, genuine wave rider. I usually never said more than hi to him, but one café evening we wound up talking.

"So, where are you from originally?" he asked.

"Northern California."

"Dude, no way. Me too. I'm from Sunnyvale."

"Really? I grew up right across the San Francisco Bay from you, in Alameda."

"No way, that's totally rad," Ryan beamed.

"So, you went to high school there?"

"Yep!"

"What year did you graduate?" I asked.

"'90."

"Cool, I'm '89."

"So, you're what—like twenty-five?" he asked.

"No, I'm twenty-four. I started first grade a year early, so I was always a year younger," I explained.

"Oh, yeah. First grade was rough—the longest two years of my life!" Ryan joked with an exuberant smile.

I couldn't help but laugh; he was a funny guy.

"So, how old are you?" I asked.

"Twenty-five."

"You're at UCSB, right?"

"Yep."

"How do you like it?"

"It's okay. I graduate this year, which is cool."

"Then what?"

"I don't know. I think I want to be an actor or a comedian. But my father was in the military, and I'm kind of interested in that too."

"Those are some pretty extreme career options," I jested. "*Saturday Night Live* or the army? Quite a choice there."

"The army?" he balked. "The marines, young lady—it's either *Saturday Night Live* or the marines," he corrected with a jovial reprimand.

We soon discovered that we adored the same NPR programs.

"I love the *Global Village* and *Morning Becomes Eclectic*. Those two shows play the best funky music from all over the world," I said.

"Yeah, those shows are way cool. How about *Thistle and Shamrock*?"

"Oh yeah, I love that show too. With Feh-ohna Ree-chie," I said with a smile, pronouncing her name in an Irish accent similar to host Fiona Ritchie's own accent.

"Ey, that 'ere's the music of me people," Ryan laughed, speaking in a Scottish accent. "I'm Scottish—Scottish American."

We both enjoyed the lively Celtic music *Thistle and Shamrock* pumped over the airwaves each week. We talked animatedly the rest of the evening. Over the next few months, we became close friends.

As the year drew to a close and the lease for Arlené's studio expired, she temporarily relocated into my one-bedroom. She moved into my living room and took the apartment by storm, while we hunted for a two-bedroom apartment. She hung a reproduction of the Mona Lisa, and faux-antique candelabras on my wall. Then she rearranged all the living room furniture.

One breezy, clear afternoon, Ryan, Arlené, and I lounged around my place, which was now Arlené's place too. It was one of those temperate, late-fall Southern California days, when you could still wear summer clothes throughout the day, but at night a mild chill set in, requiring at least a lightweight sweater if you ventured outside. As always, I'd flung the huge sliding windows in the living room wide open. The blinds slanted so late afternoon light flowed in wide bars. The breaks in the slender blinds cast horizontal patterns of golden light on the ivory walls and splattered glowing bright spots on the beige carpet.

Ryan and I sat across from Arlené, relaxed, side by side on my black faux-leather sofa. Barefoot, I rested my feet up on the coffee table, careful not to knock over the pillar candles in their steel-colored holders resting just outside the reach of my big toe. Arlené sat across from us on the futon she'd moved beneath the window, where she slept. Remakes of Jobim's famous bossa nova melodies, piped at low volume out of my stereo, filling the room with Brazilian rhythms and visions of faraway Carnaval parties on the beaches of Rio de Janeiro.

"We should call you Señor Frog," Arlené proposed, looking at Ryan.

"That's perfect," I said. Señor Frog fit. It was so much better than Preston Ryan McAlba which rang serious and straightlaced, zipped up and humorless—the polar opposite of Ryan, with his unruly, playful sense of humor.

"Yes, Señor Frog," Arlené affirmed. Then we paused, both looking at Ryan, allowing the new name to wash over him.

"You know that's a bar in Tijuana," Ryan interjected, a mischievous smile playing across his lips.

"*Your* name, Señor Frog, doesn't have anything to do with *that* Señor Frog. I like it. You are *so* Señor Frog," I grinned.

"And you," Arlené mused, turning her attention to me, "you know what the perfect name for you is?"

"What?" I asked.

"Crash," she said decidedly.

She was right. The nickname hit the mark. I was finely tethered by choice, but my unleashed, unrestrained self was as wild as a colossal train wreck.

"I've got the perfect name for you too," I returned.

"Yeah?"

"Machina—that's my new name for you."

"Crash and Machina." Ryan pondered our new names.

"Oh yeah—that totally works. Chillin' at Crash and Machina's pad," I said, trying it out.

I had pulled Machina out of a hat, just like Arlené had concocted Señor Frog out of thin air. There was no rhyme or reason to either name. It was simply appropriate to name each other—some odd natural rite of induction that always took place amongst my closest friends. I aptly tacked this newest appellation on to my long list of V Society names previously ordained by Keri and Michelle.

Arlené and my new roles as roommates fomented unexpected roller-coaster dynamics. Our quarters were small, and I was used to living alone in my space. Most times, we got along well, but sometimes we pushed each other's buttons.

"What's that smell?" I said one morning as I pulled back the sliding door that separated my bedroom from her space in the living room.

"I don't know," she mumbled, half asleep.

It was around 9:00 a.m. Saturday. I tried never to get out of bed before noon on Saturdays. The acrid stench of something burning filled my nostrils with overpowering force. It was pungent and mechanical-smelling, like burning metal. I walked through the living room to the small kitchen and dining area in the back of the apartment. An empty pan my mother had bought me sat on the burner. The heat rising beneath had charred the bottom of the pot to a deep black.

"The pot is burning!" I exclaimed. "You can't smell that?"

"What?" she replied. I couldn't see her from the kitchen. The black sofa that I had rented with the apartment blocked my view of her.

"I don't feel well. I got up to fix some tea but then just went back to sleep."

"Fine, but you should have turned the stove off. My pot is ruined."

"Sorry," she said.

"Whatever," I muttered. The whole apartment reeked of the burnt pot. "You could have burned the apartment down!"

"I said I was sorry. Calm down."

"Easy for you to say. It stinks in here," I retorted, annoyed. "Do you feel better now?"

No sooner had Arlené moved in than one of the surfers from church started dropping by the apartment looking for her. It irritated her to no end.

"I can't believe he came by here," she fussed. "He gives me the creeps. How did he even know I live here?" She looked at me for an explanation.

"How should I know? I don't even talk to him," I shot back.

Arlené's dating possibilities seemed endless in Santa Barbara. Literally, a new guy fell in love with her every week. She walked downtown, and cute guys would stop to introduce themselves to her. She waited tables in one of the upscale restaurants on State Street. Waiters at her restaurant fell in love with her. The couple that owned the restaurant was in love with her. Their kids were in love with her. Diners that came into the restaurant fell head over heels for her and left her whopping tips. Everyone was in love with her.

My normally healthy ego quietly deflated. The truth hurt. There was no one for me in Santa Barbara. My dating prospects seemed abysmal. There was zero probability of meeting my future husband anytime soon.

Excluding my former neighbor, Trevor, only three guys had asked me out the entire time I had lived in Santa Barbara. One guy worked with Arlené, probably the only single guy that worked with her that wasn't in love with her.

"One of the guys at work saw you the other night and wants to ask you out," she told me. "His name is Erol. He's Turkish, and he thinks you're beautiful."

I'd met a few of her coworkers. They were around my age, and most of them were nice looking. I couldn't picture the specific coworker she referred to, but I agreed to have dinner with him. Arlené set it up, and I went on the blind date.

"I own house in Goleta," Erol told me in broken English as we sat in a Mediterranean restaurant a few blocks from the beach. His English vocabulary was extremely limited. Funny, I didn't remember Arlené mentioning that he didn't speak English. Conversation was near impossible.

After dinner, I returned home. Arlené was waiting.

"How did it go?" she asked.

She had forgotten to clue me in on a few details beforehand. Besides the obvious language barrier, she had also overlooked a few other details, like his age—which he refused to tell me. That meant I had to apply the Age Rule. When a man is interested in a woman but refuses to tell his age, you simply double the woman's age and then subtract ten. I was twenty-four so that made him thirty-six at the youngest. He was probably closer to forty. She also didn't mention his height—he stood about five foot four, the same height as me. But Arlené had saved the best zinger for after the date.

"He said he has a house in Goleta?" she asked timidly. "That's not exactly true . . . He's homeless, so the owners let him live in the basement of the restaurant. Oh . . . and did I mention that he's not a waiter? He's a busboy."

Then there was Dan, a guy from church who asked me out. Again, applying the Age Rule, I guessed he was about thirty-six. We went out once or twice.

"So, you just moved to Santa Barbara?" I asked. "Where did you live before?"

"Out of town."

"Right, I figured that."

I had reached a dead end. He was extremely guarded about where he had lived before. But he was awfully forthcoming about other things.

"I see you and me traveling through life together," he proclaimed.

"Really? That's very interesting."

Finally, I made a little headway uncovering his past. It turned out he'd served some time in prison.

"So, why were you in prison?" I asked.

"I don't want to talk about it," he replied.

The third guy that asked me out, I met at a party in LA.

"I've known him for years," the girlfriend who took me to the party said. "He was in the hospital for months."

"For what?" I asked.

"A drinking problem," she replied.

Things were not going well in the romance realm, but at last, there was a glimmer of hope. Arlené's friend Cody had four tickets to the Santa Barbara symphony.

"Do you want to go?" she asked.

"Sure," I replied.

"I'll ask Kevin Thompson if he wants to come too. So, it will be me, you, Kevin, and Cody."

Cody and Arlené had been friends for many years. Like every other guy in Santa Barbara, he was enthralled with her. He was several years older than all of us and had taken the bar exam six times over the past six years, without passing. Kevin Thompson played the drums in the Reality worship band. He didn't fall into the male fashionista category, but he had sideburns. That was about as close to a fashionista-guy as I could find in Santa Barbara. We dressed up, and the four of us rode to the symphony in my car. Kevin and I sat together on one side of the orchestra, while Arlené and Cody sat together on the other side of the orchestra. At intermission, Kevin couldn't wait to meet back up with Arlené and Cody. Rather, he couldn't wait to meet up with Arlené. Afterward, the four of us went out and sat in the bar section of a restaurant. Cody and Kevin couldn't take their eyes off Arlené.

"That's soooooo interesting," Kevin cooed, smiling after everything Arlené said. She'd captured both under her spell. Finally, I'd had enough.

"I'm tired and ready to go home," I announced. The three of them could walk home as far as I was concerned. I wasn't sticking around to be the chauffeur for Arlené and her fan club. Arlené, Kevin, and Cody looked at me, surprised.

"What? You're ready to go already?" Arlené asked.

I hated Santa Barbara. Everyone in the entire flaky beach town was in love with my good-looking, erratic roommate. Obviously, you had to be a skinny white girl who looked like Hollywood's next big superstar to even get noticed by someone under thirty here. Guys would tell her things like, "If I don't kiss you, I'll die." She wouldn't kiss them, and of course, they'd still be alive the next day. She spurned most of her suitors, leaving a trail of lovelorn surfers, hipsters, waiters, and college guys sprinkled throughout the greater metropolitan Santa Barbara–Ventura area. Even Ryan, my closest friend in Santa Barbara, had a tiny, fleeting secret crush on Arlené.

"She's just so cute and cool," he confessed, starry-eyed.

Unbelievable! What was the matter with me? I showered every day. I didn't smell. I could hold a decent conversation. Wasn't I cute? Maybe not—not in comparison to all the Santa Barbara beach bunnies that populated the town like snow in winter.

I was having a personal crisis. I took a blunt knife from my kitchen and pried off the plastic ichthys fish symbol on the back of my car. I had proudly slapped it above my bumper when my parents delivered the brand-spanking-new car to me, direct from the dealership. Why wasn't God coming through on this simple request? Why couldn't I find a single decent guy in the entire town? I hadn't asked for much. I just wanted one attractive guy who wore socks, wasn't twice my age, had a decent IQ, loved Jesus, and was on a career track similar to mine. I didn't mind if he had a nice foreign accent too. Was that too much to ask? I felt like God had failed me.

I stopped reading my Bible. I stopped praying regularly. God wasn't talking to me, so I refused to talk to Him. I wallowed in a foul spiritual mood for weeks. For the first time in my life I'd grown angry with God. Didn't God say, "Ask and you shall receive; seek and you shall find?" I had asked and sought; in return I'd received silence. God was not blind, deaf, or unable to grant requests—so what was the problem? I couldn't figure out why he'd ignore my plea—for so long. But strangely enough, I kept playing praise CDs on my stereo. I couldn't completely cut myself loose from Jesus, regardless of how much I stewed in my own self-pity.

Chapter Twenty-Five

NEW RUMBLINGS

{Three Years after College Graduation}

IN SPITE OF MY PERSONAL CRISIS, GRAD SCHOOL WASN'T ALL BAD. All that year, I enjoyed the low-key life of a dateless, romance-deprived beach bum, wondering when a busload of Jesus-loving male-fashionistas would finally roll into town. My parents paid my rent and some expenses. I held down two part-time jobs at school: I worked a few hours a week in the school library and a few hours at the school bookstore. Students rarely came to the bookstore after the first week of school, so I spent my time behind the cashier desk reading.

"What are you reading?" one of my instructors asked, as she passed by the window opening out from the small bookstore into the main hallway of the school.

"The paper."

"*What* paper?" she asked, twisting her head sideways to read the masthead.

"The *Wall Street Journal*."

"Oh," she replied, clearly surprised.

As a Christmas gift, my dad had bought me a one-year subscription to the *Journal*, my favorite newspaper. I couldn't help it. Ever since junior high, my dad had torn interesting articles out of the *Wall Street Journal* and given them to me to read. Thanks to Dad, I was a bit of an oddball in photo school; the *Journal* wasn't exactly at the top of most fashion photographers reading lists.

But Ryan didn't see any inconsistency in my desire to shoot the cover of Italian *Vogue*—*and* follow business trends. It was all fine with him. Some Saturdays, the two of us would pile into the car and take long drives through the scenic surrounding mountains. No maps, no itinerary, just a full tank of gas and some good jams playing on the stereo. Those afternoons were near-perfect—nomadic, adventure-filled, and carefree. From the mountain peaks, we stood amazed at the awe-inspiring views of rocky cliffs and the endless shiny ocean stretching out to meet the clear sky in a sea of cyan. Ryan and I always finished off those idyllic, lazy days at the Coffee Bean and Tea Leaf. It had outdoor patio tables and chairs, strategically located in the heart of downtown, on the periphery of Paseo Nuevo, the outdoor Spanish-style shopping plaza. We'd sit and people-watch, while I sipped my favorite drink—an ice-blended mocha.

Our friendship was uncomplicated with no hidden agendas and no guesswork. We just had fun together. Not to mention Ryan was the coolest guy I knew that was in his own V Society—he'd committed himself to abstinence all these years, to honor God, just as I had.

"When you get married, and when I finally get married, do you think our spouses will be jealous of our friendship?" he asked.

"I don't know," I laughed. "I mean—I hope not. We're pretty tight, but I don't think so."

"Really? You don't think they'll care that we're best friends?"

"I don't know. That's funny—I never even thought about that. I have no idea," I shrugged. "What do you think?"

"I dunno. I think they'll be cool with it. We'd only marry people that were cool like that—right?"

"Right," I agreed.

Aside from my never-ending single status, life was pretty sweet. In January, I jetted off to Australia for a family vacation with my parents and brother. A month later, my dad called me up.

"I have some frequent flier miles I want to use up. Where would you rather go, Rome or Paris?" he asked.

"Rome," I replied. A few weeks later, Dad and I stood in front of the infamous Roman Colosseum and snapped pictures in front of the Trevi Fountain. By May, I was out of the country for the third time, this time in Mexico on a mission trip with my church. Summer arrived, and I flew the coop again—to Israel where I hung out with Keri, attended the Jerusalem Film Festival, and got baptized in the Jordan River.

"You have to see our new apartment," Keri beamed.

Many Israelis lived in high-rise, condo-style buildings. Everywhere, newly constructed multilevel buildings dotted the hillside settlement where Keri and Erez lived, just outside Jerusalem.

"I just picked out these new tiles for the kitchen," she said excitedly, pointing to a patchwork of neat, brightly colored tiles arranged in a vibrant mosaic. "And here, come see our bomb shelter," she said, ushering me into a substantial-sized windowless bedroom with an unusually thick, heavy metal door. "Every Israeli household has a bomb shelter," she explained.

I could only steal away a day and a half from my hectic touring schedule to visit with Keri. I had come to Israel with a bunch of students from Reality. Waxer, my college-group pastor, had set up a whirlwind tour of the entire country for all the students he'd brought with him. We zipped from Tel Aviv to Jaffa to Ashkelon to Nazareth, Bethlehem, Jerusalem, and just about every major biblical site in the tiny land. I couldn't keep them straight. The Sea of Galilee, the Dead Sea, Mount Hermon, Caesarea Philippi, the Golan Heights, the West Bank, Jericho, the Gaza Strip—they all blended together in a foggy conglomeration of desert, mountains, and miles of brown dust. On the tour bus, off the tour bus, into the one-hundred-degree weather, and back into the freezing air conditioning. It was exhausting, and also startling. Somehow, I expected the Holy Land to be—well, holy. I don't know what I thought I'd see, but I didn't expect to see young soldiers walking with M14 assault rifles through the streets the way I'd carry a Frappuccino.

Israel was unexpectedly secular, and divided. There were Hasidic Jews, orthodox Jews, reformed Jews, secular Jews, a tiny sliver of Messianic Jews, and other factions that I couldn't even name. None of them seemed to talk to each other but instead kept to their own distinct communities. Adding to the mix, ancient-looking Bedouins, riding ragged, beat-down-looking donkeys traveled on the roadsides. The Bedouin nomads looked like they'd been unwittingly transported in a time machine from some long-gone era, with their archaic-looking tent settlements erected in the backyards of high-rise buildings under construction. It wasn't the angel-heralding, miracle-working, storybook land I'd pictured as a child in Sunday school.

But at least I got to see Keri. She was flourishing in Israel—marriage agreed with her. Erez earned a good living, and she'd returned to school, to earn her doctorate.

After six straight months of on-and-off travel, I planned never to get a job. I had figured it out. I'd remain a perpetual student—forever roaming the world on my parents' dime. Grad school offered a socially acceptable way to skirt responsibility. I sent away for an application to the graphic design MFA program at Yale's School of Art. I enthusiastically relayed the details to my mom over the phone. How could my parents say no to Yale?

Mom was cool and collected. "That's great," she said. "But since you're about to have one master's degree, you can pay for the next one."

Mom was letting me know it was time to wind down my salad days, time to turn in my thesis and get a job. She wasn't paying my rent forever. My thesis had been complete for several months, but I couldn't find a bookbinder that I liked. In order to graduate, every master's student had to turn in three hardbound copies of his or her thesis.

The binding company recommended by the head of the graduate school produced cheap-looking, shiny leather covers. The finished product resembled slippery, black plastic snakeskin—hideous. I didn't want my life's work mistaken for a cheesy photo album. I wanted my thesis bound in smooth, matte black cloth. I also wanted a matching, hard-case slipcover, exactly like the one celebrity photographer Herb Ritts had created for his elegant book *Men/Women*.

Herb Ritts's book was a collectable of two separate photography books. The first was a black-and-white study of the female form. The second was the same, but of male models with near-perfect physiques. The slipcover sleeve that encased both books was stamped "W" (for women) in crisp gold lettering, at one end. At the other end, "M" (for men) had been stamped in identical fashion—a mirror image of the "W." After months of scattered research, I finally tracked down one lone bookbinder that would produce my coveted sleeve. The owner of the binding company was based in LA, but he promised to pick up the three copies of my thesis on his next trip to Santa Barbara.

Several weeks later, I met the bookbinder in person and handed over three thick copies of the written portion of my thesis, as well as three copies of the bodies of photographs I had created. All together, my work consisted of nearly four hundred pages. Each copy of the thesis numbered 131 pages and included an original body of fifty-five fine art photographs.

"The man that binds all the books is an extraordinary craftsman," the bookbinder stated reverently. "He is a great artisan. There are few people that can do what he does," he assured me.

The bookbinder gave me a business card that looked like he had made it himself using a typewriter and an old copy machine. The card was plain white cardstock with standard black type. He promised to return the bound books within a few weeks. Weeks and weeks went by without as much as a peep from the bookbinder. I began to believe he'd taken my thesis to Willy Wonka's Chocolate Factory to be worked on by unruly Oompa-Loompas. The weeks turned into months. Still no thesis. I passed the time in cafés, on the tennis court, improving my game, and at the beach.

Finally, I had to start looking for a job. I owed it to my parents. I would worry about turning in the thesis whenever it resurfaced from Wonka-land or wherever it had been ferried away to. Had I been a fool for entrusting my greatest work to date to an itinerant bookbinder from somewhere in the sprawling region of LA? I didn't even have an address where I could go to steal my thesis back, if the need arose. In the meanwhile, however, resumé time had arrived.

"Your new business cards will say 'graphic designer,'" my boss told me when she called to make me a job offer. It was the only position I had interviewed for so far, and I was glad that they had decided to hire me.

I'd burned out on photography, but graphic design excited me. I pored over design books and learned to make type whirl and swirl and leap off the printed page. My starting salary was tiny, but the company was exciting; the staff was young and enthusiastic. I hoped for stock options.

Several months after I began my design job, my thesis reemerged from the Oompa-Loompa's dark underworld. The mysterious little workers had done an excellent job. The three copies of my thesis were beautifully bound in black cloth with matching black slipcovers. The gold lettering read, "Judeo-Christian Themes in Modern Photography, Adele C. Moore."

"I'm sorry for the delay," the bookbinder apologized. "My binder is an artisan. He's very protective of his craft and refuses to train an apprentice. He's been sick for months, so I had to wait for him to recover to complete your books. Thanks for being so patient."

I didn't bother to go to my graduation. Brooks Institute of Photography followed a peculiar quarter system that allowed a new group of students to matriculate and commence every seven weeks. At every graduation, the undergraduates usually wore something a step up from jeans and a T-shirt. And they didn't wear caps or gowns to cover up their übercasual outfits either. That made the one graduate student, decked out in a cap and gown and the colorful master's collar, look like Bozo the Clown. I wasn't about to embarrass myself—the only graduate in a robe and cap.

"Hello, my dear," my mother said over the phone. "When should your dad and I fly down for graduation?"

"Oh, don't bother. I'm not going to graduation," I replied.

The graduation reception was the only worthwhile event. And the reception was only worth attending if you were a starving student with nothing good to eat in the fridge at home. The school dispensed lavish spreads of free food at the reception. Students often breezed through Brooks' Jefferson campus on graduation day to pile up plates of appetizers and pasta drenched in Alfredo sauce. Then they retreated to sunny corners, away from the elated, dressed-up parents, to gobble down their stacks of cubed cheese and crackers. I didn't think the plate of cubed cheese was worth my parents' time.

Truthfully, I didn't want to take the time to mount a graduation show. Mounting a photography exhibit would have been too much work now that I had a full-time job. Every graduate was required to mount photographs of their best work and hang them in the main hallway of the school. It was a tedious process. Every photograph had to be printed with painstaking accuracy in the darkroom. Then each print had to be mounted onto an archival mat board, and the mat boards had to be perfectly cut to overlay each photo. Finally, the images had to be framed in matching, impressive-looking photo frames. It was a headache.

When I dropped off my thesis with the director of the master's program, I filled out the paperwork quickly and checked the box requesting that my degree be dropped in the mail. I didn't want to be bothered driving the five miles to school to pick it up. I'd moved on. I was a working woman.

Throughout my time in Santa Barbara, I still spoke to Michelle regularly and to Milan every few weeks. Every once in a while I chatted with CJ.

I called Michelle to let her know I'd finally finished my thesis.

"Nice job," she said heartily.

Michelle still lived in Philadelphia and seemed to be doing well at her job. Her corporation—some big chemical company—loved her. Why wouldn't they? I'm sure she was the ideal employee. In addition to being industrious and always pleasant, Michelle was a strong team player and a real self-starter—an employer's dream. I bet her annual employee reviews were stellar.

I also called Milan to share my long-overdue accomplishment.

"Congratulations!" he exclaimed. "How's your new job?"

"It's great!" I said excitedly.

"Did you go suit shopping for all your new work clothes?"

"I need to," I laughed. "But actually, maybe not. They're pretty casual here. The few suits I have are okay for the office. The president of the company is the only one that really wears suits to work."

Keri was in Israel, so I couldn't call her. But I knew she'd be happy for me.

I adored my new job. My parents called often to get the scoop and hear my latest updates on work.

"What's the office like?" Mom asked.

"Really nice. My office is really bright and open—you'd like it. We have high ceilings, so it's really airy. All the walls are bright white, and there's tons of natural light. I share the end office with my boss, and we have a big window that looks out to the front of the building. My desk is cool. It's this deep purple-red molded resin or something. Above my desk I have rows of built-in bookshelves where I keep all my design magazines and paper samples."

I sketched out my new routine as Mom peppered me with questions.

I had spent my first couple of days drawing illustrations for a booklet on wireless technology. I couldn't believe it: they were paying me to sit in a brand-new office and sketch cartoons all day. And the office was only a five-minute drive from my apartment, so I could go home for lunch every day.

My very first project had been to order my new computer from Apple along with all my design software. After that I'd been tasked with selecting artwork to decorate the entire corporate office. They paid me to go to artist's studios and commission paintings and purchase photographs to hang in the conference rooms and the president's office. I was learning a ton, and I loved it.

"So, what are your coworkers like?" Mom asked.

"Super nice. Everyone is really cool. There are two groups on staff. There are all the twenty-four- and twenty-five-year-olds, like me. Most just joined the company in the past year or so. Then there are all the managers who are barely thirty years old."

My boss was really cool. She was about twenty-nine—really mellow and low key. I was learning all sorts of things about graphic design and print production from her. The president of the company was really nice too. "He's one of the only old guys here," I told my mom. "He's in his forties, but he's super friendly—very approachable."

Overall, things seemed good. I had climbed back on board with God; I wasn't angry with Him anymore. I'd reattached my ichthys back above my bumper, and I'd tabled the whole boyfriend situation for the time being. I figured I'd meet someone eventually. My social life was quite busy. Truthfully, I'd have to cut a few things out of my schedule in order to make room for a boyfriend. I hung out with Ryan just about every other day. We went out to dinner and to the movies and sat around at cafés talking all the time. My friend Brian came over most Friday nights and just hung out and talked for hours. I didn't miss dating nearly as much when I had such good guy friends to help pass the time.

Only two issues rumbled around undigested. Often, for no reason at all, my mind wandered to Milan. We spoke on the phone every once in a while. He called me. I called him.

"So, the other day I had this friend of mine run around outside in circles. She looked like a bumblebee in this yellow and black dress, so I had her make big circles outside, around me. It was great art! She didn't get it. But it was really great art. She was a bumblebee!" Milan proclaimed.

"I can't believe you made her run around like a bee for your amusement," I replied.

"No, it wasn't like that. We were just having fun. It was funny," he defended himself.

We chatted it up, and I acted the same as I always had toward him, as though nothing had changed since college. Nothing had changed really, except that with the safety of distance, I could finally explore what I'd always been afraid to examine before. When I opened my college photo album to thumb through pictures, I always lingered longest on Milan's pictures. Sometimes I'd make dinner at home and wonder what he was doing for dinner, three thousand miles away.

Besides Milan, quietly, constantly on my mind, there was the whole issue of black people—I missed them. There were only a few in my entire Santa Barbara circle. As far as I knew, they were the only six black residents, besides me, in the entire town. I'd spent the past seven years in exile from the African American community. In college, I had occasionally popped into the Baptist church on the corner of Fortieth Street, a half block from High Rise South. But I didn't have any ties there. I couldn't even remember the pastor's name. I'd been in Santa Barbara for three and a half years, and I missed seeing the faces of people that looked like me. Sometimes, walking down State Street, I'd see another black person—a tourist, no doubt—and I had to resist the temptation to run over and hug them. "Hello, my brotha. I've missed you, my sistah." I wanted to wrap my arms around them and invite them home for lunch.

My friend Blen, her sister Samra, and their mother Semret were my only ethnic connections in my black-community-deficient existence. They lived a few blocks from my office in a spacious, well-decorated two-bedroom apartment. Blen's mother was Eritrean. All three of them had moved here from Addis Ababa, Ethiopia. I never turned down an opportunity to visit them and feast at their dining room table. I'd sit down and shamelessly devour one of my favorite Ethiopian dishes—yesega wot. It consisted of lean cubes of beef cooked in berbere sauce, a spicy Ethiopian staple. Injera, the sour, spongy Ethiopian bread, satisfied me like comfort food. And nothing could compare to the sheer pleasure of eating in traditional Ethiopian style, with my hands.

The best party I went to the entire time I lived in Southern California was an Ethiopian party in Baldwin Hills, the neighborhood affectionately nicknamed "Black Beverly Hills." Blen, Samra, and I drove the two hours down the coast to LA that afternoon. We unloaded our bags at a friend's place and changed into our party clothes for the evening. I was the only non-Ethiopian and non–Amharic speaker at the party. It made no difference; I was at home.

The host of the party flew in a well-known Ethiopian singer from Washington, DC. I nearly perfected the distinct shoulder shake of traditional Ethiopian dancing, and I spent the entire night getting down on the dance floor in classic Ethiopian style. I was more than flattered when a man spoke to me in Amharic.

"You don't speak Amharic?" he asked, perplexed.

"No," I replied. "Sorry."

The man probably hadn't looked at me very closely, because a close examination would have made it obvious that I was not Ethiopian. I didn't have the keen features or voluminous tresses typical of Ethiopian women. I had the broad nose typical of non-Ethiopian blacks. I also had short, straightened hair. But hey, I was happy to have been mistaken for one of his own.

The party lifted me. The longer I danced, the higher I floated up in jubilation. I hadn't been with this many black people the entire time I had lived in Santa Barbara—it was refreshing and indescribably satisfying. How glorious just to be in their presence, enjoying traditions and culture that were distinctly black.

I got a kick out of listening to Blen's mother, Semret. She stood tall and regal—statuesque—with classic, fine Ethiopian features. Semret was also extremely opinionated about *everything*. Blen and her sister politely tuned her out when she began one of her spirited monologues on the state of the world.

"I do not understand black people who become successful and then marry white people!" Semret exclaimed. Her diction was perfect. She pronounced every syllable precisely, with extreme clarity. "It makes no sense at all. Look at Michael Jackson! Why would he marry a white woman? What is the matter with him? He is not proud of his people? We are a great people. We should marry our own. It makes no sense—at all—to marry outside of our race. I don't understand it!"

Semret didn't know that Blen's boyfriend was Lebanese. I went out with Blen and her boyfriend all the time. But Blen would never dare to introduce him to her mother as her boyfriend. Semret seemed to me like a displaced queen whose luxury ocean liner had accidentally wrecked on the shores of barbaric Santa Barbara. She was the daughter of a prominent Ethiopian ambassador and had attended the girls' equivalent of famed Eton College in England. Most of her life, she must have had servants and people available at her beck and call. Life in Santa Barbara, without a full staff of maids and butlers, seemed a tremendous inconvenience to her.

"She stopped one of my friends in the middle of the grocery store and made him carry all her groceries to the car," Blen complained to me. "She calls me at work and says, 'Blen. I cannot find the salt. Come home and find it for me.' I always have to tell her, 'This isn't like home. I'm not working for Dad. I can't just come home every time you need something.'"

I made the mistake of giving Semret my office phone number and was unwittingly enlisted as a servant.

"Adele, *a friend* is on the line." The receptionist at my office paged me on my desk phone. Normally when my friends called into the office, they would give the receptionist their name. It was customary corporate etiquette. The receptionist would page me and say, "Ryan McAlba" or "Arlené Costa is on the phone."

When the receptionist asked callers their names, no one with any respect for protocol would reply, "A friend." That was a dead giveaway that the call was personal and had nothing to do with work. Semret was blithely indifferent to protocol; rules did not apply to her.

"Hello, Adele. I have an emergency."

"Hi, Semret—what's the matter?" Panic assaulted me. A list of fatal medical emergencies raced through my head.

"Samra is going out of town, and I need her key."

I wasn't sure what type of key it was—some sort of life-and-death key? After all, she was calling me in the middle of the workday in a frenzy.

"I need you to get Samra's key for me," Semret continued.

"Okay, Semret, I'll get it right now. Where does Samra work?"

"I don't know. Come pick me up, and I can show you."

"Okay, Semret. I'll be there in a few minutes."

"I have to run a quick errand," I told my boss and shot out the door to retrieve Semret and the all-important key. I arrived on Semret's doorstep as quickly as the fire department in a five-alarm fire.

"Where are we going?" I asked her.

"Goleta," she replied. Goleta was the next town over and farther than I had expected to drive. But this was an emergency, so I snapped on my seatbelt and sped toward Goleta. Semret guided me off the freeway. She wasn't sure whether I should turn right or left, or turn back in the direction we had come. Finally, after much deliberation and a number of wrong turns, we arrived at Samra's office.

"Okay, Semret, I'll wait for you here while you go get the key from Samra."

"No. I think it is better if you go inside and retrieve the key," she replied matter-of-factly.

I couldn't walk into Samra's office in the middle of the day unannounced. It was rude; Samra would think me a lunatic. Cell phones weren't an everyday accessory back in those days, so I couldn't call Samra and warn her that I was outside her office.

"Semret, I think it's better if you go," I insisted.

"No. I think it is better if *you* go," she replied firmly.

I was stuck. I couldn't argue with her—she was my elder. I had to go inside and get the key from Samra. I walked inside the generic-looking, single-story office building. A receptionist, with a headset, sat at the front desk in the lobby.

"Hello. I'm here to see Samra Abate."

"Right through that door," the receptionist said, pointing toward a closed office door off to the right.

"Don't you want to call her first?" I asked.

"No, go on in," the receptionist assured me.

I opened the door and spotted Samra, talking to a coworker inside a cubicle. She stood in the middle of two short rows of identical gray cubicles. The room was a flurry of loitering office workers, chatting, laughing, and mingling like they were at a cocktail party. No one even noticed me coming in.

"Hi, Samra," I said, walking over to her. "Sorry to disturb you at work. Your mom said she had an emergency and needed your key."

Samra looked at me, amused. "My mom sent you all the way over here to get my mailbox key? She doesn't need the key. She's expecting some bit of mail that may not come for days. Aren't you supposed to be at work?"

"Yes, I *am* supposed to be at work. What do you mean, she doesn't need the key?" I retorted.

"I mean she doesn't *need* the key, and you're foolish to leave work in the middle of the day when Semret says she has an emergency."

I'd been had. Samra was going to LA for the weekend, to see her boyfriend, whom Semret disliked. (She seemed to dislike all of her daughters' suitors.) Samra was leaving that Friday night and coming back Sunday. Any mail that arrived on Friday or Saturday, Samra would deliver to Semret on Sunday. There was no emergency for the mailbox key.

I returned to the car and handed Semret the key.

"Thank you," she replied.

Then, like a good servant, I drove her home without a single complaint.

As the days rolled on, I realized I'd outgrown Reality. It was for college students, and I'd finished grad school. It was time to move on.

"I'm not really into Reality," I told Ryan.

"I know, everyone is so young now. They're a bunch of kids," he replied.

"Exactly. Some of those new students just graduated from high school. They look like twelve-year-olds."

A stroke of divine intervention interceded on my behalf. I usually raced through town down Anacapa Street, but that day I turned down Olive Street instead. I zipped up the street with my windows rolled down and the radio blaring. I looked to my right and was mesmerized by the scene, uncharacteristic of Santa Barbara, unfolding at the corner. A picture-perfect white church stood with a neat lawn in front. The main church building was attached to a larger, equally picturesque fellowship hall. A medium-sized, well-kept white house, designed in an architectural style that matched that of the church building, sat perpendicular to the church, attached to the hall. Sharply dressed black families poured out of the church doors and gathered on the front lawn. Old people, young people, kids. Two small boys in navy-blue suits chased each other across the lawn, weaving in and out of the grown-ups. A heavyset lady, dressed impeccably in a white suit and an ornate hat, spoke to a slender woman in a dark purple dress. Men in dark suits conversed in a small group, laughing and joking with one another.

I almost wrecked my car. I couldn't believe my eyes. Later that week, I returned to the church to find out its name. Service began at 10:00 a.m. That Sunday I put on a black suit and arrived punctually at Greater Hope Missionary Baptist Church. They welcomed me like a long-lost family member. The pastor was a small, energetic, cheerful man named J. B. Ficklin. His wife, Sister Ficklin, a warmhearted, robust matriarch, sang in the choir and greeted me with the same kindness with which she greeted her own three children. The Ficklin's three grown children were all around my age and were involved in every aspect of the church. They ensured that every service ran as smooth as clockwork.

Sister Hardeman, one of the beautiful gray-haired mothers of the church, took me under her wing like a grandchild. Deacon McNare, one of the church elders, embraced me like a niece. I had found my extended family in Santa Barbara. Greater Hope Missionary Baptist Church became my Southern California Church by the Side of the Road.

Chapter Twenty-Six

CONFESSION

{Four Years after College Graduation}

YEAR-ROUND, SANTA BARBARA REMAINED BEAUTIFUL AND SUN drenched—except in the summer. All the locals knew that from May through August, mornings were characterized by a hazy, gray marine layer. Our town's unwelcome guests—May Gray and June Gloom—settled in. My friends and I sometimes joked about the poor tourists who had saved up all their vacation time to come to Santa Barbara in the summer. I bet they looked sad and surprised, when they trekked out to the beaches in the morning, hoping to get tan. They were lucky if they could spot a single ray of sun anywhere on the horizon. All summer, the sun hibernated behind a sheath of clouds until midafternoon. Around two o'clock, the sun broke through, emancipating the dreary sky and showering the beaches with coveted warmth and light.

While my summer oscillated between contrasting weather patterns, Michelle's gleamed with excitement. It was June, and I was returning to Philadelphia for Mich's wedding reception. That summer Michelle and her boyfriend Enrique had tied the knot. She had met him while on vacation in Mexico two years earlier, and they had fallen in love. They married at City Hall with no pomp or circumstance. Her parents were hosting a party at their home to celebrate their daughter's marriage.

I flew into New York and jumped onto the airport shuttle to Midtown. I hailed a cab uptown to Justin Greco's apartment. I shaved a good chunk of change off the cost of my trip by taking the shuttle first, rather than taking a cab straight from JFK airport to the Upper East Side.

I liked talking to cab drivers. They always knew I was from out of town. No one talked to cabbies other than to call out their destination and ask for change.

"Where are you from?" I asked, afraid to call him by name, though it was posted on the glass behind his head. I was afraid I'd butcher the pronunciation.

"Egypt."

That opened it up for me to ask him everything I wanted to know about Egypt. Most people loved their homelands. Cab drivers were always glad to give me complete lessons on their countries of origin en route to my various destinations.

I arrived at Justin's, and we enjoyed a whirlwind Manhattan day, hitting all my favorite places in Soho. Late in the afternoon, Justin and I popped into an open, airy cigar lounge in the Village to meet our mutual school friend Shelly. The windows swung out toward the street, and we sat for a couple hours at a small table, talking. City dwellers whisked by outside.

Since I was in New York, I thought, *Why not celebrate a little?* I smoked a cigar with Justin and, at his suggestion, ordered a glass of cognac. I'd never tasted cognac before. I took a sip—and almost spit it out. It was as delicious as cough syrup.

"Dip the end of your cigar in it," Justin suggested.

The cigar was suddenly more flavorful with cognac tempering the smoky taste. My bill for the cognac was outrageous. I wished I could return the barely touched glass. Justin picked up the bill. It was a good thing I almost never drank and still didn't frequent bars. I could've gone broke buying tablespoon-sized glasses of nasty cough syrup. Shelly, Justin, and I finished off a perfect day with dinner at a tiny Cuban restaurant.

After dinner, I met up with CJ. He still lived in the Village and worked as a consultant during the daytime. At night, he used all the office equipment at his consulting firm to run a film festival he was putting together. I met him at his office building.

"They don't need to know I'm here at night doing this," he said. The consulting firm didn't know that their phones, copy machines, electricity, and everything else were being used to organize a major film festival. CJ hadn't changed a bit.

The look on my face must have provoked a response, because CJ looked at me and then justified his actions.

"They don't pay me enough here," he said. "I graduated from one of the top business schools. They should pay me more." Then he changed the subject. "Hey, I want to show you one of the short films I'm screening at the festival. This director is really cool."

CJ and I left his office building and walked several long blocks to his apartment to see the film. Unlike people from Southern California, New Yorkers liked to walk. My feet hurt by the time we arrived at his place. His studio was cluttered, dark, and barely big enough to fit two beds. His bed sat against one wall, and his renter's bed rested against the other wall. The small TV sat about five inches from his bed. You had to almost step over it to move through the room.

"I don't really pay rent," he explained.

"I'm subletting this place for really cheap. I rent out that side of the room to a roommate. He's just a guy that needs somewhere to sleep. I charge him almost the full cost of the rent, so I barely pay anything," he laughed.

We didn't stay long. There was nowhere comfortable to sit, and the film lasted less than ten minutes. We headed out to a dim sum restaurant.

"Aren't you going to Michelle's reception?" I asked.

"No, I've got too much going here, with the festival and all," he replied, dismissing the whole discussion.

CJ's girlfriend, an attractive blonde, met us at the restaurant. "She's really pretty," I told him when she disappeared into the bathroom.

"I could get someone even better-looking than her," he said. "After all, this *is* New York."

There was no point in addressing his comment. He spoke truthfully. She was a beautiful woman, but Manhattan abounded with them. If his girlfriend dumped him tonight, he could have another gorgeous girl in his bed by the end of the week. Within a few weeks, he might even find someone he'd keep around for more than one night. Even the savviest New Yorker couldn't immediately discern that he was a criminally in-clined man-child who rarely did his laundry and always needed rescuing by tough-actin' Tinactin to control the athlete's foot that ran wild inside his stinky boots.

I spent an hour with CJ and his girlfriend at the Chinese restau-rant in the East Village before I headed back to Justin's. My watch read a little past midnight as my cab hurried across town. I'd had an early night by New York standards. On another trip, I'd stayed out until 4:00 a.m. Even at four in the morning, the streets of the East Village usually buzzed with people and activity.

Justin had excelled in New York. He'd risen quickly through the ranks at American Express and could afford a place on the Upper East Side. He had moved out of his old apartment in Jersey—to the second-small-est apartment I'd seen in my life. CJ's was the smallest. Justin's shoebox studio was so tiny that I slept on his futon mattress, and he slept on the floor right next to me. Two grown people couldn't stretch out anywhere else comfortably, without both sleeping on the futon.

The next day, Justin and I hopped a train to Philadelphia for Michelle's reception. We enjoyed a mini V Society reunion. Mandy, Michelle, and I had a grand time. Keri still lived in Israel and couldn't make the reception. I had lost touch with Stephanie years before, shortly after Keri's wedding. Michelle seemed more reserved and less talkative than I remembered her, but otherwise, she remained unchanged. She was still one of my best friends. Michelle, Mandy, and I joyfully revis-ited all our old hangouts. We tramped through campus, and I stocked up on Penn sweatshirts, shorts, and T-shirts. It felt almost like old times.

After a couple blissful days with Michelle, I returned to Santa Barbara. Milan called after I'd been back in town a few days.

"Hey, what's up?" I said.

"Not much. What's up with you? How's work?"

"Good. I'm getting into web design now. You were so right. The Internet is blowing up. Everyone is rushing to launch their first websites. It's pretty exciting stuff."

"Don't say I didn't tell you," he laughed. "What else is going on?"

"Not much. You know . . . a little bit of this, a little bit of that. How's life in the IT world?"

"I love riding first class," he exclaimed. "All these old guys, riding first class—then there's me, on there riding with them," he laughed. "Yeah, and I'm only twenty-five!"

"That's sweet," I replied. "Hey, I just saw Michelle. She's married. I just got back from Philadelphia."

"What? You're kidding, right?" He sounded surprised.

"No, I just saw her."

"No—I mean, you were just here and you didn't come see me?"

I heard something strange in his tone—emotion. Up until that very moment, I had only hoped that he was capable of expressing more than cynicism; but had no proof. For the second time, he articulated something truly heartfelt. The first time occurred when we were in school and he'd said I could talk to him about anything after my tiff with Keri.

Disappointment hung like a lead weight in his voice. I had wounded him. I was shocked. We'd been friends for six years, and not once—not ever—had he revealed a vulnerable part of himself. I didn't think anyone could hurt him, especially not me. I was just the friend with the nice forehead.

"Ummm . . . DC is like four hours away," I offered.

"No, it isn't," he shot back. "It's two hours from Philadelphia. You know that."

"Uh—no, I didn't." In my mind, I really thought DC was farther away, even though I had made the trip from Philadelphia to DC before.

Had I doubled the distance in my head purposely so I wouldn't have to see him?

He wasn't letting it go. "Really, I can't believe you'd do that."

I didn't know what to say. What could I say? *You scare me to death, because I don't trust myself with you?* If I visited him in DC, I'd have to stay at his place. I didn't have any other friends there that I could crash with. I couldn't afford a decent hotel. Even if I did manage to find a hotel at a reasonable rate, how would I explain the need to stay in one, without an awkward discussion? After all, we were just friends. Friends spent the night at each other's places; we didn't shell out money for hotels.

I'd have been as wise to take a train to DC, as I would have been to perform my own lobotomy. One made about as much sense as the other. So, I didn't say anything. I sat there dumb. I felt terrible for letting him down. At the same time, I knew I could *never* visit him. The silence hung on the line for what seemed like forever.

Finally, he said, "Hey, do you still have those videos we made?"

"Yep, I've got them all here."

"Would you please send them to me? I'd like to watch them again."

"Sure. Of course."

"Thanks. You have my address, right?"

"Yeah."

"Okay, well drop them in the mail when you have a chance."

"Do you want all of them?"

"Yeah, send them all. I'll send them back to you after I watch them."

"Okay."

"Well, I guess I better get going."

"Yep. Okay. Bye."

"Bye."

I hung up the phone. A couple of times, I had taken the videos with me to my parents' house so I could watch our films on their VCR. I didn't have a VCR in my Santa Barbara apartment. At my parents' house, I rewound the clips of him a few times just to watch him give his absurd explanation on the meaning of life. I liked watching his expressions, remembering his gestures, seeing his smile. I wondered which clips he'd watch when he received the package of videotapes from me.

"I'm moving to Germany," he told me the next time we spoke. "I just landed a killer job with this venture capital firm that specializes in Internet communications in Eastern Europe." I knew he'd be overwhelmingly successful. I expected to read about him in the *Wall Street Journal* in a few years, "SERBIAN BUSINESSMAN BUILDS EASTERN EUROPEAN INTERNET EMPIRE."

"Here's my new phone number. You can reach me in Munich on this number. I left your videotapes with a friend. My friend will send them to you."

I never received the videotapes. The friend he had left the tapes with wasn't actually a friend. He'd given the tapes to his ex-girlfriend, with instructions to mail them to me. They'd just broken up. The last thing she probably wanted to do was mail a large package to his friend—some random woman in Santa Barbara.

Sometime before he left the country for good, he called again. This time my roommate Arlené answered the phone.

"Hello," Arlené said.

"Hello. May I speak to Adele?"

"Sure, may I tell her who's calling?"

"Milan."

"Oh—ho-ho. Milan? Milan. *Milan.* I'm so glad you called. I was just talking to Adele about you. She has something to tell you." Arlené handed me the phone receiver.

"Hey, Milan."

"Hey, Adele, how are you?"

"Good. What's new with you?"

"Not much. So hey, your roommate said you have something to tell me?" he asked.

"You'll never guess who the new creative director is!"

"What? No way. Congratulations!"

"Yeah, it's crazy cool. My boss quit to go sail around the world on her boyfriend's boat. So the president of the company promoted me to her position."

"That's so great," he replied enthusiastically. "I knew you'd do well."

"Yeah, it's awesome."

"So what do you do as creative director?"

"I get to write all the proposals for new clients and make all the pitches. And check this out—I'm free to bring in any new clients that I can win. I'm dying to get the Santa Barbara Film Festival. That would be so cool—designing all the film festival posters and advertising."

"The film festival? Oh yeah, that *would* be cool."

"I'd be willing to do the job pro bono just to get the PR."

Arlené was motioning in the background.

"What?" I snapped, covering up the mouthpiece so Milan couldn't hear.

"You need to tell him," she whispered.

"Tell him what?" I asked, playing dumb.

"Give me the phone," she requested.

"Why? What for?" I replied as I tried to move out of reach. Arlené gestured for the phone. "Hold on," I said into the mouthpiece before covering it up again quickly.

"I'm talking. Can't you see I'm talking? *Just wait*," I hissed.

"Just give it to me really quick. I need to tell him something," Arlené insisted.

Then, like a fool, I handed her the receiver.

"Hey, Milan, it's Adele's roommate Arlené again. She has something *else* important to tell you."

Clearly, Arlené had missed the memo about roommate confidentiality. She didn't seem to realize that she was violating the Number One Good-Friend Golden Rule: never tell your friend's secrets.

I couldn't believe her. She was looking at me like she'd done me a huge favor.

"You're tormented," Arlené whispered matter-of-factly, with her hand over the mouthpiece to muffle her words. "You need to come clean and fess up."

Fess up? Was she kidding? She didn't know the man we were dealing with here. It was my plan to stay friends with him forever—and never admit *anything*. We'd be ninety-five years old, and I still wouldn't fess up.

She'd messed up my whole modus operandi. For the past six years, I had perfected the art of remaining "just friends" with Milan. I would never fess up. I was in search of the right man—one that was righteous and God-seeking, not the roguish, destructive ones that were so much easier to find.

Now I sat like an idiot with the phone in my hand, and Milan on the other end.

"Your roommate said you have something else to tell me?" he asked again, perplexed.

This was so lame. Passing the phone back and forth like freakin' sixth graders. Now I was stuck. I couldn't just spit it out. I felt like I was in junior high again, nervous, perspiring, dry-mouthed, and mute.

"Uhhhh . . . ," I started. I wanted so badly to lie. I could tell him my roommate was a whack job and I had no idea what she was talking about. I could say she had forgot to take her meds that morning and often made up stuff just to provoke people.

"Umm . . . ," I stammered.

Pull it together. Pull it together!, I told myself. Why couldn't I just tell the truth? He was three thousand miles away, and I'd probably never see him again. He was moving to Munich—not a place I planned to visit anytime soon.

I could hear him on the other end of the phone. He was trying to be patient, but this was juvenile. I was hesitating, and fumbling, hemming and hawing. I just couldn't say it. "Uhhhhh . . . my roommate . . . uhhhh—right . . . something to tell you . . .ummmm . . ."

Finally, I said something coherent: "I like you."

There was silence on the other end of the line. I was going to kill Arlené when I hung up. She was now officially on my Badly Behaved Roommate list.

Then he responded, "What do you mean?"

He was kidding, right? What did I *mean*? I meant it was time to hang up the phone and end this dreadful, stinking conversation. In my entire life, I had never told a single guy (with the exception of my fifth-grade boyfriend) that I liked him, and now he wanted further explanation.

"Uhh . . . I like you," I repeated.

"Like me, how?"

"Ummm . . . like, I *like* you, like you." There was no way I would tell him the whole truth—that I loved him. That I was in love with him—and had been for years. At the beginning of sophomore or junior year, I couldn't remember which, my photography professor asked us to write down ten things about ourselves. Number three: "I've never been in love." Somewhere between the spring of junior year and the spring before graduation, that changed. I denied it, ignored it, buried it, and altogether acted like it hadn't happened. I didn't even know when it happened. Was it junior year when I first watched Milan dance and he expelled us from his room after Stephanie bit him? Or maybe it was senior year, when he came to my film class every week and sometimes walked with me to class. I honestly didn't know.

I wasn't about to give him the privilege of knowing he was the first man I had *ever* loved in my entire life. I refused to expose myself to his cool indifference. I refused to let him know that he was capable of affecting me. Ever since I had first met him, I had acted as though my interest in him never extended beyond friendship. I locked up my secret admiration in a mental vault filled with unwritten V Society notes. Only Keri suspected the truth, and she'd never tell. She wouldn't even mention it to me, unless I mentioned it first. I had told him I loved him before, but I had led him to believe it was purely platonic. I wouldn't say it again.

"So, did you give me the Bible just so you could convert me?" he asked.

"What? Of course not," I answered indignantly, without even thinking. I wasn't a pimp. I didn't push Jesus for my own benefit. Or did I?
Did I want him to make the same spiritual choice as me, just so I could
be with him? Why did I pray for him all the time? Why *did* I give him
a Bible? I didn't pray for CJ. I didn't give him a Bible. I felt totally annoyed and flabbergasted. I wanted nothing more than to hang up and
forget I'd ever met him.

"You're in love with the *idea* of me," he finally replied.

"Whatever. Gotta go," I snapped. "Bye."

I hung up the phone, numb and embarrassed. I wanted to forget the
conversation had ever happened. I sat there dumbfounded and silent.
I had a lot to think about, but I wanted to shove the conversation in
a deep closet—and then push that closet over the tallest cliff.

I'd squelched the urge to curse him out—lucky for him. Was he on
drugs? The *idea* of him? We had known each other for years. I had no
romantic ideas about him, only the raw, unsavory reality of him. He was
guarded, emotionally unavailable, and moody to the point of psycho-
sis. He was self-centered and cynical. He drank too much and smoked
too much. On top of that, he'd trampled on my best friend's heart and
treated her cruelly. Did he think I didn't know that? *He must be out of
his dark, cloudy, disillusioned mind!* No, I didn't love a fabricated, sweet,
endearing idea of him. I loved him—despite the fact that he was one of
the biggest jerks I'd ever met.

He wasn't even a good friend, as far as friends went. In direct contrast, Ryan demonstrated true friendship. I could count on Ryan; he was
honest, reliable, forthcoming, Spirit-filled, and easy to be with. None
of those things characterized Milan. Ryan stayed with me in the bathroom, and handed me a clean towel when I puked into my toilet bowl,
sick with the flu. He drove me to the doctor, bought me flu medicine,
and checked in regularly to make sure I was okay. I couldn't imagine
Milan doing that. I should have been having this conversation with Ryan,
not Milan.

I had to pull my emotions apart. I had to examine myself—peel back the onion-skin layers of all that encompassed my jumbled, interknit feelings for Milan. Desire was the first and easiest layer to peel away. Eros. Attraction. It seemed the most straightforward and uncomplicated of my tangled feelings. Desire arose as a simple, focused tinderbox. I constantly shifted its position to avoid any glimmer of heat that might cause it to erupt into an inferno. David and Bathsheba, Samson and Delilah. It was simple math. A long history of disaster befell the pursuit of temptations better left alone. I identified with David and Samson. Like them, I'd been hypnotized against my better judgment and despite my convictions. The inability to turn their eyes and lead their hearts in less treacherous directions brought on their imminent undoing.

What was the masculine word for siren? Masculine beauty tempted women as feminine beauty tempted men. My mind raced, then sputtered, stalled and then raced again in ten different directions. Ugh, thinking about the whole thing made my head hurt. I wished to ignore it. I wanted to embrace denial and exonerate myself of all but pure motives. Why had I ever set foot in Penn Film and Video so many seasons ago? Why did I listen to a nineteen-year-old boy rant about ridiculous film plots? I wished I'd avoided this—this mess.

Beneath that onion-skin layer of desire lay friendship—I thoroughly enjoyed his creative collaboration. I liked making films with him. I relished art discussions with him. I appreciated his take on visual imagery—peculiar and provocative. His ideas spurred my innovation.

Then I peeled back the final, deepest layer. I loved Milan without conditions and without expectations. Agape the Greeks called it. I loved him simply because he was Milan—flawed and dangerous, yet so impossible for me not to love. He was my imperfect friend. We were as symbiotic as water and oil. Nothing about our values and lifestyles matched. Yet, everything wily, corrupt, and volatile about him reminded me of myself—without the hand of God working out my shortcomings. He was moody; that was my natural tendency. He behaved recklessly— a fault I wished I could manifest because it would allow me to think mostly of myself. I was naturally self-centered and egotistical. His wild creativity was akin to mine, unbridled. He aimed to buck convention in the same way I rose to nonconformity. His love of all beautiful women mirrored my preoccupation with all beautiful men. Anyone paying attention could see that the superficial tantalized me. I preferred the gorgeous and fashionable, over the less spectacular.

The one and only difference between Milan and me was God—the still, mighty hand that quietly pointed me away from myself and toward something far greater, richer, and more glorious. A distinct set of parameters guided my mission, while his mission remained ambiguous, with no clear objective and no purpose. Only God's Word—the Holy Scriptures' instructions on appropriate sexual behavior—and my allegiance to the V Society had stopped me from careening with gusto toward wholeheartedly satisfying every lustful passion.

Of course, I wanted Milan. Of course, I wanted to be with him. But that wasn't the only reason I had given him a Bible. I gave him the Bible because I saw something remarkable and wholly unique in him. God had gifted him with talent and abilities unlike anyone I had ever met. His brilliance—unimaginably creative and blessed with rare business insight, bordered on clairvoyance. No doubt, he'd be successful and make a mint—but would he ever be truly satisfied? He remained bitter and broken. Only the Spirit of an all-loving, omniscient, all-powerful God could give him the wholeness and restoration he needed. Only the God that created him could show him how to best use his natural talent and fulfill his purpose in life. That's why I gave him the Bible.

I sat overwhelmed with my wildly spinning thoughts. At the core, faith compelled me toward chastity. For as long as I could remember, the hunger to stand firmly upright inside God's will had burned deep inside me. I knew the obvious potential outcomes of acting on attraction: unwanted pregnancy, STDs, getting played and the resulting broken heart.

But I never worried about any of those things either. Avoiding foreplay and practicing abstinence shielded me from all that.

Maintaining my commitment required discipline, no different than the way an athlete trains her body to respond in a certain manner. Years of practice had enabled me to enjoy the company of a man I found attractive, without acting on the attraction. As long as I had the wisdom to flee potentially compromising situations, like avoiding a trip alone to visit Milan in DC, I emerged unscathed.

Though I didn't intend it, each of my friendships with guys had always eventually revealed that he wasn't the Right One to lose my virginity to anyway. Beyond our attraction, we lacked a foundation or the motivation to sustain any sort of serious, long-term romantic relationship. Most attraction began with the thrill of the chase. After the chase ended . . . then what? What did we really have in common to keep us together longer than for a few months of impassioned hookups? Nothing. But we could always be friends. That lasted. That was good. We could look forward to that for years and years. In friendship fewer regrets existed; misunderstandings were easily pardoned and forgotten with "I'm sorry." Besides, when it came to Milan, "just friends" was complicated enough without sex.

As frustrating as my attraction to Milan had been, I knew that I'd made the right decision about him. Without a doubt, I would have regretted sleeping with him. It would have meant a lot to me, and little, if anything, to him. That one hookup would have ended our friendship quickly—on a very bitter note. I would have hated myself—and him—for allowing myself to get played like that.

The phone rang. I held my breath and picked it up. Ryan. Thank God.

"Come on, we're going out!" he exclaimed. "Girl, it's ice-blended mocha time! I'll pick you up in five minutes."

Relief. I scrambled to put on my flip-flops. Twenty minutes later, Ryan and I sat in patio chairs outside our favorite café. Both of us sipped candy-sweet adrenaline, chocolate syrup and espresso beans whirled to dizzy perfection. The breeze from the ocean swept in gently—cool, safe, refreshing. The all-too-perfect, red-roof-tiled buildings set against the never-ending blue sky comforted me. Ryan's presence comforted me. The V Society flourished. It had different members and had moved from the city of brotherly love to the shores of Santa Barbara. All was well.

I thought about Keri, Michelle, Mandy, and Stephanie. I never knew for sure which of us made it to the collective goal we set for ourselves. Maybe we all made it. Or maybe, in the frailness of our humanity, some of us lost sight of exactly what we were waiting for. Once we graduated and dispersed, we found it difficult to remain accountable to each other. But of one thing, I knew: I never would have made it across the finish line without the four of them. They walked with me, held me up, and kept me on the course during the most difficult part of the journey.

"Delie, I have an idea." Ryan looked at me seriously, with his most intent expression. Seriousness always looked out of place on Ryan's comical face. I couldn't look him straight in the eyes for too long; it made me laugh. Usually, he began every joke with his serious face, a foreshadowing of the humor to come.

"What's your idea, Señor Frog?" I replied.

"If neither of us is married by thirty, let's get married."

He was semiserious. It was a great idea from one of the truest friends and the best guy friend I'd ever had. We always had a blast, and he rarely got on my nerves. I could spend the entire day with Ryan and never get tired of him. He had a near-perfect plan with only one minor hiccup. We weren't attracted to each other. The idea of kissing him was just wrong. I knew he felt the same. Kissing me would be creepy—like making out with his sister. But aside from the lingering possibility that our marriage might be characterized by separate bedrooms, his plan was pure genius.

"That is the best idea you've had all year," I said with a smile.

"Why, thank you. I rather liked it myself." He grinned back at me.

Our agreement was like life insurance. It insured that neither of us would be in the V Society forever. We could exit honorably. We had a fail-safe. If both of us were still single at the age of thirty, we might start looking pretty attractive to each other.

Besides, turning thirty seemed a million years away. I was twenty-five, and he was twenty-six. We had so many more adventures ahead before thirty even surfaced on the horizon. I looked over at him. He'd just filled a prescription for a stylish pair of tortoise-shell eyeglasses that handsomely framed his angular face. Since his college graduation a while back, he'd shed his surfer wardrobe for semiprofessional attire. He looked good in his neatly ironed button-down shirt. Why hadn't I ever looked at him closely before? Ryan wasn't a bad-looking guy. Actually, he was kinda, sorta—well, appealing, in a way I'd never taken notice of before.

"What are you thinking?" Ryan asked.

"Nothing important."

"I know you, Delie. You've got a funny look on your face," Ryan pressed. "I've never seen that expression before."

A lot could happen in the next several years. It was bound to be one interesting ride to thirty.

EPiLOGUe

Six years after her college graduation, Adele moved from Santa Barbara. She met her future husband two years later. She joined the V Society alumnae following her marriage at age 30.

Adele remains friends with Keri, Michelle, Milan, Ryan and most of the people mentioned in this memoir.

THE V SOCIETY NOW . . .

Adele Moore Berry is married and resides in Northern California; she has a stepdaughter.

Dr. Keri Zelman and her husband live in Israel and have three children.

Michelle Schroeder and her husband reside on the East Coast with their three children.

Stephanie Schwartzbaum and her husband live in Southern California and have two children.

Dr. Amanda Johnson and her husband live in Southwest Asia with their three children.

Captain Ryan McAlba served in the United States Marine Corps in Iraq before returning to civilian life. He remains single but is on the lookout for the ideal wife.

LAST WORDS

I don't believe in settling.

Often I think we settle when we expect our lives to be characterized by a certain amount of regret—regret for things we did and regret for things we didn't do. I can honestly, say I have no regrets regarding my relationships with men, prior to my marriage.

Zilch. None.

I don't think many women can say that.

While I believe that regret and mistakes are a natural part of life, I also believe that abiding by certain bits of wisdom can lessen the frequency of regrettable mistakes.

I cherish the V Society days and my experiences for their radiant illumination of a gospel which heralds that life may be lived wildly and freely—without regret.

As the years have whipped by, the few painfully awkward situations of the V Society years have dissipated into tiny blips on the timeline of my life. As I grow older, those embarrassing situations seem less weighty, while the good decisions continue to bear a harvest in the form of life-long friendships and a memoir full of pleasant recollections.

To date, I'm still friends with many of the men I've written about. We may not speak often; sometimes years pass without so much as an e-mail. We lead busy lives, and I live in a different time zone than many of them. But, on the rare occasion that one of us takes the initiative to shoot a hello through cyberspace, I know we're both smiling with the memory of our youthful times together, which laid the foundation for our current friendship.

Finally, here's a note for those who are wondering about the transition from V Society member to alumnae status: "Was it scary? Was it weird? How did you figure out what to do?" Well, rest assured—it definitely wasn't scary, there was no weirdness, and not surprisingly, "what to do" is automatically programmed into our DNA. It didn't take me long to figure it out—at all. I think it's fair to say that most of us can be pretty fast learners when the subject matter interests us.

That said, I'll leave you with this chocolate cake analogy—since I love chocolate.

Transitioning to V Society alumnae status was similar to what I'd imagine it would be like to have this experience: One day, after following a gluten-free diet for health reasons for many years, you go to the doctor's office for a routine checkup. She runs some tests and then suddenly declares, "You're no longer allergic to wheat. Eat all the gluten you want!" If you love desserts, as I do, you're not going to wonder, "Will I enjoy eating that slice of triple-layer chocolate cake covered in rich dark chocolate ganache?" Rather, you'll already have raced out of the doctor's office and will be sitting in the nearest gourmet bakery devouring cake at lightning speed. The only thing you'll be wondering is, "Will I have a stomachache if I eat two more giant slices after this one?"

Let's just say that the Impact conference pastor was right!

ACKNOWLEDGEMENTS

First, a huge thank you to my dear friends, Keri and Michelle, who traveled with me back in time and graciously provided vital feedback on my manuscript. I am forever grateful to both of you for making college outrageous and for creating memories worth writing about. Thank you also to all of you included in the story who reviewed the manuscript and allowed me to include you in my recollection.

A million thanks, hugs, and kisses to my parents Cecelia and Hezekiah for being the best parents a girl could ask for and for giving me the freedom to be the quirky girl God made me to be. Your support and parenting make my story possible. Thank you to my awesome brother Adrian and his wife Tamica for your encouragement and investment in my first book project.

I'm incredibly appreciative for my friends and family who read the manuscript at various stages and provided invaluable encouragement and suggestions. I'm blessed by my faithful sistahs that prayed this book into publication and encouraged me with your e-mails, phone calls, and friendship. Thank you also to the prayer warriors in my home group.

Thank you to Ewurama Ewusi-Mensah of Sea Never Dry Editing and Publishing Services who guided me through the stages of the publishing process with her professional wisdom and encouraged me to share my story.

I am forever grateful to Laura, the best marketing intern *ever*.

I send a huge shout-out to the talented and experienced writers in my critique group (especially Carol Hall), who graciously allowed this new kid to join you. Your encouragement, critiques, and fellowship have been invaluable. I am also grateful for the insightful group of young women, on various college campuses, who graciously agreed to read and critique my manuscript.

Thank you to my fabulous friend Mary Beth who read my e-mails and, despite working with me for years on fashion photo shoots, said, "Hey, your e-mails are really funny; you should be writing!" You helped me awaken the sleeping writer within.

And finally, a big thank you to my husband, Berry—for waiting for me. Your sense of humor is priceless; there's never a dull moment when you are around. Thank you for constantly reminding me that God's ways are not my ways.

Share the Love...

If you enjoyed *The V Society: The True Story of Rebel Virgin-Girls*, then tell everyone you know—blog, Tweet, and post a few words on your Facebook page or favorite social media site.

In the spring of 2012, *The V Society* e-book and paperback will be available nationwide via most online retailers as well as general market and Christian bookstores!

It is available right now for preorder on Amazon.com. Preorder copies for your friends, your youth group, or as a gift for someone you know.

We want to make a *V Society* movie, but to do that we need to sell books—a *whole lot* of books, so . . .

We need your help to get the word out about *The V Society*! Share the love by writing a short review for your community or organization's newsletter. Or post a review on Amazon.com, Barnesandnoble.com, or Facebook.

And we'd love it if you'd find us on Facebook at **facebook.com/ VSocietyBook** and become a fan! There you can meet and interact with the author and the growing number of V Society fans.

Remember . . . legs crossed, nothing lost!